ART DÉCO SCHMUCK ART DÉCO JEWELRY

Katalog zur gleichnamigen Ausstellung im
Museum Idar-Oberstein unter der Felsenkirche
15.9.2002–15.1.2003
danach in weiteren Museen in Deutschland und anschließend
im Bard Graduate Center for Studies in Decorative Arts, New York,
in Zusammenarbeit mit dem Cooper-Hewitt National Design Museum, New York

CHRISTIANNE WEBER

ART DÉCO SCHMUCK ART DÉCO JEWELRY

JAKOB BENGEL

IDAR-OBERSTEIN / GERMANY

mit einem Beitrag von with a contribution by ILONKA WENK

ARNOLDSCHE

HERAUSGEBER EDITOR
Stadt Idar-Oberstein

PROJEKTLEITUNG
PROJECT MANAGEMENT
Wilhelm Lindemann

GRAFIK DESIGN
Nalbach typografik, Marion Ziegler, Stuttgart

ÜBERSETZUNG TRANSLATION
Joan Clough, München

FOTOGRAFIE PHOTOGRAPHY
Lichtblick-Fotodesign
Hiltrud + Jürgen Cullmann, Schwollen

OFFSET-REPRODUKTIONEN OFFSET REPRODUCTIONS
mb Satz und Repro, Stuttgart

DRUCK PRINTING
Karl Grammlich, Pliezhausen

Dieses Buch wurde gedruckt auf 100 % chlorfrei gebleichtem Papier und entspricht damit dem TCF-Standard.
This book has been printed on paper that is 100 % free of chlorine bleach in conformity with TCF standards.

Die Deutsche Bibliothek – CIP-Einheitsaufnahme

Ein Titeldatensatz für diese Publikation ist bei der Deutschen Bibliothek erhältlich.
ISBN 3-89790-179-X

Made in Germany, 2002

KONZEPTION DER AUSSTELLUNG
EXHIBITION CONCEPT
Prof. Dr. Kern, Anne Schlieper, Insa Schwarting, Simone Strauß, Stephanie Trauth

Organisatoren, Autorinnen und Verleger danken ganz besonders:
The organizers, authors and the editor would especially like to thank:

dem Sammler-Ehepaar | the collectors Dres. Händel

Christel und Karl-Dieter Braun, Idar-Oberstein
Dr. Elisabeth Heller, von Parish-Kostümbibliothek München
Emil Schmidt, Gescher
Museum Idar-Oberstein unter der Felsenkirche
Manfred Rauscher, Stadtarchiv Idar-Oberstein
Andrea Richter-Mahlo, Leipzig
Prof. Otto Krätz, Starnberg
Dr. Monika Rudolph, Stuttgart
Beate Manske, Wilhelm Wagenfeld Stiftung, Bremen

BILDNACHWEIS PHOTO CREDITS
Alle Fotos (einschl. Titelabbildung) | All photos (incl. cover image):
Lichtblick-Fotodesign H. + J. Cullmann, Schwollen, mit Ausnahme | except:
Kat.-Nr. 138/139, A. Bröhan, München

© VG Bild-Kunst, Bonn
Alle Nummern beziehen sich auf Text-Abbildungen
All numbers refer to figures in the text
9: Man Ray, **16:** Christian Schad, **48:** Herbert Bayer, **52:** Jean Fouquet, **76:** Fernand Léger

REPRODUKTIONEN REPRODUCTIONS:
1 aus: Salvy, Gérard-Julien: Mode des années, Paris 1991, S. 113; **2, 3** aus: Kizette: Passion by Design. The Art and Times of Tamara de Lempicka, New York 1987, **6** aus: Söderbaum, Kristina: Nichts bleibt immer so. Erinnerungen, München 1992 (Abb. 19); **7** aus: L'Art international d'aujourd'hui, Vol. 12, Paris ca. 1927; **10** aus: Owen, Elizabeth: Fashion in Photographs 1920–1040, London 1993, S. 85; **11** aus: Die neue Linie, Olympia-Heft, Berlin, Oktober 1936, S. 63; **42, 43** aus: Weber, Christianne: Art Déco Schmuck, München 2001; **46, 47** aus: Wilhelm Wagenfeld Schmuck, Wilhelm Wagenfeld Stiftung, Bremen 2001; **49, 50, 55** aus: Rudolph, Monika: Naum Slutzky, Meister am Bauhaus, Goldschmied und Designer, Stuttgart 1990; **53, 54** aus: Gabardi, Melissa: Jean Després, Mailand 1999; **69, 70** aus: Die Schaulade, 10. Jahrgang, Heft 3 (S. 141, 142); **71** aus: Weber/Möller: Mode und Modeschmuck 1920–1970, Stuttgart 1999; **72** aus: Hufnagl, Florian (Hrsg.): Plastics + Design, Stuttgart 1997 (S. 36); **73, 74** aus: Gioielli della Fantasia, Mailand 1991; **75** aus: Archiv Henkel & Grosse, Pforzheim; **76** aus: Die Form, 1929, S. 567; **77** aus: Ginelli Brunialti, Carla/ Brunialti, Roberto: American costume jewelry, Mailand 1977

5: Interfoto-Archiv, München

Ilonka Wenk
8 ZEITGEIST UND MODE DER 1930er JAHRE

Christianne Weber
20 ART DÉCO SCHMUCK AUS METALL UND GALALITH
20 Modeschmuck für die Frau von Welt – aus der Produktion Jakob Bengel, Oberstein
23 Diskussion um Materialechtheit und Materialgerechtigkeit
23 Galalith – ein Kunststoff der unbegrenzten Möglichkeiten
26 Galalith und Chrom erobern den Modeschmuck

29 DIE SCHMUCKPRODUKTION DER FIRMA BENGEL IN DEN 1930ER JAHREN
29 Musterbücher und Entwürfe
44 Inspiration und Quellen
47 Das Spiel mit Form und Farbe: der Schmuck zwischen 1931 und 1938

54 METALL- UND GALALITHSCHMUCK
54 Klein & Quenzer, Carl Keller Chr. Sohn, Oberstein
55 Henkel & Grosse, Pforzheim
57 Galalithschmuck in Frankreich
59 Galalith und Bakelit in Amerika

61 DIE UHRKETTEN- UND METALLWARENINDUSTRIE IN OBERSTEIN: 1860–1950

69 DIE KETTENHERSTELLUNG IN OBERSTEIN – DIE FIRMA JAKOB BENGEL
69 Die Bedeutung der Obersteiner Kettenindustrie
74 Die Familien Bengel und Hartenberger
83 Die Firmen- und Wohngebäude in der Wilhelmstraße in Oberstein
86 Das Werken und Wirken einer Kettenfabrik
89 Die Firmenmarke – »la marque de fabrique«
93 Die Belegschaft der Firma Bengel

KATALOG
99 Collection 1931
133 Collection 1932
211 Collection 1933
271 Collection 1935/36/38

ANHANG
279 Anhang I–IV
286 Stammbaum
287 Bibliographie
288 Register

Ilonka Wenk
8 THE 1930s ZEITGEIST AND FASHION

Christianne Weber
20 ART DÉCO JEWELRY MADE OF METAL AND GALALITH
20 Costume jewelry for the sophisticate by Jakob Bengel, Oberstein/Germany
23 The materials debate: genuine vs. simulated elegance
23 Galalith – a synthetic material with unlimted possibilities
26 Galalith and chrome triumph in costume jewelry

29 JEWELRY PRODUCTION AT BENGEL IN THE 1930s
29 Pattern books and designs
44 Sources of inspiration
46 Playing with form and color: jewelry between 1931 and 1938

54 METAL AND GALALITH JEWELRY
54 Klein & Quenzer, Carl Keller Chr. Sohn, Oberstein
55 Henkel & Grosse, Pforzheim
57 Galalith jewelry in France
59 Galalith and bakelite in America

61 THE WATCH-CHAIN AND METALWARES INDUSTRY IN OBERSTEIN: 1860–1950

69 MAKING CHAINS IN OBERSTEIN – THE FIRM OF JAKOB BENGEL
69 The importance of the Oberstein chain industry
74 The Bengel and Hartenberger families
81 The firm promises and living quarters in Wilhelmstrasse, Oberstein
83 Works and Days: operations at a chain factory
87 The factory brand – »la marque de fabrique«
91 The Bengel staff

CATALOGUE
99 Collection 1931
133 Collection 1932
211 Collection 1933
271 Collection 1935/36/38

APPENDIX
279 Appendix I–IV
286 Family tree
287 Bibliography
288 Index

GRUSSWORT

Kaum zwanzig Jahre ist es her, dass der erste Art-Déco-Schmuck im Bauhausstil auf dem internationalen Kunstmarkt Furore machte: vor allem Halsschmuck aus veredeltem Metall und dem frühen Kunststoff Galalith in faszinierenden Farben und einer zeitlosen, geometrisierenden Formensprache. Damals kannte man weder den Hersteller noch das Land, in dem diese Preziosen in den Zwanziger- und Dreißigerjahren des 20. Jahrhunderts produziert worden waren.

Mit der Ausstellung »Jakob Bengel, Idar-Oberstein – Art-Déco-Schmuck aus Deutschland«, die die schönsten Stücke aus der Musterkollektion der Firma zeigt, wird der Name »Jakob Bengel« in die Kunstgeschichte eingeführt. Die Publikation dokumentiert diese Wiederentdeckung über die Dauer der Präsentation hinaus. So wird der Name einer Firma, die sich immer nur als eine der Modeindustrie zuliefernde Metallwarenfabrik verstand, nachträglich zur Design-Marke – ein bemerkenswerter Wandel.

Der Leidenschaft und dem kriminalistischen Spürsinn eines deutschen Sammlerehepaares ist es zu verdanken, dass wir mit dem Schmuck von Jakob Bengel zugleich einen tiefen Einblick in den Geschmack der Menschen der Epoche vor dem Zweiten Weltkrieg und in die wirtschaftlichen, sozialen und politischen Verhältnisse dieser Zeit erhalten. Die Recherchen der Sammler und der Autorin Dr. Christianne Weber-Stöber haben auch die Spur zur Wiederentdeckung der historischen Uhrketten- und Bijouteriefabrik Jakob Bengel gelegt, einem Industriedenkmal der Epoche um 1900.

Ich freue mich sehr, dass das Land Rheinland-Pfalz und die Stiftung Rheinland-Pfalz für Kultur dieses Ausstellungsprojekt unterstützen konnten, das für die Edelstein- und Schmuckstadt Idar-Oberstein eine große Bedeutung hat. Ausstellung und Publikation wünsche ich großen Erfolg und vor allem begeisterte Besucher und Leser.

PROF. DR. E. JÜRGEN ZÖLLNER
Ministers für Wissenschaft, Weiterbildung, Forschung und Kultur

A FEW WORDS OF WELCOME

It was only twenty years ago that Art Déco jewelry in the Bauhaus style suddenly caused such a stir on the international art market: especially necklaces of refined metals and the early plastic Galalith in fascinating colors, timelessly fashioned in a geometricizing formal idiom. At that time neither the maker nor the country which produced these stylish 1920s and 1930s pieces was known to the public.

The exhibition »Jakob Bengel, Idar-Oberstein – Art-Déco Jewelry from Germany«, which is showing the finest pieces from the Jakob Bengel firm collection of samples, marks the introduction of the name »Jakob Bengel« to art history. The present book documents this rediscovery, which will long outlast the exhibition itself. Thus a firm which always regarded itself as merely a metalwares factory producing for the fashion industry has become a big name in fashion design – a remarkable change indeed.

The avid commitment and detecting skill of a German couple have made it possible for us to gain profound insights not only into the jewelry made by Jakob Bengel but also into the taste prevailing in the period before the second world war as well as the economic, social and political conditions of that time. The collector and author Dr. Christianne Weber-Stöber has collated and sifted the evidence in scholarly research so that the historic watch-chain and bijouterie manufacturer Jakob Bengel could be tracked down and reinstated as a major industrial monument of the period shortly before and after 1900.

I am delighted that the state of Rhineland-Palatinate and the Stiftung Rheinland-Pfalz für Kultur have been able to support this exhibition project which is so important for the gem and jewelry city of Idar-Oberstein. All my best wishes, therefore, for the success of both the exhibition and the book accompanying it. May they have many enthusiastic visitors and readers!

PROFESSOR DR. E. JÜRGEN ZÖLLNER
from the Minister for Science, Further Education, Research and Culture

VORWORT

Mit der ersten öffentlichen Präsentation der Privatsammlung »Jakob Bengel, Idar-Oberstein« unternimmt die Stadt Idar-Oberstein auch den Versuch, einen Teil ihrer Wirtschaftsgeschichte neu zu reflektieren. Ausstellung und Publikation führen in eine Epoche der Edelsteinstadt, in der sie zu den europäischen Metropolen der Schmuckindustrie gehörte. Die industrielle Produktion ermöglichte es, breiteste Bevölkerungsschichten mit modischem Schmuck, aber auch mit anderen Accessoires für die feine Dame oder den feinen Herrn auszustatten.
Die Wiederentdeckung der Galalith-Kollektion der Obersteiner Bijouteriewarenfabrik Jakob Bengel aus den Jahren 1931 bis 1938 zeigt, dass industrielle Produktion und herausragende Gestaltung kein Widerspruch sein müssen und dass die gestaltete Form dem Schmuckobjekt zu einer zeitlosen Wertigkeit verhilft. Die Sammlung von Art-Déco-Stücken im Bauhaus-Stil führt zu den Anfängen des modernen industriellen Designs. Ich bin der Überzeugung, dass es für die Bemühung der Stadt Idar-Oberstein um eine neue Profilierung auch als Schmuckstadt nur hilfreich sein kann, ihre, wie das Beispiel Jakob Bengel zeigt, ganz beachtlichen Design-Traditionen zu erforschen und herauszustellen.

Zu großem Dank ist die Stadt Idar-Oberstein allen verpflichtet, die diese Bemühungen unterstützen. Unser ganz besonderer Dank gilt dabei den Sammlern Dres. Händel, die in jahrzehntelanger mühevoller internationaler Recherche den Schmuck von Jakob Bengel und der Stadt Idar-Oberstein erneut in Verbindung gebracht haben. Unser Dank geht auch an die Autorinnen: Frau Dr. Christianne Weber-Stöber für die wissenschaftliche Bearbeitung dieses für die Schmuckgeschichte des 20. Jahrhunderts wichtigen Protagonisten Jakob Bengel, Frau Ilonka Wenk für den einleitenden Text. Der ARNOLDSCHEN Verlagsanstalt danken wir für jahrelange Vorarbeit und für die gelungene Publikation. Wir danken Herrn Prof. Dr. Kern und den StudentInnen der Fachhochschule für Edelstein- und Schmuckdesign für die Konzeption der Ausstellung sowie Herrn Lindemann, der das gesamte Projekt seitens der Stadt Idar-Oberstein betreut. Wir danken aber auch dem Land Rheinland-Pfalz, der Stiftung Rheinland-Pfalz für Kultur, der Stiftung Jakob-Bengel, der August-Becker-Stiftung, der Firma Herbert Giloy & Söhne, dem Museum Idar-Oberstein unterhalb der Felsenkirche sowie Landkreis und Kreissparkasse Birkenfeld, ohne deren Unterstützung die Realisierung der Ausstellung und der Publikation nicht möglich gewesen wäre.

HANS JÜRGEN MACHWIRTH
Oberbürgermeister der Stadt Idar-Oberstein

FOREWORD

With the first presentation to the public of the private collection »Jakob Bengel, Idar-Oberstein« the city of Idar-Oberstein is also undertaking to reconsider part of its economic history. The exhibition and the present book represent an introduction to a period in the history of the city of gems in which it was a major European center of jewelry-making. It was, after all, the industrial production of jewelry that made it possible to provide a broad public with both stylish jewelry and other fashion accessories for the elegant lady or gentleman.
The rediscovery of the Galalith collection dating from 1931 to 1938 owned by the Oberstein bijouteriewares manufacturer Jakob Bengel shows that industrial manufacture and outstanding design need by no means be a contradiction in terms and, more particularly, that the form of a piece of jewelry as designed is what makes it a timelessly valuable object in itself. The present collection of Art Déco pieces goes back to the beginnings of modern industrial design. I am convinced that researching into and emphasizing its design traditions, which are, as the example of Jakob Bengel so tellingly shows, notable indeed will have an overwhelmingly positive effect on the efforts of the city of Idar-Oberstein to regain its high profile as a jewelry city of international standing.

The city of Idar-Oberstein owes a great debt of gratitude to all those who have supported these efforts. First and foremost, our thanks go to the collectors, Dres. Händel, who have spent strenuous decades of research internationally on again linking the jewelry of Jakob Bengel and the city of Idar-Oberstein. We are indebted to Dr. Christianne Weber-Stöber for her scholarly study of Jakob Bengel, a manufacturer of outstanding importance to the history of 20th-century jewelry, and to Ilonka Wenk for her illuminating introduction. We are grateful indeed to ARNOLDSCHE Art Publishers, for making this publication a success by patiently preparing the ground for years in advance. We also thank Professor Dr. Kern and the students at the Fachhochschule für Edelstein- und Schmuckdesign for designing the exhibition and Mr Lindemann, who, as the representative of the city of Idar-Oberstein, has supervised the entire project. We also wish to thank the state of Rhineland-Palatinate, the Stiftung Rheinland-Pfalz für Kultur, the Stiftung Jakob-Bengel, the August-Becker-Stiftung, the firm of Herbert Giloy & Söhne, the Museum Idar-Oberstein unterhalb der Felsenkirche as well as the Landkreis und Kreissparkasse Birkenfeld, without whose support the exhibition and the present book would not have been possible.

HANS JÜRGEN MACHWIRTH
by the Mayor of the city of Idar-Oberstein

ZEITGEIST UND MODE DER 1930er JAHRE

Ilonka Wenk

»Wenn mir überhaupt noch mal ein Kleid gefällt, dann ist es meistens siebzig Jahre alt!« Ausgerechnet Vivienne Westwood, souveräne Stylistin eher schriller Effekte von internationalem Einfluß, ist bei der distinguierten Mode der 30er Jahre angekommen. Ihr Statement vom Juni 2002 bei einer Schau ihrer Studenten an der Berliner Hochschule der Künste ermutigt Bestrebungen, ein – was den deutschen Beitrag betrifft – vorbelastetes Retro-Thema neu zu sichten.

In der Tat: Es wird Zeit, die Eleganz und formale Geschlossenheit der 30er Jahre als klassische Moderne zu akzeptieren, die deutsche Produktion inbegriffen. Auf dem Bekleidungssektor war der »Berliner Chic« überregional ein Begriff, wie er sich den Einkäufern zweimal im Jahr auf der legendären Messe »Durchreise« darbot. Modische Impulse aus Paris fanden sich da zügig in tragbare, erschwingliche Konfektionsware »übersetzt«, ohne den Esprit des Originals dabei zu unterschlagen. Schule machte die arbeitsteilige Fertigung dieser Mode, die der Hersteller an Zwischenmeister delegierte, die ihrerseits die Näherinnen verpflichteten und für die Qualität des Endprodukts bürgten. Die Zerschlagung dieser blühenden Szene, als ab 1938 ihre überwiegend jüdischen Protagonisten vertrieben und deren Unternehmen »arisiert« wurden – voran das Nobelkaufhaus Gerson – , hat Berlin bis heute gezeichnet.

Auch der hier erstmals umfassend dokumentierte Modeschmuck der Firma Jakob Bengel aus Oberstein gehört in dieses Spannungsfeld von Produktivität und Politik. Natürlich ist auch er in Teilen ein Reflex der Geschmacksmuster, die das NS-Regime »heute Deutschland und morgen der ganzen Welt« aufzuzwingen suchte. Umso mehr überrascht die zumeist konsequent gewahrte Eigenständigkeit seines Designs. Auch beeindruckt die unternehmerische Leistung, ihn als Exportartikel selbst in Wirtschaftskrisen- und Kriegszeiten bei ersten Adressen im Ausland zu etablieren (Anhang I, S. 279).

Selten wandelt sich Mode so extrem, so aufschlußreich und exakt mit dem Jahrzehnt wie zu Beginn der 30er Jahre des 20. Jahrhunderts. Drei deutsch-sprachige Erfolgsautorinnen, Vicki Baum, Irmgard Keun und Christa Winslow, knüpfen genau da mit ihrer Zeitkritik an. Ihre – auch verfilmten – Romane und Bühnenstücke wurden vorübergehend »Kult«.

THE 1930s ZEITGEIST AND FASHION

Ilonka Wenk

»If I like a dress at all, it's usually at least seventy years old!« Vivienne Westwood of all people, the doyenne of rather brash styles with international repercussions, has fetched up at 1930s high fashion. The statement she made in June 2002 at a show of her students' work at the Berlin Hochschule der Künste encourages a burgeoning trend towards taking a new look at German retro – a subject which, as far as German period fashions are concerned, is still loaded with negative connotations.

It is indeed high time to accept 1930s fashions as classically modern, distinguished by elegance and stylistic unity and German fashions of that time are no exception. In the clothing sector, »Berlin Chic« was a supraregional buzzword when buyers attended "Durchreise" [»Passing Through«], a legendary fashion trade fair. The latest in Paris trends was picked up there and rapidly »translated« into wearable, reasonably priced off-the-rack clothes without any loss of the esprit informing the originals. The division of labor by which these fashions were created soon caught on. Work was outsourced by companies to intermediary craftsmen, who in turn hired sempstresses and were responsible for guaranteeing the quality of the end product. The demise of this flourishing fashion scene with the expulsion of its leading exponents, most of whom were Jewish and consequently lost their firms from 1938 to »Aryanisation« – notably Gerson, an upmarket department store – has left lasting scars on Berlin.

This first comprehensive survey of the costume jewelry made by Jakob Bengel at Oberstein also belongs to this highly charged field fraught with productivity and politics. Of course, this jewelry in part reflects the taste patterns which the National Socialist regime tried to impose on »Germany today and tomorrow the whole world«. What is so astonishing, however, is the consistently high degree of autonomy in design Jakob Bengel nevertheless succeeded in upholding. Equally impressive is the marketing strategy which enabled Bengel exports to establish a firm foothold at the most exclusive addresses abroad even in an era beset by economic crises followed by war (Appendix I, p. 279).

Rarely have fashions changed so radically, so tellingly and so precisely aligned with the turn of the decade as they did at the start of the 1930s. Three bestselling authors writing in German in the 1930s, Vicki Baum, Irmgard Keun and Christa Winslow, pinpointed the trends in their critical commentaries

1 Modell Castillo
Abendkleid aus rotem Satin mit passender, doppelseitig tragbarer Pelzstola.
Model Castillo
Evening dress in red satin with a reversible fur stole to match

Glanz und Elend zwischen Weimarer Republik und Drittem Reich (1918–33) demonstrieren sie am Umgang mit Schmuck- und Kleidungsstücken, die noch für das voraufgegangene Kaiserreich repräsentativ waren. Die Aura, die diese Statussymbole zu Beginn der Handlungen noch umgibt, erweist sich im weiteren Verlauf als passé, absurd, ja, verderbenbringend. Wer oder was an ihre Stelle treten wird: Auch darüber gibt diese Unterhaltungsliteratur illusionslos Auskunft.
Vicki Baum, Wahl-Berlinerin aus dem Wiener jüdischen Großbürgertum, schreibt 1929 den Roman »Menschen im Hotel«. In einem Grand Hotel à la »Adlon« kreuzen sich schicksalhaft die Wege von Aufsteigern und Verlierern nach den Regeln der neuen Zeit. Ein Baron, von den gesellschaftlichen Umbrüchen und der Weltwirtschaftskrise aus der Bahn geworfen, lebt als Hochstapler von reichen Frauen. Als er den legendären Perlenschmuck der Grusinskaja, einer alternden Primaballerina, aus deren Suite stehlen will, ertappt sie ihn in flagranti. Die beiden, entwurzelt und vereinsamt, finden sich. Um die Geliebte auf ihrer Gastspielreise ins Ausland begleiten zu können, braucht der Baron Geld. Nach einem erfolglosen Versuch, einen Buchhalter aus der Provinz zu bestehlen, der sein Erspartes in mondäne Großstadterlebnisse umzumünzen hofft, dringt er ins Zimmer eines Generaldirektors ein – ausgerechnet während dessen Rendezvous

2 Künstlerfoto Baroness de Lempicka-Foxhall, Paris, um 1930
Art photo of Baroness de Lempicka-Foxhall, Paris, ca 1930

3 Selbstporträt Baroness de Lempicka-Foxhall, 1925
Baroness de Lempicka-Foxhall, self-portrait, 1925

of contemporary issues. Their novels and plays – which were also filmed – became a »cult« and not only with the chattering classes. Such works highlight the glory and the squalor of the Weimar Republic up to the eve of the Third Reich (1918–33), demonstrated in the way they deal with jewelry and clothing representative of the defunct Wilhemine Empire. The aura which still surrounds these status symbols at the beginning of the plot is invariably exposed as passé, absurd or even corrupting as it unfolds. On the issues of who or what will replace them, such light fiction is informative and realistic.
Vicki Baum, an upper-middle-class Jewish girl from Vienna, settled in Berlin, where she wrote the novel »Menschen im Hotel« [»People in a Hotel«] in 1929. In a game played by modern rules, the trajectories of social climbers on the make criss-cross with those of losers at an elegant hotel à la »Adlon«. A baron, thrown off track by the social upheavals brought on the worldwide economic crisis, earns his living by duping rich women. Attempting to nick the fabulous pearls owned by the legendary Grousinskaya, an aging prima ballerina, from her suite, he is caught in the act by their owner. Rootless and lonely, the baron and the ballerina become lovers.
The baron needs money to accompany his mistress on tour abroad. After a fruitless attempt at robbing a provincial accountant, who hopes to transmute his savings into cosmopolitan rev-

mit seiner Sekretärin »Flämmchen«! Der Aschenbecher, den dieser nach ihm schleudert, trifft ihn tödlich. »Flämmchen« zögert keine Minute, ihren Chef der Polizei zu überlassen und mit dem bläßlichen Buchhalter nach Paris durchzubrennen.
Die Hollywood-Verfilmung des Stoffs von 1932 mit Greta Garbo, der Diva schlechthin, als Grusinskaja und der jungen Joan Crawford als umtriebiger Opportunistin »Flämmchen« macht Furore. Als eines der ersten Leinwand-Melodramen gibt dieser Film die Glamour-Version zeitgenössischer Mode für den Hausgebrauch vor: Lange, fließende Roben von kühler Erotik für die Garbo. Und auf Figur gearbeitete Kleider und »Kostümchen« mit halblangen, oft ausgestellten Röcken, adretten Garnituren und unkompliziertem Modeschmuck für »Flämmchen«, die süße Büromaus und (Über-)Lebenskünstlerin. Echte Perlen, das sieht sie richtig, bedeuten ab sofort nur noch Tränen.
Es ist dieser untere Mittelstand, der jetzt nach oben drängt, berauscht von der NS-Utopie einer »Volksgemeinschaft«, die keine Klassengegensätze mehr kennt und Marxismus, Kapitalismus und der »jüdischen Weltverschwörung« den Kampf ansagt. Ein Indikator für seine Sehnsüchte und Labilitäten ist der Pelzmantel aus dem Roman »Das kunstseidene Mädchen«, ebenfalls 1932 erschienen. Irmgard Keun, Berlinerin von großbürgerlich-liberaler Herkunft, erzählt darin von der unscheinbaren 18jährigen Doris, Sekretärin wie »Flämmchen«. In ihrer Kleinstadt hat diese ein solches Prunkstück entwendet, um ihrem ersten Freund damit zu imponieren. Jetzt ist sie im schlichten Regenmantel auf der Flucht in die Metropole, um hier endgültig zu arrivieren. »Ein Glanz« will sie werden, um welchen Preis auch immer!
Die Attribute »Flämmchen« und »kunstseiden« treffen perfekt die soziale Unbehaustheit dieser weiblichen Prototypen ihrer Generation. Zu Mitläuferinnen geboren, bringen sie zwar das Feuer des Aufbruchs mit, eine innovative Frische – aber nur in der Verkleinerungsform, einer Talmi-Version. Lebenshunger wird als Selbstzweck konsumiert, im Zugriff auf das Geld des Zufallspartners oder den feudalen Fetisch Pelz, statt sich aus eigener Kraft und Einsicht eine überzeugende urbane Existenz zu erarbeiten.
Der Glanz der Uniform schließlich: Ist wenigstens der den Trägern und Trägerinnen dieses preußischen Relikts noch garantiert? In ihrem Stück »Mädchen in Uniform« zieht Christa Winslow das 1929 anhand eines kühnen Exempels in Zweifel. Die Offizierstochter aus Darmstadt ist bekennend lesbisch – in den tollen 1920ern noch der Clou, jetzt »entartet«, ein Wagnis. Entsprechend zerbricht auf der Bühne die Internatsschülerin Manuela an ihrer Leidenschaft für eine ungewöhnliche Lehrerin. Dieser Verstoß gegen ein absolutes Tabu treibt sie in den Selbstmord.

els in the metropolis, the baron invades the office of a top manager – just when he is enjoying a tryst with his secretary, »Flämmchen« (a speaking name which literally means »Flamelet«)! An ashtray hurled by the industrialist at the intruder kills him on the spot. »Flämmchen« has no qualms at all about turning her boss over to the police and absconding to Paris with the dreary little accountant.
The 1932 Hollywood film made from the Baum novel, »Grand Hotel«, starred Greta Garbo, the diva assoluta, as Grousinskaya and, in a supporting role, the young Joan Crawford as »Flämmchen«, the adventuress with an eye to the main chance, caused a furore. One of the earliest melodramas of the talking screen, this film set trends in glamorous fashions which the public was at liberty to adore and copy: long, flowing garments redolent of cool eroticism for Garbo. By contrast, fitted dresses and »little suits« with half-length, often full skirts, stylish accessories and unabashedly fake costume jewelry for »Flämmchen«, the coquettish Girl Friday and accomplished survival artist. From now on real pearls – how right she was – only mean tears.
This is the lower middle class which was pushing up to the top, intoxicated by the Nazi utopia of a classless »people's community« which had declared war on marxism, capitalism and the »worldwide Jewish conspiracy«. An indicator of popular yearnings and foibles is the fur coat worn in another novel published in 1932, »Das kunstseidene Mädchen« [»Girl in Artificial Silk«]. In it, Irmgard Keun, an upper-middle-class Berliner from a liberal background, tells the story of Doris, a nondescript 18-year-old, a secretary like »Flämmchen«. Doris has stolen a luxurious fur coat in her provincial home town to impress her first boyfriend. Now she is on the run in the capital, wearing a simple trenchcoat but seriously on the make. She wants to be a »glamour girl« and is willing to pay the price!
The attributes »Flamelet« and »wearing artificial silk« pinpoint the social rootlessness of these female prototypes of a lost generation. Born to be nothing but fellow travelers, they nonetheless have a spark of awakening, something fresh and innovative about them – if only in diminutives, a pinchbeck version of the real thing. Lust for life is consumed as an end in itself. Taking the lolly on the run from any man they happen to have a fleeting affair with, these lovelies flaunt furs, a feudal fetish, instead of working out a convincing urban lifestyle based on strength of character and true grit.
It ultimately boils down to the glamour of uniforms. Is this still guaranteed for the men and women who wear such Prussian relics? In the play »Mädchen in Uniform« [»Girls in Uniform«], Christa Winslow casts doubts on this as early as 1929. An officer's daughter from Darmstadt, the author daringly outed herself as a Lesbian – in the Roaring Twenties it had been in to be Lesbian but by now it was coming to be regarded as »degenerate«. In the play, Manuela, therefore, is destroyed by

Mädchen in Uniform wird es ab der Machtergreifung des »Führers« Adolf Hitler 1933 wieder in Massen geben – unter anderem beim BDM, dem Reichsarbeitsdienst, als Wehrmachtshelferinnen, Sanitäterinnen und Schaffnerinnen. Daß Patriotismus und Wohlverhalten schlechthin mit Drill und Gleichmacherei nicht zu erzwingen sind, ohne daß auf Dauer die Psyche Schaden leidet, ist hier die rigide geahndete Botschaft. Nach Ablehnung durch die UFA verfilmt zwar 1931 eine (noch) freie Frauen-Produktionsfirma den Stoff mit Hertha Thiele und Dorothea Wieck. Aber Vorführungen sind verboten. Vicki Baum, Irmgard Keun und Christa Winslow mit ihrem Scharfblick für Moden und Meinungen, die einander bedingen, werden als Urheberinnen von »verbotenem Schrifttum« geächtet, in die Emigration gezwungen.

Aus der Ferne dürften sie mit Genugtuung vermerkt haben, daß die Bemühungen des 1933 gegründeten Deutschen Modeamts um Gleichschaltung des Bekleidungswesens mit der »völkischen« NS-Ideologie praktisch ins Leere gehen. Das Institut hat Order, in Anlehnung an die nationale Folklore und Historie das »reinrassig« germanische Gewand samt Zubehör zu propagieren, seine Herstellung samt Vertrieb zu fördern und zugleich aus Exportgründen mit den internationalen Standards Schritt zu halten. Ein aussichtsloses Unterfangen! Die einschlägige Profilneurose bringt der Sketch von Kurt Tucholsky »Gespräch auf einem Diplomatenempfang« zwischen zwei Nouvelles Riches auf den Punkt: »Wir in Berlin sind überall dabei, aber wir kommen zu nichts. Wir haben französischen Schick, englischen Sport, amerikanisches Tempo und heimische Hast – nur uns selbst haben wir nie gekannt.«[1]

Dem abzuhelfen, propagiert das offizielle Organ, die »NS-Frauenwarte« das Dirndl & Co, während die Ersten Damen des NS-Staats ganz anderen Begehrlichkeiten nachgehen. Magda Goebbels, Ehrenvorsitzende des Modeamts, ist zwar als Vielkindermutter das Idol ihrer Zeit, aber auch geschiedene Industriellengattin und Vorzeige-Ehefrau des Reichspropagandaministers, der auch die Filmindustrie auf Kurs bringt. Selbstbewußt reklamiert sie für die deutsche Frau

4 Strandmantel aus gefärbtem Fischernetz. 1936
Foto Max Göllner
Beach coat made of dyed fishnet. 1936
Photo: Max Göllner

a Lesbian passion for an unusual teacher at her boarding school. Infringing against an absolute taboo drives Manuela to commit suicide.

Following Adolf Hitler's accession to power in 1933, there would again be girls in uniform in droves – among them, girls saluting the »Führer« as members of the BDM [League of German Girls], serving in the Reichsarbeitsdienst [Reich Works Corps], as Wehrmacht auxiliaries, medical orderlies and tram conductors. That patriotism and good conduct simply cannot be enforced by drill and relentless leveling without causing permanent psychological damage is the message strictly insisted on here. After the UFA had refused to consider the play, a (still) independent producer of films for women did make a film of it in 1931 with Hertha Thiele and Dorothea Wieck in the leading roles. However, it was forbidden to show the film publicly. With their unerring eye for fashions and trends, which are, after all, interrelated, Vicki Baum, Irmgard Keun and Christa Winslow were outlawed as the authors of »forbidden writings« and forced to emigrate.

They must have been pleased to observe from afar that the endeavors of the Deutsches Modeamt [German Fashion office], established in 1933, to make all clothing uniform in conformity with the »ethnic« Nazi ideology were doomed to failure from the outset. The institute was ordered to disseminate propaganda for »pure-blooded« German apparel and accessories designed to match nationalist folklore and the Nazi approach to history, to promote its manufacture and marketing, yet to ensure a positive balance of trade, to keep abreast of international standards. A double-bind! A severe inferiority complex as a result of trying to keep up with the world is devastatingly captured in the Kurt Tucholsky sketch of two nouvelles riches, »Gespräch auf einem Diplomatenempfang« [»Conversation at a Diplomatic Reception«]: »We in Berlin are doing our best on all fronts but we aren't getting anywhere. We have French chic, English sports, the American pace and native hastiness – but for all that we've never got to know ourselves.« [1]

To help things along, the official organ for women's affairs, the »NS-Frauenwarte», plumped strongly for the dirndl and related

5 Marlene Dietrich, um 1933
Marlene Dietrich, ca 1933

6 Die Filmschauspielerin Kristina Söderbaum in altdeutscher Tracht vor dem Achtzylinder-Horch von Veit Harlan, während der Dreharbeiten zu dem historischen Film »Das unsterbliche Herz«, 1938. Foto: Rolf Anton

The film star Kristina Söderbaum posing in Old German costume in front of Veit Harlan's eight-cylinder Horch while the historical film »Das unsterbliche Herz« (»The Immortal Heart«) was being made in 1938. Photo: Rolf Anton

Schick, Schönheit und Klugheit, verweist den Gretchentyp ins Abseits von Heim und Herd.
Und Eva Braun, Hitlers unbedarfte Geliebte, posiert zwar auf dem Obersalzberg in der Tracht, ordert aber inoffiziell Pariser Modelle und fährt mit SS-Leibgarde nach Florenz, um dort Schuhe von Salvatore Ferragamo zu kaufen. Erst dieser Luxus an den Füßen der Rivalin überzeugt Unity Mitford, Nazi-Mitläuferin aus dem von Hitler umworbenen englischen Hochadel, bei einem Besuch im Fotoladen, wo Eva Braun anfangs noch als Verkäuferin arbeitet, von der real existenten Mesalliance des von ihr vergötterten Führers mit diesem Mauerblümchen.
Der internationale Austausch modischer Ideen funktioniert abseits aller politischen Restriktionen. Auch die deutsche Normalverbraucherin ist gut dabei, und keineswegs nur als Nehmende. Besonders das Traditionsmodeheft »Die Dame«, immerhin bis 1943 am Markt, versorgt sie über die populären Zeichnungen von »Dryden« mit Anregungen. Trotz der lässigen englischen Anspielung muss dieses Pseudonym deutsch »Drieden« ausgesprochen werden, solange sein Träger noch die »Hochmode« (Haute Couture) zeichnen darf. Denn dahinter steht der Jude Ernst Deutsch, und sein Schicksal ist absehbar. Mit kosmopolitischem Strich übersetzt er die Trends der grossen Welt, die sich dann mit etwas Improvisationstalent per Hausschneiderei umsetzen lassen.

Primär Paris brilliert da mit kontrastreicher Haute Couture von einsamer innovativer Klasse. Madeleine Vionnet erfindet den Schrägschnitt, der Kleider und Röcke aus subtilen Seiden- und zarten Wollstoffen hautnah, ohne Verschluß am Körper herabfließen läßt. In Hollywood greifen Könner wie Adrian, Chef-Kostümbildner der Filmstudios MGM, diesen Antikeneffekt unter anderem für das »blonde Gift« Jean Harlow auf. Umgekehrt verschmäht diese die Exotizismen urdeutscher Mode nicht: Auf einem Kostümfest der 1930er Jahre in Beverly Hills posiert sie aufgekratzt in Lederhosen, neben Gloria Swanson in Dirndlkleid und Tirolerhut. Ins Lodencape hüllt sich auch Marlene Dietrich bei den Salzburger Festspielen 1938. Gregor von Rezzori macht dieses Event in seinen Erinnerungen aus anderen Gründen frösteln: »Austro-Chic in Dirndl und Trachtenjoppe, während nebenan die Hofmannsthals nächt-

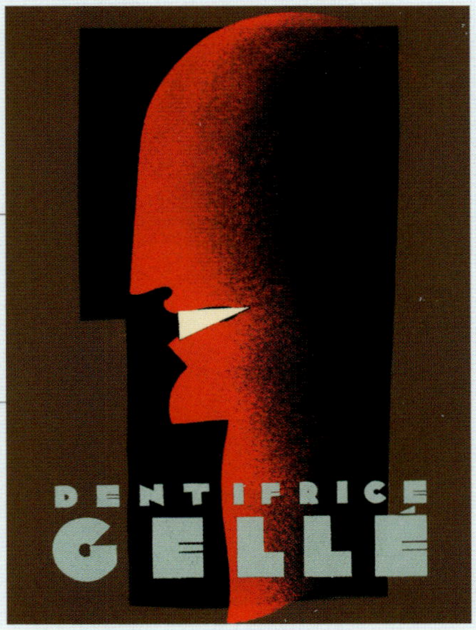

7 Jean Carlu
Entwurf für ein Plakat, Paris, 1927
Jean Carlu
Design for a poster, Paris, 1927

accessories while the first ladies of the Nazi regime were free to indulge fashion yearnings of a different order altogether. Magda Goebbels, honorary head of the Fashion Office, was a public icon of the day because she had so many children. More importantly, she had divorced an industrialist to be the Reich Propaganda Minister's model wife and he was supposed to ensure that the film industry toed the party line. With great self-assurance and poise, however, Magda Goebbels spurned the dowdy Gretchen type, banishing her to home and hob since she herself was determined to set an example for German women as chic, beautiful and intelligent.
And Eva Braun, Hitler's hapless mistress, did pose obligingly for the camera on the Obersalzberg in peasant dirndl but unofficially she ordered Paris models and went with her SS bodyguards on surreptitious shopping sprees to Florence just to splurge on Salvatore Ferragamo shoes. It was, in fact, the luxurious footwear sported by her successful rival for the »Führer«'s affections that ultimately convinced Unity Mitford, perhaps the best-known Nazi fellow traveler recruited from the English aristocracy by Hitler and his minions, on a visit to a photo shop where Eva Braun was still working behind the counter that her idol had really embarked on a mésalliance with this pathetic wallflower.
The international exchange of ideas on fashion invariably functions in the face of all political restrictions imposed on it. The elegant magazine »Die Dame«, which managed to remain on the market until 1943, supplied fashion-conscious German ladies with inspiration via drawings by »Dryden«, which were enormously popular. Although a casual allusion to the English poet, this draughtsman's pseudonym had to be pronounced »Drieden« according to the dictates of German phonology for as long as the man behind the name was allowed to take up his pen in the service of »high fashion« (haute couture). He was Ernst Deutsch, a Jew, and the fate that would overtake him was foreseeable. He translated haute couture deftly into cosmopolitan line so that, with a bit of improvisation, it might be adapted by littlesempstresses for home use.
Paris haute couture dazzled the fashion world with its innovative brilliance. Madeleine Vionnet invented the bias cut, a cross-grain cut which made it easy to form material into folds so that dress-

lings Hals über Kopf hatten flüchten müssen, um nicht als dreckige Juden misshandelt … und eingesperrt zu werden.«[2] Völlig unnachahmlich setzt sich dagegen vom Start weg die Römerin und Wahl-Pariserin Elsa Schiaparelli in Szene. Höchste Schneiderkunst verbindet sie mit einem Brillantfeuerwerk motivlicher Ideen von echter oder vorgetäuschter Plastizität, bei denen ihre Surrealisten-Freunde Cocteau und Dalí Pate stehen. Auf ihre berühmten Pullover druckt sie Schleifen, Krägen, Gürtel und Manschetten auf. Ein Kleid mit »echten« Schubladen oder einem naturgetreuen Hummer gehören zu ihrem unverkennbaren Repertoire – ebenso wie Zirkus- und Rokokodekors, alles mit passenden Hüten, Schuhen und Handschuhen. Energiegeladen wie ihre Lieblingsfarbe »Shocking Pink« und ihr Parfum gleichen Namens, ist sie Pionierin beim Einsatz von Synthetikstoffen, Reißverschlüssen und Schulterpolstern, die zunehmend zum Muß werden.

Auch diese Nouveautés finden sich in der »sophisticated comedy« wieder, dem neuen Genre des US-Films. Die Deutsche macht Augen: Wieviel kratzbürstig-witziger flirten da die intellektuelle Katherine Hepburn, die pikante Claudette Colbert mit ihren ebenso smarten Partnern Spencer Tracy oder Cary Grant! Mit der typähnlichen Marianne Hoppe und Lillian Harvey, dem »Filigrantrampel«, hält der deutsche Film zwar dagegen. Aber diese »erwachsene« Leichtigkeit fehlt!
Um eben die geht es in Paris Gabrielle, genannt Coco Chanel, mit ihrer zeitlosen Mode des strengen Luxus. Lässigkeit, Bewegungsfreiheit in ein- und demselben Outfit vom morgendlichen Marktbesuch bis zum Tagesausklang in der Oper ist ihr Credo. Einfachheit mit Raffinesse verbinden die Schnitte ihres genialen »kleinen Schwarzen«, ihrer uni Cardigankostüme aus – damals noch unüblichem – Jersey und ihrer kastigen, gepaspelten Kostüme aus federleichten Multicolor-Tweeds. Die weisse Hemdbluse, der Kaschmirpulli zur perfekt proportionierten langen Hose wurden unverzichtbare Basics, ebenso wie ihr opulenter Modeschmuck in frechem Mix von Echt und Unecht.

8 Pierre Imans
Mannequin, Paris, 1925
Pierre Imans
Mannequin, Paris, 1925

9 Man Ray
Elsa Schiaparelli, Paris, 1930
Man Ray
Elsa Schiaparelli, Paris, 1930

es and skirts made of slinky silks and clinging delicate wool fabrics flowed down the body without the need for fasteners. In Hollywood such connaisseurs as Adrian, chief costume designer at MGM, snapped up this antique effect for luminaries like Jean Harlow, the »blonde bombshell«. Conversely, she had nothing whatsoever against the exotic features of pure ethnic German fashion: at a costume ball given in Beverly Hills in the 1930s she posed defiantly dressed in Lederhosen next to Gloria Swanson sporting a dirndl and Tyrolean hat. Marlene Dietrich even wore a loden cape at the 1938 Salzburg Festival. In his memoirs, Gregor von Rezzori records that he was chilled to the bone by this event for a very different reason: »Austro-chic in dirndl and short woollen jackets while the Hofmannsthals next door had to flee under cover of night so as not to be abused as dirty Jews… and be locked up accordingly.« [2]
Born in Rome, the designer Elsa Schiaparelli moved to Paris, where she launched herself brilliantly on the international fashion scene. She combined the best of bespoke tailoring with dazzling ideas for motifs which might be three-dimensional or simply simulated plasticity, conceived in the spirit of her Surrealist friends Cocteau and Dalí. A dress with »real« drawers and one sporting a realistic-looking lobster are part and parcel of her distinctive repertoire – so are circus and Rococo decoration schemes. Bursting with energy like her signature color »Shocking Pink« and the scent bearing her name, she pioneered the use of synthetic fabrics, zips and padded shoulders, which were fast becoming a fashion must.
These novelties are also encountered in »sophisticated comedies«, the new Hollywood film genre of the day. German cinemagoers were astonished. How gruffly naughty yet sparkling with wit were the flirtations engaged in by the intellectual Katherine Hepburn and the racy Claudette Colbert with equally savvy partners such as Spencer Tracy and Cary Grant! German cinema managed to counter with two stars of similar type, Marianne Hoppe and Lillian Harvey, the »delicate tramp«. But that »adult« lightness of touch was missing.

10 Diana Mitford, Schwester von Nancy und Unity Mitford, Ehefrau des englischen Faschistenführers Sir Oswald Mosley, in geknöpftem Mantelkleid mit Cape aus geschorenem, bedrucktem Pelz, 27.1.1932. Foto Elizabeth Owen

Diana Mitford, sister of Nancy und Unity Mitford and wife of the English Fascist leader Sir Oswald Mosley, wearing a coat dress that buttons down the front with a dyed shearling cape, 27. Jan. 1932. Photo: Elizabeth Owen

Als Person dunkelhaarig, zierlich, scharfblickend, befehlsgewohnt, amüsant und elitär, lief die Chanel für einen Frauentyp Reklame, der zu einer der Ikonen der 1930er Jahre wurde – irgendwo zwischen Schneewittchen und der bösen Stiefmutter. Dazu zählen auch die Amerikanerin Wallis Simpson, für die der Prince of Wales auf die britische Krone verzichtete, mit ihrem Statement: »Man kann nicht dünn und nicht reich genug sein!« Und Simone de Beauvoir, Schriftstellerin und Gefährtin des Existenzphilosophen Jean-Paul Sartre. Wie in ihren Erinnerungen »In den besten Jahren« nachzulesen, einem akribischen Zeitpanorama, hinderten weder der Nihilismus noch die immer frugaleren Zeitläufte sie daran, auch unter den Vorzeichen von Not und Mangel die Bekleidungsrituale einer »jungen Dame« zu zelebrieren und Mahlzeiten ohne Ende bewußt zu genießen. Gala, die Muse des Malers Salvador Dalí, gehört dazu. In einer mütterlichen Variante auch die junge Königin Elizabeth und spätere «Queen Mom”. Im Film Vivien Leigh, 1939 Star in »Vom Winde verweht«, die blutjunge Elizabeth Taylor und Lida Baarova, die unglückliche Geliebte von Joseph Goebbels. Und nicht zuletzt auch »Schneewittchen« selbst – 1937 im ersten abendfüllenden Trickfilm in Farbe von Walt Disney.

Mit fortschreitender »Mobilmachung« konzentriert sich der verdeckte Austausch deutscher und ausländischer Modeideen auf den Sport. Ein Massenphänomen wie der Film, verspricht dieser ein willkommenes Propaganda-Potential. Entsprechend simuliert unter anderem das Olympia-Heft der »Neuen Linie« vom Oktober 1936 Weltoffenheit. Neben Beiträgen von Werner March (»Die Kunst im Reichssportfeld«) und Mary Wigman (»Deutscher Tanz und olympischer Geist«) stehen »Modebriefe aus vier Ländern« und Empfehlungen ausländischer Speiselokale in Berlin. Ein Feinripp-Hersteller wirbt mit kessen Schwimmtrikots. Nachhaltig und weltweit Schule macht die deutsche Skimode des Münchner Hauses Bogner zur Winterolympiade desselben Jahres in Garmisch.

11 Anzeige für Schwimmtrikots, Ribana Werke Wilhelm Benger Söhne, Stuttgart, 1936
Advertisement for knitted bathing suits, Ribana Werke Wilhelm Benger Söhne, Stuttgart, 1936

And that was what Paris was all about. Gabrielle, nicknamed Coco, Chanel with her timeless, astringently elegant fashions. Casual, comfortable to wear, a single outfit for all day from a morning visit to one's local market to an evening at the opera as a grand finale was Chanel's creed. Simplicity paired with sophistication is the hallmark of her superbly cut »little black dresses«, her jersey – at that time still an unusual tailoring fabric – suits with collarless cardigan jackets and her boxy, braid-trimmed suits made of multicolor tweeds that were as light as a feather. The Chanel white open-neck menswear shirt and cashmere sweater worn with perfectly proportioned slacks became indispensable basics and so did her opulent costume jewelry, a saucy blend of real and simulated.

A slender brunette with sharp eyes that took everything in at a glance, she herself was a commanding presence, witty and elitist. Chanel became a 1930s icon, a trendy vixen for women to emulate, evocative of both Snow White and her wicked stepmother. Another such foxy lady was the American Wallis Simpson, for whom the Prince of Wales gave up the crown. She is immortalized by her dictum »One can never be too thin or too rich.« And then there was Simone de Beauvoir, early feminist writer and companion for life to the Existentialist philosopher Jean-Paul Sartre. As she recalls in her memoir »La force de l'âge« (translated in 1962 into English as »The Prime of Life«), neither nihilism nor the increasing hardships of the era prevented her from celebrating the rites of dressing observed by »young ladies« or, despite poverty and food shortages, kept her from enjoying sumptuous meals without end. Gala, the muse of the painter Salvador Dalí, also belongs to this stellar bevy of astringent belles. A motherly variant was the young Queen Elizabeth, later beloved worldwide as the »Queen Mum«. Hollywood boasted the fragile Vivien Leigh, who starred in »Gone with the Wind« in 1939, and the violet-eyed Elizabeth Taylor, a dark rose not yet in full bloom, while Germany fell for Lida Baarova, Joseph Goebbels' ill-starred mistress. Last

Die funktional-feschen Anoraks, Keilhosen, Overalls und Nickipullover, in den USA »The Bogners« genannt«, werden auf Anhieb zu Klassikern.
Ab 1939 erfolgt die Zuteilung von Textilien für die Bevölkerung auf Kleiderkarten. Mit Kriegsbeginn bleiben die vorher schon knappen Stoffkontingente der Wehrmacht vorbehalten. Woll- und Baumwollimporte gibt es nur noch für Uniformen. Die Zivilbevölkerung geht leer aus. In einem letzten, trotz des katastrophalen politischen Hintergrunds vielleicht originellsten Kraftakt von allen, besinnt sich das Jahrzehnt noch einmal auf seine Kreativität, deutet Schwund in Herausforderung um. Aus »Ersatzstoffen« wie Zellwolle und Viskose, ursprünglich Abfallprodukten von Baumwolle und Fichtenholz, aus Fallschirmseide und Gardinentüll entstehen ansehnliche Entwürfe. Und erst recht aus den US-Synthetiks Nylon und Perlon, die der Bevölkerung als deutsche Erfindungen angedient werden! Eilig aktivierte Hilfsindustrien liefern sächsischen Flitter, einen schwachen Abglanz der Pailletten aus der Charleston-Ära, Posamenten aus dem Erzgebirge sowie Knöpfe und Schliessen aus Kunststoff in Idar-Oberstein. Falls man das Glück des Überlebens hatte, taumelt man im Frühjahr 1945 tödlich erschöpft, ausgehungert und psychisch am Ende vielfach auf kunstledernen Schuhen mit Holz- und Korksohlen in einen nicht mehr erhofften Frieden. Und, auf die Mode bezogen, in die Übergangsperiode des improvisierenden »Aus-Zwei-Mach-Eins«. Aber das ist ein anderes Kapitel.

1 Kurt Tucholsky: Gesammelte Werke Band 8, 1930. Reinbek 1980, S. 83
2 Gregor von Rezzori: Mir auf der Spur. München 1999, S. 187

but not least, »Snow White« herself swept world cinema – in 1937 she was the appealing brunette heroine of the first full-length animated cartoon film made by Walt Disney in color.
With »mobilization« in full swing, the secret exchange of German and foreign fashion ideas became increasingly limited to sportswear. A mass phenomenon like cinema, sport was promising indeed as an ideal vehicle for launching propaganda. It is not surprising that the October 1936 number of the Olympic magazine »Neue Linie« made a pretence of being cosmopolitan. Apart from articles by Werner March (»Die Kunst im Reichssportfeld« [»Art in the Reich Sport Field«]) and Mary Wigman (»Deutscher Tanz und olympischer Geist« [«German Dance and the Olympic Spirit»]), it featured »Modebriefe aus vier Ländern« [»Letters on Fashions from Four Countries«] and even recommended foreign eateries in Berlin. A maker of skinny-rib knitwear advertises pert bathing suits. The German ski fashions created by the Munich house of Bogner for the 1936 Winter Olympics in Garmisch set a trend that would survive the war. Functional and smart, Bogner anoraks, tapered ski pants, overalls and synthetic stretch velour Nicki pullovers, known in the US generically as »Bogners«, became instant classics.
From 1939 textiles were allocated to Germans on clothing ration cards. When war broke out, the textiles quota, already meager, was reserved for the Wehrmacht. Wool and cotton fabrics were now only available for making uniforms. Civilians had to make the best of what they had. Attractive designs were featured in »Ersatz materials« such as cellulose fiber and viscose, originally discarded spin-offs from cotton and conifer wood, from parachute silk and curtain tulle. And liberal use was made of the US synthetics nylon and perlon. The Germans had the wool pulled over their eyes to make them believe those fibers were German inventions! Auxiliary industries were quickly mobilized to produce Saxon Flitter, a drab substitute indeed for the sequins that had glittered in the Charleston era, gold and silver lace and braid from the Erzgebirge Mountains and buttons and buckles made of plastic at Idar-Oberstein. The lucky ladies to survive the war, physically and emotionally exhausted and famished as they were, nonetheless found the strength in 1945 to teeter on shoes with artificial leather uppers and thick wood and cork soles into a peace they had abandoned all hopes of living to see. And, as far as fashion was concerned, into a transitional era of improvisation. But that is another chapter.

1 Kurt Tucholsky: Gesammelte Werke Vol. 8, 1930. Reinbek 1980, p. 83
2 Gregor von Rezzori: Mir auf der Spur. Munich 1999, p. 187

ART DÉCO SCHMUCK AUS METALL UND GALALITH

Christianne Weber

Modeschmuck für die Frau von Welt – aus der Produktion Jakob Bengel, Oberstein

»Plötzlich auf Modediktat geschieht das Erstaunliche: der verwöhnteste Geschmack trägt ›unechten Schmuck‹. Paris hat die Mode des unechten Schmucks geschaffen, London förderte sie und nun breitet sie sich überall aus. Ein wahrer Unechtstaumel hat den Schmuckmarkt ergriffen ...«[1]

Ein Kommentar aus dem Jahr 1925, dem Jahr der großen »Exposition Internationale des Arts Décoratifs et Industriels Modernes« in Paris, auf der 40 Hersteller von Modeschmuck ihre Schmuckstücke präsentierten. Bereits 1924 lag der Umsatz des Modeschmucks in Frankreich bei 100 Millionen Francs! Auch wenn die legendäre Coco Chanel den Modeschmuck erst 1928 wirklich salonfähig machte, war er zu diesem Zeitpunkt schon längst Tagesgespräch.

Als vor beinahe zwanzig Jahren auf Antikmärkten und bei Kunsthändlern lange Halsketten und Colliers aus verchromtem Metall mit kräftig farbigem Kunststoff auftauchten, war man von diesem Modeschmuck im sachlich-kühlen »Bauhausstil« sofort begeistert. So manche Kette wurde zum Sammelobjekt in Deutschland, England und Frankreich aber auch in den USA. Eine Identifizierung der Stücke war nicht möglich, da nicht eine einzige Kette mit einer Künstler-Marke oder einem Firmensignet versehen war. Aufgrund der herausragenden Gestaltung war man sich schnell einig, daß es sich um deutschen, wohl eher französischen Modeschmuck der 1930er Jahre handelte.[2] Als nun vor einiger Zeit Musterbücher auftauchten, in denen die Vorlagen bzw. Muster für diesen außergewöhnlichen Schmuck zu finden waren, dauerte es nur kurze Zeit bis man schließlich zum Ausgangspunkt dieses Schmucks gelangte, nach Idar-Oberstein[3] zur Firma Jakob Bengel. Dort hatte man zu Beginn der 1930er Jahre mit einer unglaublichen Kreativität und einem feinen Gespür, Schmuckstücke aus Metall und Galalith geschaffen, die dem Zeitgeist und dem Typus der neuen Frau entsprachen. Nicht zuletzt war es auch die weltweit schlechte Wirtschaftslage, die dem Modeschmuck, also auch dem Schmuck der Firma Jakob Bengel, zu seinem Erfolg verhalf, wie der Kritiker Pierre Contreau 1932 sehr richtig bemerkte: »Die Frau wird in ihrem Äußeren immer einzigartig

ART DÉCO JEWELRY MADE OF METAL AND GALALITH

Christianne Weber

Costume jewelry for the sophisticate by Jakob Bengel, Oberstein/Germany

»Suddenly an astonishing thing is happening following the dictates of fashion: the most pampered taste is wearing ›simulated jewelry‹. Paris has created a fashion in simulated jewelry, London has promoted it and now it is spreading everywhere. The jewelry market is in the grip of a real craze for the simulated ...«[1]

A comment made in 1925, the year of the great »Exposition Internationale des Arts Décoratifs et Industriels Modernes« in Paris, where forty makers of costume jewelry presented their pieces. By 1924 the volume of costume-jewelry sales in France had reached 100 million francs! Even though it was not until 1928 that the legendary Coco Chanel made costume jewelry socially acceptable, by 1924 it had long been the buzz-word.

When long chains and collars of chromium-plated metal with plastic dyed in vibrant colors surfaced nearly twenty years ago on the antiques market, the fashion world was immediately enchanted with this costume jewelry in the objective, cool »Bauhaus style«. Many a necklace became a collector's item, not only in Germany, France and England, but also in the United States of America. Identification of the pieces was not possible then since not a single one of these chains bore a maker's mark or a firm stamp. The outstanding design distinguishing these pieces soon led to agreement that this must be 1930s German, or more likely, French, costume jewelry.[2] After pattern books appeared some time ago in which the models or pattern designs for this unusual jewelry were displayed, it was no time at all before its origins were traced to Idar-Oberstein[3] and specifically to the firm of Jakob Bengel. There jewelry made of metal and Galalith revealed incredible creativity and a sensitive awareness of the Zeitgeist and the new woman who was now emerging. Further, the poor economic situation worldwide was another contributing factor to making the jewelry created by the firm of Jakob Bengel so successful, as the critic Pierre Contreau aptly observed in 1932: »Women will always want to be unique in appearance. However, if they no longer have unlimited funds for this at their disposal, they will turn to inexpensive jewelry. This ushers in the era of imaginative jewelry.«[4]

sein wollen. Wenn sie dafür aber keine Unsummen mehr ausgeben darf, wird sie Schmuck zu einem billigen Preis suchen. Dann bricht die Ära des Phantasie-Schmucks aus«.[4]
Das Studium der Musterbücher von Bengel bringt die unglaubliche Vielfalt und das kaum zu überschauende Formenrepertoire dieser Schmuckproduktion ans Tageslicht. Aufgrund der beinahe lückenlosen Nachweise der Entwürfe läßt sich die Entstehung vieler Schmuckstücke auf den Tag genau datieren. Aber auch neue Erkenntnisse im Bezug auf die Modeschmuckproduktion der Firma Henkel & Grosse in Pforzheim konnten gewonnen werden. Seit langem ist bekannt, daß Henkel & Grosse seinen seit den 1950er Jahren angebotenen Dior-Schmuck in Kaufbeuren-Neugablonz fertigen läßt. Die Musterbücher der Firma Bengel zeigen jetzt, daß auch Modelle aus der Galalith- und Metallschmuckserie der 1930er Jahre nicht in Pforzheim, sondern in Oberstein für Henkel & Grosse gefertigt wurden.
Es ist dem Spürsinn und der Sammelleidenschaft eines Ehepaares in Deutschland zu verdanken, daß wir heute eine große Anzahl von Bengel-Stücken als Originale kennen und mehr, wenn auch sicher nicht alles, über diesen ausgefallenen Modeschmuck wissen. Die mehrere Hundert Bengel-Schmuckstücke umfassende Sammlung wurde im Laufe der Jahre um Dokumente, Broschüren, Auftragsbücher und weitere aufschlußreiche Unterlagen (aus ehemaligem Firmenbesitz) erweitert.
Mit der Einrichtung der Bengel-Stiftung im vergangenen Jahr war der Grundstein für die Erforschung der Obersteiner Uhrketten- und Metallwarenindustrie am Beispiel der Firma Bengel gelegt. Die Produktionsstätten und die Fabrikantenvilla stehen beispielhaft für die vielen Uhrketten- und Bijouteriewarenfirmen wie Klein & Quenzer, Carl Keller Christian Sohn oder Gottlieb & Söhne, die der Obersteiner Industrie zu ihrem weltweiten Erfolg verhalfen.

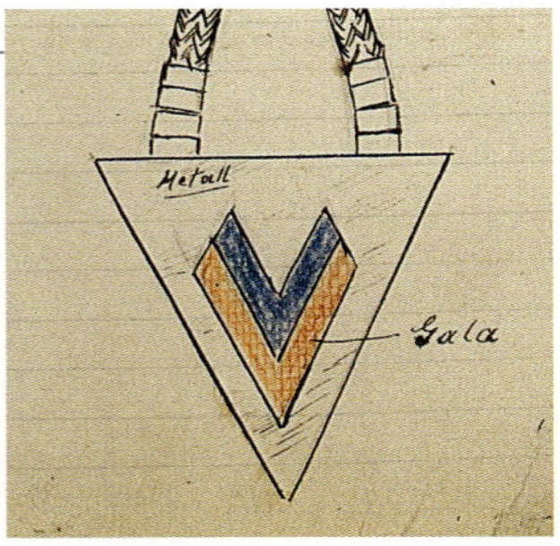

12 Musterbuch Jakob Bengel, Bd. X, S. 107, 1932/33, Ausschnitt Modell 20.209. Siehe auch Kat.-Nr. 154
Pattern Book Jakob Bengel, Vol. X, p. 107, 1932/1933, detail of model 20.209. See also Cat.no. 154

13 Taschenclip, vergl. Modell 20.209 (Halskette), Abb. 12
Handbag clip; cf. model 20.209 (necklace), fig. 12

14 Robert Bonfils, Plakat der Ausstellung »Exposition Internationale des Arts Décoratifs et Industriels Modernes«, Paris, 1925
Robert Bonfils, poster for the 1925 »Exposition Internationale des Arts Décoratifs et Industriels Modernes« exhibition in Paris

Poring over the Bengel pattern books, one is astonished at the incredible variety revealed in them and the unmistakably wide range embraced by the repertoire of forms used in producing this jewelry. Since the designs are registered in them almost without gaps, many of these pieces can be dated to the day of manufacture. Moreover, study of the pattern books has also proved informative on the production of costume jewelry at Henkel & Grosse in Pforzheim. It has long been known that Henkel & Grosse made at Kaufbeuren-Neugablonz the Dior jewelry sold from the 1950s. The Bengel pattern books show that some 1930s models from the Galalith and metal series were made, not by Bengel in Oberstein, but for Henkel & Grosse in Pforzheim.We are indebted to the infallible nose for good pieces and the passion for collection shown by a German couple for making it possible to identify a large number of Bengel pieces as original and for increasing our knowledge of this distinctive costume jewelry, even though there is much still to be discovered. Their collection, comprising several hundred pieces of Bengel jewelry, has been supplemented over the years by records, brochures, order books and other informative documentation (once owned by the firm).
Establishment of the Bengel-Stiftung (Foundation) last year laid the cornerstone for researching into the Oberstein watch-chain and metalwares industry, with the firm of Bengel as the exemplary object of study. The factories and the industrialists' mansion are typical of the numerous watch-chain and bijouterie wares firms, among them Klein & Quenzer, Carl Keller Christian Sohn and Gottlieb & Söhne, which made this Oberstein industry so successful worldwide.
Recent months and weeks have seen the collation with meticulous accuracy of additional historical material which has lain for decades in cellars and attics or has been stored in cupboards unused for a long time.

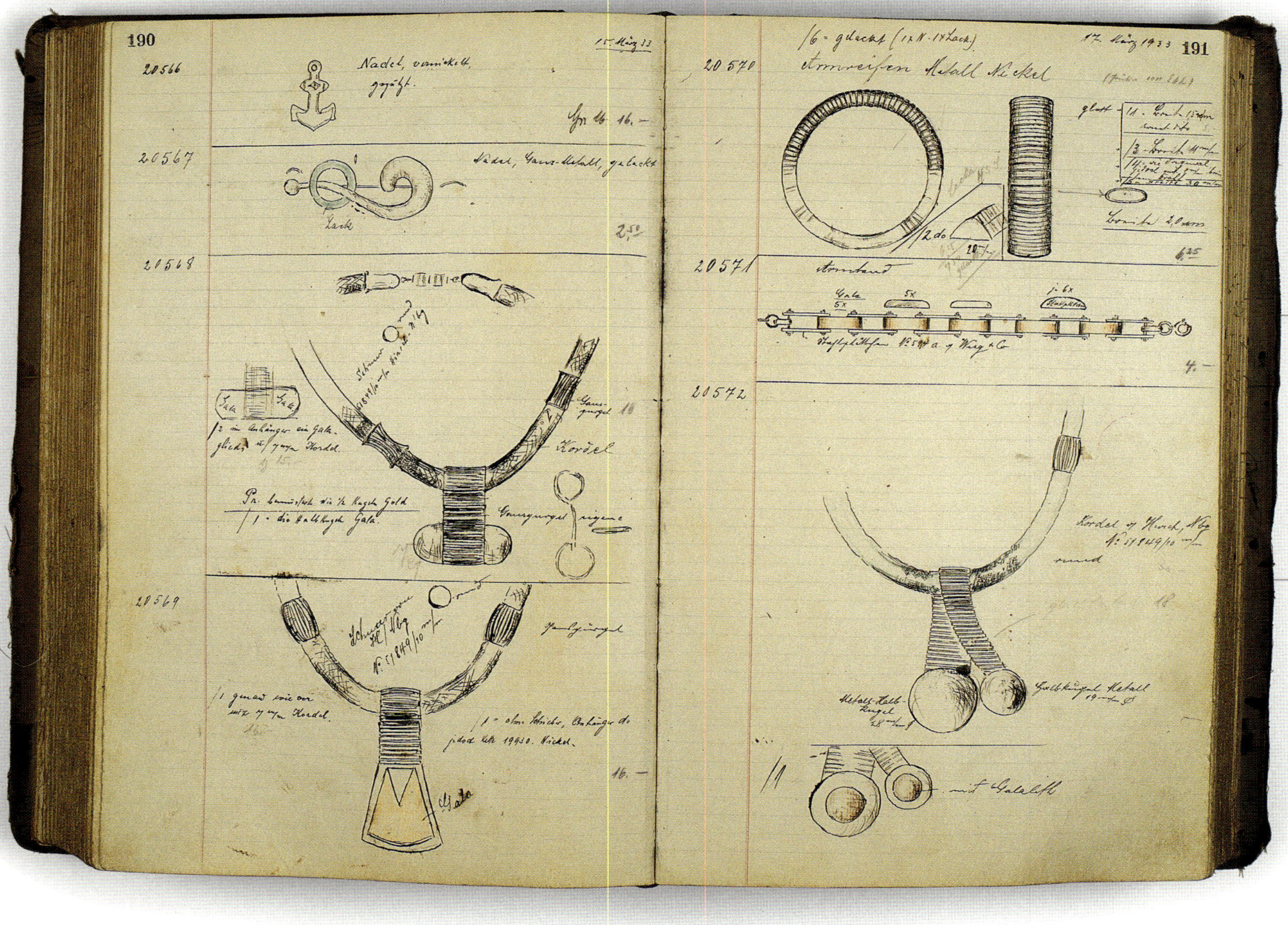

15 Musterbuch Jakob Bengel, Bd. X, S. 190/191, 1932/33
Pattern Book Jakob Bengel, Vol. X, pp. 190/191, 1932/33

In akribischer Kleinarbeit konnte in den letzten Wochen und Monaten zusätzlich weiteres historisches Material zusammengetragen werden, das über viele Jahrzehnte in Kellern, auf Dachböden oder in längst nicht mehr benutzen Schränken lagerte. Ergänzende Recherchen im Stadtarchiv Idar-Oberstein ermöglichten es, einen ersten Eindruck von der Wirtschaftsgeschichte und den produktionstechnischen Abläufen in der Metallwarenindustrie Obersteins der 1930er Jahre zu gewinnen.[5]

Diskussion um Materialechtheit und Materialgerechtigkeit

Die Forderung nach Qualitätsarbeit und Materialgerechtigkeit gehörte zu den Schlagworten des Deutschen Werkbundes, der sich mit seiner Gründung im Jahre 1907 u.a. zum Ziel gesetzt hatte, Künstler, Kunsthandwerker, Industrielle und Kunstwissenschaftler unter einem gemeinsamen ästhetischen Anspruch auf handwerkliche und industrielle Produktion zu vereinen.

Auch wenn diese hohen Ansprüche nicht nachweislich auf die Obersteiner Metallwarenindustrie gewirkt haben mögen, so müssen sie neben anderen Einflüssen, wie denen des Bauhauses und der französischen Schmuck-Avantgarde als Voraussetzung gesehen werden, daß man sich in der Firma Bengel Ende der 1920er Jahre entschlossen hatte, der billigen Massenware ohne ästhetische Wertigkeit den Rücken zu kehren und seine Produktion auf Schmuckstücke von außergewöhnlicher Innovation in materieller und gestalterischer Hinsicht zu verlegen. Als »Hilfsmittel« dienten verchromtes/vernickeltes Messing oder Tombak, das neue Kunsthorn Galalith und eine grenzenlose Phantasie bei deren Gestaltung.

Galalith – ein Kunststoff der unbegrenzten Möglichkeiten

Bereits Mitte des 19. Jahrhunderts kamen die ersten Kunststoffe auf, die auch als Surrogate in der Schmuckgestaltung eingesetzt wurden. Die Weltausstellung von 1851 in London präsentierte in Serie gefertigten Schmuck und Accessoires aus Ebonit, einem Hartgummi. Mit der Erfindung des Celluloids, einer Nitrocellulose, im Jahre 1869 erfolgte der eigentliche Start in die Kunststoffwelt. In eine Welt, in der durch chemische Umwandlungen von Naturstoffen Kunststoffe erzeugt werden konnten. Celluloid erlaubte unzählige Farb- und Effektmischungen; mit größter Sorgfalt ließ sich das Material pressen, sägen und bemalen. Täuschend ähnliche Imitationen für Elfenbein, Schildpatt und Perlmutt oder Horn waren möglich. Ein beinahe idealer Werkstoff – wäre da nicht seine leichte Brennbarkeit gewesen. Um so erfreuter war man, als zu Beginn des 20. Jahrhunderts ein Material entdeckt wurde, das Cellu-

Supplementary research conducted in the Idar-Oberstein City Archives has enabled us to gain some idea of the economic history and technical operations governing production in the 1930s Oberstein metalwares industry.[5]

The materials debate: genuine vs. simulated elegance

The call for quality of workmanship and doing justice to materials was a catchword often used by the Deutscher Werkbund. Founded in 1907, it espoused numerous goals, one of them being to unite artists, artisans, industrialists and art historians under the banner of a shared claim to a single aesthetic approach to both crafts and industrial production.

However, these lofty aims cannot be shown to have had much of an effect on the Oberstein metalwares industry. Nonetheless, with other influences such as those exerted by the Bauhaus and French avant-garde jewelry-makers, the aims of the Deutscher Werkbund can be viewed as having created the preconditions for the decision taken by the firm of Bengel in the 1920s to abandon the production of cheap, mass-produced wares of little or no aesthetic value for the creation of jewelry distinguished by extraordinarily innovative creativity in both choice of materials and design. The »indispensable aids« to creation were chromium-plated or nickel-plated brass or tombac (an alloy of copper and zinc and variously known as Prince's metal or Mannheim gold, of a more reddish color than English pinchbeck), Galalith, which was a new artificial horn, and boundless imagination in designing the jewelry made from these materials.

Galalith – a synthetic material with unlimited possibilities

The first synthetic materials had emerged by the mid-19th century and they were also used then as substitutes for genuine metals and stones in jewelry design. The 1851 London Exhibition saw the presentation of mass-produced jewelry and accessories made of ebonite, a hardened rubber. The invention of celluloid, a thermoplastic consisting of nitrocellulose polymer plasticized with camphor, in 1869 cleared the way for the making of costume jewelry from synthetic materials in a world in which synthetics could be created by the chemical transmutation of natural raw materials. Celluloid made innumerable color combinations and effects possible; this was a material which could be pressed, sawn and stained with meticulous precision. Ivory, tortoiseshell, mother of pearl and horn could now be simulated to deceive even the most knowledgeable eye. Celluloid was almost the perfect material – except for the drawback that it was highly inflammable. It was a great relief to every-

loid ersetzte und es bei weitem noch übertraf: das Kunsthorn »Galalith« war geboren. Ein Casein-Kunststoff, der dem erfinderischen Geist Wilhelm Krisches, dem Inhaber der Geschäftsbücherfabrik Edler & Krische in Hannover und dem Chemiker Adolf Spitteler aus Prien am Chiemsee zu verdanken ist. Wie so oft in der Welt der Erfindungen, war die Entstehung des neuen Kunststoffes eher einem Zufall zu verdanken. Krische hatte den Auftrag bekommen, anstatt schwarzer Schieferschultafeln, weiße Schreibtafeln zu liefern. Das leicht brennbare Zelluloid kam für diesen Auftrag nicht in Frage und es mußte nach einem anderen, neuen Material gesucht werden. Er griff zunächst auf Casein zurück, das von Milch abgetrennte Grundmaterial für die Käseherstellung, und versuchte, es mit Formaldehyd zu härten. Wochenlange Experimente führten zunächst nicht zum Erfolg, bis ihm eines Tages der Zufall zu Hilfe kam: »Krische bereitete wieder einen neuen Versuch vor. Er hatte gerade ein mit Caseinlösung belegtes Stück Papier in der Kopierpresse, als er geschäftlich abgerufen wurde. Erst am anderen Morgen konnte er an seine Arbeit zurückkehren. Sein erster Gang war zur Presse. Als er sie vorsichtig öffnete, sah er wieder das gewohnte Bild: Die Masse klebte an der Presse und löste sich auch noch vom Papier. Er öffnete die Presse ganz: Da plötzlich fiel eine feste, hornartige harte und weißglänzende Platte herunter.«[6]

Es folgten zwei Jahre intensiver Forschungen in Zusammenarbeit mit dem Chemiker Spitteler. Im Jahre 1898 wurde Wilhelm Krische und Adolf Spitteler schließlich vom Kaiserlichen Patentamt in Berlin das Deutsche Reichspatent Nr. 127 942 erteilt: »Verfahren zur Herstellung hornartiger Massen, dadurch gekennzeichnet, daß man Caseinlösung oder trockenes Casein mittels Salzen oder Säuren in seine unlösliche Verbindung überführt und auf diese Formaldehyd einwirken läßt. Das Verfahren ist dadurch gekennzeichnet, daß die unlösliche Caseinverbindung durch Verdunstung unter Druck entwässert wird, bis sie hart und durchscheinend geworden ist.«[7]

Mit der Patentanmeldung des neuen Produktes war noch lange keine Vermarktung erreicht, diese gelang erst im Jahre 1901. Krische und Spitteler schlossen mit den »Vereinigten Gummiwaren-Fabriken Harburg-Wien« einen Vertrag zur Verwertung ihres Patents. Man setzte dort die Versuche im großen Maßstab fort und gründete am 1. Januar 1904 die INTERNATIONALE GALALITH-GESELLSCHAFT HOFF & CO., die sämtliche Patente und Verfahren zur Herstellung von Kunsthorn übernahm. Die aus Milch gewonnene und hart wie Stein gewordene Masse wurde auf den Namen GALALITH (griech. Gala = Milch, lithos = Stein) getauft. Sehr bald erkannte man, daß sich Lab-Casein (Labferment = Enzym des Labmagens), das weniger porös war, noch besser zur Herstellung des Kunst-

one, therefore, when a material was discovered in the early 20th century to replace celluloid, one that far surpassed it in ductility, durability and safety: »Galalith«, a synthetic horn, was created. A synthetic material produced from casein plasticized with water, it sprang from the fertile brains of Wilhelm Krische, the proprietor of Geschäftsbücherfabrik Edler & Krische in Hannover, and the chemist Adolf Spitteler from Prien on Lake Chiemsee. As is so often the case with inventions, the new synthetic material owed its existence more to chance than to design. Krische had received an order for white boards instead of the usual blackboards made of slate. Celluloid was so highly inflammable it could not be used for this purpose; consequently, a different, new material would have to be developed. Krische turned to casein, the protein present in micellar form in skimmed milk used in cheese-making, and tried to harden it with formaldehyde. Weeks of fruitless experimentation were at last followed by success when chance came to his aid: »Krische was preparing yet another experiment. He had just put a piece of paper coated with a casein solution in the copying-press when he was called away on business. He was unable to return to his work until the following morning. The first thing he did was to go to the press. On carefully opening it, he saw what had become a familiar sight: the mass stuck to the press but detached itself from the paper. He opened up the press entirely: lo and behold, a solid, horn-like and shiny white plaque fell out of it.«[6]

There followed two years of intensive research in collaboration with the chemist Adolf Spitteler. Finally, in 1898, Wilhelm Krische and Adolf Spitteler were granted Reich Patent no. 127 942 by the Imperial Patent Office in Berlin: »Process for making horn-like solids, characterized by the plasticisation of casein solution or dry casein by means of salts or acidification into an insoluble compound which is affected by cross-linking with formaldehyde. The process is characterized by the insoluble casein compound being dehydrated by evaporation under pressure until it has become hard and translucent.«[7]

A successful market launch of the new product lagged far behind registration of the patent for it. It was, in fact, not on the market until 1901. Krische and Spitteler concluded a contract with the »Vereinigte Gummiwaren-Fabriken Harburg-Wien« to exploit the possibilities of their patent. Experiments continued there on a grand scale. On 1 January 1904 the INTERNATIONALE GALALITH-GESELLSCHAFT HOFF & CO. was founded, which took over all patents and processes for the production of synthetic horn. A solid made from milk and hard as stone, the new material was christened »Galalith« (Greek gála = milk; líthos = stone). It was not long before producers realized that insoluble protein casein (resulting from the conversion of soluble caseinogen by

horns eignete als Säure-Casein und verwendete es von nun an ausschließlich. Das Fabrikationsangebot konnte erweitert werden, die Farbskala, die bisher nur Schwarz-, Blond- und Weißnuancen aufwies, wurde um andere Farbtöne ergänzt. Schließlich gelang es, eine dem Schildpatt in Farbe, Form und Struktur sehr ähnliche Masse herzustellen und u.a. der Bijouterieindustrie ein neues Material zu liefern. Der stetig steigende Bedarf an Galalith machte die Gründung zahlreicher Niederlassungen in Deutschland und im europäischen Ausland notwendig, 1912 erfolgten die ersten Lieferungen nach Afrika. Die Jahresproduktion der Firma *Internationale Galalithgesellschaft* war 1913 auf 1500 Tonnen angestiegen, die gesamte deutsche Kunsthornfabrikation belief sich auf insgesamt 300 000 Tonnen Galalith. Während des Ersten Weltkriegs und kurz danach war der Bedarf an Casein für die Produktion von Galalith nicht zu decken. Kaum hatten sich jedoch die wirtschaftlichen Verhältnisse um 1920 wieder normalisiert, begannen unzählige Firmen mit der Herstellung von Kunsthorn.[8] Ein deutlicher Aufschwung in der Kunsthornindustrie war 1934 zu verzeichnen, ihren absoluten Höhepunkt erlebte sie 1938. Mit dem Ausbruch des Krieges mußte die Galalithproduktion aufgrund des mangelnden Casein-Rohstoffs erneut eingestellt werden. Außerdem benötigte die Kriegsindustrie größere Mengen von Galalith, das wegen seiner gut isolierenden und mechanischen Eigenschaft hoch geschätzt wurde. Neue, thermoplastische Kunststoffe ließen das einst hochbegehrte Galalith nach 1945 in Vergessenheit geraten.[9]

Was waren nun die herausragenden Eigenschaften, die Galalith zum bevorzugten Kunststoff auf dem Markt werden ließen? Galalith ist in physikalischer und chemischer Beziehung dem Naturhorn und Schildpatt sehr ähnlich. Es läßt sich wie Naturhorn verarbeiten, nämlich drehen, bohren, fräsen, prägen, löten und nachträglich in alle Töne einfärben. Neben der Nichtbrennbarkeit ist die hervorragendste Eigenschaft des Galaliths

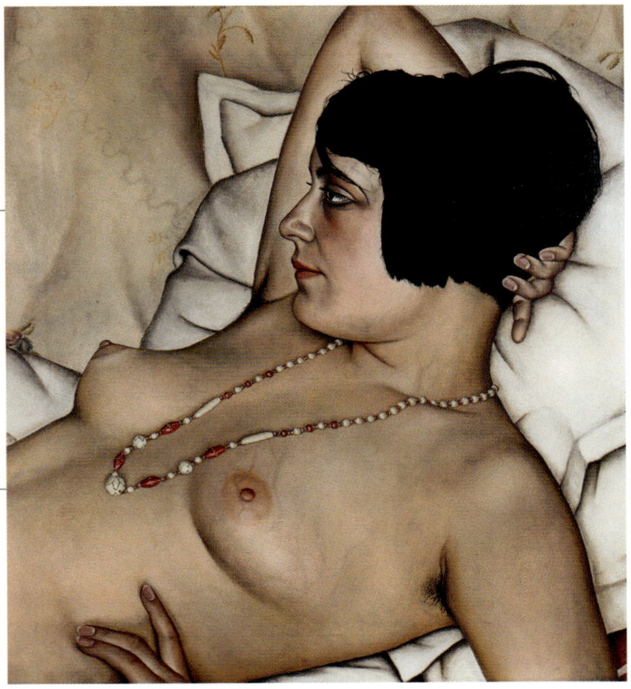

16 Christian Schad
»Halbakt«, Öl auf Leinwand, 1929
Von-der-Heydt-Museum, Wuppertal

Christian Schad
»Halbakt«, oil on canvas, 1929
Von-der-Heydt-Museum, Wuppertal

rennin = an enzyme secreted in one of the stomachs of ruminants), was better suited to the making of synthetic horn than soluble caseinogen because it was less porous and began to use insoluble protein casein from then on instead. The range of products and colors, which had hitherto included only black, blond and shades of white, was enhanced by the addition of other color tones. Ultimately it became possible to make a synthetic tortoiseshell, a solid which was very similar in color, form and structure to Galalith. One of its uses was as a new material for the jewelry-making industry. The steady growth in demand for Galalith made it necessary to found numerous branches in Germany and elsewhere in Europe. The first deliveries were made to Africa in 1912.

The annual production registered by the *Internationale Galalithgesellschaft* had increased by 1913 to 1500 tons. The total German production of synthetic horn amounted to 300 000 tons of Galalith. During the First World War and for a short while afterwards the need for casein used in the production of Galalith could not be met. No sooner had economic conditions stabilized in about 1920 than a great many firms started making synthetic horn.[8] There was a noticeable upturn in synthetic horn production in 1934, which peaked in 1938. The outbreak of the Second World War made it necessary to cease production of Galalith for civilian use once again because casein was now in short supply. Besides, the war industry required quite large amounts of Galalith, which was highly appreciated for its insulating and mechanical properties. The invention of new thermoplastic synthetic materials consigned Galalith, once so sought-after, to oblivion after 1945.[9]

What were the extraordinary properties which made Galalith the most popular synthetic material on the market? Physically and chemically, Galalith closely resembles natural horn and tortoiseshell. It can be worked like natural horn: turned, drilled, milled, stamped, soldered and afterwards stained all colors. Apart from being non-inflammable, Galalith's salient character-

seine Polierfähigkeit. Seine wunderbar leuchtenden Farben, seine Festigkeit und gleichzeitige Elastizität haben ihm zur vielseitigen Verwendung verholfen. Galalith wurde von der Industrie in Form von Platten (1/2–15 mm), Stäben (3–25 mm) und Röhren sowie in gesägten oder gestanzten Stücken geliefert. Galalith eignet sich sehr gut zur Herstellung gedrehter Massenartikel, da die Drehwerkzeuge nur wenig stumpf werden, die gedrehten Artikel lassen sich in Trommelfässern leicht schleifen und auf Hochglanz polieren.

In der Firma Bengel, Oberstein, haben sich zwei Musterkarten mit kleinen Galalith-Scheiben in jeweils 25 verschiedenen Farbnuancen erhalten, eine weitere Musterkarte zeigt Galalithstäbchen in 33 Farbtönen (siehe Abb. 17–19). Während es sich bei den Scheiben um das marmorierte und durchsichtige Galalith handelt, wurden die Stäbchen in leuchtenden Rot, Blau-,Gelb- und Grüntönen sowie Schwarz und Weiß angeboten. Ende der 1930er Jahre hatte sich das Angebot der *Verkaufsvereinigung von Kunsthornfabriken, der Internationalen Galalith-Gesellschaft Hoff & Co. Hamburg-Harburg* um ein Vielfaches erweitert: es konnten geschliffene und polierte Platten oder auch Schichtmaterial geordert werden (Abb. 20). Auch die Vielfalt der Galalithstäbe war grenzenlos: Stäbe wurden in den Farben »Schwarz extra«, »Schwarz«, Weiß, Blond, Uni, Büffel und Spezialbüffel angeboten. Es gab geschliffene und polierte Stäbe, Oval- und Kantstäbe standen zur Verfügung. Preßstäbe wurden mit Perlmutteffekten sowie in Phantasiefarben angeboten, die Galalithrohre waren sogar in buntem Schildpatt erhältlich. Auf Anfrage wurden auch Galalith-Rondelle geliefert.

Galalith und Chrom erobern den Modeschmuck

Neben anderen Industriezweigen war die Knopf- und Schmuckindustrie einer der größten Abnehmer von Galalith. Die Geschichte und Bedeutung des Galalithschmucks in Deutschland, aber auch in Europa und Amerika bedarf noch gründlicher Recherchen. Mit dem Blick auf die Galalith-Schmuckproduktion der Firma Bengel in Idar-Oberstein kann nur ein kleiner Ausschnitt dieser hochinteressanten Materie beleuchtet werden. In den 1930er Jahren hatte man diesem Schmuck aus »nur« Kunststoff keine große Bedeutung zuerkannt, so mag es auch nicht verwundern, daß man in den einschlägigen, zeitgenössischen Fachzeitschriften kaum einen nennenswerten Hinweis auf Galalith-Schmuck findet.[10] Die Deutsche Goldschmiedezeitung, das Fachblatt der Goldschmiede und Juweliere, widmete dem Modeschmuck Ende der 1930er Jahre immerhin einen Aufsatz und lobte die Vorzüge dieses Materials. Der gesetzlich geschützte Produktname »Galalith« wurde aller-

istic is the way it takes a high polish. Its wonderfully glowing colors as well as its durability accompanied by elasticity made it a highly versatile and utilitarian material. Galalith was delivered industrially in the form of plates (1/2–15 mm), rods (3–25 mm) and tubes sawn or cut by the piece. Galalith was extremely well suited to the making of turned mass-produced articles since it did not much blunt lathes and since turned articles could easily be polished to a high gloss in polishing-casks.

Two sample cards with little discs of Galalith in 25 different color shades on each have been preserved at Bengel in Oberstein. A third sample card sports discs of Galalith in 33 color tones (see figs. 17–19). The discs were in marbled and transparent Galalith; the little rods were in glowing reds, blues, yellows and greens as well as black and white. By the late 1930s the range available from the *Verkaufsvereinigung von Kunsthornfabriken and the Internationale Galalith-Gesellschaft Hoff & Co. Hamburg-Harburg* had considerably broadened: cut and polished plates or laminated material could now also be ordered (fig. 20). The variety of Galalith rods on sale was endless: rods were sold in the following colors *»extra black«, »black«, white, blond, plain, buffalo* and *special buffalo*. Cut and polished rods as well as rods which were oval and angular in section were available. Pressed rods were available with a mother-of-pearl look as well as in imaginative colors. The Galalith tubes could also be had in colored tortoiseshell. Special orders could also be placed for Galalith roundels.

Galalith and chrome triumph in costume jewelry

One of the biggest, although not the only, customers for Galalith, was the button and jewelry industry. The history and importance of Galalith jewelry, not only in Germany, but also in the rest of Europe and America has yet to be studied in any depth. Going into the Galalith jewelry produced by Bengel in Idar-Oberstein can shed light on only a small segment of this highly interesting material. Since not much importance was attached to this jewelry in the 1930s because it was »only« made of plastic, it is not surprising that hardly any mention is made of Galalith jewelry in reputable specialist journals of the time.[10] Nevertheless, Die Deutsche Goldschmiedezeitung, the goldsmiths' and jewelers' trade journal, did devote an article to this costume jewelry in the late 1930s and commended the advantages of Galalith as a material. Specific mention was not, however, made of the registered trade name »Galalith«; »high-performance resin« was as far as this article went. »...We can, therefore, say costume jewelry has been given the quality of being decorative, changing with the trends in clothing fashions. (...) Costume jewelry is usually manufactured in silver but also in simulated jewelry set with stones such as synthetic stones, glass stones

17–19 Musterkarten Galalith, 1930er Jahre
Galalith sample cards, 1930s

20 Preisliste der Internationalen Galalith-Gesellschaft Hoff & Co., Hamburg-Harburg, 1936
Price list of the Internationale Galalith-Gesellschaft Hoff & Co., Hamburg-Harburg/Germany, 1936

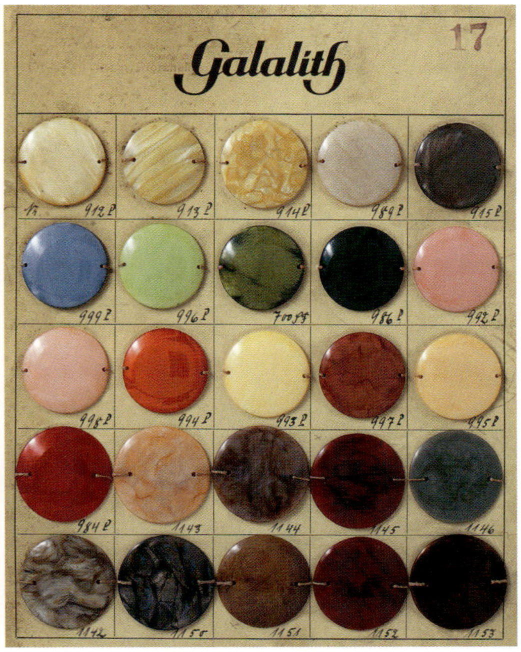

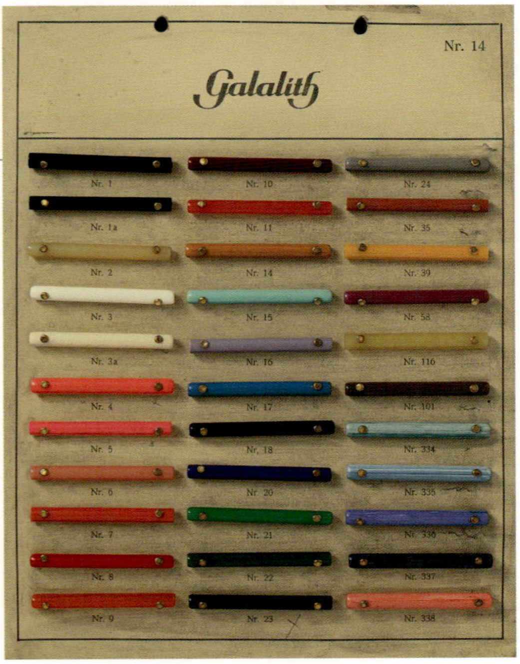

VERKAUFSVEREINIGUNG VON KUNSTHORNFABRIKEN

Internationale Galalith-Gesellschaft Hoff & Co.
Hamburg-Harburg 1

Eingetragene Schutzmarke Galalith

Fritz Behner jun., Pforzheim

Telegramm-Adresse: Galalith Hamburg-Harburg / Code used: ABC 5th Edition / Bentley's Code
Telefon: Sammel-Nr. 37 12 21

Preise für Kunsthorn

ab 1. Januar 1936

1. Platten (Preßplatten, ebenso geschnittene Platten) je kg

Farbenbezeichnung	Stärke in mm 1	1½	2–6	7–10	11–14
	RM.	RM.	RM.	RM.	RM.
Schwarz extra		2–8 mm	2.25	2.50	9–10 mm
Weiß extra			2.40	2.65	nicht für Schichtmaterial
Schwarz	3.25	2.90	2.50	2.75	3.05
Weiß, Blond, Uni	3.50	3.10	2.70	3.—	3.30
Büffel, Schildpatt, Spezialbüffel	5.—	4.40	3.50	4.30	4.80

Geschliffene Platten
Berechnung des Gewichtes der dazu verwendeten rohen Platten zuzügl. RM. 0.10 je Plattenseite netto

Polierte Platten
Berechnung des Gewichtes der dazu verwendeten rohen Platten zuzügl. RM. 0.50 je Plattenseite netto

Schichtmaterial
Berechnung des Gewichts der dazu verwendeten rohen Platten zuzügl. RM 0.80 je Leimschicht netto

2. Stäbe je kg (Stablänge etwa 1 m)

a) roh

Farbenbezeichnung	Durchmesser in mm 3–4	5–13	14–16	17–20	21–25	26–30
	RM.	RM.	RM.	RM.	RM.	RM.
Schwarz extra	(nur 5–14 mm)	2.10	—	—	—	—
Schwarz	2.40	2.25	2.25	2.50	2.80	4.40
Weiß, Blond, Uni	2.40	2.25	2.40	2.80	3.—	4.40
Büffel, Spezialbüffel	—	2.85	3.—	3.10	3.40	—

dings nicht genannt, es war lediglich vom »Edelharz« die Rede. »... Wir können also sagen, dem Modeschmuck ist das Charakteristikum des Dekorativen, des Wechselnden, und des engeren Anschlusses an den Wechsel der Kleidermode gegeben. (...) Der Modeschmuck wird meist in Silber, aber auch in Unecht fabriziert, der Steinschmuck besteht aus synthetischen Steinen, aus Glassteinen und aus Steinformen, die aus Edelharz gefertigt sind. (...) Das Edelharz kann ja in allen Farben, und ebensowohl durchsichtig wie undurchsichtig, bezogen werden. Bei seiner leichten Bearbeitbarkeit können Formen von einer Freiheit und Mannigfaltigkeit aus ihm gewonnen werden, wie sie bei Natursteinen und auch bei Glas nicht möglich sind. Ebenso ist auch ihre Befestigung im Schmuckkörper nicht an die übliche Faßtechnik gebunden. Man kann die Stücke aufstiften und aufreihen, und sie deshalb in freier und mannigfaltiger Weise mit der Metallform in Verbindung bringen.«[11] Heute faszinieren uns Leuchtkraft und Klarheit des Materials Galalith, seine ehemalige Ersatzfunktion als Kunststoff ist völlig in den Hintergrund getreten. In den 1930er Jahren konnte man dem Material diese Besonderheit nicht abgewinnen, seine Funktion als »billiger Ersatzstoff« stand im Vordergrund. In einem Zeitschriftenhinweis auf die Obersteiner Bijouterieindustrie und ihre Erzeugnisse in Metall und Galalith spiegelt sich die Zurückhaltung gegenüber dem Galalith-Schmuck deutlich wieder: »In den beiden vorstehenden Abbildungen finden wir Armreifen, Halsketten und Clips, modisch flott gearbeitete und sehr preiswerte Bijouterien, die sich an breite Käuferschichten wenden.«[12]

Als »kühle« Ergänzung, aber auch beliebter Kontrast zu dem farbigen Galalith mit seiner seidig schimmernden oder auf Hochglanz polierten Oberfläche stand das seit Ausgang des 19. Jahrhunderts bekannte und genutzte Metall Chrom, zur Verfügung. Die großindustrielle Nutzung ist etwa zeitgleich mit der des Galaliths anzusetzen.

Um 1930 war seine Verwendung noch sehr kostspielig, erst allmählich ging man dazu über, die Grundmetalle wie Messing oder Tombak nicht nur zu vernickeln sondern zu verchromen.

21 Armreif, 1932, Messing verchromt, aufgeschraubtes Galalith, Ø 75, B 9, H 24, MB Bd. X, S. 34, M-Nr. 19.918, 23.9.32, 7,25 (Kat.-Nr. 137)
Bangle, 1932, Brass, chromium-plated; Galalith, screwed-on, Ø 75, W 9, H 24, PB Vol. X, p. 34, M. no. 19.918, 23.9.32, 7,25 (Cat.no. 137)

and types of stones made from high-performance resin. (...) High-performance resin can, after all, be ordered in all colors and both translucent and opaque. It is so ductile that forms can be achieved with it in a freedom and diversity not possible with genuine stones or even glass. Nor is setting jewelry with it linked with the technique usual for mounting stones. Pieces of it can be tenoned and arrayed and, therefore, can be linked with the metal form freely and in a multiplicity of ways.«[11] Nowadays we are intrigued by the brilliance and translucency of Galalith as a material; its former function as a substitute for real stones has receded entirely into the background. In the 1930s, by contrast, the material was not regarded as anything special because emphasis was laid on its function as a »cheap surrogate material«. Reservations about Galalith jewelry are clearly reflected in a periodical of the time in which the Oberstein jewelry-making industry and its products in metal and Galalith are mentioned: »In the two present illustrations we find bangles, necklaces and clips, stylishly casual in workmanship and very reasonably priced, which are aimed at a broad segment of the market.«[12]

Chrome, well known and widely used since the late 19th century, was available as a »cool« but popular contrast to set off colored Galalith with its silky sheen or glossy polished surfaces. Industrial use of chrome set in almost concomitantly with the introduction of Galalith. In 1930 chrome was still very expensive to use. Gradually, however, base metals such as brass or tombac began to be chromium-plated as well as nickel-plated.

DIE SCHMUCK-PRODUKTION DER FIRMA BENGEL IN DEN 1930er JAHREN

Musterbücher und Entwürfe

Die ausgewählten Schmuckbeispiele der Bengelschen Produktion in den 1930er Jahren zeigen einen Querschnitt dieser äußerst kreativen Entwurfs- und Herstellungsphase. Einen lückenlosen Eindruck von der Gesamtproduktion dieser Jahre bekommt man beim Studium der erhaltenen Musterbücher (Abb. 22 ff.).

Der Wunsch der Kunden nach immer neuen Mustern war zu Beginn der 1930er Jahre größer denn je. Wie die Buchhaltungsjournale zeigen, exportierte die Firma Bengel in die ganze Welt (Anhang I, S. 279 ff.). Für jeden Markt mußten also individuelle Muster entworfen werden, die sich dem besonderen Geschmack des Landes anpaßten und der dort herrschenden Mode entsprachen. Eine große Lagerhaltung war deshalb nicht möglich. Die Vielseitigkeit in der Produktion der Firma Bengel läßt sich heute anhand der erhaltenen Musterbücher belegen. Ein großer Teil der Schmuckstücke selbst ist in alle Herren Länder zerstreut oder hat die Jahrzehnte nicht überdauert. Ein besonderes Schicksal des unechten Schmucks, der nicht wie goldene, mit Brillanten besetzte Ketten, über Generationen hinweg in Ehren gehalten wird oder seinen Weg in einen Tresor findet.

Nicht nur die Muster, sondern auch entsprechende Anmerkungen zu diesen in den Musterbüchern geben Auskunft über Produktionsweise, Materialverwendung, Kostenkalkulation, Zulieferfirmen und vieles mehr. Die Musterbücher Band I bis Band V sind wohl verschollen, deshalb läßt sich die Schmuckproduktion bei Bengel bis in das Jahr 1924 kaum nachweisen, nur einige erhaltene Materialzettel geben hierüber Auskunft (s. Abb. 111). Die im Folgenden aufgeführten Musterbücher geben Aufschluß über die Intensität der Musterentwicklung in den jeweiligen Zeiträumen.[13]

Die grenzenlose Phantasie in der Entwicklung von Mustern und Modellen für die Produktion des Metall- und Galalithschmucks bei Bengel belegt vor allem sehr eindrucksvoll das Musterbuch Band X (1932/33). Man verstand es, den unglaublichen Formenreichtum an geometrischen und stereometrischen Formen voll auszuschöpfen und immer wieder zu variieren (s. Abb. 22 ff.).

JEWELRY PRODUCTION AT BENGEL IN THE 1930s

Pattern books and designs

The examples chosen of jewelry made by Bengel in the 1930s represent a cross-section of this extremely creative phase of design and manufacture there. Studying the pattern books which have been preserved, one has a very good overall impression of production during those years (fig. 22 ff.).

Consumer desire for ever new patterns was more avid than ever by the early 1930s. As the accounting ledgers show, Bengel was exporting throughout the world (Appendix I, p. 279 ff.). Consequently, individual patterns had to be designed specially for each market to reflect the particular taste of a country and the prevailing fashions there. As a result, overstocking of inventory was not feasible. The versatility of Bengel production can be demonstrated today from the pattern books which have been preserved. Much of the jewelry is scattered across the world or has not survived. This is so often the fate of simulated jewelry, which is not, unlike gold necklaces set with diamonds, treasured for generations or kept in a bank vault. Apart from the patterns themselves, the comments on them in the pattern books are also highly instructive on production methods and materials used, cost estimates, suppliers and much more. Pattern Books Volumes I to V seem to have been lost so that jewelry production at Bengel can hardly be traced back to 1924; a few preserved slips on materials are the only evidence for this early period (see fig. 111).

The pattern books listed in the following have been preserved;[13] however, the incidence of »pattern production« varies widely and probably cannot be equated with the production of actual jewelry. Pattern Book Vol. X (1932/33) reveals the boundless imagination unleashed for the development of designs for the production of metal and Galalith jewelry at Bengel. The creators of these designs knew how to exploit to the full an incredible wealth of geometric and stereometric forms and to vary these endlessly (fig. 22 ff.). Individual elements of chains were used at will so that new variants were continually emerging (figs. 28, 29). The differing signatures and styles of drawing reveal that several people were »at work« here. The designs were also commented on by the production side and subjected to feasibility testing.

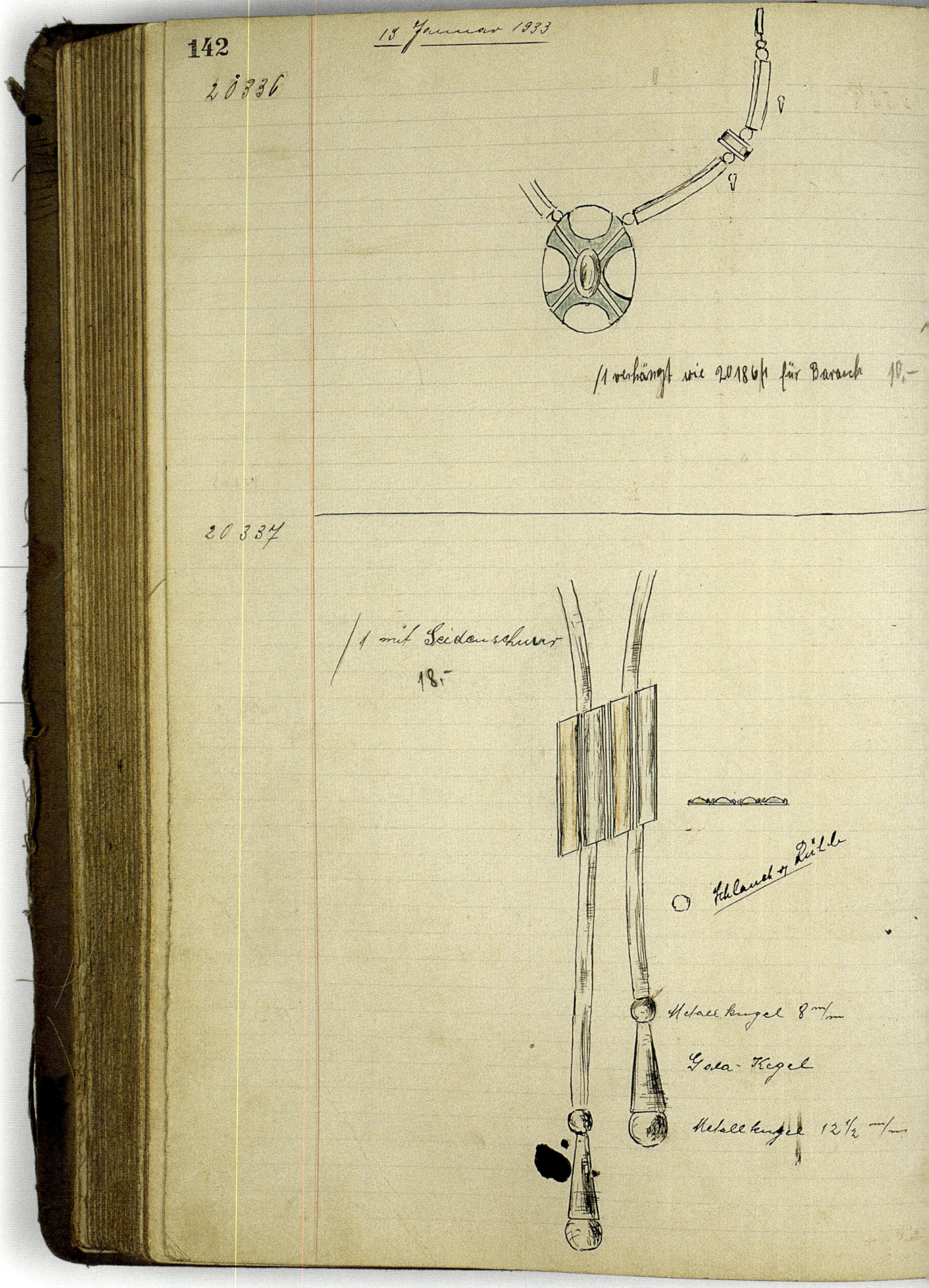

22 Musterbuch Jakob Bengel, Bd. X, S. 142/143, 1932/33
Pattern Book Jakob Bengel, Vol. X, pp. 142/143, 1932/33

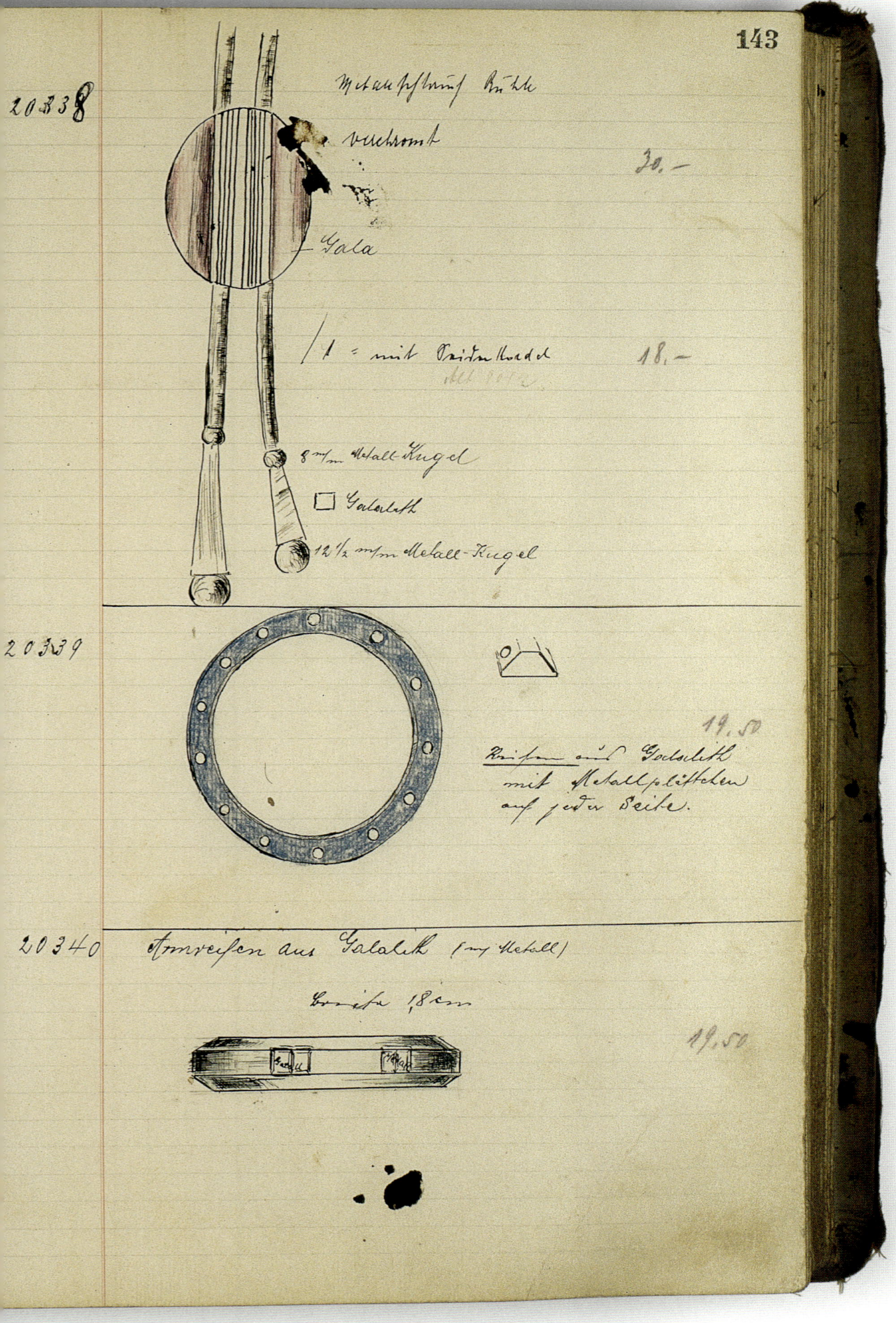
143
20338
verchromt
30.-
Gala
18.-
8 m/m Metall-Kugel
Galalith
12 1/2 m/m Metall-Kugel
20339
19.50
Reifen aus Galalith
mit Metallplättchen
auf jeder Seite.
20340
Armreifen aus Galalith (m. Metall)
Breite 1,8 cm
19.50

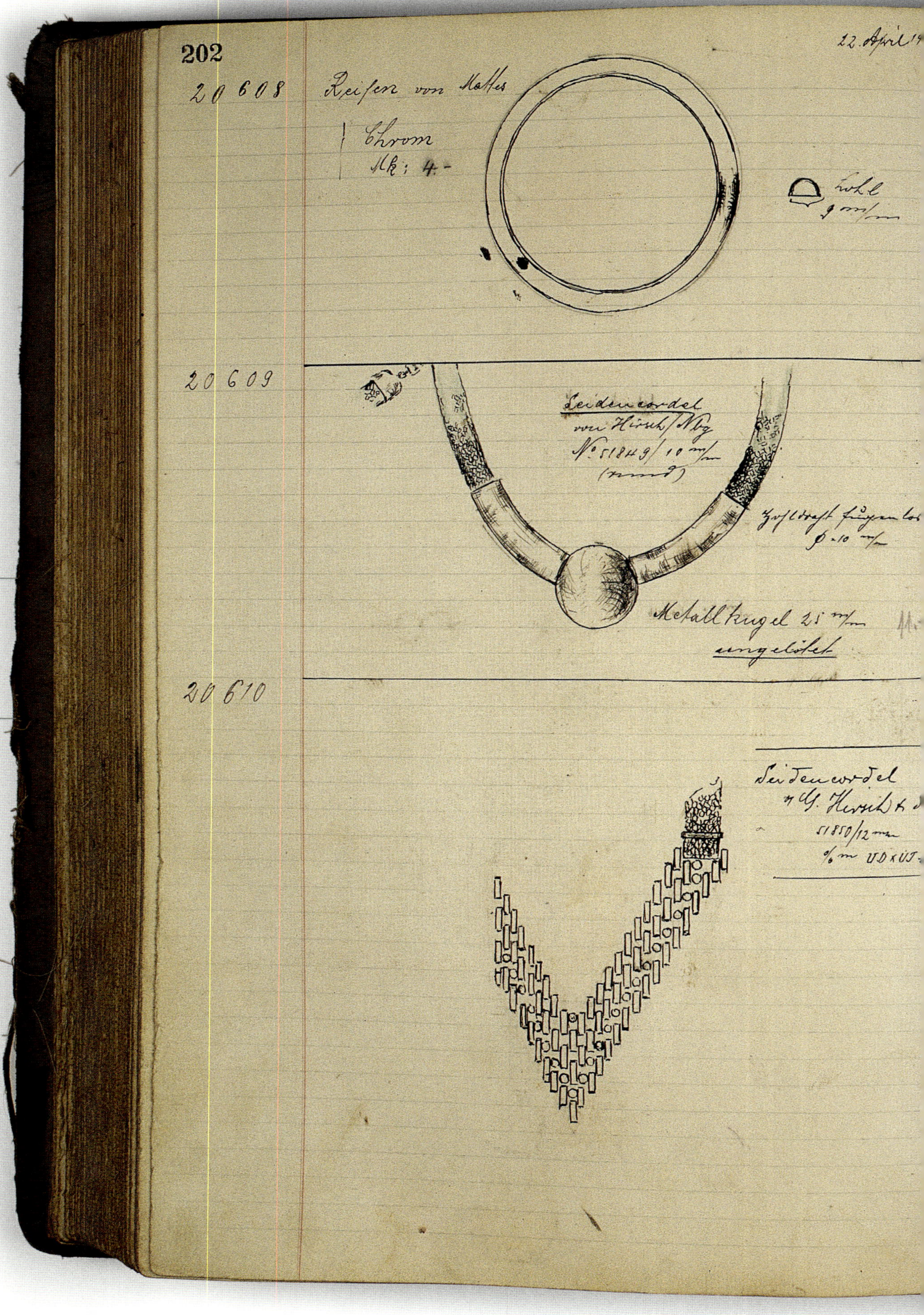

23 Musterbuch Jakob Bengel, Bd. X, S. 202/203, 1932/33
Pattern Book Jakob Bengel, Vol. X, pp. 202/203, 1932/33

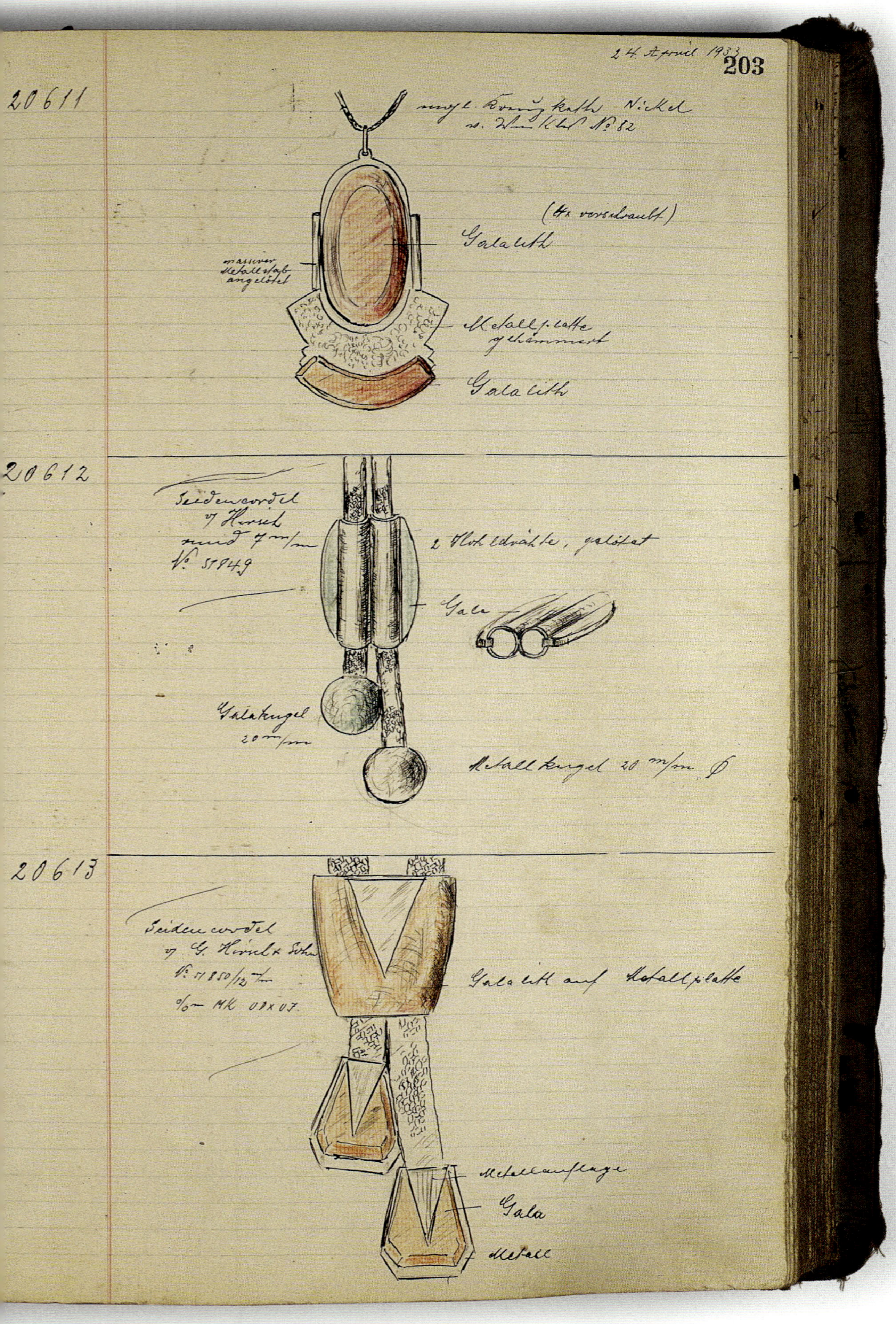
24 April 1933
203
20611
Galalith
Metallplatte gehämmert
Galalith
20612
2 Hohldrähte, gelötet
Gala
Galakugel 20 m/m
Metallkugel 20 m/m ∅
20613
Galalith auf Metallplatte
Gala
Metall

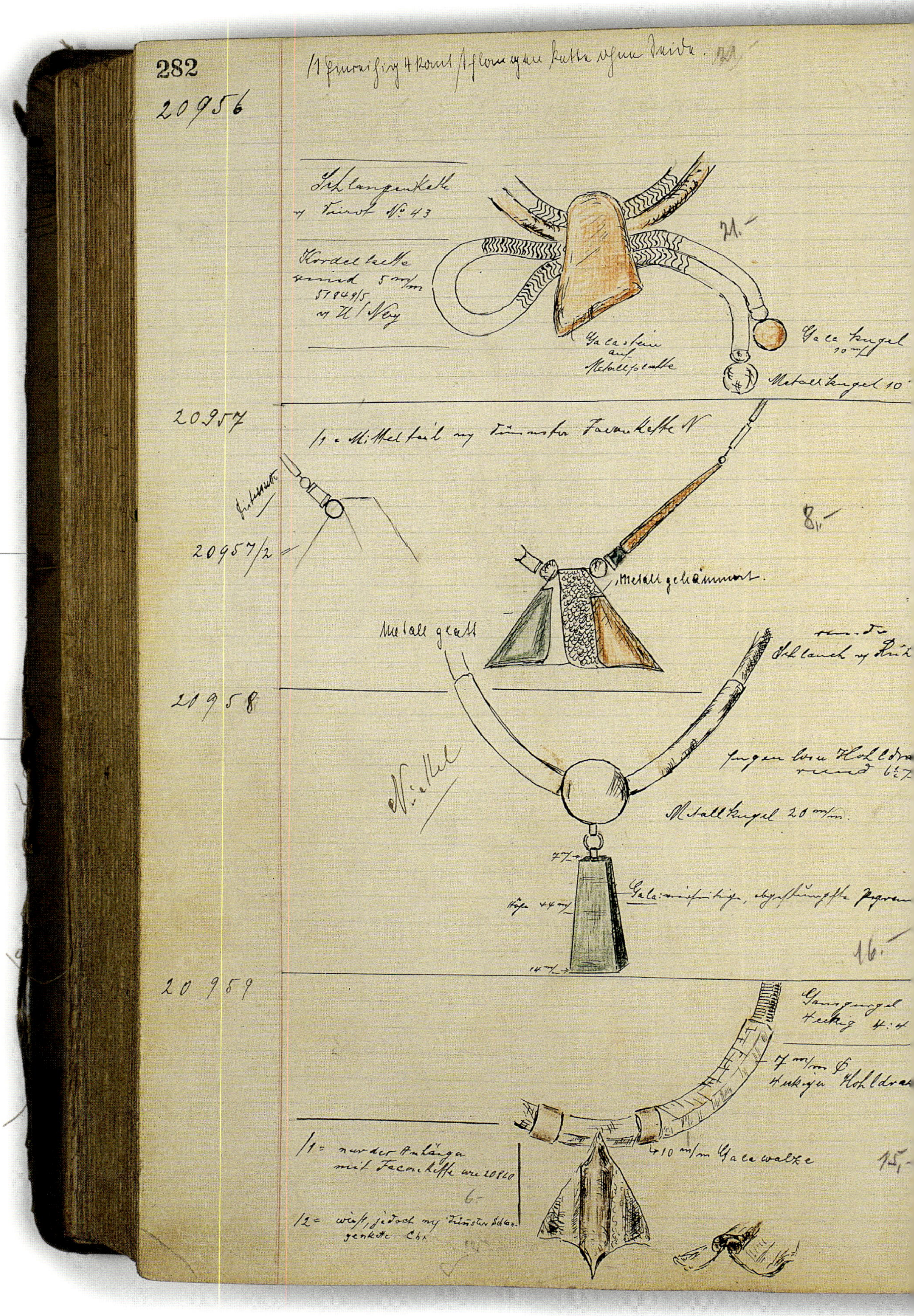

24 Musterbuch Jakob Bengel, Bd. X, S. 282/283, 1932/33 (Modell 20.956 siehe auch Kat.-Nr. 163)
Pattern Book Jakob Bengel, Vol. X, pp. 282/283, 1932/33 (model no. 20.956 see also Cat.no. 163)

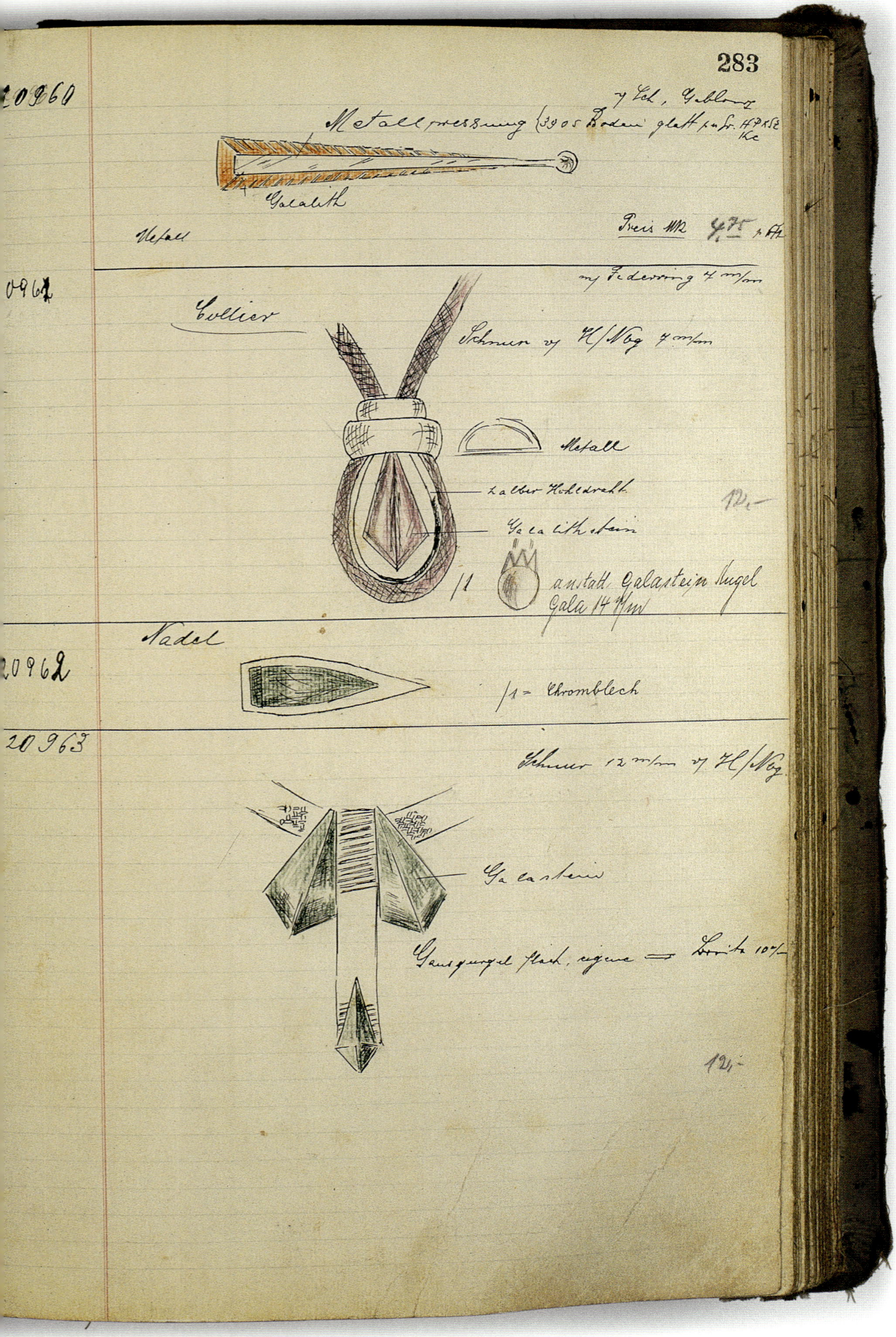
283
20960
Metallpressung
Galalith
Metall
Preis Mk 4.75
Collier
Schnur
Metall
Galalithstein
Nadel
20962
Chromblech
20963
Galastein
12,-

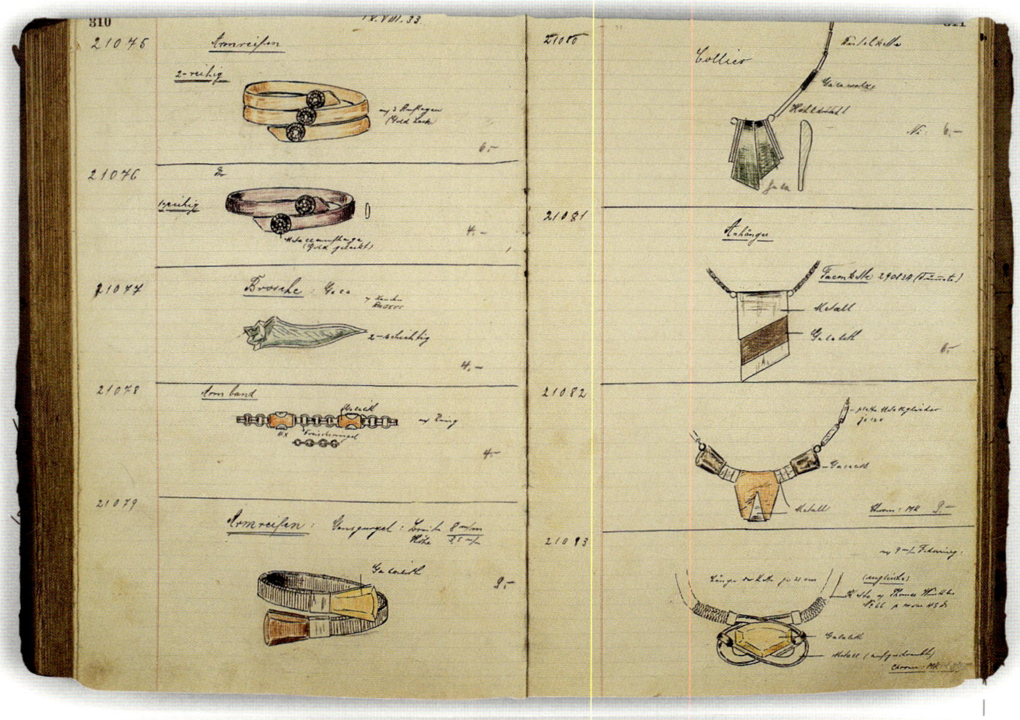

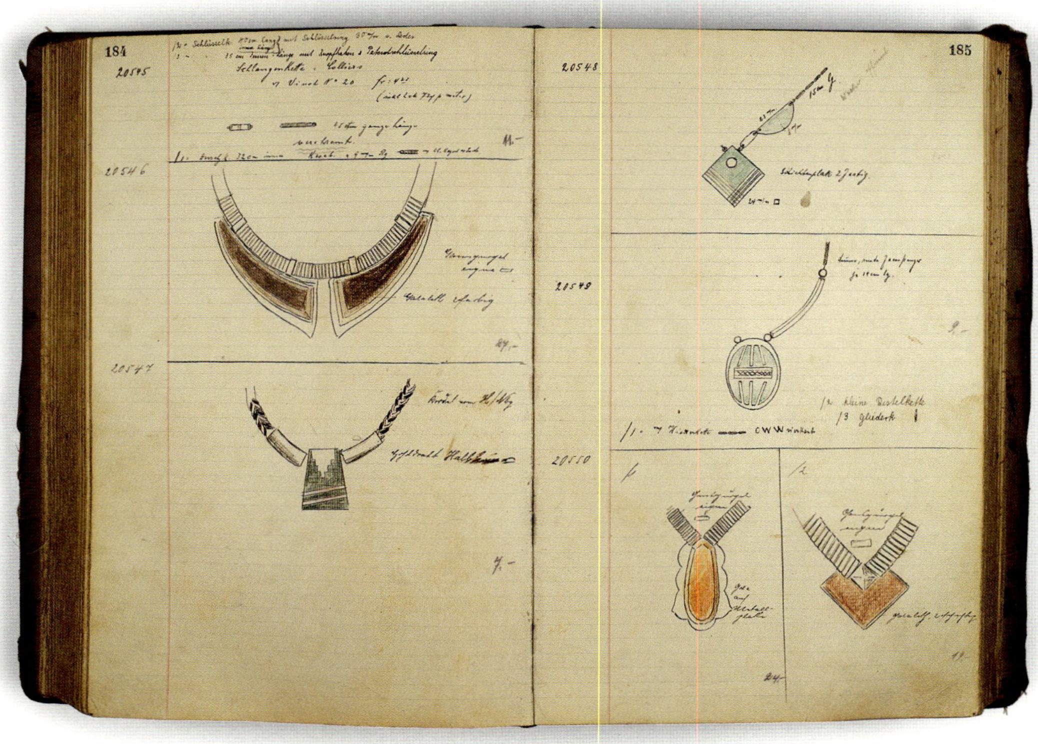

25 Musterbuch Jakob Bengel, Bd. X, S. 310/311, 1932/33
Pattern Book Jakob Bengel, Vol. X, pp. 310/311, 1932/33

26 Musterbuch Jakob Bengel, Bd. X, S. 184/185 Modell 20.546, (siehe auch Kat.-Nr. 224)
Pattern Book Jakob Bengel, Vol. X, pp. 184/185 model 20.546, (see also Cat.no. 224)

Übersicht erhaltener Musterbücher der Firma Jakob Bengel

Musterbuch Bd. VI
Dezember 1924 bis 16. März 1925, Modell Nr. 13.362–15.273 (in vier Monaten 1.911 Modelle)

Musterbuch Bd. VII
Januar 1925 bis Mitte 1929 Modell Nr. 15.274–16.818 (in drei Jahren 1.544 Modelle)

Musterbuch Bd. VIII
13. August 1929 bis 16. Juli 1931 Modell Nr. 16.819–18.317 (in zwei Jahren 1.498 Modelle)

Musterbuch Bd. IX
16. Juli 1931 bis 5. August 1932 Modell Nr. 18.318–19.788 (in einem Jahr 1.470 Modelle)

Musterbuch Bd. X
15. August 1932 bis 30. Oktober 1933 Modell Nr. 19.789–21.370 (in zehn Monaten 1.581 Modelle)

Musterbuch Bd. XI
11. November 1933 bis Januar 1935 (Modell Nrn. nicht bekannt)

Musterbuch Bd. XII
20. Februar 1935 bis 27. Januar 1937 Modell Nr. 23.230–25.115 (in zwei Jahren 1.885 Modelle)

Musterbuch Bd. XIII
29. Januar 1937 bis 1. Juni 1939 Modell Nr. 25.116–26.928 (in zweieinhalb Jahren 1.812 Muster)

Musterbuch Bd. XIV
(»Altes Musterbuch«) Modell Nr. 26.929, (26.936 = 5. Juli 1939) – 29.470

Musterbuch Bd. XIV
(»Neues Musterbuch«) Modell Nr. 29.500 (ohne Datum), (Haarspangen, Manschettenknöpfe, Münzen, Haarreifen, Ohrclips, Colliers, Brillenketten) bis 14. Februar 1966, Modell Nr. 30.783

Musterbuch Bd. XV
Modell Nr. 31.692–34.042

Musterbuch T 1
(Taschenbügel, Taschenauflagen, Gürtelschnallen, Knöpfe) 17.7.1935 = Modell-Nr. 784 Modell Nr. 1–3.036 (?)

Musterbuch T2
Keine Zeitangaben (ca. 1950/60er Jahre) Modell Nr. 3.023–3.700

Survey of preserved Jakob Bengel pattern books

Pattern Book Vol. VI
December 1924 to 16 March 1925, model nos. 13.362–15.273 In four months: 1911 patterns

Pattern Book Vol. VII
January 1925 to mid-1929, model nos. 15.274–16.818 In three years: 1544 patterns

Pattern Book Vol. VIII
13 August 1929 to 16 July 1931, model nos. 16.819–18.317 In two years: 1498 patterns

Pattern Book Vol. IX
16 July 1931 to 5 August 1932, model nos. 18.318–19.788 In one year: 1470 patterns

Pattern Book Vol. X
15 August 1932 to 30 October 1933, model nos. 19.789–21.370 In ten months: 1581 patterns

Pattern Book Vol. XI
11 November 1933 to January 1935 (model nos. not given)

Pattern Book Vol. XII
20 February 1935 to 27 January 1937, model nos. 23.230–25.115 In two years: 1885 patterns

Pattern Book Vol. XIII
29 January 1937 to 1 June 1939, model nos. 25.116–26.928 In two and a half years: 1812 patterns

Pattern Book Vol. XIV
»Old Pattern Book« model nos. 26.929 (26.936 = 5 July 1939) – 29.470

Pattern Book Vol. XIV
»New Pattern Book«, n. d., model no. 29.500 (barrettes, cuff-link, coins, hair bands, clip earrings, necklaces, spectacles chains) until 14 February 1966, model no. 30.783

Pattern Book Vol. XV
model nos. 31.692, 34.042

Pattern Book T 1
(T stands for »Tasche« = handbag handles, handbag key locks belt buckles, buttons): 17.7.1935 = model no. 784 model nos. 1–3.036 (?)

Pattern Book T 1
n. d. (ca 1950s/60s) model nos. 3.023–3.700

Einzelne Elemente der Ketten wurden beliebig oft verwendet und es konnten so immer wieder neue Varianten angeboten werden (Abb. 28, 29). Die unterschiedliche Schrift und der unterschiedliche Zeichenstil verraten, daß hier mehrere Personen »am Werk« waren. Mit Sicherheit wurden die Muster auch von produktionstechnischer Seite kommentiert und auf ihre Machbarkeit überprüft.

Die Zeichnungen sind meistens in Tusche oder Kreide ausgeführt, viele sind aber auch farbig angelegt. Die Muster reichen von flüchtigen Skizzen bis hin zu detaillierten Zeichnungen mit ausführlichen Kommentaren zu Material, Verarbeitungstechnik, Hinweisen zu Zulieferfirmen, Maß- und Größenangaben und dem kalkulierten Verkaufspreis (Abb. 22–24).

Zunächst seien einige Muster genannt, die für die vielseitige Produktion dieser Jahre stehen, ohne daß sich die ausgeführten Schmuckstücke erhalten hätten. Ein beliebtes Thema waren Monatsanhänger bzw. Astronomische Anhänger mit den Tierkreiszeichen. Beim Ansteckschmuck findet sich eine Brosche mit dem Motiv »Der Heilige Rock zu Trier 1933«, kleinere Nadeln sind mit Maiglöckchen, Schlange, Schwan oder Schmetterling geschmückt. Mit Kleiderschmuck zum Aufnähen, Taschenketten und Taschenverschlüssen wurde das Repertoire erweitert. Es mag ein bißchen verwundern, daß dieses eher unspektakuläre Warenangebot auch äußerst reizvollen avantgardistischen Schmuck einschließt.

Im Folgenden sollen einige Beispiele aus dem Musterbuch Bd. X vorgestellt werden, deren Ausführungen im Original erhalten sind. Das Muster 20.352 zum Halsschmuck (Kat. Nr. 170, Abb. 31) weist genaue Materialangaben wie »dicke runde Kordel (Kunstseide)«, »Gala 30 mm« (= Kugel), »Metall 30 mm« (= Kugel) sowie den Preis 21,– auf. Es ließ sich nicht eindeutig klären, ob sich grundsätzlich alle Preisangaben, siehe auch im Katalog (ab S. 100) auf ein Schmuckstück, oder auf ein Dutzend (= 12 Stück) beziehen. Unter der Variante/1 findet sich die Angabe: »genau dasselbe Modell nur (... unleserlich) Schnur und 20 mm Gala + Metallkugeln, 15,–«. Variante/2 »wie /1 jedoch zwei Galakugeln«. Dieses Beispiel belegt deutlich, daß ein Muster in den verschiedensten Varianten, was Material und Größe der einzelnen Elemente angeht, gefertigt

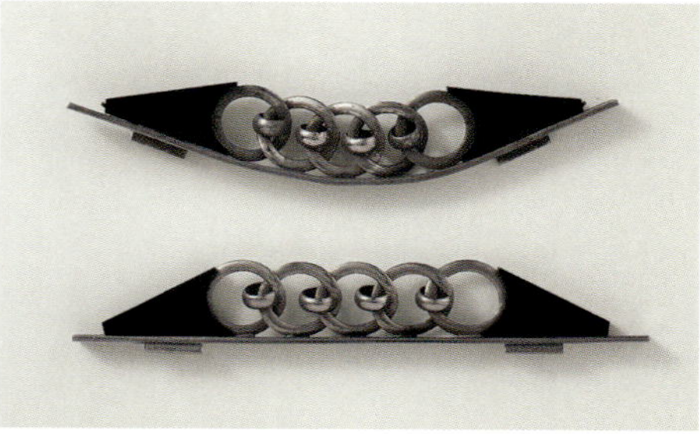

27 Taschenschnäpper von Jakob Bengel mit Ringen, 1936
Handbag snap (spring-catch) with rings, 1936

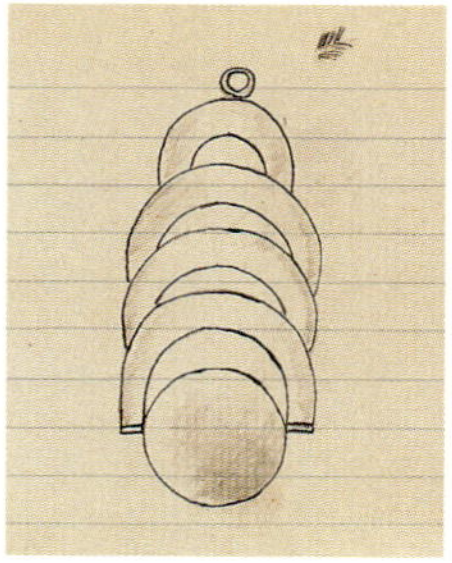

28 Modell 18.522, Musterbuch Jakob Bengel, Bd. IX, 1931/32 siehe auch Kat.Nr. 60
Model 18.522, Pattern Book Jakob Bengel, Vol. IX, 1931 see also cat.no. 60

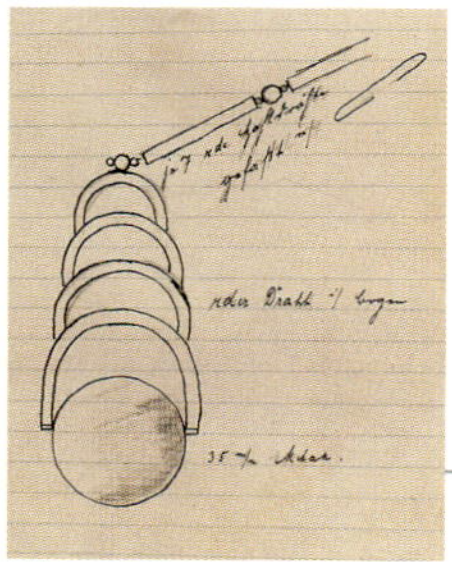

29 Modell 18.535, Musterbuch Jakob Bengel, Bd. IX, 1931/32
Model 18.535, Pattern Book Jakob Bengel, Vol. IX, 1931

The drawings are usually executed in ink or chalk. There are black-and-white drawings but many are also in color. The designs range from fleeting sketches to detailed drawings with exhaustive commentaries dealing with materials, work techniques, references to suppliers, scale and size as well as estimate sale prices (figs. 22–24).

First, let us touch on some designs which are representative of the versatile production of those years although the pieces themselves have not survived. Month and astrological pendants with the signs of the zodiac were popular as themed jewelry. Among the pins is a brooch with the motif of »The Holy Rock at Trier 1933«. Smaller pins are decorated with lilies of the valley, a serpent, swan or butterfly. The repertoire even included jewelry to be sewn on to clothes as well as handbag chains and catches. It may well seem surprising that this rather modest offering of bijouterie wares also included necklaces which were extremely attractive and avant-garde.

In the following some designs from Pattern Book Vol. X will be presented; the original pieces made from them have been preserved. Design pattern 20.352 for a necklace (Cat.no. 170, fig. 31) gives precise material specifications such as »thick round cord (artificial silk)«, »Gala 30 mm« (= sphere), »metal 30 mm« (= sphere) as well as the price 21,– (21.00 Reichsmark). It could not be determined definitely whether all prices given, see also the catalogue (from p. 100) refer to a single piece of jewelry or to a dozen (= 12 pieces of jewelry). Under Variant /1 are the following data: »exactly the same model only (... illegible) cord and 20 mm Gala + metal spheres, 15,–«. Variant /2 is »like /1 except for two Gala spheres«. This example clearly shows that a design pattern was made in all sorts of variants as far as material and the size of the individual elements were concerned. Each customer had the possibility of marketing a model tailored to his specifications. Model designs were also registered for copyright (Cat. nos. 119 and 116).

Pattern 20.471 for necklace Cat. no. 168, fig. 32 includes precise material specifications for each individual element with the size of the spheres as well as the price: »velvet thong, Galalith, metal (= slide), metal sphere 10 mm, metal, Galalith sphere 16 mm, 21,–.«

wurde. Jeder Kunde hatte die Möglichkeit, ein speziell für ihn gefertigtes Modell exklusiv zu vertreiben. Auch wurden Modelle zum Musterschutz angemeldet (Kat.-Nr. 119 und 116).
Das Muster 20.471 zum Halsschmuck (Kat.-Nr. 168. Abb. 32) gibt eine genaue Materialbeschreibung jedes einzelnen Details mit Größenangaben zu den Kugelelementen sowie die Preisangabe: »Samtkordel, Galalith, Metall (= Schieber), Metallkugel 10 mm, Metall, Galalithkugel 16 mm, 21,– «.
Das Muster Nr. 20.956 zum Collier Kat.-Nr. 163 gibt neben Preis, Material, Größe und Variante auch Zulieferfirmen an: »Schlangenkette von Weinrodt No. 43, Kordelkette rund 5 mm 51849/5 (= Modell Nr.) v. H. (= Hirsch) Nbg., Galastein auf Metallplatte, Galakugel 10 mm, Metallkugel 10 mm, /1 einreihig 4 kant Schlangenkette ohne Seide, 21,–«.
Das Muster 21.250 (Kat.-Nr. 229) zeigt, daß die im Musterbuch gemachten Angaben nicht immer auch zur Ausführung kamen: Die mittlere Kette des dreireihigen Mittelteils wurde in dem vorhandenen Original nicht in Gold ausgeführt. Wir erfahren aber auch, daß die Kettenteile nicht alle aus der Bengel-Produktion stammen, sondern zugekauft wurden: »runder Faconpanzer ungel. v. Karl Baltin, hier (= Oberstein), Schlauchkette v. E. Loch & Cie.(?), Variante/1 oben mit No. 6294/3 mm v. Loch & Cie. (?) Sohn«.
Bei dem Muster 20.546 (Kat.-Nr. 224) ist neben der Verwendung von zweifarbigem Galalith und dem Preis auch der Hinweis zu finden, daß für die Kette auf eine eigene, flache »Gansgurgel« (= Schlauchkette) zurückgegriffen wurde.
Unter Muster 20.513 (Kat.-Nr. 200) werden neun verschiedene Anhänger aufgeführt, die zum Teil mit der Faconkette No. 15989 von Fessler geliefert wurden. Bei der Variante /3 ist ver-

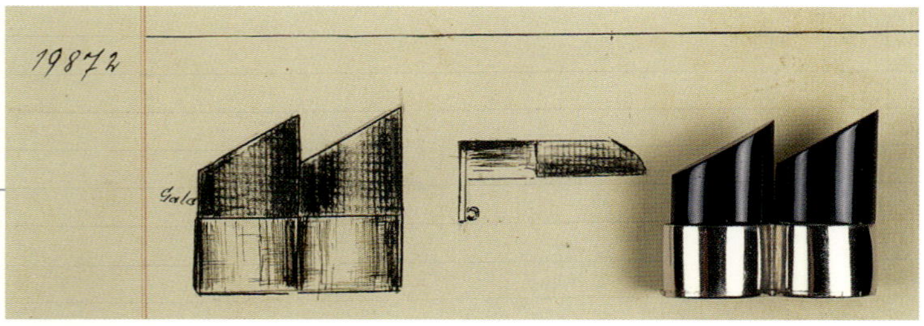

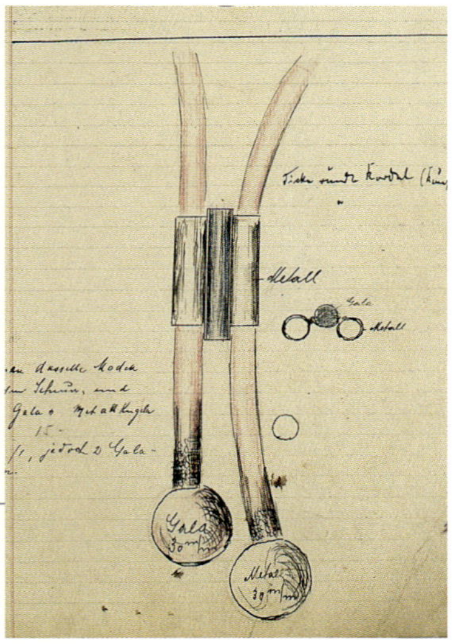

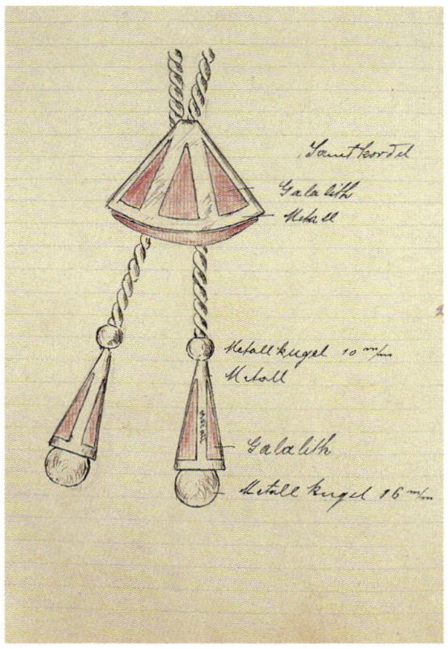

30 Musterbuch Jakob Bengel, Bd. X, Modell 19.872, Taschenschnäpper (Zeichnung und Original); Privatsammlung, Stuttgart
Pattern Book Jakob Bengel, Vol. X, model 19.872, handbag snap (drawing and original), private collection, Stuttgart

31 Musterbuch Jakob Bengel, Bd. X, Modell 20.352 (Kat.-Nr. 170)
Pattern Book Jakob Bengel, Vol. X, model 20.352 (Cat.no. 170)

32 Musterbuch Jakob Bengel, Bd. X, Modell 20.471 (Kat.-Nr. 168)
Pattern Book Jakob Bengel, Vol. X, model 20.471 (Cat.no. 168)

Pattern no. 20.956 for the collar Cat. no. 163 includes, apart from its price, material, size and variants, suppliers: »Snake necklace from Weinrodt No. 43, thong round 5 mm 51849/5 (= model no.) fr. H. (= Hirsch) Nbg., Gala stone on metal plate, Gala sphere 10 mm, metal sphere 10 mm, / 1 strand 4 cornered [= square in section] snake necklace without silk, 21,–.«
Pattern 21.250 (Cat.no. 229) shows that the guidelines entered in the Pattern Book were not always followed: the central chain of the three-strand central piece was not executed in gold in the original, which has been preserved. However, we also learn that the parts of chains were not all made by Bengel but were bought from suppliers: »*round Facon breastplate ungel. fr. Karl Baltin, here* (= Oberstein), *tubular chain fr. E. Loch & Cie.(?), variant /1 top with No. 6294/3 mm fr. Loch & Cie. (?) Sohn.*«
Pattern 20.546 (Cat.no. 224) includes, apart from the use of Galalith in two colors and the price, the information that, for the chain, a flat »goose choker« (= tubular chain) was to be used.
Under pattern 20.513 (Cat.no. 200) nine different pendants are listed, some of them delivered with the Facon chain no. 15989 by Fessler. Variant /3 bears the following remark: »w. chain fr. W. Wittmer No. 3181 col 572 black/white. Length of chain 46 cm, spherical calotte 2.2 cm«.
Most bracelets were made to form a suite with necklaces. However, many ring-bracelets and bangles were also manufactured by Bengel (figs. 33, 35). The firm had a rich array of models ranging from bangles made purely of tombac (»Mannheim gold«, similar to pinchbeck) to decorative pieces lavishly incorporating generous Galalith segments or spheres. Drawings have been preserved which imply that designs were bought in for the production of such pieces (see figs. 37–41). These drawings were used as models by the pattern makers, who were adept at trans-

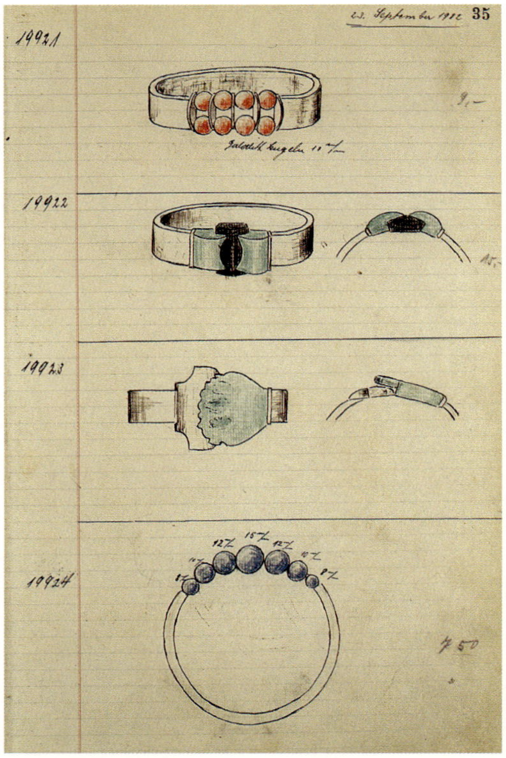

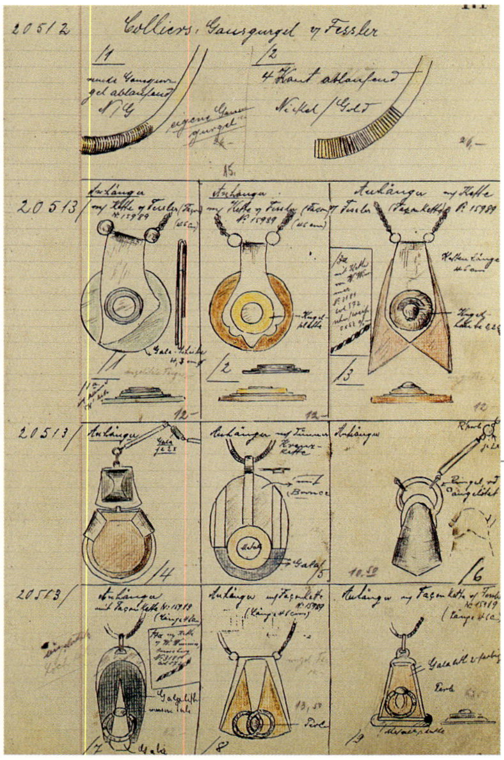

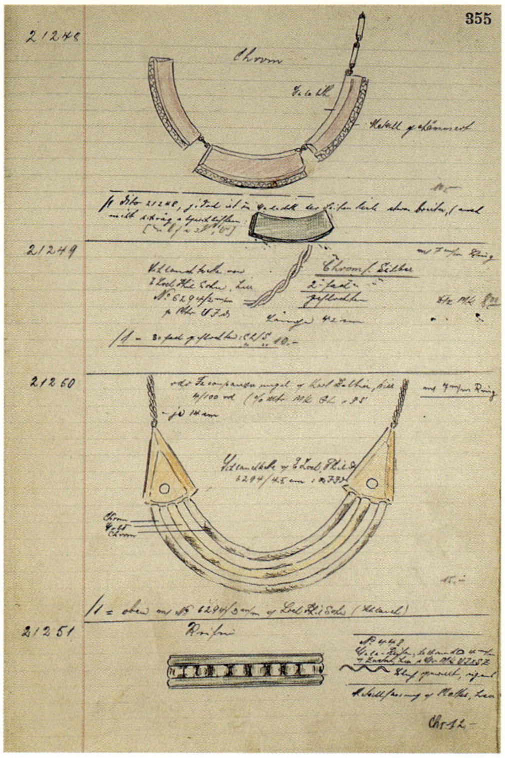

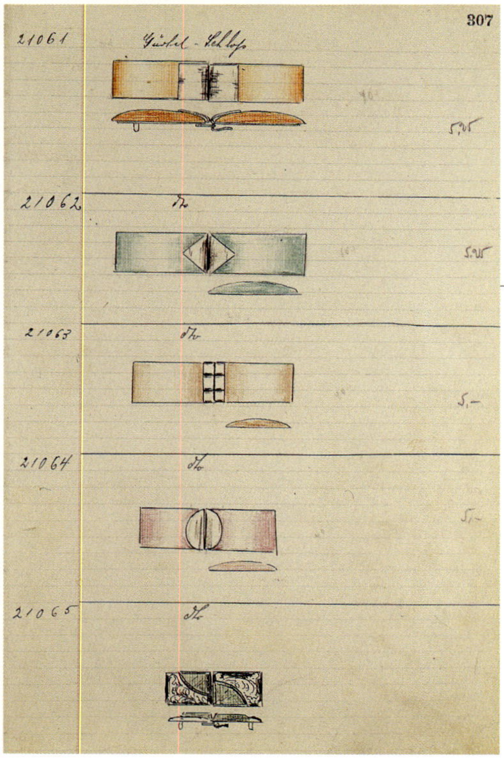

33 Musterbuch Jakob Bengel, Bd. X, S. 35, Modelle 19.921–19.924
Pattern Book Jakob Bengel, Vol. X, p. 35, models 19.921–19.924

34 Musterbuch Jakob Bengel, Bd. X, S. 171, Modell 20.512–20.553
Pattern book Jakob Bengel, vol. X, p. 171, model 20.512–20.553

35 Musterbuch Jakob Bengel, Bd. X, S. 255, Modell 21.250 (Kat.-Nr. 229), Modell 21.248 (Kat.-Nr. 230)
Pattern Book Jakob Bengel, Vol. X, p. 255, model 21.250 (Cat.no. 229) model 21.248 (Cat.no. 230)

36 Musterbuch Jakob Bengel, Bd. X, S. 307
Pattern Book Jakob Bengel, Vol. X, p. 307

merkt: »m. Kette v. W. Wittmer No. 3181 col 572 schwarz/weiß. Kettenlänge 46 cm, Kugelhaube 2,2 cm«.

Neben den meisten, als Ergänzung zum Halsschmuck gefertigten Armbändern wurden in der Firma Bengel auch viele Armreifen und Armspangen gefertigt (Abb. 33, 35). Von der reinen Gelbmetallarbeit bis hin zu dekorativen Stücken mit großen Galalithsegmenten oder -kugeln hatte die Firma eine reiche Palette im Angebot. Es haben sich Zeichnungen erhalten, die darauf schließen lassen, daß für die Produktion der Stücke Entwürfe angekauft wurden (s. Abb. 37–41). Sie dienten als Vorlagen für den Mustermacher, der sie umzusetzen verstand, wie den entsprechenden Mustern (Nr. 19.921–19.924) im Musterbuch Bd. X zu entnehmen ist (Abb. 33). Das gleiche gilt auch für die in den 1930er Jahren so beliebten kleinen Stabbroschen, deren lineare Struktur durch kleine Galalithkugeln und -segmente durchbrochen wurde. Auf einer der Zeichnungen ist mit Bleistift der Name des Zeichners »Willy Martin, Pforzheim« vermerkt (Abb. 37). Weitere Informationen zu Enwerfern haben sich nicht erhalten bzw. ließen sich nicht recherchieren. Die wenigen erhaltenen Unterlagen geben uns leider keine Auskunft darüber, wer noch bei der Firma Jakob Bengel in den 1930er Jahren für die äußerst kreativen, dem Zeitgeschmack entsprechenden, Entwürfe verantwortlich zeichnete. Ein Teil der umfangreichen Entwürfe mag von der Hand Albert Roos' stammen, der an anderer Stelle noch genannt wird. Allerdings verrät uns die unterschiedliche Handschrift der Entwürfe auch, daß hier verschiedene Mustermacher tätig waren.

Es wäre denkbar, daß man sich der Lehrer von den Fachschulen Idar-Oberstein, Pforzheim oder Hanau bediente.

Ein Blick nach Schwäbisch Gmünd zur Firma Ottmar Zieher, *Fabrik feiner Juwelen und Goldwaren*, zeigt uns, daß man sich zu dieser Zeit durchaus auch freier Mitarbeiter bediente und hier gerne bereits bekannte Künstler wie etwa Wilhelm Wagenfeld, einen ehemaligen Studenten der Hanauer Schule und des Bauhauses (Abb. 47), engagierte. Der Firmenprospekt von Zieher informiert uns, daß der Schmuck, in »enger Zusammenarbeit zwischen Künstler und Techniker« entstanden war. Immerhin haben sich 17 Skizzenblätter Wagenfelds für Ringe, Broschen und Anhänger erhalten, die zwischen 1930 und 1932 zur Ausführung kamen.[14]

Als weiteres Beispiel für eine Zusammenarbeit zwischen Künstler und ausführender Firma ist die Kooperation zwischen dem Entwerfer und damaligen Leiter der Staatlichen Zeichenakademie Hugo Leven und der Firma Hans Kreuter & Co. in Hanau zu nennen. Die Entwurfsblätter (Abb. 43) für Halsschmuck, Broschen, Anhänger sowie alle Variationen von Armschmuck – Manschettenarmband, Juwelenband, Armreif – zeugen von dem hohen gestalterischen Können Levens und gehören zu

lating them into designs, as the corresponding patterns (nos. 19.921–19.924) in Vol. X of the Pattern Book show (fig. 33). The same holds for the little bar brooches which were so popular in the 1930s. The astringent linearity of their structure was relieve by little Galalith spheres and segments. One of these drawings bears the name of the draughtsman, »Willy Martin, Pforzheim«, in pencil (fig. 37). No further information on designers at Bengel has come down to us nor was any forthcoming for research purposes.

Indeed, the few documents to have been preserved at all unfortunately tell us nothing more about who else was responsible at Jakob Bengel in the 1930s for those extraordinarily creative designs, so attuned to the taste of the times. The volume of designs was enormous; some may be from the hand of Albert Roos (who will be mentioned elsewhere). However, the variety of personal styles reveals different signatures. Several different designers must, therefore, have been at work. Possibly teachers at the Fachschule Idar-Oberstein worked for Bengel in this capacity or designers may have been recruited from other Fachschulen such as those at Pforzheim and Hanau.

The case of Ottmar Zieher, *Fabrik feiner Juwelen und Goldwaren* at Schwäbisch Gmünd shows that freelancers were employed then by jewelry-making firms. They welcomed artists who already enjoyed a considerable reputation such as Wilhelm Wagenfeld, a graduate of both the Hanau school and the Bauhaus (fig. 47). The Zieher brochure informs us that the jewelry shown in it »was the result of close collaboration between artists and technicians«. Seventeen sheets with Wagenfeld's sketches for rings, brooches and pendants have been preserved and were executed between 1930 and 1932.[14] A second example of collaboration between an artist and a manufacturer concerns Hugo Leven, a designer and director of the Staatliche Zeichenakademie at that time, and his work for Hans Kreuter & Co. in Hanau. The sheets with Leven's designs (fig. 43) for necklaces, brooches, pendants and all sorts of bracelets – cuffs, pavé-set bands, bangles – attest to his enormous talent. His designs are among the finest to have been preserved from the 1930s in Germany.[15] Both Ottmar Zieher and Kreuter & Co. were able to attract reputable designers and to attach them, at least temporarily. Even though Jakob Bengel had turned to the production of bijouterie wares – that is, was reaching out to the lower market segment in costume jewelry – it can be assumed that in Oberstein, too, the creative potential of freelance artists was appreciated and put to good use. That creative power could develop at Bengel at all was due to developments which, on the one hand, took place in Germany from 1919 at the Bauhaus, founded by Walter Gropius (figs. 49, 50), and, on the other, were inspired by French models, particularly those furnished by French avant-garde jewelry-makers (figs. 51, 52).

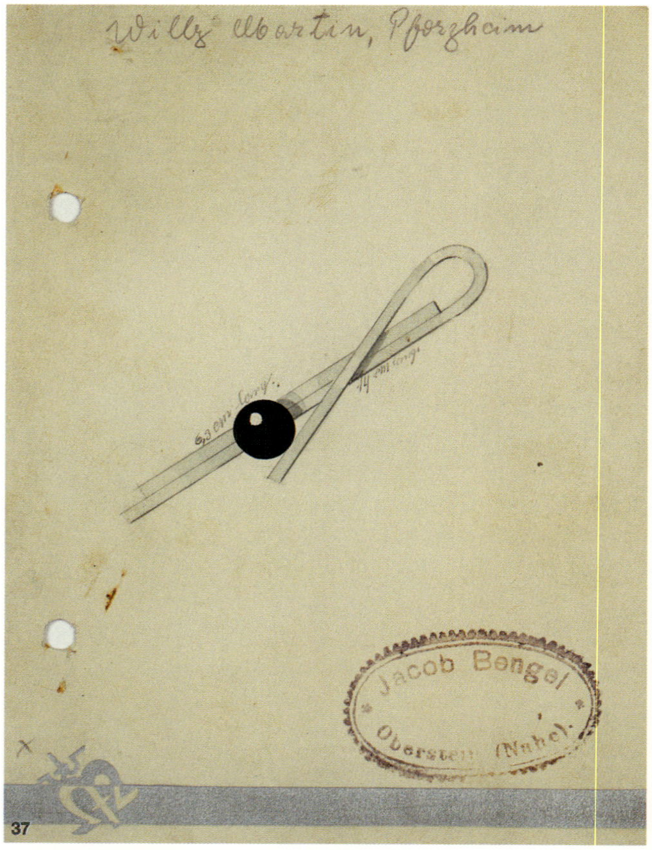

37

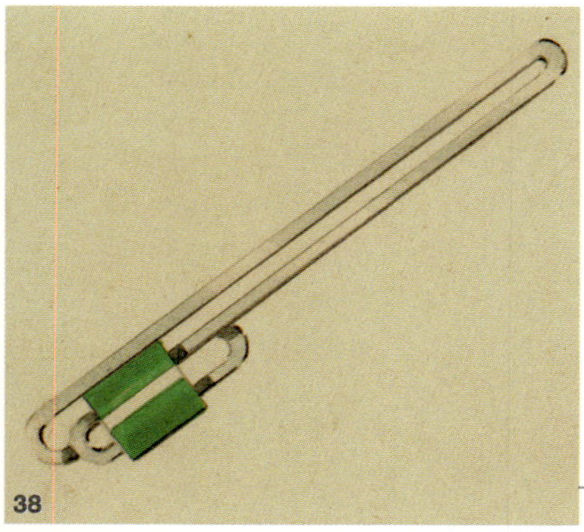
38

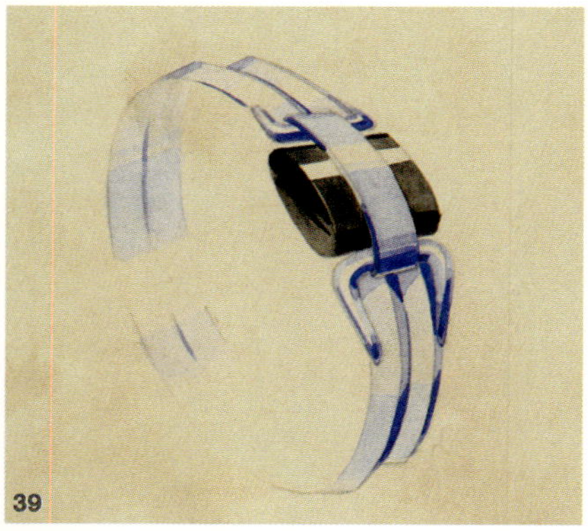
39

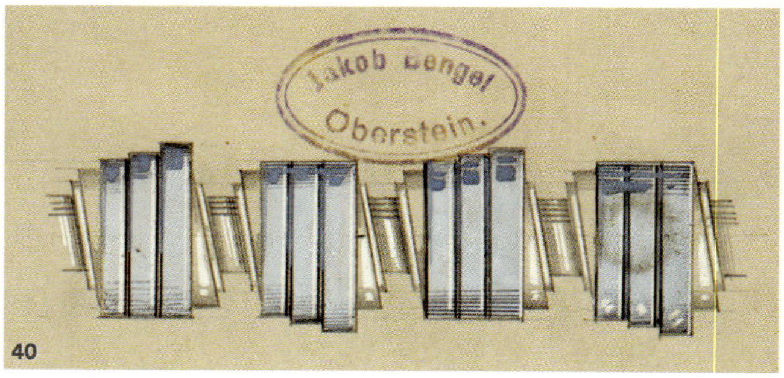

40

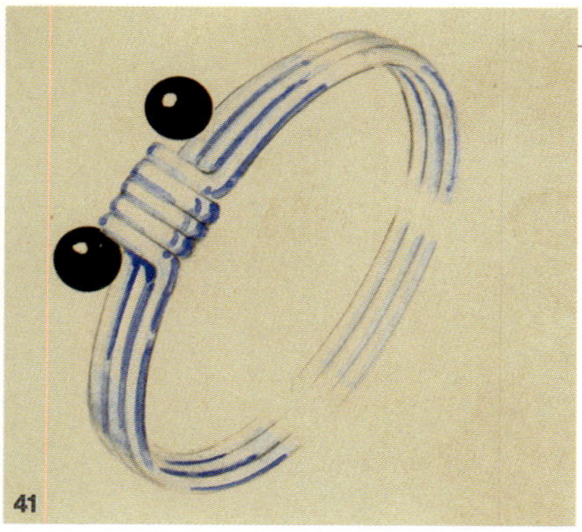
41

37 Willy Martin, Pforzheim
Entwurf »Stabbrosche« für
Jakob Bengel, Anfang 1930er Jahre
Willy Martin, Pforzheim,
»Bar brooch« design for Jakob
Bengel, early 1930s

38–41 Schmuck-Entwürfe für Jakob
Bengel, Anfang 1930er Jahre (siehe
auch Kat.-Nr. 233)
Jewelry designs for Jakob Bengel,
early 1930s (see also Cat.no. 233)

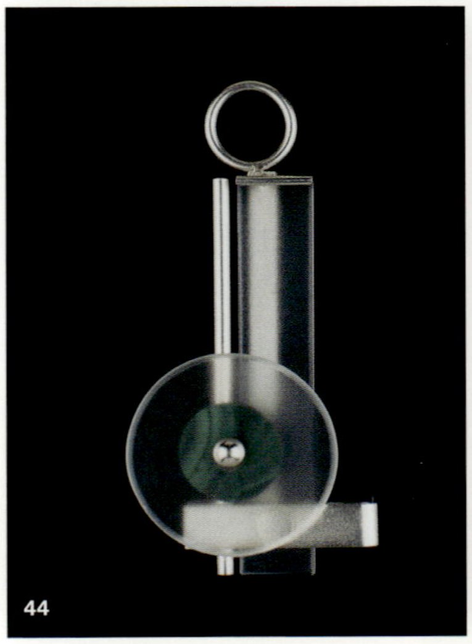

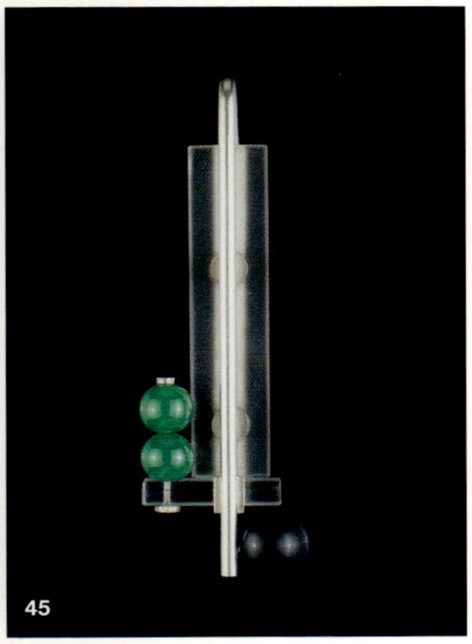

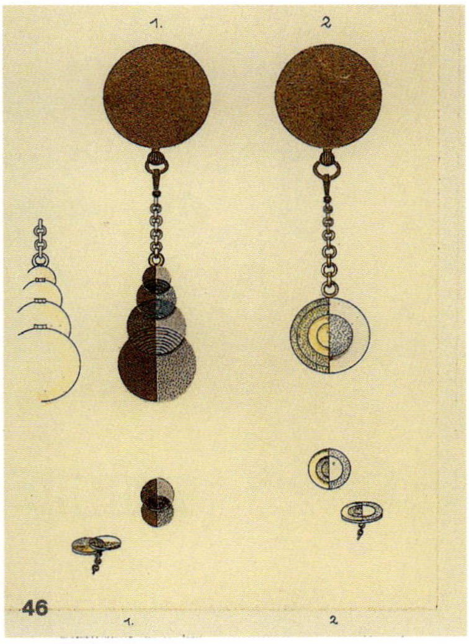

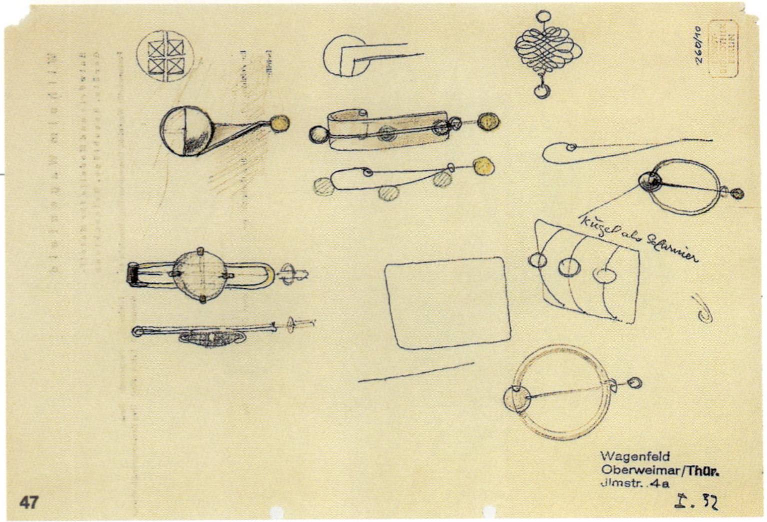

42 Hugo Leven; Entwurf für Firma Kreuter, Haar- und Ohrschmuck, um 1930
Hugo Leven; Design for Kreuter, hair and ear jewelry, ca. 1930

43 Hugo Leven für Firma Kreuter, Hanau; Entwurf für Armreifen und Armbänder, um 1930
Hugo Leven for Kreuter, Hanau; Design for bangles and bracelets, ca. 1930

44–45 Siegfried Männle; Anhänger, um 1928; Privatbesitz
Siegfried Männle; Pendant, ca. 1928; Private collection

46 Irmgard Fuß, Schwäbisch Gmünd; Entwürfe für Ohrgehänge, 1928/30
Irmgard Fuß, Schwäbisch Gmünd; Designs for drops, 1928/30

47 Wilhelm Wagenfeld, Oberweimar; Entwurfsskizze, I. 32
Wilhelm Wagenfeld, Oberweimar; Design, I. 32

48 Herbert Bayer, Zeitschriftenprospekt »Bauhaus«, 1928
Herbert Bayer, Magazine brochure: »Bauhaus«, 1928

den großartigsten Entwürfen, die sich aus der Schmuckproduktion der Zeit um 1930 in Deutschland erhalten haben.[15]
Die Firmen Ottmar Zieher und Kreuter & Co. verstanden es, zumindest zeitweilig, bekannte Entwerfernamen an ihr Haus zu binden. Auch wenn sich Jakob Bengel der Produktion der Bijouterieware – also dem preiswerten Schmuckgenre – zugewandt hatte, kann man davon ausgehen, daß man auch in Oberstein das kreative Potential freischaffender Künstler zu schätzen und nutzen wußte.
Die gestalterischen Kräfte der Firma Bengel konnten sich nur aufgrund von Entwicklungen entfalten, die sich zum einen in Deutschland ab 1919 an dem von Walter Gropius gegründeten Bauhaus vollzogen (Abb. 49, 50), aber auch an französischen Vorbildern, vor allem der französischen Schmuck-Avantgarde (Abb. 51, 52).

Inspiration und Quellen: Die Metallwerkstatt des Bauhauses – Die französische Schmuck-Avantgarde: Gerard Sandoz, Jean Puiforcat, Raymond Templier und Jean Després

Die Schmuckherstellung war nicht das eigentliche Ziel des Bauhauses und doch wurden dort die Voraussetzungen für den konsequenten Umgang mit den geometrischen und stereometrischen Formen wie Kugel, Kegel, Quadrat, Dreieck oder Rhombe gelegt. Dort wuchsen die Bereitschaft und das Verständnis aus Edelstahl, Chrom, Nickel und Glas Schmuckstücke zu schaffen. In der Bauhaus-Metallwerkstatt fand eine systematische Auseinandersetzung mit dem Werkstoff Metall statt. Dieses Atelier wird heute als eine der fruchtbarsten Werkstätten des Bauhauses gesehen.[16]
Die frühesten Erfahrungen machten die Lehrenden und Studierenden mit der Gestaltung von Gefäßen und kleinem Gerät, das sich an den stereometrischen Grundformen wie Kugel, Halbkugel, flache Kugelabschnitte, Paraboloide (= gekrümmte Flächen), Kegel, Zylinder und Würfel orientiert, die später zu den Paradigmen des legendären »Bauhausstils« werden sollen. Sachlichkeit, Material- und Produktionsökonomie sollten verbunden bleiben mit Formbewußtsein, Proportion und Eleganz, auch unter dem Aspekt der Serienproduktion. Buntmetalle wie Kupfer, Messing, Bronze, Tombak aber auch Silber, Nickel und Chrom waren wegen ihrer kühlen Ausstrahlung und der technisch anmutenden Ästhetik die bevorzugten Werkstoffe. Das Experiment in Verbindung mit handwerklicher Perfektion im Dienste der gestalterischen Qualität stand im Vordergrund. Naum Slutzky, der bekannteste und innovativste Schmuckkünstler des Bauhauses experimentierte zu Beginn der 1920er Jahre mit dem Motiv der »Rundscheibe«, die er in seiner Anfangsphase mit verschiedenen Ringteilen aus

Sources of inspiration: the Bauhaus metal workshop – French avant-garde jewelry designers: Gerard Sandoz, Jean Puiforcat, Raymond Templier and Jean Després

Making jewelry was not a stated Bauhaus goal yet the groundwork was laid there for dealing purposively and consistently with such geometric and stereometric forms as the sphere, cone, square, triangle and rhombus. It was the Bauhaus that promoted the willingness to make jewelry of stainless steel, chrome, nickel and glass and taught the skills for doing so. Systematic study of the material properties of metal was conducted at the Bauhaus metal workshop. This studio is now regarded as having been one of the most productive Bauhaus workshops.[16]
Instructors and students there first gained experience in designing vessels and small implements and utensils, using such basic forms of solids as the sphere, hemisphere, the cone, cylinder and cube as well as the paraboloid (= curved surfaces, with sections parallel to at least one plane to form parabolas) and two-dimensional forms such as the great circle (a circle drawn on a sphere that has its center at the center of the sphere) and segments of it, which would later become the signature paradigms of the legendary »Bauhaus style«. Objectivity and economical use of materials and means of production were to remain indissolubly linked with awareness of form, proportion and elegance, even under the conditions of mass production. Non-ferrous heavy metals and alloys of these such as copper, brass, bronze, tombac and even silver, nickel and chrome were the materials of choice because of their cool look and their affinity with the aesthetic of technology. Experimentation linked with consummate craftsmanship in the interests of top-quality design represented the prime Bauhaus objectives. Naum Slutzky, the best-known and most innovative of the Bauhaus art metalworkers and jewelrs, experimented in the early 1920s with the »disc« motif. In the early stages of working with it, he incorporated different materials into the various parts of his circular design (fig. 49). The pendants did not hang on gold or silver chains; instead they were worn on simple silk cords of the type also encountered in work by the French avant-garde (figs. 51, 52). Naum Slutzky's most revolutionary jewelry, however, dates not from his Bauhaus years but from about 1930, that is, from a period when the French avant-garde also attained the pinnacle of their achievement. Slutzky experimented with new materials which he translated into models for industrial or mass production although these were never made. His materials of choice were chromium-plated or silvered metals such as brass or nickel. Slutzky used simple little tubular elements, quadrilateral metal plates, lugs and wire loops to construct his pendants, chains and bangles (fig. 50).

unterschiedlichsten Materialien gestaltete (Abb. 49). Die Anhänger hingen nicht an goldenen oder silbernen Ketten, sondern wurden an einfachen Seidenkordeln getragen, wie sie auch beim Schmuck der französischen Avantgardisten zu finden waren (Abb. 51, 52). Seine revolutionärsten Schmuckstücke schuf Naum Slutzky aber nicht während seiner Bauhausjahre, sondern erst um 1930, also zu einer Zeit, als auch die französischen Avantgardisten auf ihrem Höhepunkt angelangt waren. Slutzky experimentierte mit neuen Materialien, die er in Modelle für die industrielle bzw. serielle Fertigung umsetzte, die jedoch nie ausgeführt wurden. Er bevorzugte vor allem verchromte oder versilberte Metalle wie Messing oder Nickel. Aus einfachen Röhrchen, rechteckigen Metallplatten, Ösen und Drahtschlingen konstruierte Slutzky seine Anhänger, Ketten und Armreifen (Abb. 50).

Es ist kein Zufall, daß der ausgefallene Schmuck aus Metall und Galalith oder nur Metall, der sich eindeutig an der damals aktuellen, vor allem von den Avantgardisten verwendeten Formensprache, den geometrischen, stereometrischen und maschinen-ästhetischen Elementen orientierten, erst nach 1930 in der Produktion bei Bengel auftauchten.

Ende der 1920er Jahre etablierte sich in Paris eine Gruppe von Schmuckkünstlern, um am 31. Mai 1929 die »Union des artistes Modernes (U. A. M.)« zu gründen. Zu ihnen gehörten die bedeutendsten französischen Schmuckgestalter wie Jean Fouquet, Gérard Sandoz, Jean Puiforcat und Raymond Templier. Technische Neuerungen und absolut einfache Formen standen bei ihren Schmuckstücken im Vordergrund. Diese Avantgardisten bedienten sich nicht unbedingt nur der Edelmetalle und Edelsteine – Holz, Chrom, Lack, Glas und Elfenbein waren für sie ebenso interessant. Ihre Intention stand unter dem Motto »Ein schönes Material muß nicht selten oder kostbar sein. Ein Material ist dann schön, wenn es aus sich heraus oder durch

49 Naum Slutzky
Anhänger, um 1922/23
Naum Slutzky
Pendant, ca. 1922/23

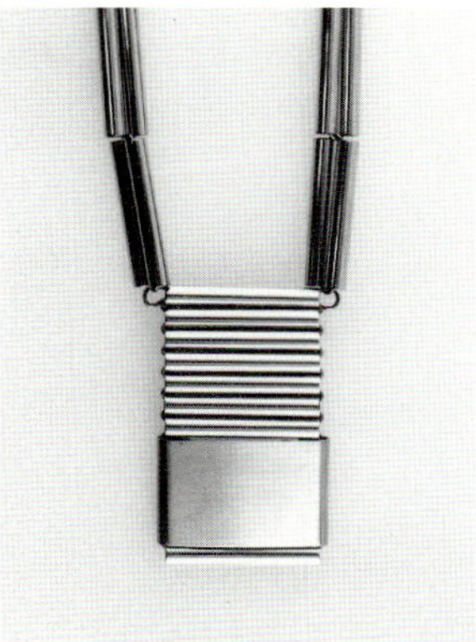

50 Naum Slutzky
Anhänger mit Halskette, Messing verchromt, 1930
Naum Slutzky
Pendant with necklace, chromium-plated brass, 1930

51 Eric Bagge, Paris
Anhänger, Ende 1920er Jahre
Eric Bagge, Paris
Pendant, late 1920s

52 Jean Fouquet, Paris
Anhänger, Ende 1920er Jahre
Jean Fouquet, Paris
Pendant, late 1920s

It is not a coincidence that the strikingly distinctive chains and pendants made of metal and Galalith or metal alone, which are so obviously influenced by the formal idiom of the French avant-garde, with its elements borrowed from geometry, trigonometry and the aesthetic of the machine, did not surface in production at Bengel until after 1930.

In the late 1920s a group of artists in jewelry established a footing in Paris to found the »Union des Artistes Modernes« (U.A.M.) on 31 May 1929. Their number included the most important French jewelry designers, such luminaries as Jean Fouquet, Gerard Sandoz, Jean Puiforcat and Raymond Templier. Technical innovations and utterly free form were the salient features of their work. These avant-garde artists did not limit themselves to using precious metals and precious stones; they were just as interested in wood, chrome, lacquer, glass and ivory. Their intention might be summarized as »A beautiful material need not be rare or costly. A material is beautiful if, of itself or through the way it has been worked, it gives aesthetic pleasure to the eye and to the sense of touch and also if it has been used with considered deliberation.«[17] The celebrated »cult of the machine« had reached its zenith to be reflected even in jewelry, for instance in Raymond Templier's pieces. Gérard Sandoz developed pendants and chains which were stringently austere in design; simple, perfect proportions were pivotal in his work. He worked with the geometry of forms such as the rectangle, the sphere and the cone and his materials were acid-treated silver and lacquer in red and black. The enthusiasm for a technical world is most apparent in Jean Després. His training as a goldsmith was interrupted by the First World War, when he was forced to occupy himself with the construction of aeroplane engines. They would influence his conception of jewelry design (figs. 53, 54). Drawing aeroplane engines, Després became enthralled with machines. In 1918 he returned to France and

seine Bearbeitung dem Auge und dem Tastsinn einen ästhetischen Genuß bereitet und mit Bedacht eingesetzt wird«.[17] Die gefeierte »Maschinenkultur« hatte ihren Höhepunkt erreicht und spiegelte sich jetzt auch im Schmuck wieder, wie etwa bei den Stücken von Raymon Templier. Gérard Sandoz entwickelte Anhänger und Ketten von äußerst strenger Gestaltung, einfache und perfekte Proportionen standen im Mittelpunkt seiner Arbeiten. Er arbeitete mit geometrischen Formen sowie geätztem Silber und Lack in Rot und Schwarz. Am deutlichsten war diese Begeisterung von einer technisierten Welt bei Jean Després zu spüren: Seine Ausbildung zum Goldschmied wurde durch den Ersten Weltkrieg unterbrochen. Er mußte sich mit der Konstruktion von Flugzeugmotoren beschäftigen, die dann Einfluß nahmen auf seine spätere Gestaltungswelt im Schmuck (Abb. 53, 54). Després zeichnete Flugzeugmotoren und erlebte eine totale Faszination durch die Maschine.

1918 kehrte er in seine Heimatstadt Avallon/Frankreich zurück und schuf in einem unnachahmlichen Stil vom Kubismus geprägten Silberschmuck. Sein Schmuck spiegelte von nun an den Zeitgeist »Technik und Maschine« wider. Zunächst scheute sich Després, mit diesem betont technischen Schmuck an die Öffentlichkeit zu treten und nahm deshalb anonym an einigen Ausstellungen teil.

Der »Motorenschmuck« von Després auf der Ausstellung »L'Aéronautique et l'Art« im Pavillon de Marsan in Paris im Jahre 1931 löste geradezu einen Skandal aus. Seine Broschen, Ringe und Armbänder erinnern in Details an Pleuelstangen, Kurbelwellen und Getriebe und sind der Höhepunkt seiner künstlerischen Kreativität und machten ihn zum Meister zwischen Art Déco und Avantgarde. Die Schmuckstücke Jean Després' müssen als Vorboten der Bengelschen Schmuckgestaltung gesehen werden, dies bestätigt auch ein Blick auf seine Musterblätter (Abb. 54).[18]

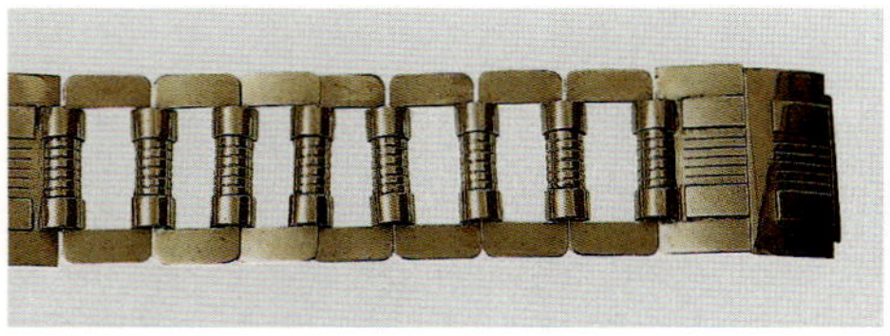

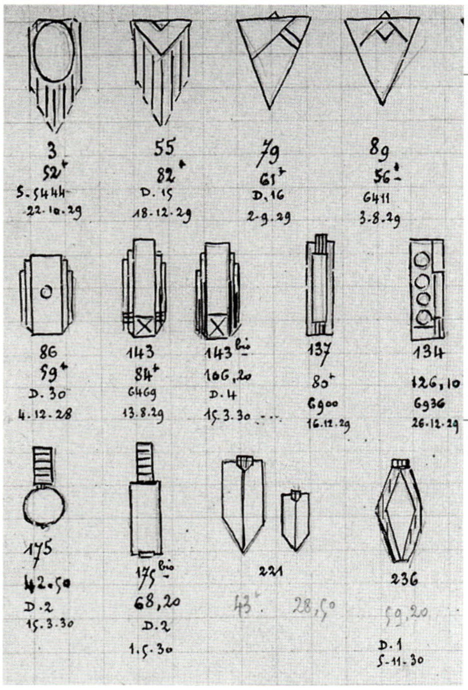

53 Jean Després
Armband, Metall, um 1928
Jean Després
Bracelet, metal, ca. 1928

54 Jean Després
Musterblatt für Anhänger (Ausriß), Anfang 1930er Jahre
Jean Després
Design sheet for pendants (excerpt), early 1930s

his native Avallon. The inimitably stylish silver jewelry he created there owed its design to Cubism. From then on his jewelry echoed the Zeitgeist, which stood for »technology and the machine«. At first hesitant to go public with such pointedly technical jewelry, Després participated anonymously in several exhibitions. The »motor jewelry« shown by Després at the 1931 »L'Aeronautique et l'Art« exhibition in the »Pavillon de Marsan« in Paris caused a scandal. Details of his brooches, rings and bracelets recall connecting rods, crankshafts and gearboxes. The supreme aesthetic achievement of this infinitely creative artist, they reveal him as a master between Art Déco and avant-garde. Jean Després' jewelry should be regarded as a precursor of Bengel jewelry design. That this is so is confirmed at a glance when one looks at the design sheets printed in a recent monograph devoted to his work (fig. 54).[18]

Playing with form and color: jewelry between 1931 and 1938

Grouping the pieces of jewelry in the collection discussed here by individual design elements facilitates stylistic classification and aesthetic evaluation of it as art and design and is, therefore, the procedure adopted in the following.

»Bauhaus elements«: square, polygon, triangle and cone

Nos. 250 and 249 recall the Naum Slutzky »disc pendants« mentioned above (see figs. 49, 55). The use of cloudy Galalith combined with tombac and faceted glass stones is what makes these two pendants such extraordinarily striking compositions. The oval pendant with translucent Galalith (no. 248) and no. 245 also belong to this group, which is notable for superb design, is very close formally to the pieces by Slutzky and in quality is certainly the equal of early 1930s French avant-garde jewelry design.

A series of necklaces is remarkable for the playful way in which triangles, semicircles, trapeziums and polygons of Galilith are

Das Spiel mit Form und Farbe: der Schmuck zwischen 1931 und 1938

Eine stilistische Einordnung und künstlerisch/gestalterische Beurteilung der vorliegenden Sammlung von Schmuckstücken ist am ehesten nachzuvollziehen, wenn man den Schmuck nach einzelnen Gestaltungselementen in Gruppen zusammenfaßt.

»Bauhauselemente«: Quadrat, Vieleck, Dreieck und Kegel

An die bereits erwähnten »Rundscheiben-Anhänger« Naum Slutzkys (s. Abb. 49, 55) erinnern Nr. 250 und Nr. 249, das gewolkte Galalith in Verbindung mit Gelbmetall und facettierten Glassteinen macht die beiden Anhänger zu außergewöhnlichen Kompositionen. Auch der ovale Anhänger mit transparentem Galalith (Nr. 248) sowie Nr. 245 gehören in diese Gruppe exzellenter Gestaltung, die formal den Slutzky-Stücken sehr nahe stehen und durchaus dem Niveau der französischen Avantgarde-Schmuckgestaltung der frühen 1930er Jahre entsprechen.

In ihrer absolut klaren Strukturierung fällt eine Reihe von Colliers auf, die mit Dreiecken, Halbkreisen, Trapez und Vielecken aus Galalith spielt (Nr. 38, Nr. 39, Nr. 107 – Nr. 110) Sehr häufig sind diese Kunststoffelemente auf gleichförmigen Metallplatten aufgeschraubt, die wiederum durch Ein- und Abknickungen das Galalith verdecken. Bis auf wenige Ausnahmen handelt es sich um Ketten, die ausschließlich als Abwicklungen in der Fläche gestaltet sind. Die verschiedenen geometrischen Elemente sind immer nur in der Mitte der Kette, sozusagen als »große Glieder«, eingefügt, die Fortführung der Kette sind meistens sehr feine Metallstäbchen, -plättchen oder -röhrchen (Nr. 148, 149, 151).

Spitz zulaufende Vielecke, gelegentlich leicht abgerundet in Form eines Blattes, werden als einzelne Glieder in Metall oder Galalith verwendet (Nr. 199, Nr. 212). Die Beispiele Nr. 211 und Nr. 230 gehören mit ihren ebenfalls spitzen Gliedern zum gleichen Repertoire, das gehämmerte Metall nimmt den Stücken, nach unserer heutigen Vorstellung, etwas von ihrer Eleganz. In zahlreichen langen Ketten und Colliers wird mit abgekanteten Bogenmotiven in Metall gespielt, in die frei drehbare Kugeln eingehängt sind (Nr. 14, Nr. 16, Nr. 19). Als Abwandlung

55 Naum Slutzky
Anhänger, 1929
Naum Slutzky
Pendant, 1929

deployed (no. 38, no. 39, nos. 107–110). These elements of synthetic materials are often screwed on to metal plates which are identical to them in form. The metal plates in turn conceal the Galalith by means of hollows and bends. In almost all cases these are necklaces which are designed exclusively to unwind in one plane. The various geometric elements are invariably only at the center, added, as it were, as »large links«. The necklace usually continues with very delicate little metal rods, discs or tubes (nos. 148, 149, 151).

Pointed polygons, sometimes slightly rounded off in the form of a leaf, are used as individual elements in either metal or Galalith (nos. 199, 212). Since their elements are also pointed, no. 211 and no. 230 draw on the same repertoire of forms. The beaten metal, however, makes these pieces somehow look less elegant, at least by today's aesthetic standards.

In numerous long chains and necklaces, beveled arc motifs in metal with freely revolving spheres suspended in them are the gambit (no. 14, no. 16, no. 19). A variation on this type sports arcs made of Galalith and combined with metal spheres.

Along with such stringently geometric models there are a great many pieces whose design is owed primarily to the conditions of mechanical production. Innumerable variations of a necklace type have been exploited with great ingenuity in endless possibilities, among them the »goose choker« and the »tubular necklace«.

The cone or cornet motif has been varied (e.g. Cat.nos. 55, 56) beyond the scope of most designers' or wearers' imaginations. The most convincing, however, of these are a long necklace sporting metal cornets alternating with black Galalith spheres (no. 58), the collar with »a cornet as central piece« and a necklace made up of tiny Galalith spheres and metal rods (no. 57). The pierced metal cones (no. 72) are an intriguing variant, which was also used in an entirely different model (no. 168). The fan-shaped metal slide of this necklace was also made in openwork.

The tubular necklace – the »goose choker« – the sautoir

The Pattern Books as well as extant pieces of jewelry reveal that the »goose choker« was an object of considerable interest for quite some time (Cat.nos. 117, 121–123, 145, 174, 177, 178). This is a type of tubular necklace, which was made with elements which are square, round, flattened, etc. in section and

dieses Typus sind die Bögen aus Galalith gefertigt und mit Metallkugeln kombiniert.

Neben diesen streng geometrischen Ausführungen finden sich sehr viele Beispiele, die in erster Linie auf die produktionstechnischen Gegebenheiten zurückzuführen sind. Unzählige Variationen eines Kettentypus wurden auf vielfältigste Art und Weise genutzt, wie bei den »Gansgurgel«- und »Schlauchketten«.

Das Kegel- oder auch Tütenmotiv wird in allen erdenklichen Möglichkeiten durchgespielt (z.B. Kat.-Nr. 55, 56). Am überzeugendsten sind allerdings eine lange Kette, in der Metalltüten mit schwarzen Galalithkugeln abwechseln (Nr. 58) und das Collier mit »Tüten-Mittelteil« und einer aus kleinen Galalithkugeln und Metallstäbchen bestehenden Kette (Nr. 57).

Die durchbrochenen Metallkegel (Nr. 72) sind eine reizvolle Spielart, die auch in einer ganz anderen Ausführung verwendet wurde (Nr. 168). Der fächerartige Schieber dieses Halsschmucks wurde auch als metallische Durchbrucharbeit gestaltet.

Schlauchkette – »Gansgurgel« – Sautoir

Über einen längeren Zeitraum hat man sich, wie aus den Musterbüchern zu entnehmen ist und auch die erhaltenen Stücke zeigen, mit dem Thema »Gansgurgelkette« beschäftigt (Kat.-Nr. 117, 121–123, 145, 174, 177, 178). Es handelt sich bei diesem Kettentypus um eine Schlauchkette, die als Vierkantschlauch, Rundschlauch, Flachschlauch u.ä. ausgebildet ist und umgangssprachlich in Oberstein »Gansgurgel« genannt wurde.

Oft sitzt vorne in der Mitte ein Galalithelement, der kühle Metallcharakter dieser Colliers steht absolut im Vordergrund. Der technoide Gestaltungsaspekt wird in den Beispielen Nr. 185 und Nr. 224 durch die Ergänzung von weißen bzw. schwarzen flachen Galalithelementen unterstrichen. Mit plastischen Galalithsegmenten wie sie bei Nr. 147 und Nr. 67 zur Anwendung kommen, wird die strenge Gestaltung wieder eher aufgehoben. Sechskant- und Achtkantschlauchketten sind ganz schmal gearbeitet, so daß ein eher zierlicher Gesamteindruck entsteht (Kat.-Nr. 70, 119, 147, 215).

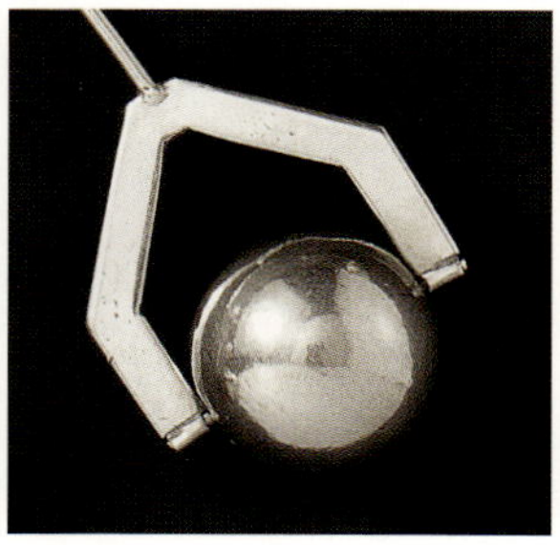

56–59 Detail aus Kat.-Nr. 39, 16, 56, 81
Detail Cat.nos. 39, 16, 56, 81

was dubbed colloquially at Oberstein »the goose choker«. The metallic coolness so characteristic of these necklaces is often set off by a Galalith central piece. The »technoid« aspect of design is underscored in nos. 185 and 224 by the addition of flat white or black Galalith elements. By contrast, the way in which plastic Galalith segments have been used in nos. 147 and 67, tends to subvert the austerity of the design. Tubular necklaces which are hexagonal or octagonal in section are very narrow in make so that they look delicate (Cat.nos. 70, 119, 147, 215). When long, tubular dresses became fashionable, long chains or »sautoirs« were worn with them. Simple tubular necklaces were particularly suited for mass-produced costume jewelry of this type. The addition of all sorts of elements made these simplest of chains look stylish (e.g. Cat.nos. 13, 69, 222, 223).

Variations in metal: the calotte – stepping – the tube

In addition to numerous variants of wire and little rods, many necklaces sported small and fairly large metal calottes as linking elements (e.g. Cat.nos. 47, 65) or as actual links (no. 81, no. 82). When there is an extremely high incidence of such calottes, combined with yellow Galalith cylindrical elements (simulated amber) mounted with little metal spheres, this design feature is at its best.

Apart from metal spheres in various sizes small and larger three-dimensional metal parts were often used in alternation with all sorts of Galalith elements; when stepped, they broadened the form canon (no. 44, no. 186). Necklaces with matching earrings (no. 23, no. 24) are representative of numerous Bengel products featuring dominant Galalith discs, spheres, cones, tubes, etc. Metal was here sparingly used for necessary linking elements. No. 65 is particularly sophisticated: three large Galalith spheres in two colors are mounted with little metal calottes and oblique »tubular triads« which continue on with white Galalith beads and metal tubes mounted in calottes. Necklace no. 40 represents a particularly harmonious blend of metal and Galalith: hexagonal concave elements are linked by tiny lugs with Galalith squares.

Der Mode des langen schmalen Kleides entsprechend wurden »Sautoirs« (lange Ketten), oft mit einem Anhänger, getragen. Für die Modeschmuck-Produktion eigneten sich die einfachen Schlauchketten besonders für deren Herstellung. Durch Ergänzung unterschiedlichster Elemente wurde diesen einfachsten Ketten eine pfiffige Note verliehen (z.B. Kat.-Nr. 13, 69, 222, 223).

Variationen in Metall: Kalotten – Abtreppungen – Röhre

Neben unzähligen Metalldraht- und Stäbchenvariationen wurden bei vielen Ketten kleine und größere Metallkalotten als Zwischenglieder (z.B. Kat.-Nr. 47, 65) oder als eigentliche Kettenglieder verwendet (Nr. 81, Nr. 82). In einer extremen Verdichtung dieser Kalotten, in Kombination mit gelben Galalithwalzen (Bernsteinimitation), die von kleinen Metallkugeln eingefaßt werden, kommt dieses Gestaltungselement sehr gut zur Geltung.

Im Wechsel mit den unterschiedlichsten Galalithelementen wurden neben unterschiedlich großen Metallkugeln auch immer wieder kleinere und größere plastische Metallteile eingefügt, die in ihrer abgetreppten Form den Formenkanon erweiterten (Nr. 44, Nr. 186). Die Halsketten mit passendem Ohrschmuck (Nr. 23, Nr. 24) stehen für die zahlreichen Beispiele der Bengel-Produktion, in denen das Galalith als Scheibe, Kugel, Kegel, Röhre oder ähnliches eingesetzt, dominiert. Das Metall wird nur als notwendiges Bindeglied sparsam eingesetzt. Von besonderer Rafinesse ist Nr. 65: drei zweifarbige, große Galalithkugeln werden durch kleine Metallkalotten und abgeschrägte »Röhrendreiergruppen« eingefaßt, die Fortsetzung bilden weiße, in Kalotten sitzende Galalithperlen und Metallröhrchen. Eine ausgewogene Verwendung von Metall und Galalith ist in dem Collier Nr. 40 zu beobachten: sechseckige Hohlprofile sind durch kleine Ösen mit Galalithquadraten verbunden.

Drahtspiralen-Colliers

Eine einfache, rund gebogene Drahtspirale bildet das eigentliche Collier bei Nr. 116, ihren »Schmuckcharakter« bekommt

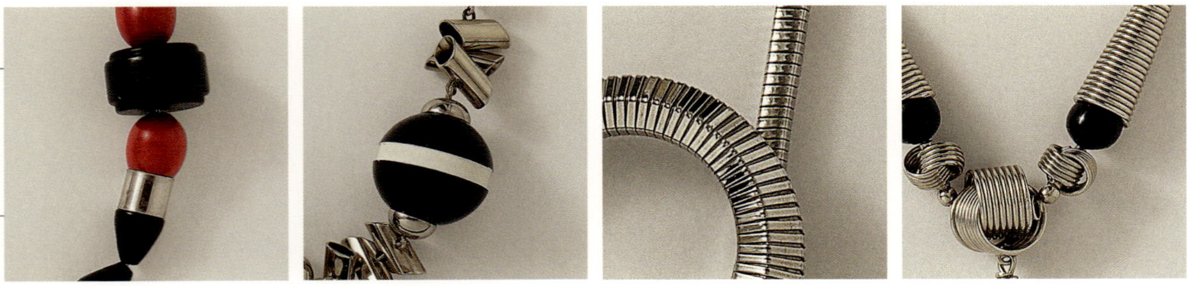

60–63 Detail aus Kat.-Nr. 23, 65, 119, 73
Detail Cat.nos. 23, 65, 119, 73

Spiral wire necklaces

The actual necklace that is model no. 116 is formed from a simple, round spiral wire. The spiral is turned into »jewelry« solely by the use of Galalith discs used in the front third of the necklace. The endless possibilities afforded by spiral wire were exhaustively explored.

Twisted into cornets, wire was no longer springy so that it could be used to form a more or less closed entity (model no. 73). Wire made of sturdy metal was even used to make the popular spiral knots so frequently found: such metal knots were suspended in twos and threes within each other to serve as linking elements. This design feature made it possible to achieve a vibrant plasticity (Cat.nos. 73, 84).

Model no. 90 consists of two elongated wire elements hung one within the other. No. 126 represents a brilliant utilization of the spiral wire knot: the necklace consists entirely of such elements, which are made to coil from front to back.

Garibaldi, cord, king's and Venetian necklaces – stylish variation

The classic necklace motifs such as Garibaldi, cord and king's were produced and used for long periods of time. These necklace types are linked in numerous Bengel designs with emphatically enhancing geometric elements (Cat.nos. 85, 87–89). Here, however, the stringent linearity of design is lost so that one has the impression that combinations were arbitrary rather than deliberate.

Necklaces with glass and Galalith rings form a design group. Although the dominant feature of no. 43 is still the contrasting juxtaposition of glass »rings of eight« and metal hemispheres, other necklaces and bracelets are designed with the glass rings fitted into dense metal knots to create a reticent yet notable touch of color.

A highly idiosyncratic version of the Venetian necklace is exemplified by objects Cat. nos. 138–141: remarkably large segments of Galalith form the central piece of both necklace and bracelet.

die Spirale nur durch die im vorderen Drittel eingesetzten Galalithscheiben.
Die vielseitigen Gestaltungsmöglichkeiten mit Spiraldraht werden in allen erdenklichen Möglichkeiten genutzt. Der Draht wird zu Tüten gebogen, so daß seine eigentliche Elastizität aufgehoben ist und er zu einem mehr oder weniger geschlossenen Körper wurde (Nr. 73).
Auch in den immer wieder verwendeten Spiraldrahtknoten wird kräftiger Metalldraht eingesetzt: diese Knoten werden zwei- und dreifach ineinander gehängt und dienen als Verbindungsglieder. Durch dieses gestalterische Element wird eine abwechslungsreiche Plastizität erreicht (Kat.-Nr. 73, 84). Bei Modell Nr. 90 handelt es sich jeweils um zwei längliche, ineinander gehängte Drahtglieder. Eine herausragende Lösung im Spiel mit diesen Spiraldrahtknoten bietet Nr. 126: das Collier besteht ausschließlich aus diesen Gliedern, die von vorne nach hinten verlaufend gestaltet sind.

Garibaldi-, Kordel-, Königs- und Venezianerketten – in modischen Variationen

Die klassischen Kettenmotive, wie Garibaldi-, Kordel- und Königskette, wurden in der Kettenproduktion über lange Zeiträume verwendet. In vielen Mustern der Firma Bengel werden diese Kettentypen mit akzentuierenden geometrischen Elementen verknüpft (Kat.-Nr. 85, 87–89). Die klare, strenge Gestaltungslinie geht hierbei allerdings verloren und es entsteht der Eindruck einer gewissen Beliebigkeit in der Kombination.
Zu einer gestalterischen Gruppe lassen sich die Ketten mit Glas- und Galalithringen zussammenfassen. Während bei Nr. 43 noch die Gegenüberstellung von »Achter«-Glasringen mit Metallhalbkugen dominiert, werden bei anderen Ketten und Armbändern die Glasringe in die dichten Metallknoten eingefügt, so daß sie nur als dezenter Farbakzent zu erkennen sind.
Eine sehr eigenwillige Spielart der Venezianerkette ist in den Objekten Kat.-Nr. 138–141 zu finden, auffallend große Galalithsegmente bilden den Mittelpunkt der Schmuckstücke.

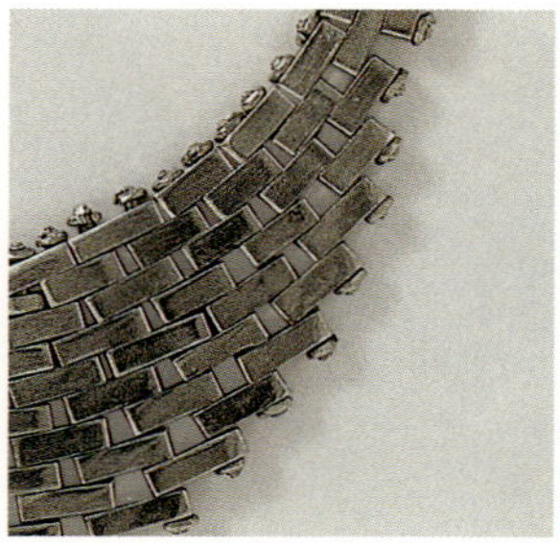

64–66 Detail aus Kat.-Nr. 33, 42, 195
Detail Cat.nos. 33, 42, 195

Brickwork necklaces and collars

Widespread throughout Europe in the 1930s and '40s, the »masonry« or »brickwork« collar was notable for the way in which the metal was worked; Galalith played only a minor role here. These collars are composed of flat, rounded or semi-rounded solid rather than meshwork links which are interlinked in such a way that a brickwork effect is created. Despite their actual flexibility, these necklaces are all quite rigid and uniform in appearance (e.g. no. 32).
The »masonry« or »brickwork« is made up of relatively large elements; Galalith plates only underscore the heaviness of such pieces. In object no. 33 the brickwork dominates the center front of the necklace; the rest of the necklace consists of individual »bricks«. A good solution has been found in no. 113: the coarse brickwork structure is relieved by skilful stepping. The severity of design has been softened in no. 2 by the addition to the front of little cornets of spiral wire with spheres.
Models e.g. Cat.nos. 4, 5–11, 226 represent yet another ingenious way of handling the »brickwork« pattern: it has been made up into stepped polygons and the surface has been lacquered in various colors and partly even with two-tone effects or lacquering on both front and back. Collar no. 41 sports little metal slides over metal beads which make decorative miniature round arches.
The dense brickwork structure can also be loosened up by the use of short and longer metal rods set between the little metal slides (nos. 111, 112). Bracelets were also made to match many of these brickwork collars (no. 5 and no. 8); some also came with matching earrings.
Women's wear in the 1930s was notable for the important role played by white lace collars. If dresses had featured collars since the 1920s, it was only logical that the motif should be echoed skeuomorphically in jewelry design.
There are interesting pieces (nos. 34–37) in the Bengel collection which were made in the »brickwork« style and varied in details. A collar boasting both reddish brown Galalith and strass decoration (no. 36) is among the most magnificent of these.

Mauerketten und Schmuck-Kragen
Bei den in den 1930er und 1940er Jahren weit verbreiteten Mauer- oder Ziegelketten steht die Verarbeitung von Metall im Vordergrund, Galalith spielt nur noch eine untergeordnete Rolle. Es handelt sich bei diesen Ketten um flache, runde oder halbrunde Glieder, die zu einem Ziegelmuster zusammengestellt werden. Den Halsketten ist eine gewisse Starre und Geschlossenheit gemeinsam (z.B. Nr. 32). Das »Mauerwerk« besteht aus relativ groben Teilen, Galalithplatten unterstreichen die Schwere des Stückes. Im Objekt Nr. 33 dominiert das Mauerwerk als Betonung in der vorderen Mitte, die Kette selbst besteht nur noch aus einzelnen »Ziegeln«. Eine gelungene Lösung wird in Nr. 113 erreicht: Die grobe Mauerwerkstruktur wird im vorderen Mittelteil durch eine geschickte Abtreppung aufgehoben. In Nr. 2 wird eine gewisse Auflockerung erreicht, indem man kleine Tüten aus Spiraldraht mit Kugeln im vorderen Bereich des Colliers hinzufügt.
Eine weitere Spielart im Umgang mit dem »Ziegelmuster« zeigen die Modelle z.B. Kat.-Nr. 4, 5–11, 226: Das Mauerwerk wird zu abgetreppten Mehrecken verarbeitet, die Oberfläche wird in verschiedenen Farben lackiert, teilweise sogar zweifarbig oder auf der Vorder- und Rückseite. Im Collier Nr. 41 laufen die kleinen Metallspangen über Metallperlen, die als kleine Rundbögen dekorativ stehen gelassen werden.
Eine Auflösung der dichten Mauerstruktur wird durch kürzere und längere Metallstäbchen erreicht, die zwischen die kleinen Metallspangen gesetzt werden (Nr. 111, 112). Zu vielen Mauerwerk-Ketten wurden die entsprechenden Armbänder gefertigt (Nr. 5 und Nr. 8) oder auch Ohrhänger.
In der Mode der 30er Jahre spielt der weiße Spitzenkragen auf den Kleidern eine große Rolle. Warum sollte man also dieses Kragenmotiv nicht auch in der Schmuckgestaltung aufgreifen. In der Bengel-Kollektion lassen sich interessante Stücke nachweisen (Nr. 34–37), die im Stile »Mauerwerk« gefertigt sind und in den Details verändert wurden. Zu den prachtvollsten Varianten gehörte der Kragen mit rotbraunem Galalith und Straßdekor (Nr. 36).

»Tulpe«, Boot, Anker, Olympiaringe, Hakenkreuz
Bei den ausschließlich aus Metall, wie etwa Messing, gefertigten Ketten fallen vor allem die aus einzelnen großen Gliedern gefertigten Stücke (Nr. 3) auf. Das Schließenmotiv (Nr. 247) – ohne Funktion – gehört mit seiner eher derben Ausführungsweise zu den weniger attraktiven Stücken. Gehämmertes Metall, das auch als kleinteiliges Element eingesetzt wird, kommt bei einer runden Brosche mit aufgelöteter Spirale (Nr. 244) und einer aus einem aufgeschnittenen Metallblech gefertigten Armspange (Nr. 243) zum Einsatz. Diese rei-

»Tulip«, boat, anchor, Olympic rings, swastika
Among the most remarkable pieces of jewelry made entirely of metal (usually brass) are those consisting solely of individual, large elements (no. 3). Clumsily worked, the clasp motif – without any function at all – makes no. 247 one of the less attractive pieces. Beaten metal, which is also used for minute details, is featured on a round brooch with a spiral soldered on to it (no. 244) and a bangle (no. 243) made of a cut piece of sheet metal. Embodying the 1930s Zeitgeist, these works all in metal went well with women's wear which tended towards either the sporty or the rustic look.
However, the prevailing taste also encompassed somewhat softer, even rather »Baroque« designs. The severity of numerous necklaces is relieved by the addition of what were known as »metal tulips« (both large and small). Chiseled and smooth nozzles embrace metal or Galalith spheres, as in Cat.nos. 42, 53, 54.
Since »going down to the sea in ships« is fun, pendants and brooches sporting anchors of various sizes, anchors in lifebelts and little sailboats featured prominently in the Bengel repertoire (Cat.nos. 196, 209, 234). Pendants and drops with a maritime theme were made as faithful tiny replicas to be worn on silk cords or ribbons. As we can see from the Pattern Books, the silk accessories were supplied by other firms such as G. Hirsch & Sohn, H./Nbg. or Altmann of Annaberg in the Erzgebirge Mountains.
The sports theme was continued in 1936, when the Olympic Games were held in Berlin. Pattern Book Vol. XII shows a great many variations on designs for jewelry featuring the Olympic rings: necklaces, pins and bangles in pinchbeck or white metal, some of them silvered or gilt (nos. 251, 252). In this Pattern Book there is an article taken from the Berlin Generalanzeiger of 1 January 1935 flaunting the headline »Sport and Games – the Five Rings«. The symbol of the five rings is mentioned in the colors blue, yellow, black, green and red and the pin with these rings for the 1936 Olympic Games in Berlin which was presented to the public is also referred to. A pin of this type has been preserved in the Bengel estate (fig. 67).
One should mention that all firms producing jewelry suffered the embarrassment in the early 1930s of having to cope with the swastika motif (fig. 68). In 1933 the Deutsche Goldschmiedezeitung did not hesitate to advertise a competition for jewelry featuring the swastika. In the commentary it says: »Swastika jewelry must be conceived as stringently simple, like the sign itself. (...) National jewelry must fulfil a twofold purpose: to adorn the wearer and proclaim his [sic] positive attitude to the new Germany.«[19] At Jakob Bengel the motif was dealt with deftly as the designs in the Pattern Book show: little Galalith swastikas, some of them in three colors, were produced to be hung by a tiny lug as a pendant on a normal chain – whenever desired or necessary.[20]

nen Metallarbeiten verkörpern den Zeitgeist der 1930er Jahre und paßten sehr gut zu der eher sportlichen, rustikalen Mode. Dem Zeitgeschmack entsprechend mußte man auch etwas gefälligere, etwas »barock« anmutende Muster anbieten. In zahlreichen Ketten wurde der strenge Charakter durch das Einfügen von so genannten (kleineren und größeren) »Metalltulpen« aufgehoben. Ziselierte und glatte Tüllen umfangen die Metall- oder Galalithkugeln, wie bei Kat.-Nr. 42, 53, 54.
Nach dem Motto »eine Seefahrt, die ist lustig« gehörten zum Repertoire der Produktion zahlreiche Anhänger und Broschen mit großen und kleinen Ankern, Ankern in Rettungsringen oder kleine Segelboote (Kat.-Nr. 196, 209, 234). Die aus Metall gefertigten maritimen Anhänger sind originalgetreu mit allen Details gefertigt und werden an verschiedenfarbigen Seidenkordeln oder -bändern getragen. Wie wir den Musterbüchern entnehmen können, wurden Seiden-Ergänzungen von anderen Firmen bezogen, z.B. Firma G. Hirsch & Sohn, Firma H./Nbg. oder Firma Altmann, Annaberg/Erzgebirge.
Das sportliche Thema wurde auch im Jahr der Olympischen Spiele 1936 fortgesetzt. Im Musterbuch Bd. XII finden sich die unterschiedlichsten Muster für Schmuckstücke mit den Olympischen Ringen: Colliers, Nadeln und Armreifen in Gelb- und Weißmetall, teilweise versilbert und vergoldet zeigen die vielseitigen Variationsmöglichkeiten (Nr. 251, 252). In besagtem Musterbuch fand sich ein Artikel des Berliner Generalanzeigers vom 1.1.1935 mit der Überschrift »Sport und Spiel – Die fünf Ringe«: es wird auf das Symbol der fünf Ringe in den Farben Blau, Gelb, Schwarz, Grün und Rot hingewiesen und die Nadel, die mit diesen Ringen für die Spiele 1936 in Berlin der Öffentlichkeit übergeben worden ist. Eine solche Brosche hat sich im Nachlaß der Firma Bengel erhalten (Abb. 67).
Man darf behaupten, daß alle schmuckproduzierenden Firmen in den 1930er Jahre in die Verlegenheit kamen, sich mit dem Motiv des Hakenkreuzes zu beschäftigen (Abb. 68). Die Deutsche Goldschmiedezeitung scheute sich nicht, 1933 einen Wettbewerb für Schmuckstücke mit Hakenkreuz auszuschreiben. Im Kommentar hierzu heißt es unter anderem: »Straff und schlicht, wie das Zeichen selbst, muß der Hakenkreuzschmuck aufgefaßt werden. (...) Nationaler Schmuck hat eine zweifache Aufgabe zu erfüllen: den Träger zu schmücken und von sei-

67 Brosche aus der Bengel-Produktion zur Olympiade 1936
Brooch produced by Bengel for the 1936 Olympic Games

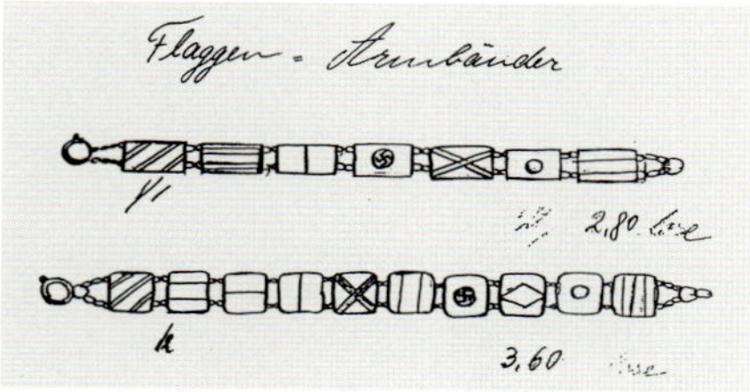

68 Flaggen-Armbänder, Musterbuch Jakob Bengel, Bd. XIII, Modell-Nr. 26.239, ca. 1938
Bracelets with flags, Pattern Book Jakob Bengel, Vol. XIII, model no. 26.239, ca 1938

The sheen of metal and textiles

French jewelrs made their gold and platinum pendants set with precious stones to be worn on simple silk cords. Naum Slutzky, too, used these simple thongs for his early »disc pendants« (fig. 49). The thick silk thongs in black, red or blue with metal or Galalith spheres produced by Jakob Bengel made attractive necklaces, often varied by the slides which were typical of the period (Cat.nos. 170–173).
In a line of short necklaces, these strong silk thongs were partly mounted with metal elements, »flat goose chokers« (thus the Pattern Book). The central pieces of such necklaces consisted of such elements, to which Galalith was added (nos. 190–193). Two other examples of the silk cord/metal/Galalith design are nos. 179, 180. Simple or double-twisted black silk cords or velvet thongs were again held together by partly movable slides in the form of circles, rectangles or polygons of metal and Galalith. The necklaces nos. 165 and 167 show an interesting material treatment although the motif idiom has remained the same – incidentally, it pervades the entire 1930s jewelry production: the Galalith and chrome slide was also available with a silk cord or snake chain. Model 162 boasts the twisted silk cord used for two strands and decorated with pendent spheres in metal and Galalith. Another metal sphere, center front, is also the clasp. Necklace no. 175 is, on the whole, less sophisticated. No. 163 boasts a combination of silk cord and snake chain; the »bow motif« makes this necklace a softer variant. The interplay of austere geometric elements, on the other hand, is the dominant feature of necklaces nos. 154, 157, 182. No. 157 is a particularly attractive design: the oval central piece of two-tone metal with black olive Galalith has been worked on both sides; the twisted silk cord is mantled with little metal slides to harmonize superbly with the central piece.
The tubular chain placed no constraints on the designer's imagination. The torque and bangle Cat.nos. 194, 195 have been formed from what looks like a piece of »flexible shower hose«; inside it run silk thongs which gleam seductively through the openings in the metal.

ner positiven Einstellung zum neuen Deutschland Kunde zu tun«.[19] Bei der Firma Jakob Bengel verstand man, äußerst geschickt mit dem Thema umzugehen, wie die Entwürfe im Musterbuch beweisen: Es wurden kleine, z.T. dreifarbige Galalith-Hakenkreuze produziert, die man an einer kleinen Öse an der ganz normalen Halskette als Anhänger befestigen konnte – wenn man wollte oder die Notwendigkeit es gebot.[20]

Metall und Textilglanz

Die französischen Juweliere verstanden es, ihre in Gold, Platin und Edelsteinen gefertigte Anhänger an einfache Seidenschnüre zu hängen. Auch Naum Slutzky benützte diese einfachen Schnüre für seine frühen »Rundscheiben-Anhänger« (Abb. 49). Bei Jakob Bengel werden dicke Seidenkordeln in Schwarz, Rot, Blau mit Metall- oder Galalithkugeln zu attraktivem Halsschmuck, der sich nicht selten durch den für die damalige Zeit typischen Schieber variieren läßt (Kat.-Nr. 170–173).

In einer Serie von kurzen Colliers werden die kräftigen Seidenschnüre durch Metallglieder, »flache Gansgurgel« (lt. Musterbuch), partiell eingefaßt. Auch die Mittelteile der Ketten bestehen aus diesen, mit Galalith ergänzten Elementen (Nr. 190–193). Zwei weitere Beispiele in der Seidenkordel/Metall/Galalith-Variation zeigen Kat.-Nr. 179, 180. Einfach und doppelt gedrehte schwarze Seiden-/Samtkordeln werden wieder durch teilweise bewegliche Schieber in Kreis-, Rechteck oder als Vieleckform aus Metall und Galalith zusammengefaßt. Eine interessante Materialverarbeitung bei gleicher Motivsprache – die übrigens die gesamte Schmuckproduktion der 1930er Jahre durchzieht – zeigen die Halsketten Nr. 165 und 167: das ovale Schieberteil aus Galalith und Chrom wird mit Seidenkordel oder Schlangenkette angeboten. Bei Modell 162 wird die gedrehte Seidenkordel zweifach verwendet und von anhängenden Kugeln in Metall und Galalith dekoriert. Eine weitere Metallkugel, vorne in der Mitte ist zugleich der Verschluß. Eher schlicht gehalten ist dagegen die Kette Nr. 175. Eine Kombination von Seidenkordel und Schlangenkette hat Nr. 163 zu bieten, das »Schleifenmotiv« macht aus dem Collier einen eher gefälligen Halsschmuck. Das Spiel mit streng geometrischen Elementen herrscht in den Ketten Nr. 154, 157, 182 vor. Ein besonders attraktives Stück ist die Nr. 157: das ovale Mittelteil aus zweifarbigem Metall mit schwarzer Galalitholive ist beidseitig ausgearbeitet, die gedrehte Seidenschnur wird von kleinen Metallspangen ummantelt und korrespondiert außergewöhnlich gut mit dem Mittelteil.

Bei der Verwendung der Schlauchkette sind der Phantasie keine Grenzen gesetzt: Halsreif und Armreif Kat.-Nr. 194, 195 sind aus einem »Brauseschlauch« gebildet, in dessen Hohlraum, Seidenbänder laufen, die sehr dekorativ durch das Metall blitzen.

METALL- UND GALALITHSCHMUCK

Die Firma Jakob Bengel war nicht die einzige Firma, die in Oberstein ausgefallenen Modeschmuck in Metall und Galalith fertigte. Der Zweite Weltkrieg hat vieles zerstört, was uns hierüber genauer Aufschluß geben könnte. Man kann aber davon ausgehen, daß die Firmen Klein & Quenzer und Carl Keller Chr. Sohn ähnlichen Schmuck produzierten.
Ein Blick nach Pforzheim zeigt, daß sich auch dort eine Firma dem Thema Metall- und Galalithschmuck im »Bauhausstil« widmete, nämlich die Firma Henkel & Grosse.
In Frankreich gab es Schmuckfirmen, hier besonders die Manufaktur Auguste Bonaz, die noch heute stellvertretend für den französischen Modeschmuck aus Galalith und Metall steht. Und schließlich darf Amerika nicht vergessen werden, das Land des »bakelite jewelry« schlechthin.

Klein & Quenzer, Carl Keller Chr. Sohn, Oberstein

Die Firma Klein & Quenzer wurde 1904 von Robert Klein und Alfred Quenzer als Engroshandelsgeschäft gegründet, bereits zwei Jahre später wurde sie in einen Fabrikationsbetrieb umgewandelt. Die ursprüngliche Fabrikation waren, wie bei der Firma Jakob Bengel auch, Uhrketten, später wurde die Produktion um Damenschmuck ergänzt. Bis zum Ersten Weltkrieg waren 80 Mitarbeiter beschäftigt. Im Vordergrund der Handelsbeziehungen stand das Exportgeschäft, durch intensive Reisetätigkeit hatte man sich die entsprechenden Märkte erobert. In den 1930er Jahren arbeiteten bei der Firma Klein & Quenzer über 300 Personen, außerdem wurden viele Aufträge an örtliche Heimarbeiter vergeben. Nach und nach stellte man die Produktion von der Erzeugung billiger Massenware auf die Herstellung von modischem Schmuck um. In den Kriegsjahren kam das Schmuckgeschäft völlig zum Erliegen, da man, wie schon im Ersten Weltkrieg, die Produktion von Orden und Militaria aufnahm. Somit konnte die Belegschaft weitgehend weiter beschäftigt werden. Kurz vor Kriegsende wurde die Firma durch zwei schwere Bombenangriffe fast völlig zerstört. Nach Auskunft eines ehemaligen Mitarbeiters, Herrn Alfred Bauer (Mitarbeiter der Firma im Jahre 1941 und 1948–1976), wurde bei Klein & Quenzer auch Metall- und Galalithschmuck hergestellt. Als Beleg für deren Produktion kann man Abbildungen dieser Schmuckstücke in der Zeitschrift *Die Schaulade* aus dem Jahre 1934 ansehen (Abb. 69, 70). »Zum Schluß möchten wir noch einige Schmuckgegenstände

METAL AND GALALITH JEWELRY

Jakob Bengel was not the only firm in Oberstein to produce distinctive costume jewelry in metal and Galalith. The Second World War destroyed much of what might have given us more precise information on this. It is, however, safe to assume that the firms of Klein & Quenzer and Carl Keller Chr. Sohn made similar jewelry.
A glance at Pforzheim reveals that there, too, a firm devoted itself to making »Bauhaus style« metal and Galalith jewelry: this was Henkel & Grosse.
In France, there were firms that made jewelry, most importantly Auguste Bonaz, which to this day stands for French costume jewelry made of Galalith and metal. Nor should the United States of America be forgotten, which was a veritable bastion of »bakelight jewelry«.

Klein & Quenzer, Carl Keller Chr. Sohn, Oberstein

Founded in 1904 by Robert Klein and Alfred Quenzer as a wholesale firm, Klein & Quenzer had been changed into a manufacturing company only two years later. Like Jakob Bengel, it originally produced watch-chains but later added ladies' jewelry to its range of goods. Until the outbreak of the First World War, Klein & Quenzer had 80 employees. It emphasized the export trade, breaking into markets by sending representatives on extensive travels. In the 1930s more than 300 employees were working for Klein & Quenzer. In addition, many orders were handled by the local cottage industry. The manufacture of cheap mass-produced goods gradually gave way to the making of stylish costume jewelry. During the war years the production of jewelry ceased entirely, as it had during the First World War, and was replaced by the manufacture of decorations and other military goods. This made it possible to keep most of the workforce on. Shortly before the Second World War ended, the firm premises were almost entirely destroyed during two severe bombing raids. According to Alfred Bauer, a former employee (in 1941 and again 1948–1976), Klein & Quenzer also produced metal and Galalith jewelry. Evidence for this is furnished by pictures of it in a 1934 number of the magazine Die Schaulade (fig. 69, 70). »Finally, we should like to show our readers some pieces of jewelry from the two jewelry manufacturers in Oberstein, Klein & Quenzer A.G. and Carl Keller Chr. Sohn. In our two illustrations we show bangles, necklaces and clips, stylishly casual and very reasonably priced costume jewelry, which is aimed at a broad market.«[21] The pieces of jewelry in these illustrations are

aus den beiden Obersteiner Bijouteriefabriken Klein & Quenzer A.G. und Carl Keller Chr. Sohn unseren Lesern zeigen. In den beiden [...] Abbildungen finden wir Armreifen, Halsketten und Clips, modisch flott gearbeitete und sehr preiswerte Bijouterien, die sich an breite Käuferschichten wenden.«[21] Die auf diesen Abbildungen zu erkennenden Schmuckstücken sind denen der Firma Jakob Bengel ähnlich. Leider haben sich weder von der Firma Klein & Quenzer noch von der Firma Carl Keller Chr. Sohn Unterlagen erhalten, die Auskunft über deren Produktionspalette geben könnten. Die Entwürfe wurden von den eigenen Mustermachern angefertigt, darüber hinaus kaufte man aber auch Entwürfe von Pariser Ateliers an. Ähnlich wie bei Jakob Bengel exportierte man weltweit, vor allem aber nach Skandinavien, Italien, England, Frankreich und Spanien, fast die gesamte Produktion ging ins Ausland. Vornehmlich wurden große Kaufhäuser wie z.B. Woolworth und andere Grossisten beliefert.

Henkel & Grosse, Pforzheim

Chrom- und Galalith/Bakelitschmuck produzierte auch die 1907 in Pforzheim durch den Goldschmied Heinrich Henkel und Florentin Grosse gegründete und heute noch existierende Firma Henkel & Grosse.

Nach dem Ersten Weltkrieg begann man mit der Produktion von Bijouterie aus Messing, Platinin, Aluminium, Holz und Galalith. Die Entwürfe für die Ketten und Armbänder fertigten die Söhne Heinrich und Artur Grosse. Es sollen persönliche Kontakte zwischen der Familie und Mitgliedern des Bauhauses bestanden haben und diese auch die Schmuckkreationen der Firma beeinflußt haben. In der anläßlich des 75jährigen Jubiläums herausgegebenen Festschrift heißt es: »Bereits 1924 reiste Heinrich Grosse im Alter von 18 Jahren nach New

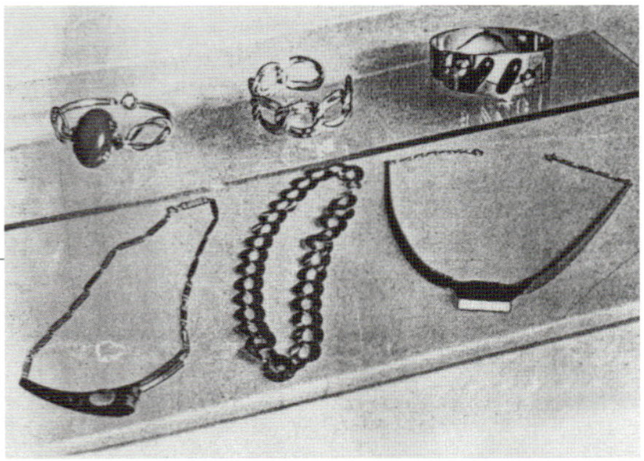

69 Klein & Quenzer, Oberstein »Arm- und Halsschmuck für die Dame«, 1934
Klein & Quenzer, Oberstein»Ladies' arm and neck jewelry«, 1934

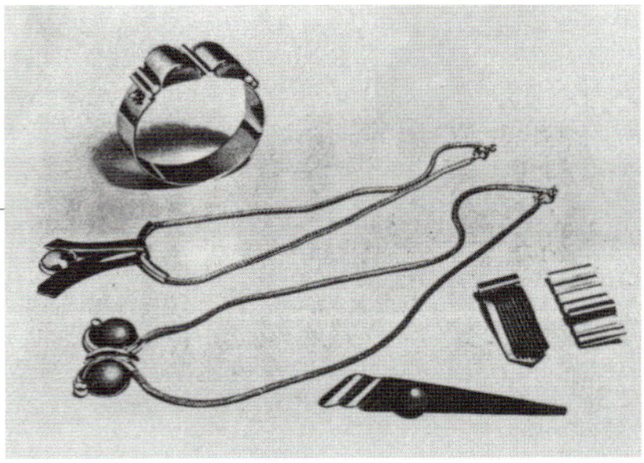

70 Carl Keller Chr. Sohn, Oberstein, »Moderner Schmuck für alle Länder der Erde«, 1934
Carl Keller Chr. Sohn, »Modern jewelry for all the countries in the world«, 1934

recognizably similar to those made by Jakob Bengel. Unfortunately, we were unable to procure records from Klein & Quenzer and Carl Keller Chr. Sohn which might have provided us with information on their ranges. The designs were executed by their own designers. Moreover, designs were also bought from ateliers in Paris. Like Jakob Bengel, these two firms exported worldwide, primarily to Scandinavia, Italy, England, France and Spain. Indeed almost their entire stock went abroad, most of it supplied to large department stores such as Woolworth's or to wholesalers.

Henkel & Grosse, Pforzheim

Chrome and Galalith/bakelite jewelry was also produced by the firm of Henkel & Grosse. Founded in Pforzheim in 1907 by Heinrich Henkel, a goldsmith, and Florentin Grosse, it is still in business today.

After the First World War Henkel & Grosse began to produce costume jewelry made of brass, platinin (= platinoid, a silvery white alloy of nickel, zinc, copper and tungsten which did not tarnish), aluminium, wood and Galalith. The sons of one of the proprietors, Heinrich and Artur Grosse, did the designs for the necklaces and bracelets. The family is said to have had personal contacts with members of the Bauhaus, who also exerted an influence on the firm's jewelry designs. A publication commemorating the 75th anniversary of the founding of the firm states: »As early as 1924 Heinrich Grosse traveled to New York at the age of 18 to overcome the narrowness of spirit he felt pervading Germany (...) He became a member of the ›Art Students League Of New York‹, where he met Alexander Calder, who, like him, was working on new jewelry designs (...) in the elegant shops lining 5th Avenue and 57th Street he found inspi-

York, um die Enge zu überwinden, die er überall in Deutschland spürte (...) Er wurde Mitglied der ›Arts Students League Of New York‹ wo er Alexander Calder kennenlernte, der wie er selbst an neuen Schmuckentwürfen arbeitete (...) in den eleganten Geschäften der 5th Avenue und der 57. Straße fand er für sich und seine Arbeit die Anregungen, die später mit in die neue Konzeption der Schmuckfertigung eingingen. Bei der Rückkehr 1927 über Paris kamen die Ideen des Art Déco hinzu.« Artur und Adalbert reisten bereits in den 1920er Jahren nach Nord- und Südamerika, England, Frankreich und Italien um geschäftliche Kontakte zu knüpfen. Adalbert Grosse studierte in Amerika die revolutionären Techniken moderner Vertriebssysteme, die er später in Europa realisierte. In den 1930er Jahren bestanden Kontakte zu den Modeschöpfern Lanvin und Schiaparelli sowie zu den großen Kaufhäusern wie Harrods in London und Saks in New York.

Marcel Breuer interessierte sich für die neuen Schmuckideen des Hauses und besuchte die Firma 1933 in Pforzheim. 1937 wird die Firma Henkel & Grosse auf der »Exposition Internationale des Arts et Technique dans la Vie Modernes«, Paris, für eine aus Metall gestanzte, vergoldete Brosche mit dem »diplôme d'honneur« ausgezeichnet.

Aus der sicher sehr vielseitigen Produktion in Metall und Galalith/Bakelit haben sich nur einige wenige Stücke erhalten, die immer wieder abgebildet werden (Abb. 71, 75). Die Musterbücher der Firma Bengel zeigen, daß zahlreiche Modelle von Bengel für Henkel & Grosse angefertigt wurden; sie sind absolut identisch mit den in der Literatur als Henkel & Grosse-

71 Henkel & Grosse, Pforzheim, Anhänger mit Kette, Metall, Bakelit (?), 1931
Henkel & Grosse, Pforzheim, Pendant with chain: metal, bakelite (?), 1931

72 Maison Auguste Bonaz, Oyonnax/Frankreich; Collier, Galalith, um 1928 Privatsammlung, München
Maison Auguste Bonaz, Oyonnax, France; Collar, Galalith, ca. 1928 Private collection, Munich

ration for himself and his work, which later went into his new conception of jewelry-making. On his return via Paris in 1927, the ideas of Art Déco were added.« By the 1920s Artur and Adalbert Grosse had traveled throughout North and South America, England, France and Italy to make business contacts. In America Adalbert Grosse studied the revolutionary techniques of modern marketing and distributing systems, which he would later implement in Europe. In the 1930s the firm had contacts with the haute couture houses of Lanvin and Schiaparelli as well as large department stores such as Harrods in London and Saks Fifth Avenue in New York. Intrigued by the new ideas in jewelry launched by Henkel & Grosse, Marcel Breuer visited the firm in Pforzheim in 1933. Henkel & Grosse was represented in 1937 at the »Exposition Internationale des Arts et Techniques Appliqués à la Vie Moderne« in Paris and were awarded a »diplôme d'honneur« for a gilt cut-card brooch.

Only very few pieces have been preserved from what must have been a prolific and diverse range in metal and Galalith/bakelite – they are shown again and again (figs. 71, 75). The Bengel Pattern Books show that many of their models were made for Henkel & Grosse; they are identical with the pieces shown in specialist publications as Henkel & Grosse jewelry. A bangle (Cat.no. 184) was beyond any doubt made for Henkel & Grosse as the reference to it in the Pattern Book (Pattern 20.560) shows.[22] Modell 20.117, however, was made exclusively for other firms, e.g. for the firm of Leon Meyer.[23] Even though the col-

Schmuck abgebildeten Stücken. Eine Armspange (Kat.-Nr. 184) ist durch den entsprechenden Hinweis im Musterbuch (Muster 20.560) eindeutig als Produkt für die Firma Henkel & Grosse zu identifizieren.[22] Aber auch für andere Firmen, so z.B. für die Firma Leon Meyer, wurde das Modell 20.117 exklusiv gefertigt.[23]

Auch wenn die vorgestellte Schmuckkollektion der Firma Bengel sicher nicht singulär gesehen werden kann, so muß man sich doch fragen, wie kam es zur Produktion dieser ausgefallenen, auf dem Sammlermarkt heute so begehrten Objekte bei der Firma Bengel. Hatte Ernst Hartenberger sen. die geniale Idee, das neue Material Galalith für seine Schmuckgestaltung zu nutzen?

Galalith-Schmuck in Frankreich: Maison Auguste Bonaz, u.a.

Auch in Frankreich verstand man es mit Galalith/Bakelit einen ganz eigenen Weg zu beschreiten. Als Wegbereiter der Kunststoffschmuckherstellung muß die französische Manufaktur Bonaz genannt werden. César Bonaz hatte in Oyonnax im Osten Frankreichs 1910 eine Firma für Haarschmuck gegründet und sich auf die Herstellung von geschnittenen Hornkämmen spezialisiert. Sein Sohn Auguste (1877–1922) übernahm das Erbe des Vaters. Nach seinem frühzeitigen Tod verstand es seine Frau Marguerite Marie Bailly (1882–1970), den Namen Bonaz in die ganze Welt zu tragen, er steht noch heute für außergewöhnlich schönen Halsschmuck aus Galalith und Chrom (Abb. 72). Im Repertoire der Manufaktur sind sowohl ganz aus Galalith gefertigte Stücke zu finden, aber auch die Materialkombination Metall/Galalith gehörte zum Programm. Bis in die 1930er Jahre wurden Ketten, Armreifen und Broschen produziert, bei denen man Kugeln, Stäbchen, Dreiecke und andere geometrische Metallelemente mit farblich und formal darauf abgestimmten Galalithformen verknüpfte. Die ganz in Kunststoff gefertigten Stücke setzen sich in ihrer Farbigkeit deutlich von denen der Amerikaner ab, es sind nicht die grellen, knallbunten man möchte fast sagen, schrillen Farben des »American way of life«, es sind die dezenten, sensibel aufeinander abgestimmten Farbklänge des französischen »savoir vivre.« Gemäß der Haarkammtradition des Hauses wurden in den 1920er Jahren so genannte Mantilla-Kämme gefertigt, deren Zierelemente kleine Blütchen waren. Steckkämme mit orientalischem Design in Gold und mit Straßeinlagen ergänzten das Repertoire der Manufaktur Bonaz. Anstecker für Hüte und Schals oder Knöpfe waren mit bunten Pinguinen, Eulen, Vögeln, Mohren oder japanischen Figuren dekoriert. Entsprechend der damaligen Schwarzweiß-Mode wurden geometrische Clips in dieser Farbe in Handarbeit gefertigt. Diese

lection of jewelry by Bengel presented here cannot be regarded as the only one of its kind, the question nonetheless arises of how Bengel came to produce these distinctive objects, which are now sought-after collector's items. Was it Ernst Hartenberger, sen., who had the brilliant idea of using the new material Galalith for his jewelry designs?

Galalith jewelry in France: Maison Auguste Bonaz et al.

In France, too, jewelry designers were going their own way in using Galalith and bakelite. The French manufacturer Bonaz must be credited with pioneering the manufacture of jewelry made of synthetic materials. In 1910 César Bonaz had founded a firm at Oyonnax in eastern France to make jewelry to be worn in the hair. Cut horn combs were his specialty. His son Auguste (1877–1922) inherited the firm. After his untimely death, his widow, Marguerite Marie Bailly (1882–1970), succeeded in making the name of Bonaz world-famous. It is remembered even today for exquisitely beautiful jewelry to be worn in the hair made of Galalith and chrome (fig. 72). The Bonaz range included pieces fashioned entirely of Galalith as well as combinations of metal and Galalith. On into the 1930s Bonaz was making necklaces, bangles and brooches, in which spheres, triangles and other geometric metal elements were linked with Galalith shapes which harmonized with them in color and style. The Bonaz pieces made entirely of synthetic materials are strikingly different in color quality to those made by American manufacturers. The French pieces are not the lurid, shockingly unrestrained or, one is even tempted to say, shrill colors defining certain aspects of the »American way of life«. By contrast, they are, one might say, the sensitively nuanced colors of French »savoir vivre«. True to the proprietary tradition of haircomb-making, Bonaz manufactured what were known as mantilla combs, decorated with minute flowers, in the 1920s. Haircombs of orientalizing design in gold and set with strass completed the Bonaz range. Pins to be worn on hats and scarves as well as buttons were decorated with colorful penguins, owls, birds, blackamoors or Japanese figures. Since black-and-white was then fashionable, geometric clips were made by hand in this color combination. These stylish pieces of jewelry were sold at hairdressers, haberdashers, dress shops, perfumeries and at large department stores. By 1925 the house of Auguste Bonaz was represented by a stall at the important exhibition »Arts Décoratifs et Industriels Modernes« in Paris. Painted celluloid combs and a wide variety of toilet articles guaranteed success at the exhibition, which amounted to an advertising campaign (fig. 73).[24] Unlike Bengel Bengel in Oberstein, Bonaz aimed at addressing their target market in specialist magazines such as La Coiffure Française Illustrée, La Coiffure de Paris (May 1926, fig. 74) or Vogue.[25]

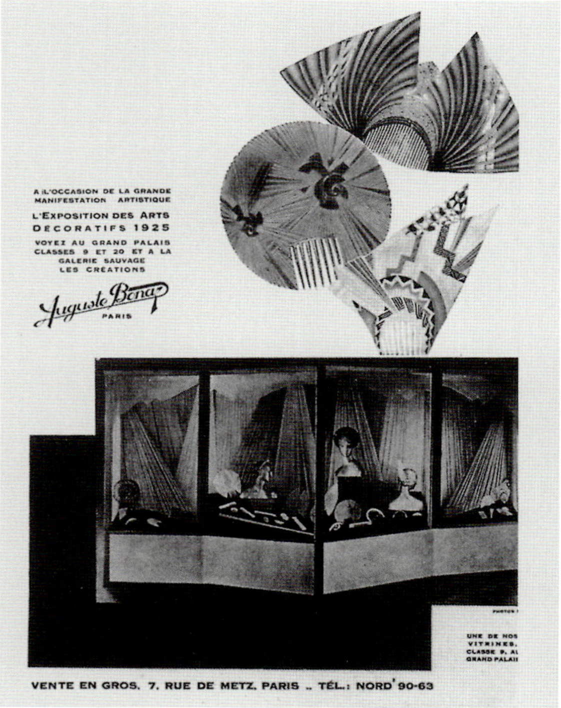

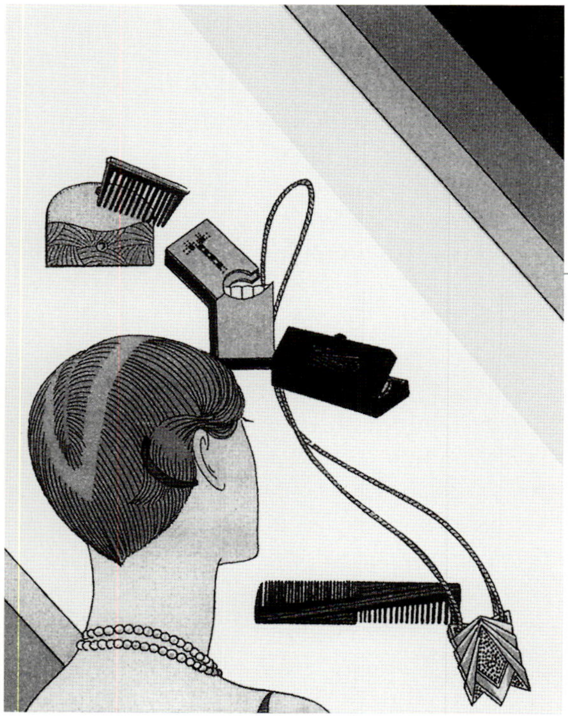

73 Werbeanzeige der Maison Auguste Bonaz für die Ausstellung »Exposition Internationale des Arts Décoratifs et Industriels Modernes«, Paris, 1925
Maison Auguste Bonaz: advertisement for the 1925 »Exposition Internationale des Arts Décoratifs et Industriels Modernes« exhibition in Paris

74 Werbeanzeige der Maison Auguste Bonaz, aus: La Coiffure de Paris, März 1926
Maison Auguste Bonaz: advertisement from: La Coiffure de Paris, March 1926

75 Henkel & Grosse, Pforzheim, Gruppe von Schmuckstücken aus Chrom und Galalith, 1925–1930 (?)
Henkel & Grosse, Pforzheim, Chrome and Galalith jewelry, 1925–1930 (?)

76 Fernand Léger
Katalog-Titelblatt zur Ausstellung »Machine-Age Exposition«, New York, 1927
Fernand Léger
Catalogue cover for the 1927 exhibition »Machine-Age Exposition«, New York, 1927

modischen Schmuckstücke wurden bei Friseuren, Kurzwarenhändlern, Modegeschäften, Parfümerien und in den großen Kaufhäusern angeboten. Bereits auf der großen Ausstellung »Arts Décoratifs et Industriels Modernes« in Paris im Jahre 1925 war das Haus Auguste Bonaz mit einem eigenen Stand vertreten. Mit bemalten Celluloidkämmen und zahlreichen Artikeln für den Toilettentisch konnte man eine erfolgreiche Ausstellungsbeteiligung verbuchen und diese auch als Werbekampagne einsetzen (Abb. 73).[24] Im Gegensatz zur Firma Bengel in Oberstein war man im Hause Bonaz durchaus daran interessiert, in den entsprechenden Fachzeitschriften den Endverbraucher anzusprechen, wie etwa in *La Coiffure Française Illustrée, La Coiffure de Paris, Mai 1926* (Abb. 74) oder in *Vogue*.[25] Ferner ist für die Kunsstoffschmuckgestaltung in Oyonnax auch Louis Collomb zu nennen, der ebenfalls mit Celluloid-Accessoires begonnen hatte und dann zu Galalith-Arbeiten überging. Sein Sohn Paul entwarf ab 1939 den Schmuck, besonders beliebt waren schwarze Galalitharmreifen mit silbernen Blüten.
Kurze Erwähnung sollen hier auch die »colliers de Paris« der Schriftstellerin Elsa Triolet finden, die in dem gleichnamigen Buch die Geschichte ihrer Nebenbeschäftigung, Modeschmuck zu fertigen, erzählt. In enger Zusammenarbeit mit den Couturiers wie Coco Chanel, begann sie Ende der 1920er Jahre ganz einfachen Modeschmuck zu fertigen, gewissermaßen als schönste Nebensache der Welt. Wie ihrer Erzählung zu entnehmen ist, bediente sie sich vieler verschiedenen Materialien wie Porzellan, Glas, Perlmutt aber auch unterschiedlicher Metalle und Kunststoff! Auf einer Abbildung in ihrem Buch trägt Elsa Triolet eine Kette aus Metallringen, auf Kordel gezogen, die – wäre sie nicht von der Hand Triolets gefertigt worden – durchaus aus der Produktion Jakob Bengel stammen könnte.[26]

Galalith und Bakelit in Amerika

Ganz anders ging man in Amerika mit dem dort weit verbreiteten Kunststoff Bakelit um, dessen Produktion ab 1910 eingesetzt hatte. In den 1930er Jahren war man vom «Bakelit-Fieber« ergriffen, es gehörte zum Lebensinhalt und wurde in allen Lebensbereichen akzeptiert. Bereits 1936 wurden 70 % des amerikanischen Modeschmucks in Bakelit gefertigt. Bei B. Altmann, Lord & Taylor oder Bergdorf Goodman in der 5th Avenue in New York riß man sich förmlich um den Bakelitschmuck. Bei Woolworth konnte man witzige Stücke schon für 50 Cents ergattern. Dem Bakelit widmete man eine eigene Zeitschrift mit dem Titel »Modern Plastics«.
Galalith, das in Amerika unter den Handelsnamen »Erinoid«, »Karolith« und »Aladdinik« verkauft wurde, spielte in Amerika im Vergleich zu Europa nur eine untergeordnete Rolle. Der

Another substantial contributor to jewelry designed to be made at in synthetic materials at Oyonnax was Louis Collomb. He, too, had started out making celluloid accessories before switching to Galalith. From 1939 his son Paul designed jewelry for Collomb. His black Galalith bangles with silver flowers were a smash hit.
The »colliers de Paris« made by the writer Elsa Triolet should also be touched on briefly here. This was the title of the book she wrote on her sideline, which was making costume jewelry. Collaborating closely with couturiers such as Coco Chanel, Elsa Triolet began to make very simple costume jewelry in the 1920s, which might be called the most exquisite irrelevance in the world. As her account reveals, she actually used a great variety of materials, including porcelain, glass, mother of pearl and various metals as well as, most importantly, synthetics! A photo in her book shows Elsa Triolet wearing a necklace of metal rings strung on cord which – had it not been from Triolet's own hand – could easily be mistaken for a Jakob Bengel piece.[26]

Galalith and bakelite in America

Bakelite was widespread in America and it was handled in an entirely different way. Production of bakelite began in 1910. In the 1930s America was in the throes of the »bakelite craze«. It was an integral part of life and was accepted everywhere. By 1936 seventy per cent of American costume jewelry was being made of bakelite. At such august New York department stores as B. Altmann, Lord & Taylor and Bergdorf Goodman in 5th Avenue, bakelite jewelry sold like the proverbial hot cakes. At the other end of the market, Woolworth's sold witty pieces of bakelite jewelry for only 50 cents. A magazine, Modern Plastics, was dedicated to bakelite.
Galalith, which was marketed in the US under the trade names of »Erinoid«, »Karolith« and »Aladdinik«, played only a very minor role there compared with its conquest of Europe. The biggest costume-jewelry manufacturer in America, Cohn & Rosenberger, which was founded in New York in 1901, did use this material for some small product lines in 1930. An advertisement alludes to this revolutionary material, which would become known there under the registered trade name »Corolite«: »Corolite (simulated prystal) is the season's huge jewelry success« raved the headline (fig. 77). The text explaining the necklaces, bracelets and earring illustrated in the brochure runs: »About every other piece of new jewelry one sees is of this strikingly new, utterly different material. Bely-cur beads, combinations of Corolite, crystal, beads and metal ornaments make the new line of bestsellers. All the new muted pastels in necklaces, bracelets and earrings.« Prystal itself, also a registered trade name, was a phenolic resin which came in different colors, both translucent and opaque.

größte Modeschmuckproduzent in Amerika, die 1901 in New York gegründete Firma Cohn & Rosenberger, verwendete im Jahre 1930 für einige kleinere Serien dieses Material. In einer Anzeige wird auf das revolutionäre Material hingewiesen, das dort unter dem eingetragenen Namen *Corolite* bekannt wird: »Corolite (simulated prystal) is the seasons huge jewelry success« lautete die Überschrift (Abb. 77). Zu den abgebildeten Ketten, Armbändern und Ohrgehängen erklärt der nebenstehende Text: »About every other piece of new jewelry one sees is of this strikingly new, utterly different material. Bely-cur beads, combinations of Corolite, crystal, beads and metal ornaments make the new line of bestsellers. All the new muted pastels in necklaces, bracelets and earrings.« Prystal selbst, ebenfalls ein eingetragener Markenname, ist ein Phenolharz, das es in verschiedenen Farben, luzid und opak gibt. Kleiderclipse und verschiedene Schmuckstücke wurden in Weiß und Schwarz gefertigt. Unter dem Motto »Pompadour Line« verkaufte Cohn & Rosenberger Ketten, die aus Metallgliedern und Corolite-Kugeln bestanden. Die Serie »Neptune Blue Jewelry« bestand aus Chrom und Bakelit, wobei es sich nur um ein chromähnliches Material mit garantiertem Anlaufschutz handelte, das unter dem Namen »CoroChrome« bekannt wurde.[27] Auch wenn die Amerikaner Chrom oder chromähnliche Materialien in ihrem Modeschmuck verwendeten, so blieb doch immer ein entscheidender Unterschied zum europäischen Metall- und Kunstoffschmuck, wie auch schon Davidov/Redington Dawes in ihrem Buch sehr richtig bemerkten: im europäischen Schmuck war der Metallanteil wesentlich höher. Die verchromten Kettenglieder entsprachen dem kühlen, sachlichen Zeitgeschmack, das farbige Galalith oder Bakelit wurde meistens nur als Dekor, als farbkräftiger Akzent verwendet. Die Amerikaner liebten es, Bakelit großflächig und voluminös einzusetzen, die knallbunten Schmuckstücke entsprachen ihrem Lebensgefühl und ihrer Lebenslust.[28]

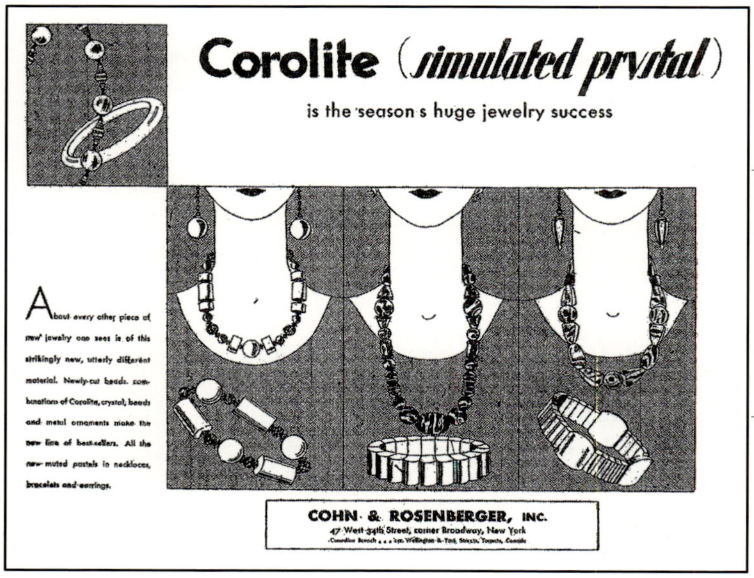

77 Werbeanzeige für die Schmuckserie »Corolite«, Cohn & Rosenberger, New York, um 1930
Cohn & Rosenberger, New York: advertisement for the »Corolite« line in jewelry, ca. 1930

Although American manufacturers used chrome and materials similar to it for costume jewelry, it remained different in one respect at least from European metal and synthetics jewelry, as Davidov/Redington Dawes have aptly observed in their book: European costume jewelry had a much higher metal content. The chromium-plated chain links matched the European taste, which was cool and objective. Colored Galalith or bakelite was usually used only as decoration to add vibrant touches of color. American designers, on the other hand, used bakelite lavishly over large surfaces. Brightly colored jewelry might be said to have suited what Europeans view as the breezy American lifestyle with its carefree casualness.[28]

Clips and various other pieces of jewelry were made in black-and-white. The Cohn & Rosenberger »Pompadour Line« featured necklaces consisting of metal links and Corolite balls. Their »Neptune Blue Jewelry« was made of bakelite and chrome, or, more precisely, of a material resembling chrome which was guaranteed not to tarnish and was marketed as »CoroChrome«.[27]

DIE UHRKETTEN- UND METALLWAREN-INDUSTRIE IN OBERSTEIN: 1860–1950

Wirtschaftlicher Aufschwung im ausgehenden 19. Jahrhundert

Als Jacob Bengel 1873 seinen Betrieb zur Herstellung von Uhrketten gründete, existierten in Oberstein schon mehrere Firmen dieses Produktionszweiges. Bereits 1826 werden erste kleinere Hersteller von Uhrketten in Oberstein erwähnt. In das Jahr 1865 fällt die Gründung der Uhrketten- und Schmuckwarenfabrik Gottlieb & Wagner, die erste Uhrkettenfabrik in Oberstein. Viele Jahre war sie die bedeutendste Fabrik am Platz. Nur ein Jahr später, 1866, nahm die Uhrketten- und Bijouterie-Fabrik Louis Gottlieb & Söhne ihre Tätigkeit auf, weitere Firmen folgten. Für Jahrzehnte war die Uhrketten-Produktion, der sich immer neue Fabriken zuwandten, zum beherrschenden Zweig der Obersteiner Industrie geworden. Die Vollendung der Rhein-Nahe-Eisenbahn zwischen 1856 und 1860 war eine wichtige wirtschaftliche Verbesserung, sie erleichterte die verkehrstechnische Anbindung Obersteins an die entsprechenden Absatzmärkte. Die 1870er Jahre waren ein Jahrzehnt des Aufschwungs. Nach der Reichsgründung 1870/71 verbesserten sich die wirtschaftlichen Verhältnisse, der Wegfall der Zollgrenzen zwischen den einzelnen Fürstentümern erleichterte den Handel. »Das nach der allgemeinen Krisis von 1873 infolge der gedrückten Kaufkraft des konsumierenden Publikums eingetretene Verlangen nach möglichst billiger Ware förderte in der Obersteiner Industrie vor allem den Absatz billiger Uhrketten.«[29] Die zunächst als Gewerbe mit viel Handarbeit tätigen Unternehmen entwickelten sich zu großen Betrieben, die sich im Laufe der Jahre immer mehr Maschinen zulegten.

Allmählich wurde auch in Deutschland das Verfahren bekannt, auf galvanischem Wege zu vernickeln, zu versilbern oder zu vergolden. Mitte der 1870er Jahre hielten Gasmotoren in die heimischen Betriebe Einzug, die es erlaubten, Poliermaschinen, Dreh- und Ziehbänke in größerem Ausmaß zu betreiben. Im Jahre 1877 kam es schließlich zur Gründung der Obersteiner-Idarer-Gasanstalt. Mit der Inbetriebnahme von Dampfmaschinen und Elektromotoren wurden diese produktionstech-

THE WATCH-CHAIN AND METALWARES INDUSTRY IN OBERSTEIN: 1860–1950

Economic upturn in the late 19th century

By the time Jacob Bengel founded his firm for making watch-chains in 1873, there were already several others manufacturing this specialized product in Oberstein. As early as 1826 the first makers of watch-chains, albeit on a small scale, are recorded. Gottlieb & Wagner, *Uhrketten- und Schmuckwaren Fabrik*, was founded in 1865. Gottlieb & Wagner were the most important industrial manufacturers of watch-chains in Oberstein and for many years they continued to lead the field locally. Founded a year after Gottlieb & Wagner, the *Uhrketten- und Bijouterie-Fabrik* Louis Gottlieb & Söhne was soon followed by other watch-chain and bijouterie makers. For decades the manufacture of watch-chains was the most important Oberstein industry.

Completion of the Rhine-Nahe railway line between 1856 and 1860 sparked off a major economic upturn since the rail link ensured Oberstein ready access to the market. In any case, the 1870s were a decade of prosperity. After the German Empire was founded in 1870/71, the economic situation improved because elimination of customs barriers between what had been the individual territorial states facilitated trade and commerce. »The demand for wares which were as cheap as possible resulting from the reduced purchasing power inflicted by the general crisis of 1873 on consumers was particularly instrumental in promoting sales of inexpensive watch-chains produced at the Oberstein factories.«[29] Businesses which had begun by making their products mainly by hand developed into large-scale industrial operations, adding more plant and machinery with the years.

Like other countries, Germany, too, became familiar with the process of electroplating base metals with nickel, silver or gold. Moreover, by the mid-1870s gas-driven engines were in general use in German industry. This innovation made it possible to operate polishing-casks, lathes and wire-drawing frames on a larger scale. In 1877 the Obersteiner-Idarer-Gasanstalt [Oberstein Idar Gas Works] was founded. Finally, the introduction of steam-driven factory machinery and electric engines promoted further technical advances. »The late 1870s saw an economic

nischen Vorteile nochmals erweitert. »Ende der 1870er Jahre trat eine Konjunktur-Belebung ein. Aus Amerika kam zu jener Zeit die Herstellung vernickelter Uhrketten nach Deutschland. Der größte Teil der Hausindustriellen stellte sich auf die Herstellung dieser Nickelketten um. Es begann eine Periode der Hochkonjunktur, die ununterbrochen 10 Jahre lang anhielt.«[30]
In den 1890er Jahren hatten sich die in Oberstein ansässigen Uhrketten- und Bijouteriefabriken bestens etabliert, auch die Firma Jakob Bengel gehörte, knapp 20 Jahre nach ihrer Gründung, zu den ersten am Platze. »Die bijouterie fausse stellt alle möglichen Gegenstände her, insbesondere ist die Uhrkettenfabrikation zu außerordentlichem Umfang gediehen. Von Metallen kommen vorzugsweise in Anwendung Tombak, ein Gemisch von Kupfer und Messing, ferner Nickel, Neusilber, aber auch in Gold und Silber wird gearbeitet. (...) Firmen von erster Bedeutung sind die Uhrkettenfabrikation von Peter Hermann, Gottlieb und Wagner, Leopold Keller Sohn, Jakob Bengel (...).«[31]
Schon damals waren die wirtschaftlichen Erfolge der Firmen von starken Schwankungen betroffen. In den Jahresberichten der Handelskammer zum Thema »Bijouterie« wird im Jahre 1893 berichtet: »In der ersten Hälfte des verflossenen Jahres lag das Geschäft in diesen Artikeln so sehr darnieder, daß die Fabriken ihre Arbeiter nur halbe Tage beschäftigen konnten. Seitdem ist ein Aufschwung zu bemerken gewesen, der hoffentlich von Bestand sein wird. Eine allgemeine Besserung der Geschäftslage wäre im Interesse der Arbeiterbevölkerung dringend zu wünschen, die nun schon so lange Jahre in äußerst gedrückten Verhältnissen lebt.«[32]

Das 20. Jahrhundert

Mit dem Beginn des 20. Jahrhunderts verbesserte sich auch wieder die Lage der Bijouteriewarenindustrie Obersteins. Bereits 1905 konnte die Handelskammer wieder Erfolge vermelden. In ihren Mitteilungen heißt es unter der Rubrik »Echte und unechte Bijouterie«: »Die Obersteiner Fabriken von Uhr-, Hals- und Muffketten waren voll beschäftigt, und es

78 Uhrketten einer Obersteiner Firma, vor 1900
Museum Idar-Oberstein
Watch-chains from an Oberstein firm, before 1900

upturn. The manufacture of nickel-plated watch-chains was introduced to Germany from America at that time. Most local industrialists switched to making such nickel chains. A boom began, which lasted without a break for ten years.«[30]
By the 1890s the Oberstein manufacturers of watch-chains and bijouterie wares were doing well. Barely twenty years after Jakob Bengel was founded, it was one of the most successful in this sector. »The bijouterie fausse [industry] makes all sorts of objects. The manufacture of watch-chains has seen tremendous growth. Of the metals used, tombac, an alloy of copper and brass, as well as nickel, German silver and even gold and silver, are being worked. (...) Enterprises of the first rank are the watch-chain manufacturers Peter Hermann, Gottlieb und Wagner, Leopold Keller Sohn, Jakob Bengel (...).«[31] Even in those days business fluctuated considerably. The Jahresberichten der Handelskammer [Annual Reports published by the Chamber of Commerce] have the following to say under the heading of »bijouterie« for 1893 berichtet: »In the first half of the previous year business was so poor that the factories could only employ workers half days. Since then an upturn has made its appearance, which will, one hopes, continue. A general amelioration of business conditions would be an urgent desideratum in the interest of the working classes, who have been living for so many years in extremely straitened circumstances.«[32]

The 20th century

The 20th century ushered in better times for the Oberstein bijouterie wares industry. By 1905 the local chamber of commerce was once again reporting successes. In the Annual Reports under the heading »Genuine and Simulated Jewelry« it says: »The Oberstein manufacturers of watch, neck and muff chains were working at full capacity and even the troubles in Russia, which is a prime market for these Oberstein products, have so far not affected production. In some factories overtime has been implemented so that growth in demand has also resulted in increased earnings for the workforce.«[33]

haben sogar die Wirren Rußlands, das ein Hauptabnehmer dieser Obersteiner Fabrikation ist, bis jetzt nichts daran geändert. In manchen Fabriken wurden Überstunden eingelegt, so daß die vermehrte Nachfrage auch ein Steigen der Arbeiterverdienste im Gefolge hatte.«[33]

Der Streik von 1907

Hatte die günstige Konjunktur der Uhrketten-Erzeugung mit einigen Hochs und Tiefs beinahe dreißig Jahre angehalten, so war das Streikjahr 1907 ein schwerer Schlag für Oberstein: »volle vier Monate, seit Mitte August ds. Jahres war unsere gewerbefleißige Stadt mit ihrer weltbekannten Uhrketten-, Bijouterie- und Metallwarenfabrik der Schauplatz eines erbitterten Kampfes zwischen dem Deutschen Metallarbeiter-Verband und dem hiesigen Arbeitgeber-Verband.«[34] Begonnen hatte die Arbeitsniederlegung bei der Firma Gebrüder Schmidt und weitete sich dann auf andere Betriebe aus. Sogleich erkannte die Pforzheimer Industrie ihre Chance und nahm den Kampf um den Absatz am Weltmarkt auf. Ein lohnender Einsatz, denn immerhin entfielen von den 227 Betrieben, die sich in Deutschland 1907 mit der Herstellung von Schmuckwaren aus unedlen Metallen und Legierungen befaßten, wobei die Uhrkette als Schmuckware gesehen wurde, allein 173 Firmen mit 2086 Beschäftigten auf Oberstein.[35]

Die Obersteiner Bijouterie- und Kettenindustrie erholte sich jedoch auch von dieser Entwicklung rasch, es gelang ihr sogar die Wiedergewinnung ihrer Absatzmärkte, die Pforzheimer Bijouteriefabriken blieben allerdings eine ernst zu nehmende Konkurrenz. Die führende Stellung am Weltmarkt entfiel wieder auf Oberstein – bis 1914 der Erste Weltkrieg ausbrach.

Die Auswirkungen des Ersten Weltkriegs

In der Deutschen Goldschmiedezeitung vom 24. August 1918 beschäftigte man sich mit der Obersteiner Uhrketten- und Metallwarenindustrie unter den Einwirkungen des Krieges. »... Erst gegen Ende des Jahres 1916 hob sich die Nachfrage nach Obersteiner Artikeln, sowohl vom neutralen Auslande, als auch von der deutschen Kundschaft. Jedoch der Mangel an Rohstoffen schränkte den Umsatz erheblich ein. Infolge der Beschlagnahmung der Sparmetalle sah sich die Fabrikation genötigt, mit der Verarbeitung von Eisen zu beginnen, und mit Beginn des Jahres 1917 stieg die Nachfrage nach Obersteiner Erzeugnissen sehr, so daß die alten Lager fast vollständig aufgeräumt und abgesetzt werden konnten. (...) Infolge des bereits erwähnten Mangels an den vor dem Kriege verarbeiteten Materialien, konnte die Ausführung von Aufträgen auf Grund der früher herausgegebenen Muster und Proben nicht mehr erfolgen, sondern die Abnehmer haben sich dazu ver-

The 1907 strike

Despite some fluctuation, prosperity in the watch-chain industry lasted for nearly thirty years. The 1907 strike amounted to an enormous setback for Oberstein:

»For four months on end, since mid-August of this year, our commercially thriving city with its world-famous watch-chain, bijouterie and metalwares industry was the scene of a bitter struggle between the German Metalworkers' Union and the local Employers' Association.«[34]

Workmen first laid down their tools at Gebrüder Schmidt and the strike spread from there to other factories. Pforzheim, on the other hand, immediately saw the Oberstein strike as an opportunity to corner the world market.

This was a clever move because, of the 227 firms in Germany which had been making jewelers' wares – watch-chains were thus classified – since 1907, Oberstein was home to 173 businesses employing a total workforce of 2086.[35]

Nevertheless, the Oberstein bijouterie and watch-chain industry was quick to recover, even regaining its share of the world market. The factories in Pforzheim, however, remained serious competition. Oberstein once again led the world market – until the Great War broke out in 1914.

The aftermath of the First World War

The Deutsche Goldschmiedezeitung of 24 August 1918 featured article on the effects of the war on the Oberstein watch-chain and metalwares industry.

»...Only towards the close of 1916 did demand grow for Oberstein articles both from neutral countries and from the German domestic market. However, the shortage of raw materials considerably limited turnover. Due to the requisitioning of scarce metals needed for the war effort, the industry was forced to start processing iron and, early in 1917, there was such a growth in demand for Oberstein products that the old inventory backlog was almost entirely exhausted and could be sold off. (...) Owing to the above mentioned shortage of materials processed before the War, it was no longer possible to fill orders on the basis of the patterns and samples which had formerly been issued. Instead, customers had to agree to make do with such articles as could be manufactured from available semi-finished wares in conjunction with substitute materials, especially iron. Watch-chains made of iron were the main product. (...) Lobster and bolt-ring clasps were much sought-after and their makers achieved good earnings with them (...) The collateral war industry (Iron Crosses) was kept busy and was able to enlarge considerably the scale of operations (...). Some firms had procured orders to manufacture the so-called Imperial Watch-Chains late

79 Firma Jakob Bengel
Maschinensaal mit Fuß- und Exzenterpressen, heutiger Zustand
Jakob Bengel, the factory floor with foot-driven and eccentric cutters as it is today

stehen müssen, mit solchen Artikeln vorlieb zu nehmen, die aus vorhandenen halbfertigen Waren in Verbindung mit Ersatzmaterialien, besonders Eisen, hergestellt werden konnten. Uhrketten aus Eisen waren der Hauptartikel. (...) Sehr gesucht waren Karabiner und Federringe, und deren Hersteller hatten gute Verdienste aufzuweisen (...) Die Fabrikation der mittelbaren Kriegsindustrie (Eiserne Kreuze) war gut beschäftigt und konnte den Betrieb bedeutend vergrößern (...). Einige Firmen hatten mit den sogenannten Reichsuhrketten Ende des Jahres 1916 und Anfang 1917 Beschäftigung gefunden. (...) Die der Obersteiner Industrie erteilten Heeresaufträge haben im Laufe der Zeit einen ganz erheblichen Umfang angenommen, und die Industrie ist dafür auf das Äußerste in Anspruch genommen. Die Herstellung von Uhrketten geht neben der Munitionsindustrie rüstig weiter. Die Nachfrage ist groß, und man ist kaum in der Lage, die übernommenen Aufträge auszuführen (...).«[36]

Die Jahre zwischen den beiden Weltkriegen

Nach dem Ersten Weltkrieg folgten erneute Einschränkungen für die Obersteiner Industrie, auch sie hatte unter der Erhebung einer 26 % Reparationsabgabe auf deutsche Waren durch Frankreich zu leiden. Die Anfang 1923 einsetzende Ruhraktion seitens der französischen Besatzung brachte Oberstein für längere Zeit die vollständige Absperrung von der Außenwelt und damit den fast völligen Stillstand der gesamten Industrie.

Wie bereits 1907 boten sich auch jetzt wieder für Pforzheim gute Gelegenheiten, entsprechende Marktanteile zu erobern. Die oft so gepriesenen »Goldenen Zwanziger Jahre« waren für die Obersteiner Metallwarenindustrie längst nicht so »golden«. Nach einer Aufstellung des Berufsamtes Oberstein waren 1924 in sämtlichen Fabrik- und Hausindustriebetrieben noch 1950 Personen beschäftigt, gegenüber 1907 mit 2911 Beschäftigten.

Die allgemein schwierige wirtschaftliche Lage in Deutschland schlug sich auch in Oberstein nieder. Produktionszweige wie Schmuck, und sei er auch aus preiswertem Material, ließ sich schwer verkaufen. Unter den Stadtnachrichten der National-Zeitung findet man am 11. Dezember 1934 die Überschrift: »Die heimische Industrie liefert Frontkämpfer-Ehrenkreuze. Wie wir soeben erfahren sind bei der hiesigen Metallindustrie 465 000 Frontkämpfer-Ehrenkreuze in Auftrag gegeben worden. Wir freuen uns darüber, daß die in letzter Zeit nicht mehr voll beschäftigte heimische Industrie dadurch wieder für eine längere Spanne lohnende Beschäftigung gefunden hat und geben uns der Hoffnung hin, daß der Auftrag in Bälde noch erhöht wird.« Stolz verkündete die gleiche Zeitung nur

in 1916 and early in 1917. (...) The orders placed by the military with the Oberstein industry have, with time, grown to a considerable volume and the industry is working at full capacity to fill them. The manufacture of watch-chains is proceeding briskly apace alongside the munitions industry. Demand is strong and it is almost impossible to fill orders that have been taken on (...).«[36]

The years between the world wars

Watch-chain and jewelry manufacture in Oberstein again felt the pinch following the First World War. It, too, suffered from the reparation payments amounting to 26 % levied by France on German wares. The occupation of the Ruhr by the French from early in 1923 completely isolated Oberstein for quite some time and industry there ground to a halt. As it had in 1907, Pforzheim again seized the opportunity of cornering as large a share of the world market as possible.

The much vaunted »Roaring Twenties« were certainly not a »Golden Age« for the Oberstein metalwares industry. Figures collated by the Oberstein Berufsamt (Employment Office) show that only 1950 persons were employed in 1924 in all manufacturing and cottage industries as compared with a total of 2911 employed in 1907. The poor economic conditions prevailing throughout Germany also affected Oberstein. Products such as jewelry, and this included jewelry made of the cheapest materials, found few buyers. The local news section of the »National-Zeitung« of 11 December 1934 ran the headline: »Local industry provides decorations for combat veterans. As we have just heard, 465 000 crosses honoring combat veterans have been ordered from the local metals industry. We are delighted that local manufacturing, which has not been working to full capacity recently, has thus found worthwhile work for quite some time ahead and we hope that this order will soon be followed by others.« The same newspaper was proud to announce only a few days later: »Work for 1000 comrades. Reich government places an order with the precious stone and metal jewelry industry.«[37] This order was for producing the final plaquette of the Winterhilfswerk (a National Socialist compulsory charity, ostensibly for relieving hardship during cold weather), the WHW badge for collecting for the needy between 23–31 March 1935. The industry expected to make 6 million badges and was of the opinion that this number might even be increased to 10 million. In an essay entitled »Vom ›Schorstegold‹ to Eloxal«, Walther Fischer had this to say on the subject: »Costume jewelry experienced an upswing when the Third Reich unleashed a rampant inflation of badges, enameled pins and Winterhilfe plaquettes decorated with gemstones, until the Second World War forced many metal factories to switch to war production.«[38]

80–82 Firma Jakob Bengel, Kettenmaschinen-Saal (rechts), Kettenmaschinen (links unten), Maschinensaal zur Herstellung von Halbfabrikaten (rechts unten), heutiger Zustand
At Jakob Bengel, hall with chain-making machinery (right), chain-making machines (bottom left), factory hall for half-finished products (bottom right) as they look today

wenige Tage später: »Arbeit für 1000 Volksgenossen. Reichsregierung vergibt Auftrag für Edelstein- und Metallschmuckindustrie.«[37] Hierbei ging es um den Auftrag, die Schlußplakette des Winterhilfswerks, also die WHW-Abzeichen für die Sammlung vom 23.–31. März 1935, zu produzieren. Man rechnete mit einer Stückzahl von 6 Millionen Plaketten und war der Meinung, daß sich diese noch auf 10 Millionen erhöhen könne.
Walther Fischer bemerkt in seinem Aufsatz »Vom ›Schorstegold‹ zum Eloxal« zu diesem Thema: »Die unechte Bijouterie erlebte einen Auftrieb, als das 3. Reich eine Abzeichenhausse brachte, die sich in emaillierten Anstecknadeln oder mit Schmucksteinen verzierten Winterhilfsplaketten austobte, bis dann der 2. Weltkrieg die Umstellung vieler Metallfabriken auf Kriegsbedarf bedingte.«[38]
Die Produktion aller Arten von unechtem Schmuck, zu dem u.a. Reißverschlüsse, Uhrenketten, Puderdosen, Zigarettenetuis und Taschenbeschläge zählten, wurde nach Nord- und Südamerika exportiert, nach ganz Europa, in den Orient und nach Afrika. Im Jahre 1938 hatte der Umsatz dieser Industrie trotz der nicht einfachen Ausfuhrbestimmungen noch 5 421 124 RM betragen, während er im Dezember 1945 nur noch bei ungefähr 191 000 RM lag.

Die Nachkriegsjahre – Neubeginn und wirtschaftlicher Aufschwung

Die Wiederaufnahme der Produktion in den Obersteiner Metallwaren- und Bijouteriefirmen zwischen 1945 und 1949 erfolgte nur langsam. Verantwortlich dafür waren der Rohstoffmangel und nicht zuletzt aber auch die anhaltende Demontage von Maschinen wie Stanzautomaten, Pressen und Drehbänken durch die französische Besatzung.
Die Schmuck- und Metallwarenindustrie in der seit 1933 vereinigten Stadt Idar-Oberstein hatte erheblich zu kämpfen, das Exportgeschäft war fast völlig zum Erliegen gekommen: »Der Export ruhte bis auf ganz geringfügige Einzelgeschäfte vollkommen. Durch die Demontage-Aktion wurden der Industrie zahlreiche wertvolle Maschinen entzogen.«[39]
Erfreulicherweise ist im Jahre 1950 zu lesen, daß sich der Devisenerlös bei der Obersteiner Metall- und Schmuckwarenindustrie wieder günstiger gestaltet hatte und somit erste Anzeichen des Aufschwungs zu vermelden waren.[40] Die Beschreibung in Idar-Oberstein spiegelt die allgemein eintretende Situation im Deutschland dieser Jahre wieder.

Costume jewelry and bijouterie accessories of all kinds, including, among so many other things, zips, watch-chains, compacts for face powder, cigarette cases and handbag fittings, were exported to North and South America, throughout Europe, to the Far East and Africa. In 1938 the volume of sales in this industry still amounted to 5 421 124 Reichsmark whereas in December 1945 it totaled only about 191 000 Reichsmark.

The postwar years – a fresh start with the economic miracle

The Oberstein metalwares and costume-jewelry manufacturers got off to a slow start when production began again between 1945 and 1949. The reasons for this were shortage of raw materials and, not least, the continuing dismantling of machines such as blanking and cutting presses as well as lathes by the French occupation.
The jewelry and metalwares industry in the city of Idar-Oberstein, amalgamated since 1933, was faced with a hard battle since the export trade had come virtually to a standstill: »Export was dormant except for a very few minor individual businesses. The dismantling operation deprived the industry of numerous valuable machines.«[39]
It is, therefore, reassuring to read that, by 1950, profits were looking up in the Oberstein jewelry and metalwares industry heralding the economic miracle to come.[40] This description from Idar-Oberstein reflects the situation about to set in generally in Germany during those years.

DIE KETTENHERSTELLUNG IN OBERSTEIN – DIE FIRMA JAKOB BENGEL

Die Bedeutung der Obersteiner Kettenindustrie

Die Gründung der Firma Bengel fiel in eine Zeit wirtschaftlicher Prosperität. Der findige Schlossermeister Jacob Bengel hatte sich mit der Errichtung einer Uhrkettenfabrik im Jahre 1873 einen damals einträglichen Produktionszweig ausgesucht. »Die unechte Uhrkettenherstellung war nämlich in Schwung gekommen und allmählich das Genre geworden, was im Anfang reichlich Aufträge und schönen Verdienst brachte. Die Uhrkette war nun der courante Artikel geworden, der mit Hilfe und Anwendung von Maschinenarbeit emporgekommen war (...) Von der Anfertigung des einfachen Ringglieds aus der Drahtspirale auf der Drehbank bis zur Prägung und Stanzung des ciselierten Glieds auf der großen Präge- und Stanzpresse wurde die Uhrkette und ihre verschiedenen Teile Gegenstand fabrikmäßiger Herstellung; nur einfache und von der Maschine schwer auszuführende Hantierungen, wie das Ineinanderhängen der Ringe und Glieder wurde noch in hausindustrieller Tätigkeit besorgt ...«[41]

Von allen schmuckproduzierenden Zweigen in Oberstein hatte die Kettenfabrikation die größten technischen Innovationen, denn ursprünglich war die Herstellung von Uhrketten reine Handarbeit. Eine maschinelle Kettenherstellung setzte Ende der 1880er Jahre ein, eine erste Maschine aus England soll 1888 aufgestellt worden sein.[42] Einen weiteren Fortschritt brachte die von dem Mechanikermeister Hauschild 1902 konstruierte Kettenmaschine. Es dauerte noch einige Jahre bis die maschinelle Kettenfertigung in Oberstein von Anker-, Panzer-, Erbs- und sonstigen Fassonketten an den Qualitätsanspruch der Handarbeit heranreichte.

Jacob Bengel verstand es schon sehr früh, seine Kettenproduktion von der Handarbeit auf die Maschinenfertigung umzustellen. Dies war absolut notwendig, um auch der Konkurrenz vor Ort standhalten zu können. Er fuhr mit seinem Bruder in das damals deutsche Elsaß und erwarb dort die ersten Kettenmaschinen. Diese Kettenmaschinen wurden von Frauen per Hand bedient, etwa so wie die ersten Nähmaschinen. Dadurch konnte die Produktion der bisher von Hand geformten und anein-

MAKING CHAINS IN OBERSTEIN – THE FIRM OF JAKOB BENGEL

The importance of the Oberstein chain industry

The firm of Jakob Bengel was founded in an era of prosperity. The resourceful master metalworker Jacob Bengel had discovered a lucrative market niche for himself when he founded a watch-chain factory in 1873. »The manufacture of watch-chains in base metals had just begun to take off and they were gradually becoming the most popular genre, which initially brought in a great many orders and good profit margins. The watch-chain was now an article in everyday use and had become so with the aid and use of the machine ... From the manufacture of a simple ring link from a wire spiral on the lathe to blanking and cutting a chiseled link on the big blanking and cutting press, the watch-chain and its various parts were the object of industrial production; only simple operations that were difficult for the machine to perform, such as the interlinking of rings and links, was still done by the cottage industry ...«[41]

The manufacture of chains called for more innovation than all the other branches of jewelry-making practized at Oberstein. Watch-chains were originally made entirely by hand. Chains began to be industrially made towards the end of the 1880s. The first machine is said to have been brought from England and set up in 1888.[42] The machine for making chains constructed by Hauschild, a master mechanic, in 1902 represented a further technical advance. It would take several more years before the industrially made anchor chains, curb chains, round belcher chains and other fancy-shaped chains attained the quality of hand-crafted ones.

Jacob Bengel was clever enough to switch early on from handcrafting chains to making them industrially by machine. This step was necessary if he wanted to be competitive even on the local level. He went with his brother to Alsace, which was then German, to buy the first chain-making machines. Women operated them by hand, rather like the first sewing machines. They made it possible to accelerate by a multiple factor the production of chain links, which had previously been shaped by hand and soldered together. Over the years, the plant was enlarged considerably, with the number of machines growing to several dozen (fig. 80–82).

83 Firma Jakob Bengel
Blick in den Maschinensaal mit Fuß- und Exzenterpressen, heutiger Zustand.
At Jakob Bengel, a present-day view of the factory floor with foot-driven and eccentric cutters

84 Firma Jakob Bengel
Teilansicht des Lagers der Prägestempel, Gesenke und Folgewerkzeuge, heutiger Zustand.
At Jakob Bengel today, a glimpse of the storeroom for the dies, swage and finishing tools

ander gelöteten Kettenglieder um ein Vielfaches gesteigert werden. Im Laufe der Jahre wuchs der Maschinenbestand auf mehrere Dutzend (Abb. 80–82). Später wurden die Maschinen über Transmissionen durch Dampfmaschinenkraft angetrieben. Zu den eindrucksvollsten Maschinen gehören die gewaltigen Spindelpressen, die noch heute mit ihrer 80-Tonnen bzw. 120-Tonnen-Kraft Prägearbeit verrichten können. Geradezu zierlich wirken dagegen die zahlreichen Fußpressen, die gelegentlich heute noch im Einsatz sind (Abb. 79, links).
Der Schritt von der Uhrkettenfabrikation zur Bjouteriewarenindustrie war streng genommen nur eine Erweiterung des bisherigen Sortiments. Insbesondere bei den Damenuhrketten blieb die Grenze zwischen Schmuck- und Gebrauchskette immer fließend. Die Muster der Chatelâines sind auch bei den Halsketten und Colliers zu finden. Nach wie vor nahmen die Schmuckketten für Damen neben Armbändern, Ohrgehängen, Broschen, Fingerringen und Gürtelschnallen den Hauptanteil bei der Produktion ein.
Die Herstellung der Kette läßt sich in drei Arbeitsschritte unterteilen: 1. die Herstellung aller Einzelteile aus denen eine Kette besteht, 2. das Zusammensetzen dieser Teile und 3. die weitere Bearbeitung der rohen Ketten. Die Fertigung der Einzelteile hat einen hohen maschinellen Anteil, während das Zusammensetzen der Einzelteile meistens von Hand, zum großen Teil in Heimarbeit ausgeführt wurde. Metallblech und -draht sind die wesentlichen Bestandteile der maschinell gefertigten Kette. Besondere Aufmerksamkeit soll der Kettenfabrikation gelten, denn sie hatte damals in technischer Hinsicht die größten Fortschritte aufzuweisen.
Das älteste Kettenmuster bildete die Panzerkette, bei der einzelne aus aufgewundenem Draht geschnittene Ringe ineinander gehängt und verlötet werden.

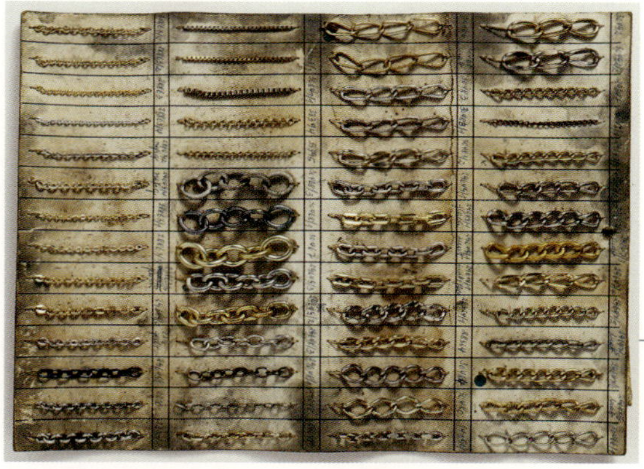

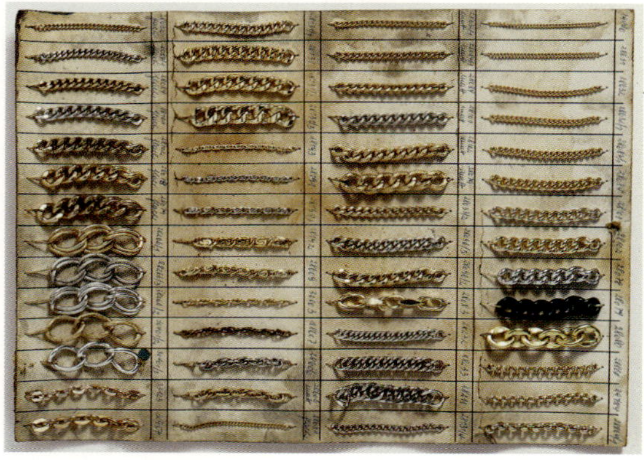

85–86 Musterkarten unterschiedlicher Ketten der Firma Jakob Bengel, wohl nach 1950
Jakob Bengel samples cards with chains, after 1950s

Later such machines were driven by steam via gearboxes. Among the most impressive machines are the mighty screw-presses, which even today can stamp out chains by exerting a pressure of 80 or 120 tons. The numerous foot-driven presses, on the other hand, which are occasionally still in use, look dainty by comparison (fig. 79 left).Strictly speaking, the switch from making watch-chains to manufacturing costume jewelry merely represented broadening the range of goods already available. Ladies' watch-chains (chatelaines) especially have always shown how fluid the boundaries are between chains used as jewelry and those that are solely utilitarian. The designs for chatelaines are interspersed between those for necklaces and collars. The production of necklaces for ladies, as well as bracelets, earrings, brooches, finger rings and belt buckles still continued to take up the lion's share of production. The process of manufacturing chains can be divided into three work phases: 1) the manufacture of all the individual components of which a chain is made; 2) assembly of these parts and 3) finishing the rough chains. The individual components were largely machine-made whereas they were usually assembled by hand, with much of this work farmed out to cottage industry. Industrially manufactured chains consist largely of sheet metal and wire. The manufacture of chains is being focused on here because at that time it made the greatest technological advances in the costume-jewelry sector.The oldest chain pattern was the curb chain (*Panzer*) necklace. Its individual rings, cut from unrolled wire, are interlinked and soldered. Made in all widths and sizes, these necklaces were for the most part electroplated with gold, silver or nickel.»For many businesses it marked a great change when the First World War ushered in the fashion of wearing watches on a strap on the wrist instead of a chain. However, it was not long before the industry began to manufacture articulated and one-piece watchbands. Soon the watchbands, usually of chromium-plated metal in a

Diese Ketten wurden in allen Weiten und Größen gefertigt, vorwiegend wurden sie galvanisch vergoldet, versilbert oder vernickelt.
»Eine gewaltige Umwälzung bedeutete es für viele Betriebe, als mit dem Ersten Weltkrieg die Mode aufkam, die Uhren nicht mehr an der Kette, sondern am Armband zu tragen. Aber sehr bald begann die Industrie, Glieder- und Zugarmbänder herzustellen, und bald hatte das Uhrarmband aus meist verchromtem Metall in vielseitiger Ausführung die gleiche Stellung errungen wie vordem die Uhrkette. Allerdings fand das Metall-Uhrarmband stets einen starken Konkurrenten im Lederarmband, auch sind die modischen Wandlungen nicht in dem Ausmaße betont wie einst bei der Uhrkette!«[43]
Die Deutsche Goldschmiedezeitung berichtet 1920 ausführlich über die Bedeutung der deutschen Schmuckkettenindustrie und ihre Problematik: »So umfangreich die ganze Industrie bei uns ist, so wenig reine Kettenfabriken gibt es, d.h. Betriebe, welche nur mit der Herstellung von Schmuckketten zu tun haben. Zum mindesten stellen sie außer der Kette auch noch die sogenannte Kettenbijouterie her, also Anhänger, Schieber, Medaillons und dergleichen. (...) Die Herstellung von Maschinen für die Kettenindustrie ist zu einem bedeutsamen Sonderzweige des Maschinenbaues geworden, und manche mechanischen Betriebe, die als Spezialität Kettenmaschinen herstellen, nutzten die von ihnen gebauten Maschinen dazu aus, daß sie für eigene Rechnung durch dieselben Maschinenketten fabrizieren ließen.« Am Ende dieses Artikels finden sich interessante Anmerkungen, die gerade auch im Bezug auf die Produktion der Firma Bengel relevant sind: »Das Herstellen neuer Muster ist im Schmuckkettenfach eine besonders schwierige und verantwortungsvolle Aufgabe, die ohne genaue technische Kenntnis und Erfahrung nicht zu lösen ist. (...) Der Mustermacher spielt bei Schmuckketten eine große Rolle, und der entwerfende Zeichner vermag nur in ständiger Zusammenarbeit mit diesem Ersprießliches leisten. Ein Stamm gut geschulter Arbeiter und Arbeiterinnen (...) ist die erste und wichtigste Grundlage zu einem erfolgreichen Betrieb. (...) Schon die Bedienung und Instandhaltung der Kettenmaschinen, bei denen es sich um äußerst komplizierte Bewegungsmaschinen handelt, kann nur durch Leute ge-

87 Gürtelschließen aus der Produktion Jakob Bengel auf Musterkarte, nach 1936
Sample card with belt buckles produced by Jakob Bengel, after 1936

great variety of models, had achieved the status once boasted by the watch-chain. However, the metal watchband always faced strong competition from the leather watchstrap; even dressy models were not emphasized to the extent that watch-chains once were!«[43]
In 1920 the Deutsche Goldschmiedezeitung reported at length on the importance of the German jewelry industry and the problems besetting it: »As extensive as the industry, taken as a whole, is, there are few businesses manufacturing chains alone, i.e., firms which only have to do with the manufacture of chains as jewelry. Apart from chains, they also make at least what is known as chain bijouterie, that is, pendants, slides, medallions and the like. (...) The making of machinery for the chain industry has become an important sideline of mechanical engineering and some mechanical engineering firms which specialize in the making of machinery for manufacturing chains have used the machines they have constructed to manufacture machine chains with them for their own profit.« At the end of the above article there are some interesting footnotes which are also particularly relevant to production at Bengel: »The making of new designs is, in the jewelry chain sector, a particularly demanding task entailing great responsibilities, problems which cannot be resolved without precise technical knowledge and experience. (...) The pattern maker plays an important role in the manufacture of chains for jewelry and the designer and draughtsman can only achieve productive work by collaborating closely at all times with the pattern maker. A workforce of well-trained men and women. (...) is the foremost and most important foundation for a successful business. (...) The operation and maintenance of the chain-making machines, which are machines operating with extremely sophisticated movements, can only be handled by people who are trained mechanics and thoroughly familiar with the entire manufacturing process. (...) On into the early years of this century [the 20th century] American chain manufacturers were superior to their German counterparts in the rational use of machinery whereas the latter surpassed the Americans in the great variety of design patterns they made. Nowadays the machine manufacture and finishing of chains is so highly developed in Germany that it can in any case be said to be the most advanced in the world.«[44]

schehen, die gelernte Mechaniker und mit der gesamten Fabrikation aufs Gründlichste vertraut sind. (...) Bis in den Anfang dieses Jahrhunderts [20. Jhd.] hinein waren die amerikanischen Kettenfabrikanten den deutschen in Bezug auf rationelle Maschinenverwendung überlegen, während diese jene in der Mannigfaltigkeit der Muster übertrafen. Heute ist die maschinelle Herstellung und Bearbeitung der Kette in Deutschland so hoch entwickelt, daß sie in dieser Beziehung jedenfalls als die erste in der Welt bezeichnet werden kann.[44]

Die Familien Bengel und Hartenberger

Jacob Bengel – vom Sohn eines Tagelöhners zum Uhrkettenfabrikanten

Die Firma Jakob Bengel wurde als Uhrketten- und Kleinmetallwarenfabrik im Jahre 1873 von dem begabten und erfinderischen Schlossermeister Friedrich Jacob Bengel (15.6.1848 – 6.7.1921 Oberstein), Sohn des Tagelöhners Friedrich Bengel und dessen Ehefrau Elisabetha, geb. Krummenauer, in der Wilhelmstraße 42 in Oberstein gegründet (Abb. 89, 92).[45] Mit dem Erlös aus dem Verkauf von Ländereien in der Luisenstraße, war es dem jungen Mann möglich gewesen, eine eigene Firma aufzubauen.

Im selben Jahr der Firmengründung heiratete er Luise Catharina Wild (24.7.1850 – 17.5.1940 Oberstein). Luise Bengel (Abb. 90, 91) arbeitete nicht nur in der Produktion an der Seite ihres Mannes mit, sie war ihm auch eine kluge Ratgeberin bei der Abwicklung der Geschäfte. Über die privaten und beruflichen Lebensumstände Jacob Bengels gibt uns eine Abschrift der Versicherungspolice Nr. 96 der »Magdeburger Allgemeine Versicherungs-Actien-Gesellschaft« aus dem Jahre 1887 Aufschluß. Dort heißt es unter

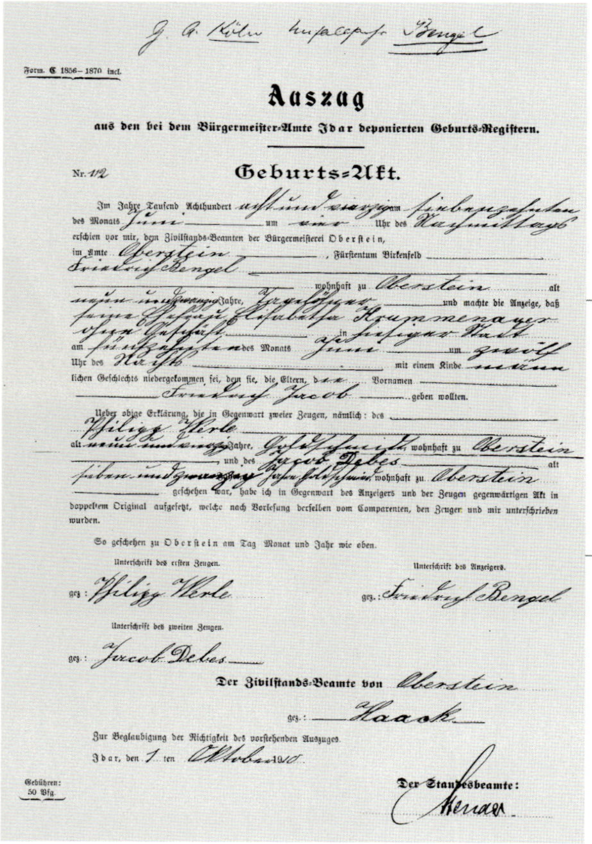
Form. C 1856–1870 incl.

Auszug

aus den bei dem Bürgermeister-Amte Idar deponierten Geburts-Registern.

Nr. 112 **Geburts-Akt.**

Im Jahre Tausend Achthundert ... am ... des Monats Juni um ... Uhr des Nachmittags erschien vor mir, dem Zivilstands-Beamten der Bürgermeisterei Oberstein, im Amte Oberstein, Fürstentum Birkenfeld Friedrich Bengel wohnhaft zu Oberstein alt ... Jahre, ... und machte die Anzeige, daß seine Ehefrau Elisabetha Krummenauer ... in ... am ... des Monats Juni um zwölf Uhr des ... mit einem Kinde ... lichen Geschlechts niedergekommen sei, dem sie, die Eltern, den Vornamen Friedrich Jacob geben wollten.

Ueber obige Erklärung, die in Gegenwart zweier Zeugen, nämlich: des Philipp Werle alt ... Jahre, Goldschmied, wohnhaft zu Oberstein und des Jacob Debes alt ... wohnhaft zu Oberstein geschehen war, habe ich in Gegenwart des Anzeigers und der Zeugen gegenwärtigen Akt in doppeltem Original aufgesetzt, welche nach Vorlesung derselben vom Comparenten, den Zeugen und mir unterschrieben wurden.

So geschehen zu Oberstein am Tag Monat und Jahr wie oben.

Unterschrift des ersten Zeugen. gez.: Philipp Werle

Unterschrift des Anzeigers. gez.: Friedrich Bengel

Unterschrift des zweiten Zeugen. gez.: Jacob Debes

Der Zivilstands-Beamte von Oberstein gez.: Haack

Zur Beglaubigung der Richtigkeit des vorstehenden Auszuges.

Idar, den 1ten Oktober 1910

Der Standesbeamte:

Gebühren: 50 Pfg.

88 Geburtsurkunde Friedrich Jacob Bengel (späterer Register-Auszug vom 1. Oktober 1910)
Friedrich Jacob Bengel's birth certificate (later registry-office copy, 1 October 1910)

The Bengel and Hartenberger families

Jacob Bengel – from day-laborer's son to industrial manufacturer of watch-chains

The firm of Jakob Bengel was founded in 1873 to make watch-chain and small metal wares by the talented and inventive master machinist Friedrich Jacob Bengel (15.6.1848 – 6.7.1921 Oberstein), at 42 Wilhelmstrasse in Oberstein. His parents were Friedrich and Elisabetha Bengel, née Krummenauer (figs. 89, 92).[45] With the proceeds from selling properties in Luisenstrasse, the young man was able to establish and build up a firm of his own.

The year he founded the firm he married Luise Catharina Wild (24 July 1850 – 17 May 1940 Oberstein). Luise Bengel (figs. 90, 91) not only worked in the factory beside her husband. She was also an intelligent adviser when it came to doing business. The copy of an insurance policy, policy no. 96 issued by the Magdeburger Allgemeine Versicherungs-Actien-Gesellschaft in 1887, supplies informative details of Jacob Bengel's private and professional life. There it says, among other things: »The Magdeburger Allgemeine Versicherungs-Actien-Gesellschaft insures (...) *Herrn Friedrich Jacob Bengel* in *Oberstein*, who, as he informs us, currently holds the undersigned position, respectively practises the trade or undersigned profession: Proprietor of a bijouterie wares factory operating with gas-driven motor, supervising the business and at times working in it, going on short business trips and on occasion obliged to hunt.«

From these scanty remarks we learn that Jacob Bengel worked hands-on in his factory, already had the newest technical advances at his disposal and that he was given to hunting, which must have been a favorite pastime.

By 1890 Jacob Bengel and his own employees had built a private dwelling for himself on the factory premises as well as a building, then known as works quarters, to house employees.

anderem: »Die Magdeburger Allgemeine Versicherungs = Actien = Gesellschaft versichert (...) *den Herrn Friedrich Jacob Bengel* in *Oberstein* welcher nach seiner Angabe zur Zeit nachbezeichnete Lebensstellung einnimmt resp. nachbezeichnetes Gewerbe betreibt oder nachbezeichnetem Berufszweig angehört: ›Besitzer einer Bijouteriewarenfabrik mit Gasmotorbetrieb, den Betrieb beaufsichtigend, zeitweise mitarbeitend, kleinere Reisen ausführend und zuweilen der Jagd obliegend‹«.
Aus diesen wenigen Anmerkungen erfahren wir, daß Jacob Bengel aktiv in seiner Fabrik mitarbeitet, bereits über die neuesten technischen Errungenschaften verfügte und die Jagd seine große Leidenschaft war.

Bereits 1890 baute Jacob Bengel auf dem Fabrikgelände mit seinen eigenen Mitarbeitern zusätzlich ein Wohnhaus, so genannte Werkswohnungen, in denen Mitarbeiter der Firma wohnen konnten.

»Vom Firmengründer Jakob Bengel weiß ich nur, daß er einer der erfolgreichsten Fabrikanten der Stadt war und eine Menge Kinder hatte. Sein einziger ihm verbliebener Sohn, Bengels Rudi, war ein starker, gutmütiger, aber auch eigenwilliger junger Mann, der in Schillings im Eck Werkzeugmacher lernte, später nach Südamerika auswanderte und dort eine Menge Nachwuchs hinterließ.«

Luise Bengel entwickelte sich im Laufe der Jahre zum guten Geist der Firma, sie war eine geschätzte und beliebte Persönlichkeit, die man liebevoll die »Bengels Bas« nannte. »Wie sie mir geschildert wurde, fühlte sie sich am wohlsten inmitten ihrer 40 bis 50 Goldschmiedsmädchen, die sie beaufsichtigte. Sie war eine gute Menschenkennerin. Wenn die Mädchen zuviel plapperten, wobei die Zangen öfter, wenn auch nur für fünf Sekunden ruhten, rief sie: ›Ihr Mädchen, singt einmal eins (= Lied)‹. Die Mädchen stimmten ein Lied an, die Zangen bewegten sich pausenlos in gleichmäßigem Rhythmus, und die Bengels Bas hatte ihre Freude an den meist wehmütigen alten Volksweisen, die gedämpft auch auf der Straße zu hören waren und manchen Passanten zum stehenbleiben bewegten.«[46]

89 Friedrich Jacob Bengel, um 1875
Friedrich Jacob Bengel, ca. 1875

90 Luise Catharina Bengel, um 1875
Luise Catharina Bengel, ca. 1875

91 Luise Catharina Bengel, um 1900
Luise Catharina Bengel, ca. 1900

92 Friedrich Jacob Bengel, um 1900
Friedrich Jacob Bengel, ca. 1900

▸ siehe auch Stammbaum, S. 286
see also family tree, p. 286

»Of the founder of the firm, Jakob Bengel, all I know is that he was one of the most successful industrialists in the city and had a great many children. The only surviving son, Rudi Bengel, was a sturdy, good-natured young man, who nonetheless had a mind of his own. He trained as a tool-maker at Schillings »im Eck«, later emigrated to South America and left to posterity there a great many offspring.« Over the years, Luise Bengel grew into the guiding spirit of the business. A greatly appreciated and popular person, she was fondly nicknamed »Bengels Bas«, »Bengel's boss«. »As she was described to me, she was never happier than when she was surrounded by her 40 to 50 girl goldsmiths, whom she supervised. She had a good knowledge of people. If the girls chattered too much, leaving their pliers to rest, which quite often happened, even for only five seconds, she would call out: ›Girls, sing us one [= a song].‹ The girls would strike up a song, the pliers would move ceaselessly in a uniform rhythm and Bengel's boss enjoyed the usually melancholy old folksongs, which were even audible, albeit in muffled tones, in the street, moving many a passer-by to stand and listen.«[46] According to Emil Schmidt (see also p. 91ff.), later apprenticed to the firm, Anna Bengel was strict. It was well-known that she was given to saing on Monday mornings at about 10 past 7 am: »Allez, allez, quick, the day after tomorrow half the week is over and we haven't delivered anything.«

Ernst Hermann Hartenberger, sen. – from ironmonger's son to manufacturer of watch-chains and jewelry

Ernst Hermann Hartenberger, sen. (18 November. 1877–8 October 1951 Oberstein), whose father was an ironmonger, had owned a thriving ironmongery in Oberstein. Profits were so good that in 1900 he was able to marry a young lady named Anna Bengel (14 June 1881–30 January 1973), the industrialist's daughter (fig. 94, 98).

Not long after marrying into this family, Hartenberger sold his own business, bringing the proceeds with him to his father-in-law's firm. The Bengel factory was taken over by young Hartenberger between 1901 and 1910.

»Bengel's Boss had a son-in-law after her own heart, from the hard-working Hartenberger family, a hard-headed, pragmatic businessman, with a sense of humor that sometimes bordered

93 Ernst Hartenberger d. Ä. (links) mit Mitarbeitern in der Firma Jacob Bengel, vor 1914
Ernst Hartenberger, sen. (left), with staff at Jacob Bengel, before 1914

Dem späteren Lehrling der Firma, Emil Schmidt (siehe auch S. 93ff.) zufolge, ist über Anna Bengel bekannt, daß sie ein strenges Regiment führte. Ein bekannter Spruch von ihr montags morgens um 10 Minuten nach 7 Uhr war: »Allez, allez, macht schnell, übermorgen ist schon die halbe Woche vorbei und wir haben noch nichts geliefert.«

Ernst Hermann Hartenberger sen. – vom Eisenwarenhändler-Sohn zum Uhrketten- und Bijouteriewaren-Fabrikanten

Der Eisenwarenhändlers-Sohn Ernst Hermann Hartenberger sen. (18.11.1877–8.10.1951 Oberstein) hatte in Oberstein einen florierenden Eisenhandel besessen, seine guten finanziellen Verhältnisse erlaubten ihm, im Jahre 1900 die junge Fabrikantentochter Anna Bengel (14.6.1881–30.1.1973) zu heiraten (Abb. 94, 98). Bald nach der Einheirat verkaufte Hartenberger sein eigenes Geschäft und brachte den Erlös in die Firma seines Schwiegervaters ein, die Übernahme der Bengel-Fabrik durch den jungen Hartenberger erfolgte zwischen 1901 und 1910.
»Die Bengels Bas bekam einen Schwiegersohn nach ihrem Herzen; aus der tüchtigen Familie der Hartenberger, mit einem ausgeprägten kaufmännischen Realitätssinn und einem manchmal ans makabre grenzenden Humor. Unter ihm herrschten strenge Bräuche (...).«[47]

Jacob Bengel blieb der engagierte Techniker, der in Zusammenarbeit mit seinen Gesellen, die für die Produktion notwendigen Maschinen auch selbst baute und hin und wieder kleine Erfindungen machte, wie etwa die heute noch im Gebrauch befindliche Bengel-Zange. Ein Handwerkszeug, das es ermöglichte, die Kette bequem mit der linken Hand zu fassen, um mit der Spitzzange weitere Kettenglieder einzuhängen (Abb. 99). Mit seinem Schwiegersohn hatte Jacob Bengel einen weltoffenen Kaufmann an seiner Seite, der es verstand, den europäischen Markt, ja später sogar die Weltmärkte zu erobern.
Ernst und Anna Hartenberger hatten zwei Söhne und eine Tochter. Das älteste Kind, die Tochter, wurde nach der Mutter auf den Namen Anna getauft (22.2.1903–9.1.1946 Oberstein). Sie heiratete 1922 Eugen Gottlieb, der aus der Familie der Uhrketten- und Schmuckwarenfabrik Gottlieb & Söhne stammte (Abb. 95). Ernst Hartenberger und sein Bruder Hugo Hartenberger kauften später eine Villa in der Mainzer Straße 244, die sich heute noch im Besitz der Familie Gottlieb befindet.
Der älteste Sohn wurde nach dem Vater benannt, Ernst Hermann Hartenberger jun. (13.8.1905 Oberstein – 14.1.1978 Idar-Oberstein). Wie seinem Arbeitsbuch von 1935 zu entnehmen ist, besuchte er 1920 die Handelsschule in Kirchheim und 1923 die Wirtschaftsschule, das »Lycée Jaccard« in Lausanne (Abb. 96, 120). In den Jahren 1922/23 absolvierte er ein kaufmän-

on the macabre. Under him the business was strictly run (...).«[47]
Jacob Bengel remained committed to technology. Working with his journeymen, who also built the machines needed for manufacturing, he even made minor inventions now and then, among them the Bengel pliers, which is still used today. This is a tool which enabled an employee to hold the chain comfortably in his/her left hand so that other links could be added to a chain with needle-nose pliers (fig. 99).
In his son-in-law, Jacob Bengel had a cosmopolitan businessman at his side, one who know how to corner the European market and later even the world market.
Ernst and Anna Hartenberger had two sons and a daughter, who was the eldest child and was christened Anna after her mother (22 Feb. 1903–9 Jan. 1946 Oberstein). In 1922 she married Eugen Gottlieb, a member of the family who owned Gottlieb & Söhne, manufacturers of watch-chains and jewelry (fig. 95). Ernst Hartenberger and his brother, Hugo, later bought a mansion at 244 Mainzer Strasse, which is still owned by the Gottlieb family. The Hartenbergers' eldest son was named Ernst Hermann Hartenberger, jun. (13 Aug. 1905 Oberstein – 1978 Idar-Oberstein), after his father. As can be seen in his 1935 works log, he attended trade school in Kirchheim in 1920 and, in 1923, the »Lycée Jaccard«, a commercial college in Lausanne (figs. 96, 120). In 1922/23 he served an internship at Gebr. Levy, a firm in Frankfurt am Main. The works log notes that his special skills were in »French and English, both spoken and written«. From 1 January 1924 until 2 September 1940 he was employed in his father's firm and traveled abroad as its representative. By 1935 he was married to Else Laub (1911 Oberstein – 26.6.1978 Idar-Oberstein).
The Hartenberger's younger son, Walter (16 Aug. 1916 – early 1945), a lieutenant in the German Air Force, suffered the fate of so many young men in the Second World War. Wounded in Hungary, he was sent to a field hospital in Czechoslovakia. Nothing further is known about him and he was later listed as missing (fig. 97).
As an industrialist with international business links, Ernst Hartenberger, sen., attached enormous importance to ensuring that his children received good basic education and professional training. Consequently, it was only natural that he should have sent his sons abroad. Ernst went to Lausanne to experience life in an elegant, sophisticated city and Walter attended the Institut Schaffner in Geneva. A brochure of this school setting out its educational aims and detailing the course program shows that it offered everything that was important for a cosmopolitan firm such as Jakob Bengel: in addition to »harmonious formation and development of character (...)«, value was attached to a thorough education: »The school prepares pupils for all examina-

94 Anna Hartenberger, geb. Bengel und Ernst Hartenberger d.Ä., um 1903
Anna Hartenberger, née Bengel, and Ernst Hartenberger, sen., ca. 1903

95 Eugen Gottlieb (Firma Gottlieb & Söhne) und Frau Anna, geb. Hartenberger, um 1920
Eugen Gottlieb (of Gottlieb & Söhne) and his wife Anna, née Hartenberger, ca. 1920

96 Ernst Hermann Hartenberger jun., im Internat Lycée Jaccard, Lausanne, 1923
Ernst Hermann Hartenberger, jun., at boarding school Lycée Jaccard, Lausanne, 1923

97 Walter Hartenberger, um 1936
Walter Hartenberger, ca. 1936

98 Anna und Ernst Hartenberger jun., 1930er Jahre
Anna and Ernst Hartenberger, jun., 1930s

nisches Volontariat bei der Firma Gebr. Levy in Frankfurt am Main. Als besondere Fertigkeiten werden im Arbeitsbuch »Französische und englische Sprache in Wort und Schrift« angegeben. Vom 1. Januar 1924 bis 2. September 1940 war er als kaufmännischer Angestellter und Auslandsreisender in der Firma seines Vaters tätig. Bereits 1935 hatte er Else Laub (1911 Oberstein – 26.6.1978 Idar-Oberstein) geheiratet.
Den jüngsten Sohn Walter (16.8.1916 – Anf. 1945), Leutnant der Luftwaffe, ereilte das Schicksal vieler junger Männer im Zweiten Weltkrieg. Er wurde in Ungarn verwundet und kam in ein Lazarett in Tschechien. Sein weiteres Schicksal ist unbekannt, er wurde später als verschollen gemeldet (Abb. 97).
Ernst Hartenberger sen. kam es als Fabrikant mit internationalen Geschäftsverbindungen darauf an, daß seine Kinder eine adäquate Erziehung und Ausbildung erhielten. So war es nur selbstverständlich, daß er seine Söhne ins Ausland schickte: Ernst ging nach Lausanne, um das Flair der großen weiten Welt zu erleben, Walter besuchte das Institut Schaffner in Genf. Ein erhaltener Prospekt dieses Hauses, weist auf die Ausbildungsziele und das Unterrichtsprogramm hin, was für ein weltoffenes Unternehmen wie die Firma Jakob Bengel wichtig war: Neben einer »harmonischen Bildung und Entwicklung des Charakters (...)« legte man dort auf eine solide Ausbildung Wert: »Die Schule bereitet auf alle Examen vor. Sie schenkt dem Studium der modernen Sprachen (...) besondere Aufmerksamkeit. Der Unterricht wird in französischer Sprache erteilt. Das Institut ist zur Vorbereitung auf eine Laufbahn in Industrie, Handel, Transport, Bank, Versicherung und Verwaltung speziell geeignet.« Walter und Ernst jun. waren also zu unternehmerisch denkenden, weltoffenen Menschen erzogen worden. So war es für sie auch selbstverständlich, daß sie ihren Vater auf seinen Reisen nach Paris und London begleiteten, um dort Geschäftsverbindungen zu pflegen oder neue Kontakte zu knüpfen. Später reisten die Söhne alleine ins Ausland, um die Produktion der Firma dort vorzustellen.
Aus den Jahren vor dem Zweiten Weltkrieg haben sich – wie in so vielen Familien und Betrieben – kaum Unterlagen erhalten. So sind Erzählungen und Berichte aus zweiter Hand eben-

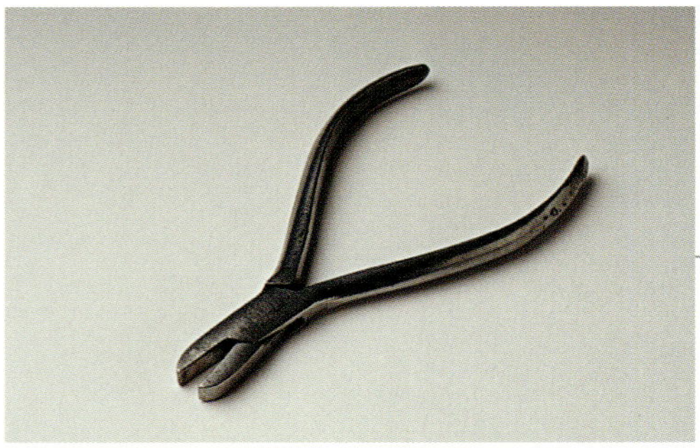

99 Bengel-Zange
Bengel pliers

100 Gürtelschließen und Knöpfe der Firma Bengel, nach 1945
Belt buckles and buttons from Bengel, after 1945

tions. It pays particular attention to the study of modern languages (...). Instruction is in the French language. The Institute is particularly suited to preparing for careers in industry, commerce, transportation, banking, insurance and administration.« Walter and Ernst jun. were, therefore, brought up to be both shrewd businessmen and men of the world. Of course they accompanied their father on business trips to Paris and London to cultivate business links or make new contacts. Later the sons would travel abroad on their own to present the firm's wares.
Only very few records exist for the years preceding the Second World War – a situation common to many families and businesses alike. As a result, accounts and reports, even at second hand, are just as import as a casual mention in the press. In the National-Zeitung of 19 November 1934 there is a note which implies that Hartenberger was still financially able to donate quite a considerable sum to the Winterhilfswerk: »For the Winterhilfswerk 1934/35 the following donations of money were received in Gau Koblenz – Trier – Birkenfeld from industrial circles amounting to over 300,– Reichsmark. Follow their example and give an offering.« Ernst Hartenberger, sen., of Oberstein, is one of the names mentioned here: he donated 600 Reichsmark.
The two world wars left their mark on the Hartenberger family, as they did on so many families, and, of course, also on the firm of Bengel. Ernst Hartenberger, sen., fought in the First World War (in an infantry battalion); his two sons fought in the second war. He refused to allow one of his sons to be exempt from military service to manage the firm, which would have been his right by law. Walter never returned from the war but Ernst jun., a non-commissioned Air Force officer, survived. On his return from internment as a prisoner of war in the south of France, he was again employed from January 1946 in his father's firm. Together father and son built up the jewelry-making business again and renewed the business contacts that had lain fallow during the war – the 1950s economic miracle was ahead of them. Production now concentrated on making chains of Eloxal for curtains and decoration purposes.[48] In the Allgemeinen Zeitung, Birkenfelder Anzeiger no. 203, 2/3 Sept. 1950 there is

so wichtig wie eine beifällige Anmerkung in der Tagespresse. In der National-Zeitung vom 19. November 1934 findet man eine Notiz, aus der man schließen kann, daß die finanziellen Verhältnisse Hartenbergers es damals noch zuließen, eine nicht unerhebliche Spende für das Winterhilfswerk zu leisten: »Für das Winterhilfswerk 1934/35 gingen im Gau Koblenz – Trier – Birkenfeld aus den Kreisen der Wirtschaft folgende Geldspenden im Werte von über 300,– Reichsmark ein. Folgt ihrem Beispiel und opfert.« Unter anderen wird hier auch Ernst Hartenberger sen., Oberstein, mit einer Spende von 600,– Reichsmark erwähnt.
Wie in vielen Familien hinterließen die beiden Weltkriege ihre Spuren in der Familie Hartenberger und somit auch in der Firma Bengel. Ernst Hartenberger sen. war selbst Teilnehmer des Ersten Weltkrieges (Infanteriebataillon), seine beiden Söhne nahmen am Zweiten Weltkrieg teil. Er lehnte es ab, einen seiner Söhne zur Führung der Firma freistellen zu lassen, wie es ihm laut Gesetz zugestanden hätte. Während der Sohn Walter nicht mehr aus dem Krieg zurückkehrt, überlebte Ernst jun. den Krieg als Unteroffizier der Luftwaffe. Von der Kriegsgefangenschaft in Südfrankreich heimgekehrt, arbeitete er ab Januar 1946 wieder als kaufmännischer Angestellter in der Firma seines Vaters. Gemeinsam bauten sie die Schmuckproduktion wieder auf und erneuerten die kriegsbedingt brachliegenden Geschäftsbeziehungen – die guten 1950er Jahre standen bevor. Ein Schwerpunkt der Produktion war die Fertigung von Ketten aus Eloxal für Vorhänge und Dekorationszwecke.[48] In der Allgemeinen Zeitung, Birkenfelder Anzeiger Nr. 203, 2./3.9.1950 ist ein Artikel zu »250 Jahre Idar-Obersteiner Schmuck- und Metallwarenindustrie« zu finden. Unter diesem Artikel haben einige Firmen eine Anzeige geschaltet, so auch die Firma Bengel: »Uhrketten-Bijouterie- und Metallwarenfabrik JAKOB BENGEL, Idar-Oberstein 1, Telefon 2229.«
Nach dem Tod des Vaters im Jahre 1951 übernahm Ernst Hartenberger jun. die Geschäfte seines Vaters, die zu dieser Zeit sehr gut florierten. In den 1950er Jahren ist im ABC der Deutschen Wirtschaft zur Produktion der Firma Bengel folgender Eintrag zu finden: »Unechte Bijouterie, Eloxal-Schmuckwaren, Meterketten in Alu, Messing, Eisen, Tombak, Silber, Gold, roh und veredelt, Bügel für Klein-Lederwaren, mod. Damentaschenbügel, Auflagen, Verzierungen, Schnallen und Beschläge, Schuhornamente, Goldschmuck, Fingerringe, Anhänger und Broschen.«
Bereits vor dem Zweiten Weltkrieg hatte die Familie Hartenberger in einem gepflegten Wohlstand gelebt, man gehörte zu den wenigen Familien, die in Oberstein bereits ein Auto ihr Eigen nennen konnten und man hatte in Meddersheim, in der Nähe Obersteins, eine eigene Jagdhütte. Es haben sich zahl-

an article on »Two hundred and fifty years of the Idar-Oberstein jewelry and metal wares industry«. Below the article several firms placed advertisements, among them Bengel: »Watch-Chain, Bijouterie and Metal Wares Factory JAKOB BENGEL, Idar-Oberstein 1, Telephone 2229.«
On the death of his father in 1951, Ernst Hartenberger, jun., took over his father's business, which was flourishing at the time. In the 1950s, the ABC der Deutschen Wirtschaft has the following entry on Bengel: Costume bijouterie, Eloxal jewelry, chains by the metre in aluminium, brass, steel, tombac, silver and gold, unfinished and plated, handles for small leather goods, stylish handles for ladies' handbags, decorations, buckles and fittings, show ornaments, gold jewelry, finger rings, pendants and brooches.
Before the Second World War the Hartenbergers were well-to-do and lived very comfortably. They were among the few families in Oberstein to own a motor car and they had a hunting lodge of their own in Meddersheim, near Oberstein. Family photographs from that time show jolly hunting parties. Ernst Hartenberger, sen., hunted regularly with friends or employees such as Otto Feikert.
Ernst Hartenberger, jun., and Else Hartenberger, née Laub, had three daughters: Christel (*1937 in Idar-Oberstein), Anna Maria (*1938 in Idar-Oberstein) and Freya Gabriele (*1948 in Idar-Oberstein). After their father's death in 1978, they continued to manage the firm on into the 1990s (fig. 104). However, the changes wrought by German reunification in 1989 caused a drastic drop in orders from which Bengel has yet to recover.

The firm premises and living quarters in Wilhelmstrasse, Oberstein

A drawing dating from 1910 conveys a very good idea of how impressive the premises of the Jakob Bengel watch-chain factory at 40/42 Wilhelmstrasse were in the early 20th century. The smoking chimneys stand for the diversity and prosperity of the firm during those years (fig. 106).[49]
The buildings are part of a complex comprising the Bengel housing and plant which were built in Wilhelmstrasse in Oberstein between 1873 and 1906. When the firm was founded, it occupied a building on the banks of the Nahe. Its 35-metre factory chimney rising between the factory and the housing built for employees in about 1890 was a »local landmark« visible for miles. The proprietor's mansion (at 44 Wilhelmstrasse), built in the late Jugendstil or German Art Nouveau style with an ornamental garden, was designed and built in 1910/11 by the architect Max Jager for Ernst Hermann Hartenberger sen., the proprietor at that time (figs. 107–109). The building is two-storeyed and symmetrical in plan. The pronounced central gable with the bay win-

Einladung zur Jagd

auf ....

am .... in ....

Treffpunkt um .... Uhr in ....

101 Firmenschild Jakob Bengel Bijouterie- und Schmuckwarenfabrik
Firm plate of Jakob Bengel Bijouterie- u. Schmuckwarenfabrik

102 Postkarte »Einladung zur Jagd«, 1950er Jahre
Postcard: »invitation to a hunt«, 1950s

103 Ernst Hartenberger d. Ä. auf der Jagd, 1950er Jahre
Ernst Hartenberger, sen., hunting, 1950s

104 Anna Maria (links) und Christel Hartenberger, um 1942
Anna Maria (left) and Christel Hartenberger, ca. 1942

105 Ernst Hartenberger d. Ä. in seinem Verkaufsstand auf der Frankfurter Messe, vermutlich 1950
Ernst Hartenberger, sen., in his stall at the Frankfurt Trade Fair, probably 1950

106 Zeichnung der Fabrik- und Wohngebäude auf dem Briefbogen »Jacob Bengel Uhrkettenfabrik Oberstein« (Ausriß), vor 1910
Drawing of the factory premises and living quarters on the letterhead of »Jacob Bengel Uhrkettenfabrik Oberstein« (excerpt), before 1910

reiche Familienfotos erhalten, die fröhliche Jagdgesellschaften belegen. Mit Freunden oder seinen Mitarbeitern, wie zum Beispiel Otto Feikert, ging Ernst Hartenberger sen. regelmäßig auf die Jagd.

Aus der Ehe Ernst Hartenbergs jun. mit Else Laub gehen drei Töchter hervor, Christel (*26.2.1937 in Idar-Oberstein), Anna Maria (*1938 in Idar-Oberstein) und Freya Gabriele (*1948 in Idar-Oberstein), die nach dem Tode des Vaters im Jahre 1978 die Firma Bengel bis in die 90er Jahre weiterführen (Abb. 104). Mit der wirtschaftlichen Veränderung in Deutschland nach 1989 hatte die Firma drastische Auftragseinbußen zu verzeichnen, die bis heute nicht mehr aufgefangen werden konnten.

Die Firmen- und Wohngebäude in der Wilhelmstraße in Oberstein

Einen sehr schönen Eindruck von dem imposanten Firmengelände der Uhrkettenfabrik Jakob Bengel in der Wilhelmstraße 40/42 zu Beginn des 20. Jahrhunderts vermittelt eine Zeichnung aus den Jahren vor 1910. Die rauchenden Schlote stehen für eine vielseitige und prosperierende Produktion dieser Jahre (Abb. 106).[49]

Die Gebäude der Firma Bengel gehören zu einem Komplex von Wohn- und Fabrikbauten in Oberstein, die zwischen 1873 und 1906 in der Wilhelmstraße entstanden. Mit der Gründung der Firma entstand zunächst das eigentliche Firmengebäude am Ufer der Nahe. Der 35 Meter hohe Fabrikschlot ragt zwischen dem Fabrikbau und den um 1890 erbauten Werkswohnungen als »Wahrzeichen« weithin sichtbar empor.

Die Fabrikantenvilla (Wilhelmstraße 44), im späten Jugendstil mit einem Ziergarten, wurde 1910/11 von dem Architekten Max Jager für den damaligen Inhaber Ernst Hermann Hartenberger sen. erbaut (Abb. 107–109). Die Villa besteht aus einem zweigeschossigen, symmetrischen Bau. Ein besonderer Akzent setzt der übergiebelte Mittelrisalit, mit einem für die Zeit typischen Erker. Die aus Effusivgestein mit Sandsteinteilen gefertigte Fassade, zeugt von einer bescheidenen Prächtigkeit.[50]

Tritt man durch den Haupteingang in die Villa (Abb. 109), dann wird man im Hausflur von interessanten Landschaftsmalereien überrascht, die 1920 von dem Maler R. Minn ausgeführt wurden (restauriert). Erhalten haben sich auch die Inneneinrichtung und Ausstattung des Hauses, beeindruckend sind die schwere Holzvertäfelung an den Wänden der Wohnzimmer und die gut erhaltenen Stuckdecken. Besonders zu erwähnen sind die farbigen, bleiverglasten Fenster im Flur wie auch im Treppenhaus und in der ersten Wohnetage. Die Motive auf den zehn Fenstern erzählen aus dem bürgerlichen Leben und der heimischen Märchenwelt und sind mit volkstümlichen Sinnsprüchen ergänzt.

dow so typical of the period is a salient feature. The façade in effusive stone (tuff lava) articulated with sandstone radiates both modesty and grandeur.[50]

On entering the mansion through the front door (fig. 109), you are pleasantly surprised by some interesting landscapes (they have undergone restoration) painted in 1920 by R. Minn. The furnishings and appointments of the house are in their original condition. The massive paneling on the living-room walls and the beautifully preserved stucco ceilings. The stained-glass and leaded windows in the hall, the stairwell and on the first floor are remarkably fine. The motifs in the ten windows tell stories from everyday life and local legend and bear vernacular mottoes. The mansion has never been remodeled. When you step on to the cobbled courtyard entrance leading to the back door, you see that this period house has kept its charm. The decorative garden with its old trees is still as it was. The complex bears witness even now to early 20th-century architecture at its best. In 1932, however, the business grew to such an extent that it became necessary to build a factory annex between the buildings as they were then.

When you walk into the Bengel factory, you really feel as if you have stepped back to the early years of the past century. A realistic description gives a good idea of how a factory operated in those days (figs. 79–84).

Works and Days: operations at a chain factory

An article in the specialist journal Die Schaulade is illuminating on the Oberstein bijouterie and watch-chain industry in 1934. The impression jotted down can easily be applied to Bengel as the firm was in the years just before the Second World War. You reel the author might have been on the spot: »The layman has no idea of how much hard work goes on in buildings which were often only marked by a sign saying ›Bijouteriefabrik‹ and in larger businesses. The bijouterie industry works with all metals which were made by German foundries and plants: brass, tombac, German silver, tin and steel, to name only a few. Another product that is used in vast quantities is Galalith, which, as is well known, is made from casein. Finally, glass, too, is used in such design as ›gemstones‹ or beads of all shapes and sizes. If you go into one of the larger factories, you must first get used to the noise level there. Strangers cannot help but think that pandemonium reigns yet they soon realize that everyone has his particular job and the whole business operates according to a prescribed system. This is where the huge die-presses stand, greedily »devouring« strips of sheet-metal from which they cut out pieces – for a ring bezel, for chain links or for some other purpose. If these plates which are stamped out already bear decoration, such a drawing will have been engraved in advance by the firm's own engraver on the die of hardened steel

107 Fabrikanten-Villa Bengel/Hartenberg, Wilhelmstraße 44, heutiger Zustand
The proprietor's mansion, 44 Wilhelmstrasse, in 2002

108 Wohnzimmer mit Erker, heutiger Zustand
Sitting-room with bay window, 2002

109 Treppenaufgang, heutiger Zustand
The stairwell as it looks today

110 Zeichnung der Fabrik- und Wohngebäude auf einer Visitenkarte, um 1930
A drawing of the factory and employee housing on a visiting card, ca. 1930

Die Villa blieb von jeglichen Veränderungen verschont. Trifft man über die mit Kopfsteinpflaster befestigte Hofeinfahrt auf den rückwärtigen Eingang des Hauses, so hat sich noch viel von der einstigen Idylle des Anwesens erhalten, so auch der Ziergarten mit dem alten Baumbestand.
Der Gebäudekomplex zeugt noch heute von der architektonischen Anlage des frühen 20. Jahrhunderts, jedoch wurde 1932 aufgrund der Expansion zwischen den bestehenden Gebäuden der Anbau einer Maschinenhalle notwendig.
Betritt man heute die Maschinenhallen der Firma Bengel, so glaubt man sich wirklich in die Jahre zu Beginn des vergangenen Jahrhunderts zurückversetzt. Die plastische Beschreibung vom Funktionieren einer damaligen Fabrikanlage gibt uns einen absolut realistischen Eindruck (Abb. 79–84).

Das Werken und Wirken einer Kettenfabrik

In einem Artikel des Fachblattes »Die Schaulade« wird 1934 ein Schlaglicht auf die Bijouterie- und Uhrkettenindustrie Obersteins geworfen. Der hier skizzierte Eindruck läßt sich ohne weiteres auf die Firma Bengel in den Jahren vor dem Zweiten Weltkrieg übertragen, ja man könnte fast meinen, der Autor sei dort gewesen: »Der Laie macht sich keinen Begriff davon, welch rastlose Arbeit sich in den oftmals außen nur durch ein Schild ›Bijouteriefabrik‹ gekennzeichneten Häuser und in den größeren Betrieben abspielt. In der Bijouterie-Industrie werden alle Metalle verarbeitet, die in deutschen Hütten und Werken hergestellt werden: Messing, Tombak, Neusilber, Blech, Eisen u.a.m. Ein weiteres Produkt, das in riesigen Mengen verwendet wird und das der Bijouterie-Industrie ganz neue Anregungen gegeben hat, ist das Galalith, das bekanntlich aus Casein gewonnen wird. Schließlich findet auch Glas in seiner Gestaltung als ›Schmuckstein‹ oder Perlen in den verschiedensten Formen Verwendung. Betritt man einen größeren Betrieb, so muß man sich erst an den dort herrschenden Lärm gewöhnen. Der Fremde hat unwillkürlich den Eindruck, als wenn ein heilloses Durcheinander herrschte, doch erkennt er recht bald, daß jeder seine besondere Beschäftigung hat und der ganze Betrieb nach einer vorgeschriebenen Systematik arbeitet. Hier stehen große Stanzen, die gierig Blechstreifen in allen Breiten ›fressen‹, aus denen sie Stücke – für eine Ringplatte, für Kettenglieder oder irgendeinen anderen Zweck – herausstanzen. Sollen diese Platten, die herausgeschlagen werden, schon eine Verzierung zeigen, so wird vom eigenen Graveur vorher diese Zeichnung in die Stanze aus gehärtetem Stahl hineingraviert (sowohl die Urzeichnungen als auch die Entwürfe werden von eigenen Künstlern angefertigt). Dort arbeiten an langen Tischen Arbeiter oder Arbeiterinnen, die die Platten auf Ringe auflöten, Kettenglieder zusammenhängen,

(both the original drawings and the designs are done by the firm's own artists). Workmen or women labor there at long tables, soldering bezels on to rings, putting chain links together, attaching spirals (much of this work is also done by the cottage industry) and, while they are still blanks, send them to the electroplating division for further treatment, where they are nickel-plated, polished or scoured. If they have already received the desired finished, they are set with decorative stones and pieces of Galalith, chains are fitted out with lobsters or other clasps etc., etc. (...) The machines on which chains – known as Panzer chains – are made are marvels of precision and ingenuity. The way these machines, which are now made in Germany – formerly they had to be imported – operate borders on magic. The wire enters the machine on one side, is gripped there by several flat-nosed pliers, is wound and cut, the individual chain links are joined together, the complete, albeit still unfinished, chain emerges from the other side and falls on to a slightly domed plate so that it cannot get tangled up or even form a ball which cannot be disentangled. (...) There is not enough space here to go into everything else there is to be seen there. Let us, therefore, be content with just mentioning a few things. There are mighty drops or swage-hammers to process or stamp out larger metal elements, then there are gigantic electroplating vats for gilding or silvering, nickel-plating or chromium-plating, acid baths for cleaning and biting, casks filled with petrol for cleaning, shaking-troughs, casks filled with sawdust for drying or producing a high-gloss finish and much, much more.
The Oberstein bijouterie industry makes all sorts of things: necklaces, key-rings, bracelets, earrings, finger rings, watch-chains, hat pins, clips, cuff-links of all types and in all models imaginable.
Roughly 3000 people are employed in the Oberstein bijouterie industry, with 1400 more in the cottage industry. Most products, about 75% of what is made, is exported. Oberstein bijouterie products are found in all countries in the world; they bear witness everywhere to the imaginative German approach to form and to German quality. But domestic specialist dealers are also called upon to devote their energies to promoting this industry, which is a major economic factor to be reckoned with (...).«[51]
It cannot be shown from the records which have been preserved when exactly Bengel added its line in bijouterie wares but this was probably done in the early years of the 20th century. Cost-estimate sheets for manufacture and materials preserved from the period between 21 Dec. 1907 to 4 March 1911 refer to model numbers 8001–10.000. They show that, in about three years, 2000 bijouterie models were made. This implies that the production of approx. 2000–2500 bijouterie models a year at Jakob Bengel must have set in shortly after 1900.

Spiralen einhängen (diese Arbeiten werden auch viel in Heimarbeit vergeben) und, falls sie noch roh sind, in die Galvanisierungsanstalt zur Weiterbehandlung schaffen, wo sie vernickelt, poliert oder gescheuert werden. Sind sie jedoch schon fertig behandelt, so werden sie mit Ziersteinen oder Galalithstücken komplettiert, Ketten mit Karabinern oder Verschlüssen versehen u.a.m. (...) Ein Wunderwerk von Präzision und Erfindungsgeist stellen die Maschinen dar, auf denen Ketten – die sogenannten Panzerketten – gearbeitet werden. Die Arbeitsweise dieser Maschinen, die jetzt in Deutschland gebaut werden – früher mußte man sie aus dem Ausland beziehen – grenzt an Zauberei. An einer Seite der Maschine tritt der Draht hinein, wird dort von mehreren Flachzangen gepackt, gewickelt und zerschnitten, die einzelnen Kettenglieder werden ineinander gehängt, auf der anderen Seite tritt die fertige, wenn auch noch rohe Kette heraus und fällt auf einen etwas gewölbten Teller, damit sie sich nicht verwickelt oder gar ein unentwirrbares Knäuel bildet. (...) Es würde zu weit führen, wollte man alles das aufzählen, was es noch zu sehen gibt. Begnügen wir uns daher nur mit einigen kurzen Andeutungen. Da sind mächtige Fallhämmer zur Bearbeitung oder Ausstanzung größerer Metallteile, da gibt es die riesigen galvanischen Bäder zur Vergoldung und Versilberung, zur Vernickelung und Verchromung, die Säurebäder zum Reinigen und Abbeizen, die mit Benzin gefüllten Auswaschtrommeln, die Schüttelfässer, die mit Sägespänen gefüllten Trommeln zum Trocknen oder auch zur Hochglanzerzeugung und vieles andere mehr.

Die Obersteiner Bijouterie-Industrie stellt vielerlei her: Halsketten, Schlüsselketten, Armbänder, Ohrringe, Reifen, Fingerringe, Uhrketten, Hutschmuck, Clips, Manschettenknöpfe in allen erdenklichen Arten und Ausführungen.

In der Obersteiner Bijouterie-Industrie sind in den Fabriken rund 3000 Personen beschäftigt und nahezu 1400 Personen in der Heimarbeit. Der größte Teil der Erzeugnisse, etwa 75 % der Produktion, wird exportiert. Obersteiner Bijouterieerzeugnisse gibt es in allen Herren Ländern, sie legen überall Zeugnis ab von deutscher Formenphantasie und deutscher Arbeit. Aber auch für den inländischen Fachhändler besteht die Aufgabe, diese Industrie, die einen bedeutenden Wirtschaftsfaktor darstellt, tatkräftig zu fördern (...).«[51]

Es läßt sich anhand der noch vorhandenen Unterlagen nicht nachweisen, wann genau die Erweiterung der Produktion um Bijouteriewaren bei Bengels erfolgte, sie dürfte aber zu Beginn des 20. Jahrhunderts anzusetzen sein. Erhaltene Kalkulations- bzw. Materialzettel aus der Zeit vom 21.12.1907 bis 4.3.1911 reichen von den Modellnummern 8001–10.000. In gut drei Jahren wurden also 2000 Bijouterie-Modelle angefertigt. Daraus

The 1913 firm address book describes the range of articles manufactured as follows: »watch-chains, châtelaines, necklaces, bracelets, collars made in all possible sizes, shapes and models, nickel-plated, silver-plated, gilt, copper-plated, blackened and German silver. Bengel, therefore, was a trend-setting chain manufacturer in Oberstein even before the First World War. The letterhead of a collection letter bearing the pre-printed date »191..« provides a convenient summary of the broad range of wares available from Bengel prior to the Great War: »Manufacture of watch-chains, chatelaines, necklaces, bracelets, collars in every size, shape and model desired, such as nickel-plated, silvered, gilt, copper-plated, oxidized and German silver. Leather thongs and leather chatelaines. Metal wares. Manufacture of watch-chain accessories and all related mass-produced articles.«

Scraps of invoices from 1922/23 list Bengel product lines in lockets, soldered brass chain-mail collars, unsoldered brass chain-mail necklaces being discontinued, celluloid belts in various models and gilt créoles.

Material was handled economically at Bengel; this is shown by the circumstance that documents no longer needed were cut into four pieces and cost calculations for products written on the back (fig. 111). Under no. 12.904/1 of 20 Nov. '22 we find the cost estimate for a »Key chain of broad chain-mail links 1.30 mm 100 m = 5 kg«; under no. 12.872 of 24 Nov. '22 »Metal belt nickel-plated brass« and under no. 12.746 of 21 Aug. 1923 »Celluloid = Collar 40 cm long comprising 25 elements 481/0.50 mm«. It is worthwhile taking a closer look for once at a cost-calculation sheet of this kind. Under no. 12.487 of 26 July 1921 the costs of a making »Tula chain [model] 13 [elements] of uniform length« are set down in detail:[52] (see fig. 111)[53]

Jacob Bengel's ingenuity as an inventor was boundless. This is shown by an offer consisting of individual elements of steel balls of varying diameter for polishing, sold by the kilo, with the cost depending on size. In the text it also says: »my prices are for Oberstein, net cash down, packing at cost. The balls are hard and give just as good a polish as precisely round balls ...« Instructions for use are included with these steel polishing balls.[54]

The factory brand – »la marque de fabrique«

Products made by Bengel do not bear a trade mark so that it is not all that easy to attribute them to the firm. Labels stuck on them with the firm mark and indicating material have been lost over the years (figs. 113, 116). Most of the costume jewelry made by Bengel went wholesale to retailers, who then sold it under their own stamp, as the label marked »Original Julienne« clearly shows (figs. 116).[55] We know that, by 1913, Jacob Bengel was manufacturing a »gun carriage with cannon-ball ball-bearings« (figs. 112, 114) under the trade name »JACOB BENGEL«.[56]

könnte man schließen, daß die Bijouterieproduktion bei ca. 2000–2500 Modellen pro Jahr bei Jakob Bengel kurz nach 1900 eingesetzt haben dürfte.

Im Adreßbuch des Jahres 1913 wird die Produktion der Firma wie folgt beschrieben: »Uhrketten, Chatelaînes, Halsketten, Armbänder, Colliers in jeder gewünschten Aufmachung und Ausführung in vernickelt, versilbert, vergoldet, verkupfert, oxydiert und Altsilber.« Bereits vor dem ersten Weltkrieg gehörte die Firma Bengel also zu den maßgebenden Kettenfabriken in Oberstein. Der Briefkopf eines Mahnschreibens, daß als gedrucktes Datum mit »191..« versehen ist, gibt einen Überblick über die große Produktionspalette vor dem Ersten Weltkrieg: »Fabrikation von Uhrketten, Chatelaines Halsketten, Armbändern, Kolliers in jeder gewünschten Aufmachung u. Ausführung, wie vernickelt, versilbert, vergoldet, verkupf. Oxyd. u. Altsilb. Lederketten und Lederchatelaines. Metallwaren. Fabrikation von Uhrketten-Fournituren und aller ins Fach einschlagenden Massenartikel.«

In Fragmenten erhaltene Rechnungen aus den Jahren 1922/23 nennen als Firmenprodukte Klappmedaillons, gelötete Messingpanzerketten, ungelötete Messingpanzerketten ablaufend, Celluloid-Gürtel in verschiedenen Ausführungen und vergoldete Creolen.

Daß man in der Firma Bengel sparsam mit dem Material umging zeigt die Tatsache, daß nicht benötigte Firmenpapiere in vier Teile zerschnitten wurden und die Rückseite dann als Papier für die Berechnung der Herstellungskosten einzelner Produkte diente (Abb. 111). Unter der Nr. 12.904/1 vom 20.11.22 finden wir etwa die Berechnung für »Schlüsselkette aus weiter Panzerkette 1.30 mm 100 m = 5 kg«, unter der

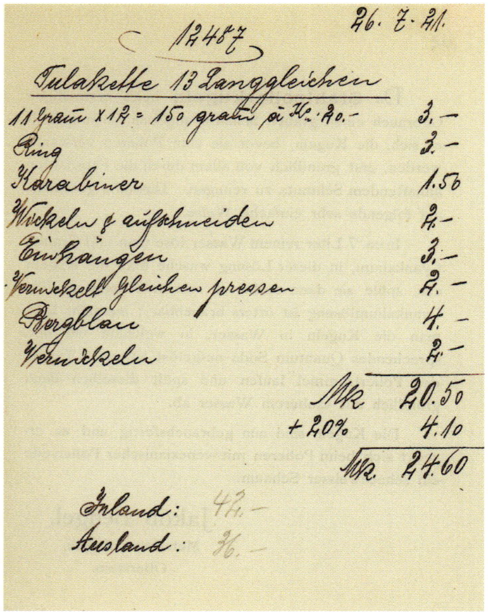

12487	26. 7. 21
Tulakette 13 Langgleichen	
11 Gramm | Grammes x 12 = 150 Gramm à | at Kr. 20,–	3,–
Ring | Ring	3,–
Karabiner | Lobster	1,50
Wickeln und aufschneiden | Winding and cutting	2,–
Einhängen | Linking	3,–
Vernickelt gleichen pressen | Stamping nickel-plated elements	2,–
Bergblau | Mountain blued	4,–
Vernickeln | Nickel plating	2,–
Mk	20,50
+ 20 %	4,10
Mk	24,60
Inland: | Germany:	42,–
Ausland: | Abroad:	36,–

111 Material- und Kalkulationszettel für Modell 12.487, 26.7.1921
Sheet with material costs estimate for model 12.487, dated 26.7.1921

The trade name occurs on the firm writing paper and product labels which have survived.

From about 1930 Ernst Hartenberger, sen., used a postcard-sized business card printed in French on which this mark appears with the additional reference »Marque de Fabrique« (fig. 117). In the left half of this postcard there is a sketch of the factory premises and buildings, with the employee housing and the proprietor's mansion and the factory chimney towering over it all. This extremely important primary source also reveals much more.

The firm must, therefore, have had a large clientele in French-speaking countries. Second, it is also pointed out that special orders can be placed by clients from all countries and that the firm kept abreast of new and novel developments in fashions. Finally, the metal and Galalith necklaces and bracelets produced between 1931 and 1938 are expressly mentioned as a firm specialty!

Another firm mark has been shown to have existed in 1940 yet nothing is known about how it was used.[57]

Advertising – Marketing and distribution – Export

Further important information to be gleaned from this business card is that the firm was represented at the Leipzig Fair in the Speckshof, the most important trade fair for the bijouterie wares industry before the Second World War. That is where the new designs for the collection were presented and orders taken for wares.

For the first time, in the 1926 Leipzig Fair address book, the firm is listed, under the heading of »Bijouterie and Jewelry Wares«, as *Bengel, Jakob, Oberstein (Nahe), Bijouterie-, Uhrket-*

Nr. 12.872 vom 24.11.22 »Metallgürtel Messing vernickelt«, unter der Nr. 12.746 vom 21.8.1923 ist zu finden »Celluloid = Collier 40 cm lang bestehend aus 25 Glieder 481/0.50 mm«. Es lohnt sich einen solchen Berechnungszettel für die Herstellungskosten einmal genauer anzusehen. Unter Nr. 12.487 vom 26.7.21 wird die Ausführung einer »Tulakette 13 Langgleichen« berechnet:[52] (siehe Abb. 111)[53]

Der Erfindergeist des alten Jacob Bengel war nicht zu bremsen, dies belegt ein aus mehreren Einzelteilen bestehendes Angebot für Stahl-Polier-Kugeln mit verschiedenem Durchmesser zu entsprechenden Preisen per Kilo. Im Text heißt es dann weiter »meine Preise verstehen sich loco Oberstein, netto Cassa, Verpackung selbstkostend berechnet. Die Kugeln sind hart und eignen sich zum Polieren ebenso gut wie präcis runde Kugeln ...«. Diesen Stahlpolierkugeln wurde auch gleich eine entsprechende Gebrauchsanweisung beigefügt.[54]

Die Firmenmarke – »la marque de fabrique«

Die Produkte der Firma Bengel tragen keine Firmenmarke, sie sind deshalb dieser Firma nicht ohne weiteres zuzuordnen. Angehängte Etiketten mit dem Firmenzeichen und der Materialangabe, wie das nebenstehende Beispiel, haben sich natürlich im Laufe der Jahre verloren (Abb. 113, 116). Der bei Bengel produzierte Schmuck wurde außerdem zum größten Teil an Wiederverkäufer abgegeben, die den Schmuck unter ihrem eigenen Signet verkauften, wie das Etikette mit der Aufschrift »Original Julienne« (Abb. 116) deutlich zeigt.[55]

Wir wissen, daß Jacob Bengel bereits 1913 die Marke »Lafette mit einer Kanonenkugellagerung« (Abb. 112, 114) sowie der Umschrift »JACOB BENGEL« führte.[56] Auf seinem Briefpapier und erhaltenen Produktetiketten ist die Marke zu finden.

Ernst Hartenberger sen. verwandte etwa ab 1930 eine postkartengroße, in französischer Sprache gedruckte Visitenkarte, die ebenfalls diese Marke mit dem zusätzlichen Hinweis »Marque de Fabrique« trägt (Abb. 117). Dieses äußerst wichtige Dokument verrät aber noch viel mehr.

112

112 Petschaft mit Siegelabdruck »Jacob Bengel Oberstein«
Official firm seal with impression »Jacob Bengel Oberstein«

113

114

115

116

113 Etikette »Garantiert Alpacca« der Firma Jacob Bengel
Jacob Bengel label »Guaranteed Alpacca« [White Metal]

114 Fabrik-Marke »Jacob Bengel Oberstein«, vor 1913
Factory mark »Jacob Bengel Oberstein«, before 1913

115 Fabrik-Marke »Jacob Bengel Oberstein«, um 1930
Factory mark »Jacob Bengel Oberstein«, ca. 1930

116 Etikette »Original Julienne«, um 1933
Label »Original Julienne«, ca. 1933

ten- u. Metallwarenfabr. Gegr. [founded] 1873: V, 911/13. It was represented at both the spring and autumn fairs and again at both in 1927 and 1928. Business seems to have been booming during those years because by 1929 the firm had added two stalls to the one it already occupied at the fair. It is safe to assume that this went on twice a year, in spring and autumn, during much of the 1930s, when Bengel presented their products in the Speckshof. The following entry appears in the 1938 spring Leipzig fair address book: *1. Spezialfabrik moderner Bijouterie, Uhrarmbänder, Uhrketten/Specks Hof, V, Std. 911/14.* The last entry is in the 1939 address book of the Leipzig autumn fair. In 1938/39 Bengel had made their stall smaller, which may have been due to the worsening economic situation.[58]

The constant changes in fashion exacted a great deal of flexibility in costume-jewelry production. New designs had to be produced non-stop to keep consumer demand high with ever-changing incentives to buy. Larger businesses brought out two collections a year, with such collections quite often comprising up to 2000 designs. Since so much of production went abroad, the fact that tastes so often differed widely from those prevailing at home had to be taken into consideration. No advertising in the form of advertisements in specialist journals could be found nor have any brochures come to light (fig. 119).[59]

Much of the costume jewelry produced in Oberstein went abroad, yet the export trade did not proceed without hitches. In the 1930s, for instance, an export currency declaration had to be submitted to the German Reichsbank in compliance with the provisions of the regulations governing currency exchange. Since every country had its own import formalities and customs regulations, it would not have been possible – or it would have been extremely time-consuming and expensive – to prosecute dilatory debtors should Bengel have needed to do so. As correspondence on the subject reveals, in 1935, the firm did try to arrange to have money owed by an Algerian customer paid via the German Consulate-General in Algiers. Other records show how difficult it sometimes was to collect money owed from

Die Firma Bengel hatte also einen großen Kundenstamm im französischen Sprachraum. Man weist aber auch darauf hin, daß man in der Lage ist, spezielle Kundenwünsche für alle Länder zu fertigen und man sich an den modischen Neuheiten orientierte. Letztendlich werden hier ausdrücklich die zwischen 1931 und 1938 produzierten Metall/Galalith-Ketten und -Armbänder genannt, also eine Spezialität der Firma!
Eine weitere Firmenmarke ist für das Jahr 1940 nachzuweisen, über ihre Verwendung ist allerdings nichts bekannt.[57]

Werbung – Vertrieb – Export

Ein ebenso wichtiger Hinweis auf dieser Visitenkarte ist die Vertretung der Firma auf der Leipziger Messe im Speckshof, die wichtigste Messe der Bijouteriewaren-Industrie überhaupt vor dem Zweiten Weltkrieg. Dort wurden die neuen Muster der Kollektion ausgestellt und die Bestellungen der Waren angenommen.
Im Messe-Adreßbuch des Jahres 1926 wird unter der Rubrik »Bijouterie- und Schmuckwaren« zum ersten Mal »Bengel, Jakob, Oberstein (Nahe), Bijouterie-, Uhrketten- u. Metallwarenfabr. Gegr. 1873: V, 911/13« genannt; auf der Frühjahrs- und Herbstmesse war die Firma vertreten. Dies gilt auch für die Jahre 1927 und 1928. Die Geschäfte scheinen in diesen Jahren gut gelaufen zu sein, denn bereits 1929 vergrößert die Firma ihren Messestand um zwei weitere Stände. Auch im darauffolgenden Jahr, und es ist davon auszugehen, daß dies kontinuierlich im Frühjahr und Herbst der 1930er Jahre geschieht, bietet die Firma Bengel ihre Produktion im Speckshof an. Zur Frühjahrsmesse des Jahres 1938 erscheint der Eintrag im Messe-Adreßbuch: »1. Spezialfabrik moderner Bijouterie, Uhrarmbänder, Uhrketten/Specks Hof, V, Std. 911/14«. Eine letzte Eintragung findet sich zur Herbstmesse 1939. In den Jahren 1938/39 hatte man den Messestand verkleinert, was möglicherweise auf die jetzt schlechtere Wirtschaftslage zurückzuführen war.[58]

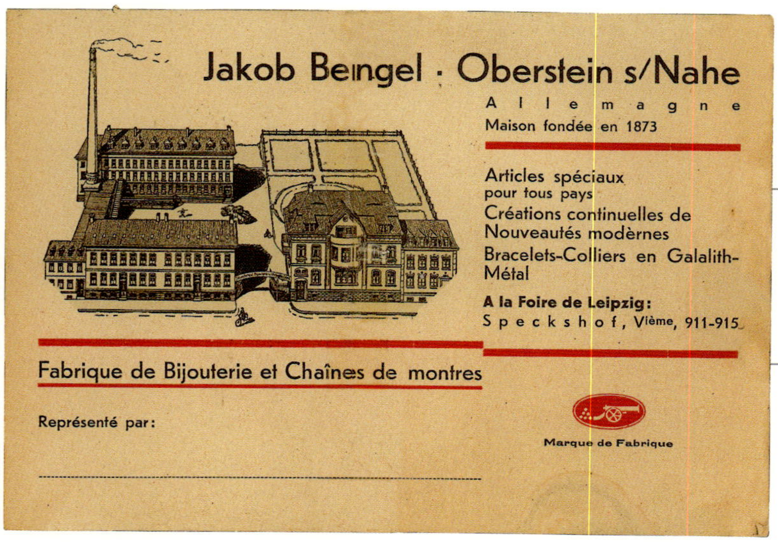

117 Visitenkarte von Ernst Hartenberger d. Ä., um 1930
Visiting card of Ernst Hartenberger, sen., ca. 1930

abroad. Bengel also had to resort to using the Bank for International Settlements as a clearing house representing the firm's interests as an exporter.
A a conscientious and scrupulous businessman, Ernst Hartenberger, sen., established a precise code of regulations for invoices to be used by foreign suppliers. In about 1930 the firm had a form to be used for collection letters printed in four languages – German, English, French and Spanish.[60] Politely (as the firm saw it) but firmly (and this is the operative word), dilatory customers were given a nudge that was anything but gentle to remind them that they owed Bengel money.
The German Chamber of Industry and Commerce issued precise regulations governing the export trade. Emil Schmidt, a former employee of the firm, has a clear recollection of the guidelines for sending goods abroad: »The regulations governing dispatch of goods abroad were set down precisely in a post-office manual [Postbuch]. Several customs declarations of content, sometimes even a certificate of origin of the goods in the consignment, had to be included. The postal language was French then.«
Sales abroad were handled mainly by foreign representatives or German exporters. Since foreign buyers rarely came to Oberstein to the bijouterie and chain dealers, Oberstein businesses that exported goods had representatives at many German and foreign spas and resorts. In 1936 Bengel offered the Milan wholesalers Ercole Leoni nickel-plated and German silver bracelets, gilt pins, chromium-plated bangles, nickel-plated children's watches, ear clips and nickel-plated collars. A 1938 invoice for devotional articles has been preserved. In 1938 zip chains were exported to Switzerland. Even as late as 1943 during the war, Bengel continued to export nickel-plated and chromium-plated wrist-watches, key chains and silver necklaces to Italy.
Immediately following the Second World War, Bengel re-established old business ties abroad. There is an entire file containing letters, confirmation of orders and invoices relating to the

Die ständig wechselnde Mode erforderte von den Bijouteriewaren-Herstellern eine sehr hohe Flexibilität in der Produktion, es mußten also unablässig neue Muster produziert werden, um den Kunden immer wieder neue Kaufanreize zu bieten. Die größeren Unternehmen gaben zweimal im Jahr eine neue Kollektion heraus, eine Kollektion bestand nicht selten aus bis zu 2000 Mustern. Bei dem großen Verkaufsanteil ins Ausland mußten die dort herrschenden, oft sehr unterschiedlichen Geschmacksrichtungen berücksichtigt werden. Werbung über Anzeigen in entsprechenden Fachzeitschriften ließen sich nicht nachweisen, ebenso haben sich keine Werbeprospekte erhalten.[59] (Abb. 119)

Der hohe Exportanteil der Obersteiner Firmen trug zwar den dort produzierten Modeschmuck in die ganze Welt, die geschäftliche Abwicklung solcher Auslandsgeschäfte war jedoch nicht ganz unproblematisch. In den 1930er Jahren mußte u.a. eine Exportvaluta-Erklärung gemäß Durchführungs-Verordnung zur Devisenverordnung an die Reichsbank abgegeben werden. Jedes Land hatte auch damals schon seine eigenen Einfuhrformalitäten und Zollbestimmungen, eine notwendige Rechtsverfolgung im Streitfall war nur mit erheblichem Aufwand möglich.

Wie aus einem erhaltenen Schriftwechsel hervorgeht, versuchte die Firma Bengel 1935 das Geld eines algerischen Schuldners über das Deutsche Generalkonsulat in Algier zu erhalten. Auch andere Unterlagen beweisen, wie schwierig es manchmal war, ausstehende Gelder aus dem Ausland einzutreiben. Die Firma Bengel holte sich auch Unterstützung bei einer Auslandsincasso- und Export-Interessenvertretung. Als gewissenhafter Geschäftsmann stellte Ernst Hartenberger sen. eine genaue Fakturenregulierung für ausländische Lieferanten auf. Um 1930 hatte man sich ein viersprachiges – Deutsch, Englisch, Französisch, Spanisch – Mahnschreiben drucken lassen.[60] Höflich aber bestimmend, machte man seine säumigen Kunden auf ausstehende Gelder aufmerksam.

Die Industrie- und Handelskammer gab genaue Anweisungen für das Auslandsgeschäft vor. Emil Schmidt, ein ehemaliger Mitarbeiter der Firma, erinnert sich noch genau an die Anweisungen für den Auslandsversand: »Die Versandvorschriften ins Ausland waren in einem Postbuch genau vorgeschrieben. Es mußten mehrere Zollinhaltserklärungen, manchmal auch noch ein Ursprungszeugnis der Sendung beigefügt werden. Die Postsprache war damals Französisch.«

Der Absatz ins Ausland erfolgte in der Hauptsache durch ausländische Vertreter oder deutsche Exporthäuser. Selten kam ein fremder Einkäufer zu den Bijouterie- und Kettenhändlern nach Oberstein. In vielen deutschen und ausländischen Badeorten waren Obersteiner Handelsfirmen vertreten.

wholesalers Ercole Leoni in Milan. In 1949 Oberstein inquires whether Leoni might be interested in chrome or gold-plated or »costume-jewelry bracelets«. Brooches are advertised as »delicate fantasy with stones or simulated ones«. In 1951 gilt bands are offered to Leoni for DM 1.65 each and chromium-plated bands for DM 1.50 each. A dozen were sold for DM 19.80 or DM 17.40, respectively.

One of Bengel's regular clients was Woolworth's, the world's largest emporium with rock-bottom prices serving the poor, founded by the American businessman Charles Summer in New York in 1879. The Frankfurt branch, F.W. Woolworth Co. GmbH, was founded in 1926. The largest continental European department store of its day, Karstadt, born of a merger in 1920 between Rudolph Karstadt (founded in 1881) and Theodor Althoff (founded in 1885), was another Bengel customer. Jewelry was sold primarily to department stores in Germany and abroad. Wholesalers, too, were Bengel customers; they sold to perfumeries and hairdressers. Bengel exported a major part of what they produced to France.

Two thick ledgers from the 1930s convey interesting insights into how export was handled at Bengel. These clients were both wholesalers and retailers (fig. 118). The ledgers are organized as follows: Vol. 1 is for »France and Overseas« whereas vol. 2 covers »Non-French countries«.

In France the great Paris department stores were the most important Bengel clients. (Appendix I, p. 279)

It goes without saying that Bengel, too, had suppliers since they did not manufacture all parts of a piece of jewelry: outsourcing was practized then as now. Some of these suppliers are revealed in the firm records that have come down to us. (Appendix II, p. 282)

The Bengel staff – reminiscences of Emil Schmidt, an employee

Manufacturers of bijouterie wares depended on having a staff that was loyal and worked efficiently, with the know-how to deal with what was, for its time, »high-tech« machinery. Employees, therefore, had to be highly skilled and trained mechanics and tool-makers. Even then competition was stiff; all such firms tried to manufacture products which others could not imitate and they even guilt chain-making machines and tools themselves to secure their competitive edge.

Works diaries and logs kept in the Idar-Oberstein City Archives are informative on the Bengel staff of the 1930s and 1940s. The personnel profile included goldsmiths and metalworkers specialized in jewelry-making, setters, tool-makers, tool-makers and machinists, turners, milling cutters, stores supervisors, errand boys and unskilled labor (Appendix IV, p. 284). In addition, there

Im Jahre 1936 wurden der Firma Ercole Leoni, Großhändler in Mailand, von Bengel vernickelte Armbänder, Armbänder in Altsilber, vergoldete Nadeln, verchromte Armreifen, vernickelte Kinderuhren und Ohr-Clips sowie vernickelte Colliers angeboten. Von 1938 hat sich eine Rechnung für gelieferte Heiligenartikel erhalten.
1938 wurden Reißverschlußketten in die Schweiz exportiert. Auch noch während des Krieges, 1943, lieferte die Firma Bengel vernickelte und verchromte Uhrarmbänder, Schlüsselketten und silberne Halsketten nach Italien.
Unmittelbar nach dem Zweiten Weltkrieg knüpfte man wieder Kontakte ins Ausland. Es hat sich ein ganzer Ordner mit Briefen, Auftragsbestätigungen und Rechnungen im Bezug auf den Großhändler Ercole Leoni in Mailand erhalten. 1949 fragt man aus Oberstein an, ob Uhrarmbänder in Chrom oder vergoldet von Interesse sind oder »Fantasie Armbänder«, als Broschen werden »feine Fantasie mit Steinen oder Simili« angeboten. Im Jahre 1951 werden vergoldete Bänder zu DM 1,65 das Stück bzw. verchromte Bänder zu DM 1,50 das Stück angeboten. Das Dutzend gibt es für DM 19,80 bzw. DM 17,40.
Zu den Einkäufern von Bengel-Produkten gehörte auch das größte Einheitspreisgeschäfts-Unternehmen der Welt, Woolworth, das 1879 von dem nordamerikanischen Kaufmann Charles Summer in New York gegründet worden war. Die Frankfurter Niederlassung F. W. Woolworth Co. GmbH wurde 1926 gegründet. Auch das größte europäische Warenhausunternehmen Karstadt, das 1920 durch die Fusion der Unternehmen Rudolph Karstadt (1881 gegr.) und Theodor Althoff (gegr. 1885) zustande kam, war Kunde bei Bengel. In erster Linie wurde der Schmuck an Kaufhäuser im In- und Ausland verkauft. Ebenso zählten Großhändler zu den Kunden, die dann wiederum Parfümerien und Friseure belieferten. Einen maßgeblichen Anteil ihrer Ware exportierte die Firma Bengel nach Frankreich.
Aus den 1930er Jahren haben sich zwei umfangreiche Buchhaltungsjournale der Firma Bengel erhalten, die einen interessanten Einblick in das Auslandsgeschäft der Firma geben. Bei den Kunden handelt es sich sowohl um Großhändler wie auch um Einzelhändler (Abb. 118). Diese Buchhaltungsjour-

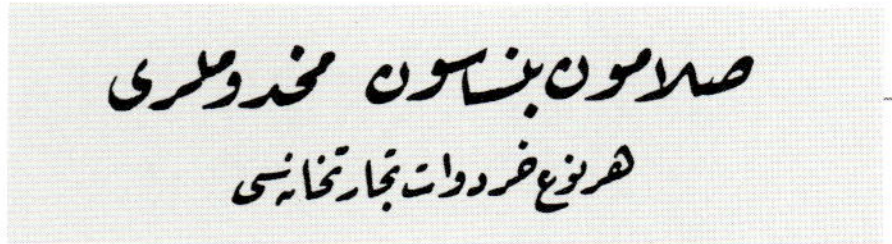

118 Klischee in arabischen Lettern einer vermutlich pakistanischen Schmuckfirma: »SALAMON BENSON, WIR FÜHREN JEDE ART VON SCHMUCK«, wohl 1930er Jahre, Nachlaß J. Bengel
Stamp of a presumably Pakistani jewelry firm in Arabic letters: »SALAMON BENSON, WE CARRY ALL KINDS OF JEWELRY«, probably 1930s, estate J. Bengel

119 Anzeigen-Klischee Jakob Bengel, 1930er Jahre
Advertisement block used by Jakob Bengel, 1930s

was the white-collar staff: Klara Wilhelm and Herta Kleine from Nahbollenbach, Lotte Muth from Oberstein (who married the machinist Willi Stumm, a Bengel employee). Albert Hügel managed the domestic trade. Otto Caesar was the accountant, a man who wrote all business correspondence by hand. Handwritten copies of this correspondence are kept in a special ringbinder, which is very thick. Copying the firm's correspondence required painstaking care since carelessness might cause ink to blot the letters, rendering them illegible. If that happened, they had to be rewritten. Otto Feikert was both a packer and errand boy. He did not even have a chair in the office, just his large packing table and a lectern. Ernst Hartenberg, sen., seems to have been on quite good terms with Feikert because he enjoyed taking him hunting, as old photos show. A Herr Heinz was one of the employees responsible for dispatch. Then there were sales representatives for both Germany and abroad such as Herr Rink and Herr Hügel. Finally, design pattern makers round off the personnel picture. Albert Roos, the pattern maker, lived in a flat provided by the firm. In the 1950s he set up on his own as a goldsmith.
The cottage industry, which employed mainly women, such as Hilde Knapp (1955–59, 1973–78), was extremely important. Women working at home had to prepare, couple and solder chain links which they took home with them from the factory for further processing. This work was done as a rule by women and even children. Bolt-ring and lobster clasps were also made in the cottage industry. According to Hilde Knapp, the blanks were brought to her home in the morning and picked up again the same evening or the next day.
Goldsmiths' apprenticeships could be served and commercial training certificates taken at Bengel. During the Second World War, a munitions worker was also on the staff – as in all firms at that time.
When researching into the history of any German firm during the 1930s, one soon realizes that almost no eyewitnesses are left alive to talk about those years. What a pleasant surprise it is, therefore, to come across a man like Emil Schmidt (b. 3 Dec. 1914 in Oberstein). Now he lives far from his native city in Gescher, Sauerland, but he enjoys reminiscing about Oberstein and

nale sind nach Band 1 »Frankreich und Überseegebiete« sowie Band 2 »Nichtfranzösische Länder« aufgeteilt.
In Frankreich spielten vor allem die großen Kaufhäuser in Paris als Auftraggeber eine große Rolle. (Anhang I, S. 279)
Selbstverständlich hatte auch die Firma Bengel ihre Zulieferfirmen, denn nicht alle Bestandteile eines Schmuckstücks wurden selbst hergestellt. Einige Geschäftspartner sind den erhaltenen Unterlagen zu entnehmen. (Anhang II, S. 282)

Die Belegschaft der Firma Bengel – Die persönlichen Erinnerungen des Mitarbeiters Emil Schmidt

Die Bijouteriewarenfirmen waren auf eine gut funktionierende Belegschaft angewiesen, die es verstand, mit den für die damalige Zeit »hochtechnischen Maschinen« umzugehen.
Es waren also Mitarbeiter nötig, die als ausgebildete Schlosser und Werkzeugmacher arbeiten konnten. Denn schon damals mußte man seine Produkte konkurrenzfähig machen: Jeder versuchte mit dem Bau eigener Kettenmaschinen und Werkzeuge eigene Produkte herzustellen, die nicht ohne weiteres zu kopieren waren, um damit einen Vorsprung am Markt zu haben.
Wie sich aus den im Stadtarchiv Idar-Oberstein erhaltenen Arbeitsbüchern entnehmen läßt, waren bei der Firma Bengel in den 1930er/40er Jahren vor allem Goldschmiede/Metallschmuckwarenarbeiter, Fasser, Werkzeugmacher, Werkzeugschlosser, Werkzeug-/Maschinenschlosser, Dreher, Fräser, Lagerverwalter, Packer, Botengänger und Hilfsarbeiter beschäftigt (Anhang IV, S. 284). Daneben gab es Angestellte im kaufmännischen Bereich: Klara Wilhelm und Herta Kleine aus Nahbollenbach, Lotte Muth aus Oberstein, letztere heiratete den bei Bengel beschäftigten Schlosser Willi Stumm. Albert Hügel war für das Inlandsgeschäft verantwortlich. Als Buchhalter war Otto Caesar angestellt. Er schrieb sämtliche Briefe mit der Hand. Die Zweitschrift dieser Korrespondenz wurden in einem besonders dafür vorgesehenen dicken Buch festgehalten, also handschriftlich kopiert. Diese Arbeit mußte besonders sorgfältig geschehen, da bei unsachgemäßer Ausführung die Tinte auslief, der Brief unleserlich wurde und noch einmal neu geschrieben werden mußte. Otto Feikert war

Arbeitsbuch
(Gesetz vom 26. Februar 1935, RGBl. I S. 311)
Nr. 190/8651
Hermann Ernst Hartenberger
(Vor- und Zuname, bei Frauen auch Geburtsname)
(Eigenhändige Unterschrift des Inhabers)

120 Arbeitsbuch Nr. 190/8651 von Hermann Ernst Hartenberger d.J., ausgestellt am 1.2.1936
Works log no. 190/8651 issued to Hermann Ernst Hartenberger, jun., on 1 Feb. 1936

the first firm he trained in, Jakob Bengel. From 1 September 1930 until 31 January 1934 Emil Schmidt trained as a clerk at Bengel. In the 1950s, from 1955 to 1959, he returned to Bengel as an employee at management level. He was responsible for acquiring new orders calculating production costs and supervising production.
To convey some idea of the »business climate«, working conditions and employer-employee relations in a firm like Bengel during the early 1930s, it is essential to include at least extracts of Emil Schmidt's recollections of that time.[61] (Appendix III, p. 282)
In the 1920s and 1930s Bengel employed a workforce of about 100. A photo of the workforce, which dates from about 1935, shows almost 60 employees: roughly one third women and two thirds men (fig. 121).
The Idar-Oberstein City Archives have kept the works logs and diaries of some of the Bengel workforce. A law that came into force on 26 February 1935 (RGBl. I S.311) required that all employees kept such logs. They give birth date and other personal data as well as all employers and the employment of the person keeping the log. (Appendix IV, p. 284)

The firm of Jakob Bengel in the 21st century

The foundation of the Stiftung Bengel by Christel Braun, née Hartenberger, the proprietor's eldest daughter, in 2001 ensured that the legacy of Jakob Bengel with its history of almost 130 years would continue. The importance of the Idar-Oberstein bijouterie and chain-manufacturing industry becomes clear when one looks into the infrastructure of the factory, some of which has been preserved and even, in part, put into operation again so that this legacy can be kept for future generations. The building of an industrial museum has given the old factory a new lease of life. Concomitantly, the establishment of a »Laboratory for Contemporary Jewelry Design«, which will be used by the »Fachbereich Edelstein- und Schmuckdesign der Fachhochschule Trier« [Precious stones and Jewelry Design Department of Trier Polytechnic], is to link up with the extremely creative phase the firm of Jakob Bengel underwent during the 1930s.

Packer und Botengänger. In der Firma hatte er gar keinen Stuhl, sondern nur seinen großen Packtisch und ein Stehpult zum Schreiben. Ernst Hartenberg sen. scheint aber ein recht freundschaftliches Verhältnis zu seinem Mitarbeiter Feikert gehabt zu haben, er nahm ihn gerne als Begleiter auf die Jagd mit, wie alte Fotos belegen. Im Versandbereich war u.a. Herr Heinz tätig. Ferner sind Inlands- und Auslandsreisende wie Herr Rink und Herr Hügel sowie Mustermacher zu nennen. Der Mustermacher Albert Roos hatte eine Wohnung in der Firma und machte sich in den 1950er Jahren als Goldschmied selbständig.

Auch bei der Firma Bengel spielten die Heimarbeiterinnen, wie Hilde Knapp (1955–59, 1973–78) eine wichtige Rolle. Die Tätigkeit der Heimarbeiterinnen bestand aus dem Einhängen, Richten und Zusammenlöten der Kettenglieder, die sie vorgearbeitet aus der Fabrik erhielten. In der Regel wurde diese Tätigkeit von Frauen und Kindern verrichtet. Auch Federringe und Karabiner wurden in Heimarbeit hergestellt. Nach Aussagen von Hilde Knapp wurde die Ware am Morgen zu ihr nach Hause gebracht und am Abend oder am folgenden Tag wieder abgeholt. Bei der Firma Bengel konnte man auch eine Goldschmiedelehre oder eine kaufmännische Ausbildung absolvieren. Während des Zweiten Weltkriegs waren bei der Firma Bengel – wie bei allen Firmen dieser Zeit – einige Rüstungsarbeiter beschäftigt.

Bei der Aufarbeitung einer Firmengeschichte, aus den 1930er Jahren, muß man leider sehr schnell feststellen, daß beinahe keine Zeitzeugen mehr greifbar sind, die aus diesen Jahren berichten könnten. Um so erfreulicher ist es, wenn man auf einen Mann wie Emil Schmidt (geb. 3.12.1914 in Oberstein) trifft, der heute zwar weit entfernt von seiner Heimatstadt in Gescher im Sauerland lebt, aber sich gerne an Oberstein und seine erste Ausbildungsstätte, die Firma Jakob Bengel, erinnert. Vom 1. September 1930 bis zum 31. Januar 1934 absolvierte Emil Schmidt seine kaufmännische Lehre bei Bengel. In den 50er Jahren, von 1955 bis 1959 war er dann nochmals als kaufmännischer Angestellter dort tätig. Ihm oblagen die Akquisition neuer Auftraggeber, die Kalkulation der produzierten Ware aber auch die Überwachung der Produktion. Um einen Einblick in das »Firmenklima«, die Arbeitsbedingungen und das Verhältnis zwischen Fabrikant und Arbeiter/Angestellter in einer Fabrik zu Beginn der 1930er Jahre zu bekommen, ist es wichtig, die persönlichen Erlebnisse Emil Schmidts in Auszügen wiederzugeben.[61] (Anhang III, S. 282)

In den 1920er und 1930er Jahren dürften ca. 100 Mitarbeiter bei der Firma Bengel beschäftigt gewesen sein. Auf einem Foto der Belegschaft, das um 1935 zu datieren ist, sind fast 60 Mitarbeiter zu sehen: etwa ein Drittel weibliche und zwei Drittel männliche Personen (Abb. 121).

121 Mitarbeiter der Fa. Jakob Bengel, um 1935:
Jakob Bengel employees, ca. 1935:

1. Ernst Hartenberger d.Ä. | sen.
2. Herr Späth, Aufseher | foreman
3. Herr Cullmann
4. Allwich Kessler
5. Otto Feikert
6. Ernst Bender
7. Otto Caesar
8. Hulda Schneider
9. Albert Roos
10. Sohn von Albert Hügel | Albert Hügel's son

Von einigen Mitarbeitern der Firma Bengel haben sich im Stadtarchiv Idar-Oberstein Arbeitsbücher erhalten. Zur Führung eines solchen Arbeitsbuches war man laut Gesetz vom 26. Februar 1935, RGBl. I S. 311 verpflichtet. In diesen Arbeitsbüchern sind Geburtsdatum, weitere persönliche Daten und alle Arbeitgeber sowie die Funktion des Beschäftigten genannt. (Anhang IV, S. 284)

Die Firma Jakob Bengel im 21. Jahrhundert

Mit der Gründung der Stiftung Bengel durch die älteste Tochter Christel Braun, geb. Hartenberger, im Jahre 2001, kann das Erbe der Firma Jakob Bengel mit einer fast 130jährigen Firmengeschichte, weitergeführt werden. Die Bedeutung der Idar-Obersteiner Bijouterie- und Kettenindustrie läßt sich anhand der erhaltenen und auch teilweise wieder in Gang gesetzten Infrastruktur der Fabrik nachvollziehen und für zukünftige Generationen bewahren. Mit dem Aufbau eines Industriemuseums wird der einstige Fabrikationsbetrieb zu neuem Leben erweckt. Mit der gleichzeitigen Einrichtung eines »Labors für zeitgenössisches Schmuckdesign«, das dem Fachbereich Edelstein- und Schmuckdesign der Fachhochschule Trier zur Verfügung stehen wird, soll an die künstlerisch äußerst kreative Phase der Firma Jakob Bengel in den 1930er Jahren angeknüpft werden.

1 Karl Meitner-Heckert: Modischer Zeitschmuck – Echt oder unecht?, in: DGZ Nr. 2, 1925, S. 3f.
2 In der einschlägigen Literatur zum Thema Modeschmuck werden die Schmuckstücke als deutsche oder französiche Arbeiten der frühen 1930er Jahre genannt: Berlin 1972, Nr. 100; Berlin 1977, S. 136; Hartleb 1985, S. 6, 7 Abb. 1, 2, Abb. 7; Raulet 1985, S. 262f; Erfurt 1987/88, S. 27 Nr. 273–275, Nr. 279, 295, 298, 301; Davidov/Redington 1988, S. 53–55; Weber 1990, S. 216 Nr. 336, 337, S. 259 Nr. 496, 497; Farneti 1991, S. 78 Nr. 120, 121, S. 80 Nr. 123, 124, S. 81 Nr. 125, S. 82 Nr. 127, 128, S. 136 Nr. 208, 209; Moro 1995, S. 47, 124–126; Möller 1996, S. 125; Darmstadt/München 1997/98. In Weber/Möller 1999 konnte der Schmuck zum ersten Mal in einer Publikation als Bengel-Schmuck vorgestellt werden.
3 Die beiden Städte Idar und Oberstein wurden am 1.10.1933 vereint zu Idar-Oberstein.
4 Raulet 1985, S. 256
5 Für hilfreiche Unterstützung bei meinen Recherchen danke ich sehr herzlich: Herrn Rauscher, Stadtarchiv-Idar-Oberstein; Herrn Lindemann, Stadtverwaltung Idar-Oberstein; Andrea Richter-Mahlo, Leipzig; Herrn und Frau Braun, Fa. Jakob Bengel; dem Sammlerehepaar gilt mein besonderer Dank für die großzügige Unterstützung
6 Galalith. Die Geschichte eines Kunststoffs 1904–1954, 1954, S. 8; Ullmann, Enzyklopädie, 2. Aufl. V. S. 28–30
7 Galalith, 1954, S. 9
8 Galalith, 1954, S. 23ff.: 1909/10 Fa. M. Oechsler in Weißenburg, Bezeichnung »Osalith«, 1912: in England wurde die Erinoid Ltd. gegründet, Bezeichnung »Erinoid«; 1919: in Frankreich nimmt die Fa. Compagnie du Celluloid Petitcollin-Oyonnithe die Kunsthornerzeugung auf, Bezeichnung »GALA«; 1920/21 in Wien wird die Akalit Kunsthornwerke AG gegründet, Bezeichnung »AKALIT«. Weitere Kunsthornprodukte kommen in den 20er Jahren in Europa auf den Markt: ERGOLITH; ROALIT; CASELITH; MODELITH; IDEALITH; LITHOCORN. 1927 wurde in Japan Kunsthorn unter dem Namen LACTOLOID hergestellt.

1 Karl Meitner-Heckert: Modischer Zeitschmuck – Echt oder unecht?, in: DGZ Nr. 2, 1925, p. 3f.
2 In specialist publications dealing with costume jewelry, these pieces are called early 1930s German or French work: Berlin 1972, Nr. 100; Berlin 1977, p. 136; Hartleb 1985, p. 6, p. 7 figs. 1, 2, fig. 7; Raulet 1985, p. 262f; Erfurt 1987/88, p. 27 nos. 273–275, nos. 279, 295, 298, 301; Davidov/Redington 1988, pp. 53–55; Weber 1990, p. 216 nos. 336, 337, p. 259 nos. 496, 497; Farneti 1991, p. 78 nos. 120, 121, p. 80 nos. 123, 124, p. 81 no. 125, p. 82 nos. 127, 128, p. 136 nos. 208, 209; Moro 1995, p. 47, 124–126; Möller 1996, p. 125; Darmstadt/Munich 1997/98. In Weber/Möller 1999 the jewelry was published for the first time as Bengel jewelry.
3 The two cities of Idar and Oberstein were united on 3 Oct. 1933 and are since then known as Idar-Oberstein.
4 Raulet 1985, p. 256
5 For their help and support of my research I would like to express my thanks to: Herr Rauscher, Stadtarchiv-Idar-Oberstein; Herr Lindemann, Stadtverwaltung Idar-Oberstein; Andrea Richter-Mahlo, Leipzig; Herr and Frau Braun, of Jakob Bengel. I owe an enormous debt of gratitude to the above mentioned collectors for their generous support.
6 Galalith. Die Geschichte eines Kunststoffs 1904–1954, 1954, p. 8; Ullmann, Enzyklopädie, 2nd ed. V. pp. 28–30
7 Galalith, 1954, p. 9
8 Galalith, 1954, p. 23f.: 1909/10 the firm of M. Oechsler in Weißenburg, called ›Osalith‹ in 1912: in England Erinoid Ltd was founded, with its product called ›Erinoid‹; in 1919: the French Compagnie du Celluloid Petitcollin-Oyonnithe began to make synthetic horn, called ›GALA‹; in 1920/21 Akalit Kunsthornwerke AG was founded in Vienna to make ›AKALIT‹. Other synthetic horn produced in Europe came on the market in the 1920s as: ERGOLITH; ROALIT; CASELITH; MODELITH; IDEALITH and LITHOCORN. In 1927 artificial horn was produced in Japan under the trade name of LACTOLOID.
9 I would like to thank Professor Otto Krätz, Starnberg, for kindly imparting this information to me.
10 Between 1912 and 1921 a »Fachzeitschrift für Fabrikation und Handel von Kunsthorn Marke ›Galalith‹ und Kunsthorn-Waren« [»Specialist journal for the manufacture of and trade in synthetic horn, trade name ›Galalith‹, and synthetic horn wares«] was published in Leipzig.
11 DGZ, Nr. 27, 1938, p. 262
12 Die Schaulade, 10.Jg. Heft 3, p. 143
13 Not all, however, were available for in-depth research.
14 Catalogue *Wilhelm Wagenfeld Schmuck*, ed. Beate Manske, Wilhelm Wagenfeld Stiftung, Bremen 2001
15 Catalogue *Hugo Leven: Entwürfe und Objekte zwischen Jugendstil und Art Déco*, compiled by the Kulturamt der Stadt Hanau Verwaltung der Museen, Museum Hanau Schloß Philippsruhe, 2001
16 Die Metallwerkstatt am Bauhaus, Berlin 1992, p. 7
17 Raulet, 1985, p. 255
18 Gabardi, 1999: Jean Després, pp. 194–201
19 Rudolf Rücklin, Nationaler Schmuck, in: DGZ, Nr. 49, 1933, p. 528
20 It can be assumed that the firm could not entirely avoid making final plaquettes for the Winterhilfswerk, as is mentioned elsewhere, nor did it want to avoid making them even though no evidence for this is extant.
21 Die Schaulade, 10. Jg. Heft 3, 1934, p. 141, p. 143
22 Almost all pieces shown in Becker 1991, p. 199 and elsewhere can be traced to the Bengel Pattern Books. Cf. patterns 19.058 (Cat.no. 79), 18.505 (Cat.no. 38), (Cat.no. 39), (Cat.no. 80), (Cat.no. 97).
23 See PB, vol. X, reference at mod. no. 20.117
24 Farneti 1991, p. 122
25 Farneti 1991, p. 116, p. 135, p. 140. The Musée du Peigne et des Matières Plastiques, Place Georges Pompidou, in Oyonnax presents an excellent survey of what was produced at Bonaz.
26 Triolet 1999, p. 70
27 Brunialti 1997, p. 42, p. 43
28 Davidov/Redington, 1988, p. 53
29 Worreschke 1925, p. 23
30 Festschrift 1928, p. 43
31 Deutsche Illustrierte Zeitung 1892, p. 37

9 Für freundliche Auskünfte danke ich Herrn Professor Otto Krätz, Starnberg
10 Zwischen 1912 und 1921 war in Leipzig eine »Fachzeitschrift für Fabrikation und Handel von Kunsthorn Marke »Galalith« und Kunsthorn-Waren« erschienen.
11 DGZ, Nr. 27, 1938, S. 262
12 Die Schaulade, 10. Jg. Heft 3, S. 143
13 Nur ein Teil der Musterbücher stand für eingehende Recherchen zur Verfügung.
14 Katalog *Wilhelm Wagenfeld Schmuck,* hrsg. Beate Manske, Wilhelm Wagenfeld Stiftung Bremen 2001
15 Katalog *Hugo Leven – Entwürfe und Objekte zwischen Jugendstil und Art Déco,* hrsg. Kulturamt der Stadt Hanau Verwaltung der Museen, Museum Hanau Schloß Philippsruhe, 2001
16 Die Metallwerkstatt am Bauhaus, Berlin 1992, S. 7
17 Raulet, 1985, S. 255
18 Gabardi, 1999: Jean Després, S. 194–201
19 Rudolf Rücklin, Nationaler Schmuck, in: DGZ, Nr. 49, 1933, S. 528
20 Es ist davon auszugehen, daß man sich auch der Produktion von Schlußplaketten für das Winterhilfswerk, von der noch an anderer Stelle berichtet wird, nicht ganz entziehen konnte und wollte, auch wenn sich hierfür keine Belege erhalten haben.
21 Die Schaulade, 10. Jg. Heft 3, 1934, S. 141, 143
22 Die u.a. bei Becker 1991, S. 199 abgebildeten Schmuckstücke lassen sich fast alle in den Musterbüchern bei Bengel nachweisen. Vergleiche Muster 19.058 (Kat.-Nr. 79), Muster 18.505 (Kat.-Nr. 38), (Kat.-Nr. 39), (Kat.-Nr. 80), (Kat.-Nr. 97).
23 s. MB, Bd. X, Hinweis bei Mod.-Nr. 20117
24 Farneti 1991, S. 122
25 Farneti 1991, S. 116, 135, 140. Im Musée du Peigne et des Matières Plastiques am Place Georges Pompidou in Oyonnax kann man sich einen guten Überblick über die dort entstandene Produktion verschaffen.
26 Triolet 1999, S.70
27 Brunialti 1997, S. 42, 43
28 Davidov/Redington, 1988, S.53
29 Worreschke 1925, S. 23
30 Festschrift 1928, S. 43
31 Deutsche Illustrierte Zeitung 1892, S. 37
32 Jahresberichte der Handelskammer 1893, S. 23, Stadtarchiv Idar-Oberstein
33 Jahresberichte der Handelskammer 1905, S. 34, Stadtarchiv Idar-Oberstein
34 Im Stadtarchiv Idar-Oberstein hat sich eine Abschrift eines Textes zum Streik von 1907 erhalten
35 Worreschke, 1925, S. 2
36 DGZ, 24.8.1918, Nr. 35–36, S. 178f.
37 Nationale Zeitung vom 11.12.1934, Stadtarchiv Idar-Oberstein
38 Fischer, 1956, S. 53
39 Die Aufgabe, Zeitschrift für Wirtschaft und Forschung, 2. Jg. Januar 1949, S. 35: Jahresbericht 1948 der Fachgruppe Schmuck- und Metallwaren Idar-Oberstein
40 DGZ, Nr. 5, 1950, S. 116
41 Hisserich 1890, S. 148
42 Roth 1986, S. 199
43 Fischer, 1956, S. 53
44 DGZ, Nr. 24, 1920, S. 407
45 Geburtsakte Nr. 112: Im Jahre Tausend Achthundert achtundvierzig am siebenzehnten des Monats Juni um vier Uhr des Nachmittags erschien vor mir, dem Zivilstands-Beamten der Bürgermeisterei Oberstein, im Amte Oberstein, Fürstentum Birkenfeld Friedrich Bengel wohnhaft zu Oberstein alt neunundzwanzig Jahre, Taglöhner und machte die Anzeige, daß seine Ehefrau Elisabetha Krummenauer ohne Geschäft in hiesiger Stadt am fünfzehnten des Monats Juni um Zwölf des Nachts mit einem Kinde männlichen Geschlechts niedergekommen sei, dem sie, die Eltern, den Vornamen Friedrich Jacob geben wollten. Über obige Erklärung, die in Gegenwart zweier Zeugen, nämlich: des Philipp Werle alt neunundzwanzig Jahre, Goldschmidt, wohnhaft zu Oberstein und des Jacob Debes alt siebenundzwanzig Jahre Goldschmied, wohnhaft zu Oberstein, geschehen war, habe ich in Gegenwart des Anzeigers und der Zeugen gegenwärtigen Akt in doppeltem Original aufgesetzt, welch

32 Jahresberichte der Handelskammer 1893, p. 23, Stadtarchiv Idar-Oberstein
33 Jahresberichte der Handelskammer 1905, p. 34, Stadtarchiv Idar-Oberstein
34 A copy of a text on the 1907 strike has been preserved in the Idar-Oberstein City Archives (Stadtarchiv Idar-Oberstein).
35 Worreschke, 1925, p. 2
36 DGZ, 24.8.1918, Nr. 35–36, p. 178f.
37 Nationale Zeitung of 11 Dec. 1934, Stadtarchiv Idar-Oberstein
38 Fischer, 1956, p. 53
39 Die Aufgabe, Zeitschrift für Wirtschaft und Forschung, 2. Jg. January 1949, p. 35: Jahresbericht 1948 der Fachgruppe Schmuck- und Metallwaren Idar-Oberstein
40 DGZ, Nr. 5, 1950, p. 116
41 Hisserich 1890, p. 148
42 Roth 1986, p. 199
43 Fischer, 1956, p. 53
44 DGZ, Nr. 24, 1920, p. 407
45 Birth certificate no. 112: »In the year one thousand eight hundred and forty-eight there appeared before me on the seventeenth of the month of June at four o'clock in the afternoon, Friedrich Bengel, civil servant of the Oberstein mayoralty, in the Oberstein office, Duchy of Birkenfeld, inhabitant of Oberstein, twenty-nine years of age, day-laborer, and made known that his spouse, Elisabetha Krummenauer, without a profession in this city, bore a child of male sex on the fifteenth of the month of June at midnight, to whom they, the parents, desired to give the Christian names Friedrich Jacob. Of the above declaration, which was made in the presence of two witnesses, namely Philipp Werle, twenty-nine years of age and domiciled in Oberstein, and Jacob Debes, twenty-seven years of age, domiciled in Oberstein, I have, in the presence of the declarant and the witnesses, had two certified copies made which, after having been read, were signed by the comparant, the witnesses and me ...«.
46 Casper, n. d. [1975] pp. 42, 43
47 Casper, n. d. [1975] p. 42, p. 43
48 Eloxal consists of pure aluminium. It can be colored by certain processes and hardened; it is light-weight and does not oxidize.
49 Preserved as a letterhead, this drawing can be viewed at the Idar-Oberstein Department of Building Control and Inspection (Bauamt) and elsewhere; cf. Kulturdenkmäler in Rheinland-Pfalz. Kreis Birkenfeld, Vol. 11, 1993, p. 216, p. 248
50 Plans in color of the front and back of the mansion as well as the employee housing are kept at the Bauamt in Idar-Oberstein.
51 Die Schaulade, 10. Jg. Heft 3, 1934, p. 141, p. 142
52 Even then individual parts for objects to be manufactured were bought in. As this example shows, individual elements came from Czechoslovakia (Kr. = Kronen/er).
53 It is astonishing that lower costs were calculated for wares sent abroad. It must be assumed, however, that customs duties, tax, carriage and packing would be added.
54 »Since steel polishing balls produce grey scum on first use, it is recommended that the balls be thoroughly cleansed of all impurities adhering to them from manufacture before they are used. That is done very simply as follows. In approx. 7 liters of distilled water dissolve 250 grams of potassium cyanide, wash the balls in this solution, then rinse them clean in distilled water (the potassium cyanide solution can be used more than once): now run the balls in the polishing-cask for about 1 day and then rinse this out thoroughly with clean water. The balls are now ready for use and a snow-white lather is induced when Venetian polishing soap is used in polishing. Jakob Bengel, Metallwarenfabrik, Oberstein«
55 The necklace Cat.no. 218 still has its original tag marked »Original Julienne«.
56 No explanation has been found for why the firm name is written »Jakob« with a »k« although the founder's name is entered on his birth as »Jacob« with a »c«.
57 The Deutscher Goldschmiedekalender, Leipzig 1940, p. 118, has the entry »JB Bengel, Jakob Idar-Oberstein (Chrom-Durchziehketten/Chrome chain with slide)«.
58 A postcard with a view of the »Trade Fair Palace Specks Hof, Leipzig« has been preserved in the estate. The building in which the Leipzig Fair was held was very showy and grand, with several storeys.

nach Vorlesung derselben vom Comparenten, den Zeugen und mir unterschrieben wurden ...«.

46 Casper, o. J. (1975) S. 42, 43

47 Casper, o. J. (1975) S. 42, 43

48 Eloxal besteht aus Reinaluminium. Es kann in bestimmten Verfahren gefärbt und gehärtet werden, es hat ein leichtes Gewicht und oxidiert nicht.

49 Erhalten hat sich diese Zeichnung als Briefkopf, der sich u.a. im Stadtbauamt Idar-Oberstein befindet; vergl. Kulturdenkmäler in Rheinland-Pfalz. Kreis Birkenfeld, Bd. 11, 1993, S. 216, S. 248

50 Im Bauamt von Idar-Oberstein haben sich farbig angelegte Pläne von Vorder- und Rückansicht des Wohnhauses sowie der Werkswohnungen erhalten.

51 Die Schaulade, 10. Jg. Heft 3, 1934, S. 141, 142

52 Schon damals hat man Einzelteile für die Produktion zugekauft. Wie dieses Beispiel zeigt, kamen einzelne Bestandteile aus der Tschechoslowakei (Kr. = Kronen).

53 Es ist erstaunlich, daß die Ware für das Ausland preiswerter kalkuliert wurde. Man muß davon ausgehen, daß noch Zoll, Steuer, Fracht und Verpackung hinzukamen.

54 »Da Stahlpolierkugeln beim erstmaligen Gebrauch einen grauen Schaum abgeben, so empfiehlt es sich, die Kugeln, bevor sie zum Polieren verwandt werden, erst gründlich von allem durch die Fabrikation anhaftenden Schmutz zu reinigen. Dasselbe geschicht auf folgende sehr einfache Weise. In ca. 7 Liter reinem Wasser löse man 250 Gramm Cyankalium, in dieser Lösung wasche man die Kugeln aus, spüle sie dann sauber in reinem Wasser ab (die Cyankaliumlösung ist öfters brauchbar): nunmehr läßt man die Kugeln in Wasser, in welchem ein entsprechendes Quantum Soda aufgelöst ist, ca. 1 Tag in der Poliertrommel laufen und spült dieselben dann gründlich mit sauberem Wasser ab. Die Kugeln sind nun gebrauchsfertig und es erzeugt sich beim Polieren mit venezianischer Polierseife ein schneeweiser Schaum. Jakob Bengel, Metallwarenfabrik, Oberstein«

55 An dem Collier Kat.-Nr. 218 hat sich ein Anhänger mit der Aufschrift »Original Julienne« erhalten.

56 es konnte nicht geklärt werden, warum im Namenszug der Firma »Jakob« mit »k« geschrieben wird, obwohl sich der Firmengründer laut Geburtsurkunde mit »c« schrieb.

57 Im deutschen Goldschmiedekalender, Leipzig 1940, S. 118, ist die Eintragung »JB Bengel, Jakob Idar-Oberstein (Chrom-Durchziehketten)« zu finden.

58 Im Nachlaß hat sich eine Postkarte mit Ansicht des »Meßpalast Specks Hof, Leipzig« erhalten, einem äußerst repräsentativen mehrstöckigen Messegebäude.

59 Im Nachlaß hat sich ein kleiner Druckstempel erhalten »Unechte Bijouterie aller Art Jakob Bengel Oberstein« mit Abbildungen von kaum zu erkennenden Schmuckstücken. Die Verwendung dieses Klischees konnte nicht geklärt werden.

60 »Ich mache hiermit darauf aufmerksam, daß die nebenstehend aufgeführten Rechnungen bisher von Ihnen nicht beglichen wurden. Unter Bezugnahme auf die zwischen uns vereinbarten Bedingungen bitte ich hiermit höflich um sofortige Überweisung meines Guthabens im Betrage von ... Sollte dieser Betrag nicht bis zum ... in meinem Besitz sein, oder ich bis dahin nichts Gegenteiliges von Ihnen hören, werde ich mir erlauben, mein Guthaben zuzüglich der enstehenden Kosten am ... durch Postnachnahme/Bankquittung/Tratte einzuziehen, wovon Sie gefl. Vormerkung nehmen wollen. Für Ihren ferneren Bedarf empfehle ich mich Ihnen hochachtungsvoll Jakob Bengel.

61 Herrn Emil Schmidt danke ich sehr herzlich für seine freundlichen Auskünfte.

59 There is a little stamp is in the estate bearing the words »Unechte Bijouterie aller Art Jakob Bengel Oberstein«/»Simulated bijouterie of all kinds Jakob Bengel« with representations of pieces of jewelry which are virtually unidentifiable. The use of such stamps could not be clarified.

60 »Herewith I wish to draw your attention to the circumstance that the enclosed invoices have not yet been paid. With reference to the conditions agreed on between us, I hereby request you to transfer at once the money owed to the sum of ... Should this sum not be in my possession by ... or if I have not heard anything from you to the contrary, I shall take the liberty of debiting to my account the sum owed on ... by carriage forward/banker's order/draft/ for which you will be so kind as to make provision. Should you need anything else, I look forward to receiving further orders from you, Your obedient servant, Jakob Bengel.«

61 I am greatly indebted to Herr Emil Schmidt for so kindly imparting this information.

Alle Maßangaben in mm

h.L	=	halbe Länge
L	=	Länge
H	=	Höhe
B	=	Breite
Ø	=	Durchmesser
Bd.	=	Band
Kat.-Nr.	=	Katalog-Nummer
MB	=	Musterbuch
M-Nr.	=	Modellnummer
Nr.	=	Kat.-Nr.
p. Dtz.	=	per Dutzend
Rs	=	Rückseite
V	=	Variante in einer anderen Galalithfarbe vorhanden
Vs	=	Vorderseite

Kursiv gesetzte Informationen stammen aus den Musterbüchern.

Zur Angabe der Modell-Nummer: Das ausgeführte Schmuckstück entspricht in Gestaltung und Materialzusammensetzung genau den Angaben im Musterbuch (Modellnummer). Es gibt aber auch Schmuckstücke, bei denen nur Details der Entwürfe mit der tatsächlichen Ausführung übereinstimmen. Einzelne Entwurfsmotive sind somit in mehreren Modellen wiederzufinden.

Detaillierte Angaben zu Technik und Material der Schmuckstücke finden Sie ab S. 47 ff.

All measurements in mm

h.L	=	Half length
L	=	Length
H	=	Height
W	=	Width
Ø	=	Diameter
B	=	Back
Cat. no.	=	Catalogue number
F	=	Front
M. no.	=	Model number
No.	=	Cat. no.
PB	=	Pattern book
V	=	Variant available in a different Galalith color
Vol.	=	Volume

Data given in italics is taken from the pattern books.

Refering to the model number: In design and material composition the pieces of jewelry are identical with the information given in the pattern book (model number). However, there are also examples in which only details of the drafts correspond to the actual pieces of jewelry. Some motifs of design can therefore be found in several models.

You can find detailed information on techniques and materials on pp. 46 ff.

A U S W A H L

COLLECTION 1931

S E L E C T I O N

HALSKETTE MIT KRAWATTEN-ANHÄNGER, 1931
Gelbmetall, ohne Verschluß
Halskette: L 780, Anhänger: H 105
MB Bd. VIII, S. 324, M-Nr. 18.116

01

CHAIN WITH TIE FOB, 1931
Pinchbeck, no clasp
Chain: L 780; fob: H 105
PB Vol. VIII, p. 324, M. no. 18.116

COLLIER, 1931/32
Messing, Federringverschluß, Glas
Halskette: L 400

▸ **02**

NECKLACE, 1931/32
Brass; bolt-ring clasp; glass
Chain: L 400

COLLIER, 1931
Gelbmetall, Schraubverschluß
Halskette: L 600
MB Bd. X, S. 216, M-Nr. 20.671,
2.5.31, 10,–

03

NECKLACE, 1931
Pinchbeck, screw clasp
Chain: L 600
PB Vol. X, p. 216, M. no. 20.671,
2.5.31, 10,–

COLLIER, 1931
Messing verchromt, Federring-verschluß »GARANTIE***«, teilweise zweifarbig lackiert
Halskette: L 390
MB Bd.VIII, S. 329, M-Nr. 18.136, vor 16.7.31

▶ **04**

NECKLET, 1931
Brass, chromium-plated; bolt-ring clasp »GARANTIE***«; partly lacquered in two colors
Chain: L 390
PB Vol.VIII, p. 329, M. no. 18.136, before 16.7.31

ARMBAND, 1931
Messing verchromt, Federringverschluß »GARANTIE***«, teilweise dreifarbig lackiert
L 180, B 30
MB Bd. VIII, S. 328, M-Nr. 18.133, vor 16.7.31

05

BRACELET, 1931
Brass, chromium-plated; bolt-ring clasp »GARANTIE***«; partly lacquered in three colors
L 180, W 30
PB Vol. VIII, p. 328, M. no. 18.133, before 16.7.31

ARMBAND, 1931
Messing verchromt, teilweise zweifarbig lackiert, Federringverschluß
L 170, B 42
MB Bd. IX, S. 51, M-Nr. 18.515, 24.8.31

06

BRACELET, 1931
Brass, chromium-plated; partly lacquered in two colors; bolt-ring clasp
L 170, W 42
PB Vol. IX, p. 51, M. no. 18.515, 24.8.31

ARMBAND, 1931
Messing, Federringverschluß
L 175, B 26
MB Bd. IX, S. 61, M-Nr. 18.551A,
24.8.31, 12,–

07

BRACELET, 1931
Brass, bolt-ring clasp
L 175, W 26
PB Vol. IX, p. 61, M. no. 18.551A,
24.8.31, 12,–

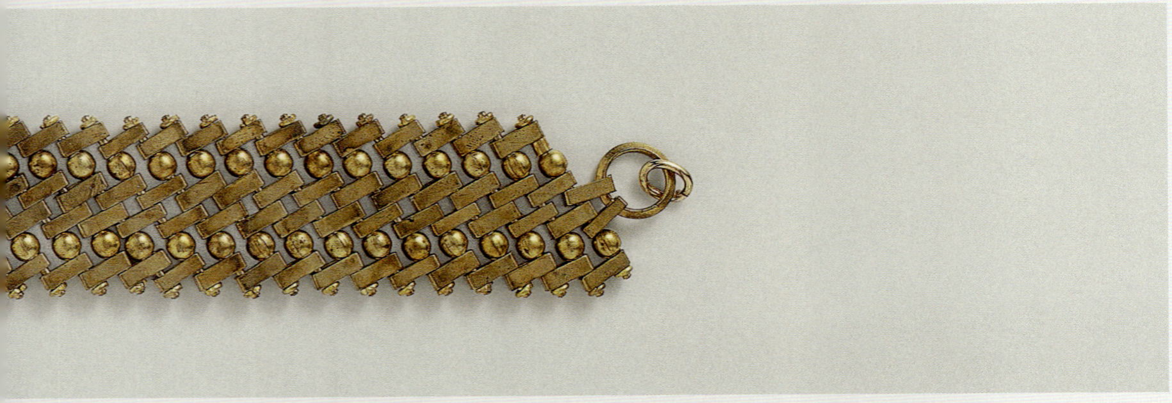

ARMBAND, 1931
Messing verchromt, Federring-
verschluß »GARANTIE***«, teilweise
lackiert
L 180, B 35
MB Bd. VIII, S. 130, M-Nr. 17.337,
vor 16.7.31

08

BRACELET, 1931
Brass, chromium-plated; bolt-ring clasp
»GARANTIE***«; partly lacquered
L 180, W 35
PB Vol. VIII, p. 130, M. no. 17.337, before
16.7.31

COLLIER, 1931
Messing verchromt, Federringverschluß, teilweise dreifarbig lackiert
Halskette: L 390
MB Bd.VIII, S. 329, M-Nr. 18.135, vor 16.7.31

09

NECKLET, 1931
Brass, chromium-plated; bolt-ring clasp; partly lacquered in three colors
Chain: L 390
PB Vol.VIII, p. 329, M. no. 18.135, before 16.7.31

COLLIER, 1931
Messing verchromt, Federringverschluß, teilweise lackiert
Halskette: L 390
MB Bd.VIII, S. 329, M-Nr. 18.136, vor 16.7.31

10

NECKLET, 1931
Brass, chromium-plated; bolt-ring clasp; partly lacquered
Chain: L 390
PB Vol.VIII, p. 329, M. no. 18.136, before 16.7.31

COLLIER, 1931
Messing verchromt, Federringverschluß »GARANTIE***«, zweifarbig lackiert Vs und Rs
Halskette: L 390
MB Bd. VIII, S. 329, M-Nr. 18.134, vor 16.7.31

11

NECKLET, 1931
Brass, chromium-plated; bolt-ring clasp »GARANTIE***«; lacquered in two colors F and B
Chain: L 390
PB Vol. VIII, p. 329, M. no. 18.134, before 16.7.31

HALSKETTE MIT ABHÄNGUNG, 1931
Messing vernickelt, teilweise schwarz lackiert, Federringverschluß Stempelung GERMANY, marmoriertes Galalith
Halskette: L 450, Anhänger: H 88
MB Bd. IX, S. 79, M-Nr. 18.689, 2.12.31

▶12

CHAIN WITH PENDANT, 1931
Brass, nickel-plated, partly lacquered black; bolt-ring clasp stamped GERMANY; marbled Galalith
Chain: L 450; pendant: H 88
PB Vol. IX, p. 79, M. no. 18.689, 2.12.31

SAUTOIR, 1931
Messing vernickelt, Federringverschluß, »GARANTIE***«, Galalith
Halskette: L 560, Anhänger: L 100
MB Bd. IX, S. 59, M-Nr. 18.546,
14.8.31, 25,–

◀ 13

GUARD CHAIN, 1931
Brass, nickel-plated; bolt-ring clasp »GARANTIE***«; Galalith
Chain: L 560; pendant: L 100
PB Vol. IX, p. 59, M. no. 18.546,
14.8.31, 25,–

HALSKETTE MIT ANHÄNGER, 1931
Messing verchromt, Federringverschluß, Galalith
Halskette: L 570, Anhänger: H 100
MB Bd. IX, S. 72, M-Nr. 18.586,
22.10.31, 24,–

14

CHAIN WITH PENDANT, 1931
Brass, chromium-plated; bolt-ring clasp; Galalith
Chain: L 570; pendant: H 100
PB Vol. IX, p. 72, M. no. 18.586,
22.10.31, 24,–

HALSKETTE MIT ANHÄNGER, 1931
Messing verchromt, Federringverschluß »GARANTIE***«, Galalith
Halskette: L 500, Anhänger: H 90
MB Bd. IX, S. 101, M-Nr. 18.697, 2.12.31

15

CHAIN WITH PENDANT, 1931
Brass, chromium-plated; bolt-ring clasp »GARANTIE***«; Galalith
Chain: L 500; pendant: H 90
PB Vol. IX, p. 101, M. no. 18.697, 2.12.31

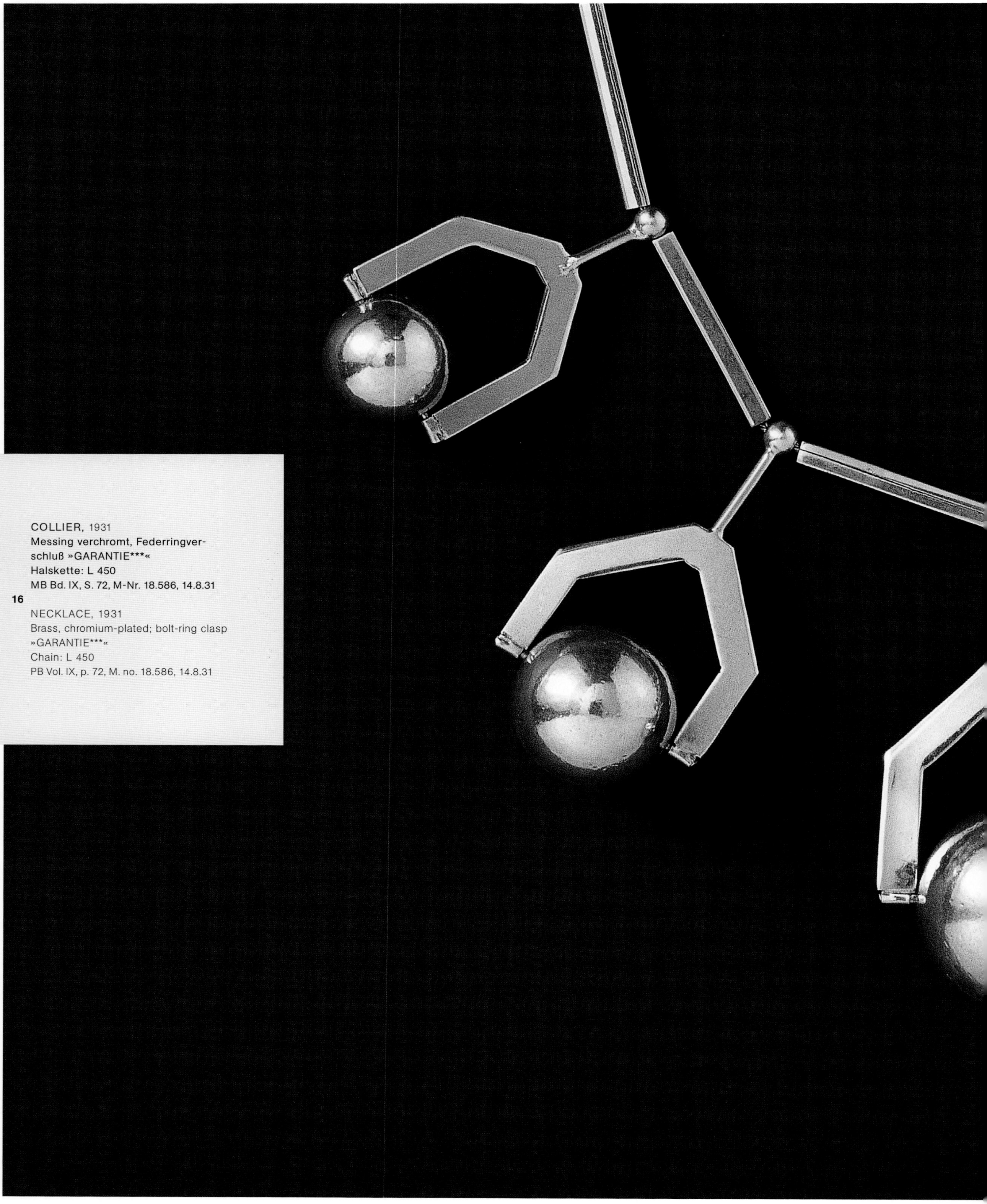

COLLIER, 1931
Messing verchromt, Federringverschluß »GARANTIE*«**
Halskette: L 450
MB Bd. IX, S. 72, M-Nr. 18.586, 14.8.31

16

NECKLACE, 1931
Brass, chromium-plated; bolt-ring clasp »GARANTIE***«
Chain: L 450
PB Vol. IX, p. 72, M. no. 18.586, 14.8.31

HALSKETTE MIT ANHÄNGER,
UM 1931
Messing vernickelt, Federringverschluß, Galalith
Halskette: L 580, Anhänger: H 100

17

CHAIN WITH PENDANT, CA 1931
Brass, nickel-plated; bolt-ring clasp; Galalith
Chain: L 580; pendant: H 100

HALSKETTE MIT ANHÄNGER, 1931
Messing vernickelt, Federringverschluß, Glas/Galalith, Wolkengalalith
Halskette: L 730, Anhänger: H 100
MB Bd. VIII, S. 375, M-Nr. 18.312, 6.7.31

18

CHAIN WITH PENDANT, 1931
Brass, nickel-plated; bolt-ring clasp; glass/Galalith, cloudy Galalith
Chain: L 730; pendant: H 100
PB Vol. VIII, p. 375, M. no. 18.312, 6.7.31

HALSKETTE MIT ANHÄNGER, 1931
Messing verchromt, Federringverschluß »GARANTIE***«, Galalith
Halskette: L 610, Anhänger: H 95
MB Bd. VIII, S. 375, M-Nr. 18.311, 6.7.31

19

CHAIN WITH PENDANT, 1931
Brass, chromium-plated; bolt-ring clasp »GARANTIE***«; Galalith
Chain: L 610; pendant: H 95
PB Vol. VIII, p. 375, M. no. 18.311, 6.7.31

HALSKETTE MIT ANHÄNGER, 1931
Messing vernickelt, Federringverschluß, Galalith (V)
Halskette: L 460, Anhänger: H 90
MB Bd. VIII, M-Nr. 17.890 (laut Etikett), vor 16.7.31

20

CHAIN WITH PENDANT, 1931
Brass, nickel-plated; bolt-ring clasp; Galalith (V)
Chain: L 460; pendant: H 90
PB Vol. VIII, M. no. 17.890 (according to label), before 16.7.31

HALSKETTE, 1931
Messing verchromt, Schraubverschluß, Galalith
Halskette: L 450
MB Bd. IX, S. 93, M-Nr. 18.670, 2.12.31, 27,–

21

CHAIN, 1931
Brass, chromium-plated; screw clasp; Galalith
Chain: L 450
PB Vol. IX, p. 93, M. no. 18.670, 2.12.31, 27,–

COLLIER, 1931
Messing verchromt, Schraubverschluß
Halskette: L 450
MB Bd. IX, S. 70, M-Nr. 18.579, 24.8.31

22

NECKLACE, 1931
Brass, chromium-plated; screw clasp
Chain: L 450
PB Vol. IX, p. 70, M. no. 18.579, 24.8.31

HALSKETTE MIT OHRHÄNGER, 1931
Metalldraht, Messing vernickelt, Federringverschluß, Galalith
Halskette: L 530, Ohrhänger: H 40
MB Bd. IX, S. 15, M-Nr. 18.372, 3.8.31, 15,50 (Halskette)

▸ 23

CHAIN WITH DROP, 1931
Wire; brass, nickel-plated; bolt-ring clasp; Galalith
Chain: L 530; drop: H 40
PB Vol. IX, p. 15, M. no. 18.372, 3.8.31, 15,50 (chain)

HALSKETTE MIT OHRHÄNGER, 1931
Metalldraht, Messing vernickelt, Federringverschluß, Galalith
Halskette: L 530, Ohrhänger: H 40
MB Bd. IX, S. 15, M-Nr. 18.372, 3.8.31, 15,50 (Halskette)

◂ 24

CHAIN WITH DROP, 1931
Wire; brass, nickel-plated; bolt-ring clasp; Galalith
Chain: L 530, drop: H 40
PB Vol. IX, p. 15, M. no. 18.372, 3.8.31, 15,50 (chain)

UHRKETTEN , 1931
Messing verchromt, Karabinerhaken, Galalith
L 115–135

25

WATCH CHAINS, 1931
Brass, chromium-plated; lobster clasp; Galalith
L 115–135

ARMBAND, 1931
Gummi, verchromtes Galalith, Galalith
L 70, H 40
MB Bd. IX, S. 6, M-Nr. 18.338, 29.7.31, 9,–

26

BRACELET, 1931
Rubber; chromium-plated Galalith; Galalith
L 70, H 40
PB Vol. IX, p. 6, M. no. 18.338, 29.7.31, 9,–

HALSKETTE MIT ANHÄNGER, 1931
Gelbmetall, Federringverschluß,
Galalith
Halskette: L 530, Anhänger: H 46
MB Bd. IX, S.11, M-Nr. 18.357, 21.7.31

27

CHAIN WITH PENDANT, 1931
Pinchbeck; bolt-ring clasp; Galalith
Chain: L 530; pendant: H 46
PB Vol. IX, p. 11, M. no. 18.357, 21.7.31

HALSKETTE MIT ANHÄNGER, 1931
Messing verchromt, Federring-
verschluß »GARANTIE***«, Galalith,
teilweise gesprenkelt
Halskette: L 580, Anhänger: H 60
MB Bd. IX, S. 43, M-Nr. 18.485, 24.8.31

28

CHAIN WITH PENDANT, 1931
Brass, chromium-plated; bolt-ring clasp
»GARANTIE***«; Galalith, partly mottled
Chain: L 580; pendant: H 60
PB Vol. IX, p. 43, M. no. 18.485, 24.8.31

HALSKETTE MIT ANHÄNGER, 1931
Messing verchromt, Schraubver-
schluß, aufgeschraubtes Galalith
Halskette: L 580, Anhänger: H 60
MB Bd. IX, S. 54, M-Nr. 18.528, 14.8.31

29

CHAIN WITH PENDANT, 1931
Brass, chromium-plated; screw clasp;
Galalith, screwed on
Chain: L 580; pendant: H 60
PB Vol. IX, p. 54, M. no. 18.528, 14.8.31

27

29

HALSKETTE MIT ANHÄNGER, 1931
Messing vernickelt/verchromt, Federringverschluß »GARANTIE***«, Galalith
Halskette: L 720, Anhänger: H 65
MB Bd. IX, S. 11, M-Nr. 18.357/1, 21.7.31

30

CHAIN WITH PENDANT, 1931
Brass, nickel and chromium-plated; bolt-ring clasp »GARANTIE***«; Galalith
Chain: L 720; pendant: H 65
PB Vol. IX, p. 11, M. no. 18.357/1, 21.7.31

HALSKETTE MIT ANHÄNGER, 1931
Messing vernickelt, Federringverschluß »GARANTIE***«, Galalith in zwei Farben, genietet
Halskette: L 610, Anhänger: H 42
MB Bd. IX, S. 58, M-Nr.18.541, 30.9.31

31

CHAIN WITH PENDANT, 1931
Brass, nickel-plated; bolt-ring clasp »GARANTIE***«; Galalith in two colours; riveted
Chain: L 610; pendant: H 42
PB Vol. IX, p. 58, M. no.18.541, 30.9.31

32

COLLIER MIT ANHÄNGER, 1931
Messing verchromt, Federringverschluß »GARANTIE***«, Glas
Halskette: L 440, Anhänger: H 90
MB Bd. VIII, S. 227, M-Nr. 17.749, vor 16.7.31

NECKLACE WITH PENDANT, 1931
Brass, chromium-plated; bolt-ring clasp »GARANTIE***«; glass
Chain: L 440; pendant: H 90
PB Vol. VIII, p. 227, M. no. 17.749, before 16.7.31

▶ 33

COLLIER, 1931
Messing verchrom, Federringverschluß (»Made in Germany«), Galalith
Halskette: L 390
MB Bd. IX, S. 48, M-Nr. 18.504, 24.8.31

COLLAR, 1931
Brass, chromium-plated; bolt-ring clasp (»Made in Germany«); Galalith
Chain: L 390
PB Vol. IX, p. 48, M. no. 18.504, 24.8.31

34
KRAGEN-COLLIER, 1931
Messing verchromt, Hakenverschluß vorne in der Mitte, teilweise lackiert, Galalithkugeln
Halskette: L 400
MB Bd. IX, S. 69, M-Nr. 18.506, 24.8.31

COLLAR-NECKLACE, 1931
Brass, chromium-plated; strung-bead hook, centre front; partly lacquered; Galalith spheres
Chain: L 400
PB Vol. IX, p. 69, M. no. 18.506, 24.8.31

35
KRAGEN-COLLIER, 1931
Signatur: »DEPOSE« (geschützt)
Messing, ornamental lackiert, Hakenverschluß vorne in der Mitte, Glaskugeln
Halskette: L 400
MB Bd. VIII, S. 228, M-Nr. 17.752, vor 16.7.31
MB Bd. IX, S. 47, M-Nr. 18.499, 24.8.31, 18,–

COLLAR-NECKLACE, 1931
Signature: »DEPOSE« [»registered«]
Brass, decoratively lacquered; strung-bead hook, centre front; glass spheres
Chain: L 400
PB Vol. VIII, p. 228, M. no. 17.752, before 16.7.31
PB Vol. IX, p. 47, M. no. 18.499, 24.8.31, 18,–

KRAGEN-COLLIER, 1931
Messing verchromt, Federring-verschluß »GARANTIE***«, Galalith mit Strass
Halskette: L 410
MB Bd. IX, S. 48, M-Nr. 18.504, 24.8.31

36

COLLAR-NECKLACE, 1931
Brass, chromium-plated; bolt-ring clasp »GARANTIE***«; Galalith with strass
Chain: L 410
PB Vol. IX, p. 48, M. no. 18.504, 24.8.31

KINDER-KRAGEN-COLLIER, 1931
Messing verchromt, lackiert, Hakenverschluß vorne in der Mitte, zwei Galalithkugeln
Halskette: L 390
MB Bd. IX, S. 45, M-Nr. 18.493, 14.8.31

37

CHILD'S COLLAR-NECKLET, 1931
Brass, chromium-plated, lacquered; strung-bead hook, centre front; two Galalith spheres
Chain: L 390
PB Vol. IX, p. 45, M. no. 18.493, 14.8.31

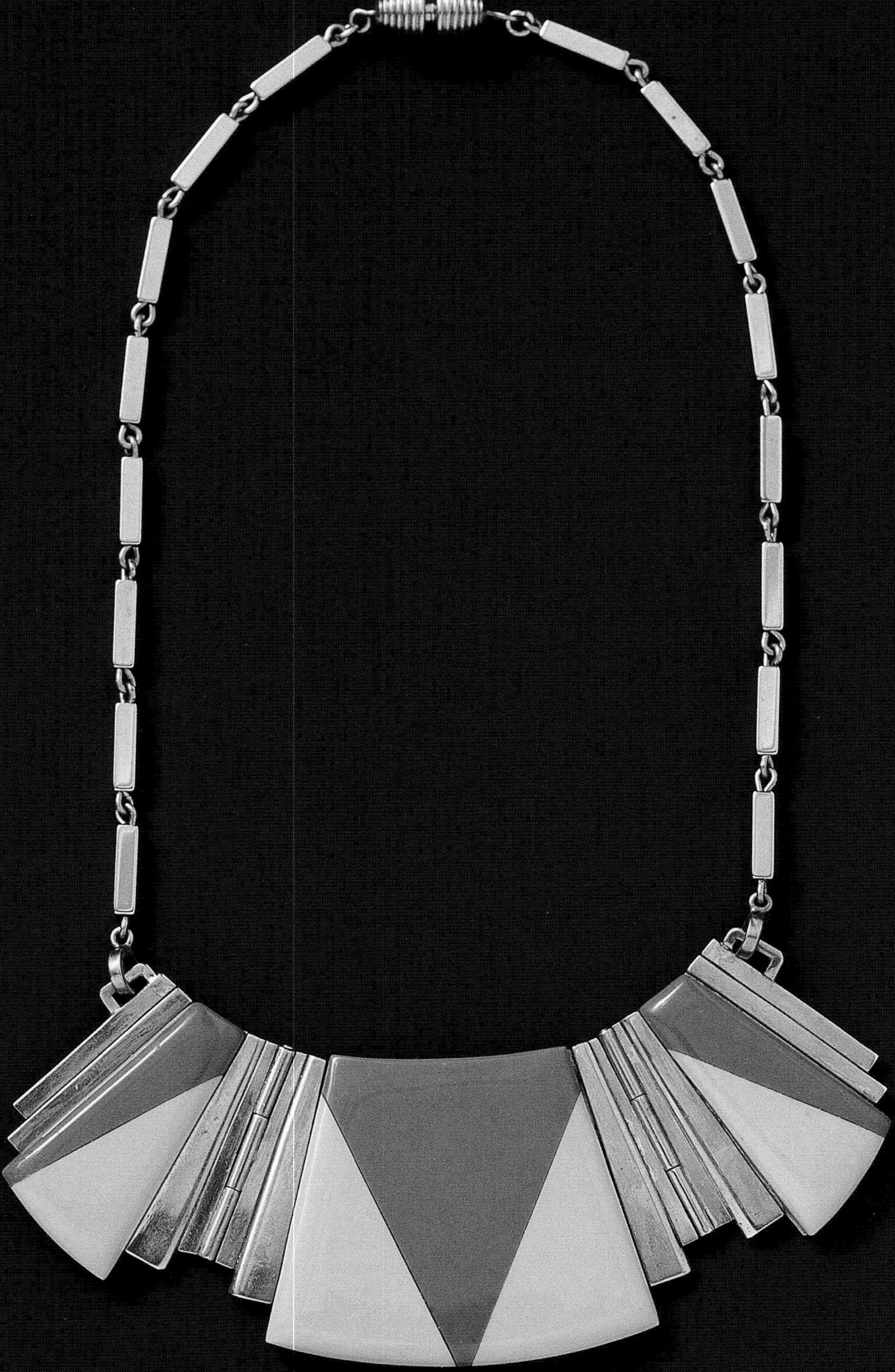

COLLIER, 1931
Messing verchromt bzw. vernickelt, Schraubverschluß, aufgeschraubtes Galalith
Halskette: L 380
MB Bd. IX, S. 48, M-Nr. 18.505, 24.8.31, 27,–

◀**38**

NECKLET, 1931
Brass, chrome or nickel-plated; screw clasp; Galalith, screwed on
Chain: L 380
PB Vol. IX, p. 48, M. no. 18.505, 24.8.31, 27,–

COLLIER, 1931
Messing verchromt, Schraubverschluß, Galalith
Halskette: L 430, Mittelteil: H 27
MB Bd. IX, S. 48, M-Nr. 18.505, 24.8.31, 27,–

39

NECKLACE, 1931
Brass, chromium-plated; screw clasp; Galalith
Chain: L 430; central piece: H 27
PB Vol. IX, p. 48, M. no. 18.505, 24.8.31, 27,–

COLLIER, 1931
Nickel, Federringverschluß, Galalith
Halskette: L 405
MB Bd. IX, S. 74, M-Nr. 18.592/3, 22.10.31

40

NECKLACE, 1931
Nickel; bolt-ring clasp; Galalith
Chain: L 405
PB Vol. IX, p. 74, M. no. 18.592/3, 22.10.31

COLLIER, 1931
Messing verchromt, Federringverschluß
»GARANTIE***«, zweifarbig lackiert
Halskette: L 390
MB Bd. IX, S. 63, M-Nr. 18.555, 30.9.31

41

NECKLET, 1931
Brass, chromium-plated; bolt-ring clasp
»GARANTIE***«; lacquered in two colours
Chain: L 390
PB Vol. IX, p. 63, M. no. 18.555, 30.9.31

COLLIER, 1931
Metalldraht, Messing vernickelt, »Alt Nickel«, Federringverschluß, Glaskugeln
Halskette: L 420
MB Bd. IX, S. 94, M-Nr. 18.591, 22.10.31

42

NECKLACE, 1931
Wire, nickel-plated brass, »German nickel«; bolt-ring clasp; glass balls
Chain: L 420
PB Vol. IX, p. 94, M. no. 18.591, 22.10.31

COLLIER, 1931
Nickel, Glas, Federringverschluß
»GARANTIE***«
Halskette: L 430
MB Bd. IX, S. 83, M-Nr. 18.628, 17.11.31

43

NECKLACE, 1931
Nickel, glass; bolt-ring clasp
»GARANTIE***«
Chain: L 430
PB Vol. IX, p. 83, M. no. 18.628, 17.11.31

44

KETTE, 1931
Metalldraht, Messing vernickelt, Schraubverschluß, Galalith
Halskette: L 500
MB Bd. IX, S. 106, M-Nr. 18.717, 2.12.31

CHAIN, 1931
Wire, nickel-plated brass; screw clasp; Galalith
Chain: L 500
PB Vol. IX, p. 106, M. no. 18.717, 2.12.31

45

COLLIER, 1931
Metallschnur, Messing verchromt, Federringverschluß »GARANTIE***«, Wolkengalalith
Halskette: L 430
MB Bd. IX., S. 90, M-Nr. 18.656, 2.12.31

NECKLACE, 1931
Metal cord, chromium-plated brass; bolt-ring clasp »GARANTIE***«; cloudy Galalith
Chain: L 430
PB Vol. IX., p. 90, M. no. 18.656, 2.12.31

46

COLLIER, 1931
Messing verchromt, Schraubverschluß, Holz, Galalith
Halskette: L 500
MB Bd. IX, S. 91, M-Nr. 18.661, 2.12.31, 36.–

NECKLACE, 1931
Brass, chromium-plated; screw clasp; wood; Galalith
Chain: L 500
PB Vol. IX, p. 91, M. no. 18.661, 2.12.31, 36.–

47

COLLIER, 1931
Metalldraht, Messing verchromt, Federringverschluß »GARANTIE***«, Galalith
Halskette: L 410
MB Bd. IX, S. 100, M-Nr. 18.694, 2.12.31

NECKLACE, 1931
Wire, chromium-plated brass; bolt-ring clasp »GARANTIE***«; Galalith
Chain: L 410
PB Vol. IX, p. 100, M. no. 18.694, 2.12.31

COLLIER, 1931
Messing verchromt, Schraubverschluß, Galalith
Halskette: L 450
MB Bd. IX, S. 93, M-Nr. 18.670, 2.12.31, 27,–

48

NECKLACE, 1931
Brass, chromium-plated; screw clasp; Galalith
Chain: L 450
PB Vol. IX, p. 93, M. no. 18.670, 2.12.31, 27,–

HALSKETTE, 1931
Messing vergoldet (»Amerikanisch Doublé«), Federringverschluß »AM DOUBLE«, Galalith
Halskette: L 390
MB Bd. IX, S. 87, M-Nr. 18.646, 2.12.31, 16,–

49

CHAIN, 1931
Brass, gold-plated (American rolled gold); bolt-ring clasp »AM DOUBLE«; Galalith
Chain: L 390
PB Vol. IX, p. 87, M. no. 18.646, 2.12.31, 16,–

50

HALSKETTE, 1931
Messing verchromt, Federringverschluß »GARANTIE*«, Galalith**
Halskette: L 450
MB Bd. IX, S. 87, M-Nr. 18.646, 2.12.31, 16,–

CHAIN, 1931
Brass, chromium-plated; bolt-ring clasp »GARANTIE***«; Galalith
Chain: L 450
PB Vol. IX, p. 87, M. no. 18.646, 2.12.31, 16,–

51

COLLIER, 1931
Messing verchromt, Federringverschluß, Galalith
Halskette: L 430
MB Bd. IX, S. 87, M-Nr. 18.646, 2.12.31, 16,–

NECKLACE, 1931
Brass, chromium-plated; bolt-ring clasp; Galalith
Chain: L 430
PB Vol. IX, p. 87, M. no. 18.646, 2.12.31, 16,–

SAUTOIR, 1931
Messing vernickelt, Federringverschluß, Galalith
Halskette: L 660, Abhängung: L 80
MB Bd. IX, S. 59, M-Nr. 18.544/3, 24.8.31, 30,–

52

GUARD CHAIN, 1931
Brass, nickel-plated; bolt-ring clasp; Galalith
Chain: L 660; pendant: L 80
PB Vol. IX, p. 59, M. no. 18.544/3, 24.8.31, 30,–

A U S W A H L

COLLECTION 1932

S E L E C T I O N

COLLIER, 1932
Metalldraht, Messing vernickelt,
Federringverschluß »GARANTIE ***«,
Galalith
Halskette: L 450
MB Bd. IX, S. 154, Nr. 18.917, 6.1.32, 12,–

53

NECKLACE, 1932
Wire, Brass nickel-plated, bolt-ring
clasp »GARANTIE ***«; Galalith
Chain: L 450
PB Vol. IX, p. 154, no. 18.917, 6.1.32, 12,–

HALSKETTE, 1932
Messing vernickelt, Schraubverschluß,
Glas (Rumpelperlen)
Halskette: L 460
MB Bd. IX, S. 283, M-Nr. 19.435, 27.5.32

▶ **54**

CHAIN, 1932
Brass, nickel-plated; screw clasp; glass
(irregular beads)
Chain: L 460
PB Vol. IX, p. 283, M. no. 19.435, 27.5.32

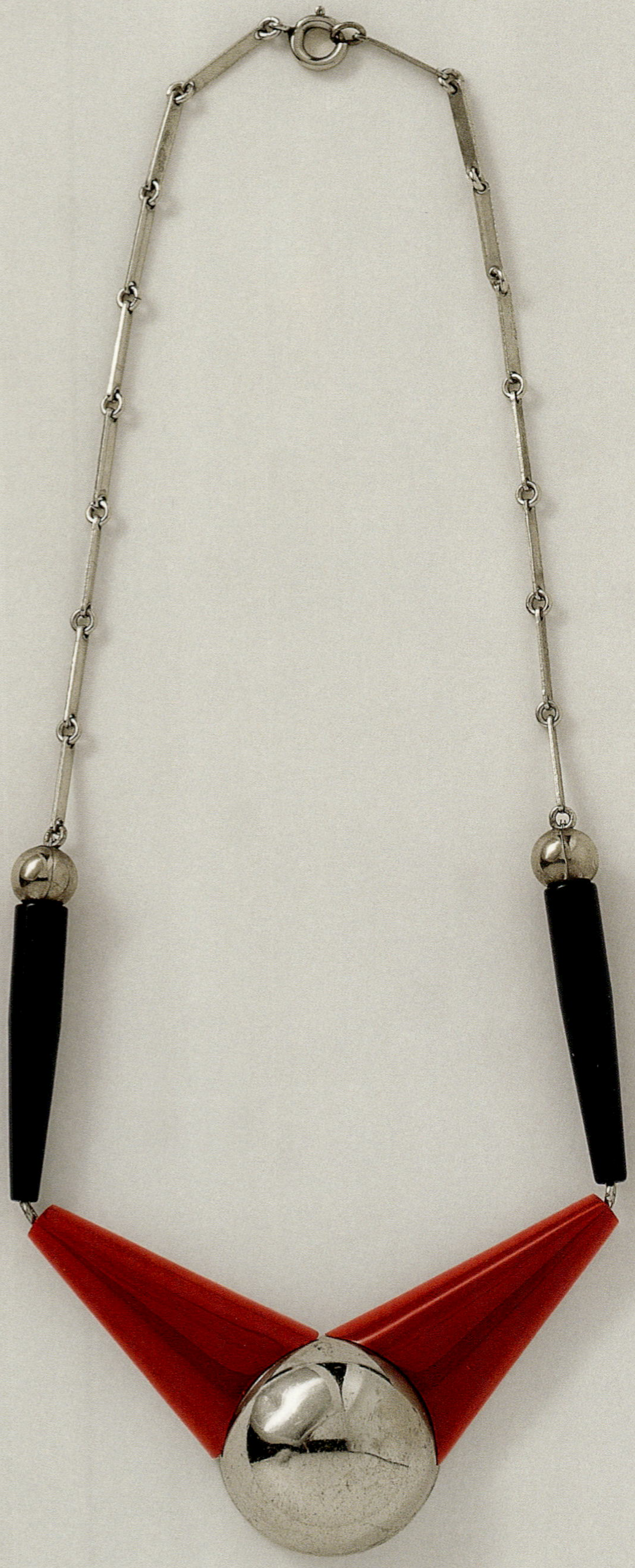

HALSKETTE, 1932
Metalldraht, Messing vernickelt, Federringverschluß, Galalith
Halskette: h.L 270
MB Bd. IX, S. 215, M-Nr. 19.157, 18.3.32, 12,–

◀ **55**

CHAIN, 1932
Wire, nickel-plated brass; bolt-ring clasp; Galalith
Chain: h.L 270
PB Vol. IX, p. 215, M. no. 19.157, 18.3.32, 12,–

COLLIER, 1932
Messing verchromt, Federring-verschluß, Galalith
Halskette: L 420
MB Bd. IX, S. 341, M-Nr. 19.651, 15.7.32

56

NECKLACE, 1932
Brass, chromium-plated; bolt-ring clasp; Galalith
Chain: L 420
PB Vol. IX, p. 341, M. no. 19.651, 15.7.32

COLLIER, 1932
Metalldraht, Messing vernickelt, Galalith (Lapislazuliimitat)
Halskette: L 470
MB Bd. IX, S. 244, M-Nr. 19.269, 2.5.32, 16,50

57

NECKLACE, 1932
Wire, nickel-plated brass; Galalith (imitation lapis lazuli)
Chain: L 470
PB Vol. IX, p. 244, M. no. 19.269, 2.5.32, 16,50

HALSKETTE, 1932
Metalldraht, Messing verchromt, Schraubverschluß, Galalith (V)
Halskette: L 600
MB Bd. IX, S. 308, M-Nr. 19.532, 23.6.32, 36,–

58

CHAIN, 1932
Wire, chromium-plated brass; screw clasp; Galalith (V)
Chain: L 600
PB Vol. IX, p. 308, M. no. 19.532, 23.6.32, 36,–

HALSKETTE, 1932
Messing vernickelt, Schraubverschluß, Galalith
Halskette: L 370
MB Bd. IX, S. 185, M-Nr. 19.037, 7.3.32, 21,–

▸ **59**

CHAIN, 1932
Brass, nickel-plated; screw clasp; Galalith
Chain: L 370
PB Vol. IX, p. 185, M. no. 19.037, 7.3.32, 21,–

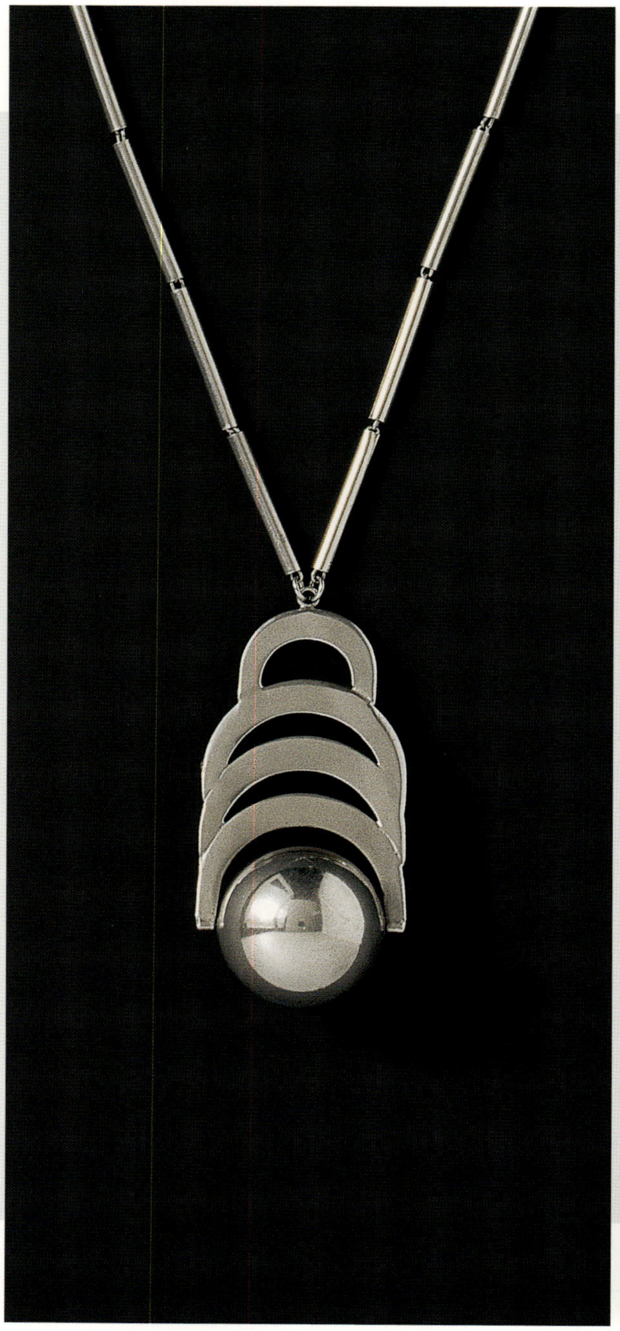

HALSKETTE MIT ANHÄNGER, 1932
Messing verchromt, Federringverschluß
Halskette: L 580, Anhänger: H 65
MB Bd. IX, S. 58, M-Nr. 18.522, 24.8.32
(siehe auch S. 38, Abb. 28)
Privatsammlung, Stuttgart

60

CHAIN WITH PENDANT, 1932
Brass, chromium-plated; bolt-ring clasp
Chain: L 580; pendant: H 65
PB Vol. IX, p. 58, M. no. 18.522, 24.8.32
(see also p. 38, fig. 28)
Private collection, Stuttgart

HALSKETTE MIT ANHÄNGER, 1932
Messing vernickelt, Schraubverschluß, Galalith
Halskette: L 480, Anhänger: H 55, B 45
MB Bd. X, S. 172, M-Nr. 20.513/11, 14.2.32, 10,–

61

CHAIN WITH PENDANT, 1932
Brass, nickel-plated; screw clasp; Galalith
Chain: L 480; pendant: H 55, W 45
PB Vol. X, p. 172, M. no. 20.513/11, 14.2.32, 10,–

COLLIER, 1932
Messing vernickelt, Schraubverschluß, Galalith
L 450
MB Bd. IX, S. 274, M-Nr. 19.397, 27.5.32, 6,– p. Dtz.

▶ **62**

NECKLACE, 1932
Brass, nickel-plated; screw clasp; Galalith
L 450
PB Vol. IX, p. 274, M. no. 19.397, 27.5.32, 6,– per dozen

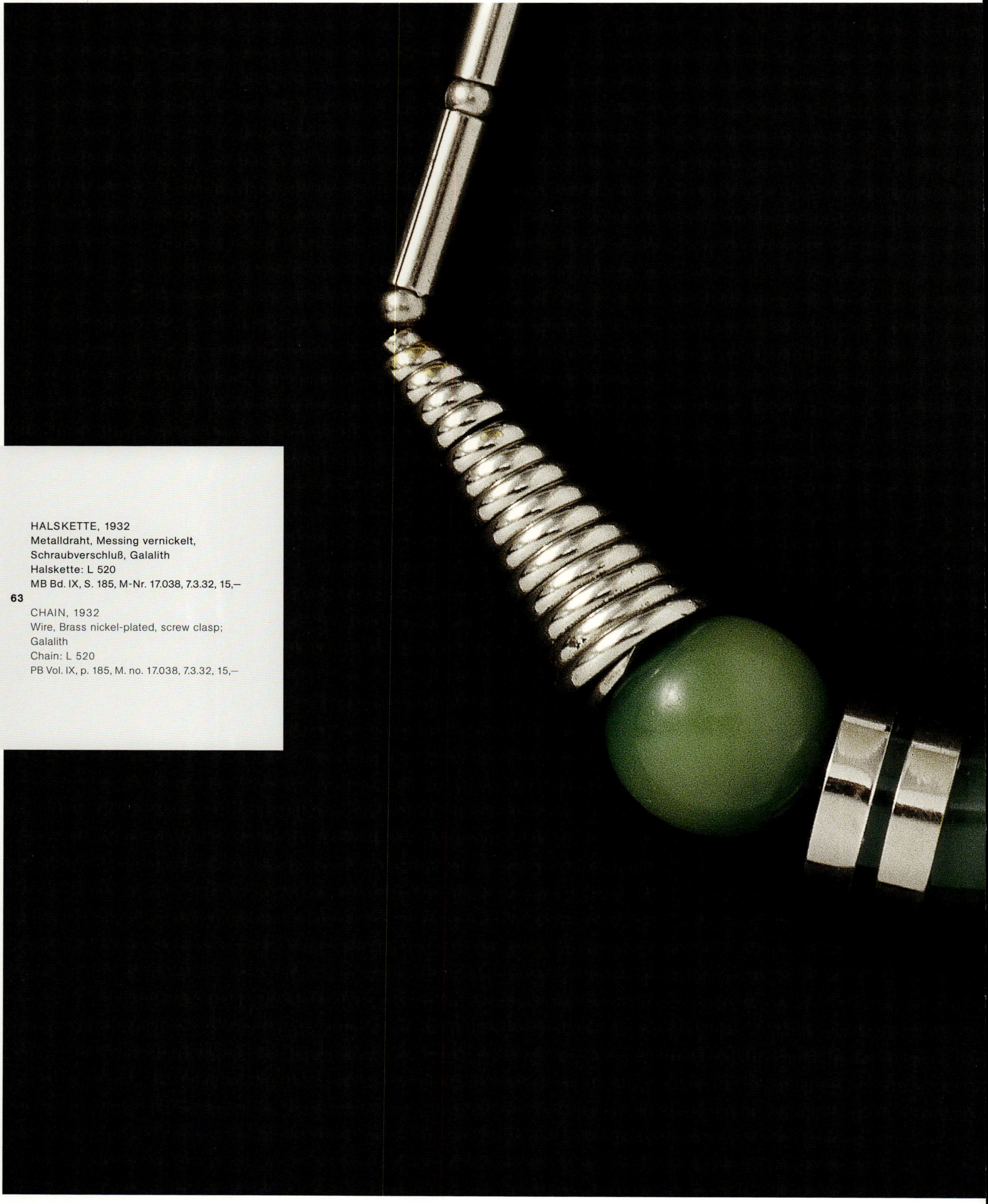

63

HALSKETTE, 1932
Metalldraht, Messing vernickelt, Schraubverschluß, Galalith
Halskette: L 520
MB Bd. IX, S. 185, M-Nr. 17.038, 7.3.32, 15,–

CHAIN, 1932
Wire, Brass nickel-plated, screw clasp; Galalith
Chain: L 520
PB Vol. IX, p. 185, M. no. 17.038, 7.3.32, 15,–

HALSKETTE, 1932
Metalldraht, Messing vernickelt,
Schraubverschluß, Galalith
Halskette: L 485
MB Bd. IX, S. 251, M-Nr. 19.296, 2.5.32

64

CHAIN, 1932
Wire, nickel-plated brass; screw clasp;
Galalith
Chain: L 485
PB Vol. IX, p. 251, M. no. 19.296, 2.5.32

HALSKETTE, 1932
Messing vernickelt , Schraubverschluß,
Galalith
Halskette: L 440
MB Bd. IX, S. 351, M-Nr. 19.696,
30.7.32, 15,–

65

CHAIN, 1932
Brass, nickel-plated; screw clasp;
Galalith
Chain: L 440
PB Vol. IX, p. 351, M. no. 19.696,
30.7.32, 15,–

66

HALSKETTE, 1932
Messing verchromt, Federringverschluß, Galalith
Halskette: L 465
MB Bd. IX, S. 251, M-Nr. 19.296, 2.5.32

CHAIN, 1932
Brass, chromium-plated; bolt-ring clasp; Galalith
Chain: L 465
PB Vol. IX, p. 251, M. no. 19.296, 2.5.32

67

COLLIER, 1932
Messing vernickelt, Schraubverschluß, Galalith
Halskette: L 400
MB Bd. X, S. 127, M-Nr. 20.282, 24.12.32, 27,–

NECKLACE, 1932
Brass, nickel-plated; screw clasp; Galalith
Chain: L 400
PB Vol. X, p. 127, M. no. 20.282, 24.12.32, 27,–

HALSREIF, 1932
Messing verchromt, Federringverschluß, Galalith
Halskette: Ø 140
MB Bd. X, S.61, M-Nr. 20.038, 2.11.32, 10,–

68

TORQUE, 1932
Brass, chromium-plated; bolt-ring clasp; Galalith
Chain: Ø 140
PB Vol. X, p. 61, M. no. 20.038, 2.11.32, 10,–

HALSKETTE, 1932
Messing vernickelt, Federringverschluß, Galalith
Halskette: L 470
MB Bd. X, S.61, M-Nr. 20.038, 2.11.32, 10,–

◀ 69

CHAIN, 1932
Brass nickel-plated; bolt-ring clasp; Galalith
Chain: L 470
PB Vol. X, p. 61, M. no. 20.038, 2.11.32, 10,–

COLLIER, 1932
Messing vernickelt, Schraub-
verschluß, Galalith
Halskette: L 470
MB Bd. X, S. 61, M-Nr. 20.037, 2.12.32, 21,–

70

NECKLACE, 1932
Brass, nickel-plated; screw clasp; Galalith
Chain: L 470
PB Vol. X, p. 61, M. no. 20.037, 2.12.32, 21,–

HALSKETTE, 1932
Messing vernickelt, Federringverschluß
»GARANTIE***«, Galalith
Halskette: L 440
MB Bd. IX, S. 81, M-Nr. 18.623/1, 12.11.31 r.
MB Bd. IX, S. 223, M-Nr. 19.189, 18.3.32, 21,–

▸ **71**

CHAIN, 1932
Brass, nickel-plated; bolt-ring clasp
»GARANTIE***«; Galalith
Chain: L 440
PB Vol. IX, p. 81, M. no. 18.623/1, 12.11.31 r.
PB Vol. IX, p. 223, M. no. 19.189, 18.3.32, 21,–

HALSKETTE, 1932
Messing vernickelt, Schraubverschluß, Galalith
Halskette: L 500, Mittelteil: H 50
MB Bd. X, S. 10, M-Nr. 19.826, 23.8.32, 27,–

72

CHAIN, 1932
Brass, nickel-plated; screw clasp; Galalith
Chain: L 500; central piece: H 50
PB Vol. X, p. 10, M. no. 19.826, 23.8.32, 27,–

COLLIER MIT ANHÄNGER, 1932
Messing vernickelt, Federringverschluß, Galalith
Halskette: L 420, Mittelteil: H 60
MB Bd. X, S. 23, M-Nr. 19.879, 8.9.32, 15,–

73

NECKLACE WITH PENDANT, 1932
Brass, nickel-plated; bolt-ring clasp; Galalith
Chain: L 420; central piece: H 60
PB Vol. X, p. 23, M. no. 19.879, 8.9.32, 15,–

COLLIER, 1932
Messing vernickelt, Schraubverschluß, Galalith,
Halskette: L 460
MB Bd. IX, S. 247, M-Nr. 19.284, 2.5.32, 16,–

74

NECKLACE, 1932
Brass, nickel-plated; screw clasp; Galalith
Chain: L 460
PB Vol. IX, p. 247, M. no. 19.284, 2.5.32, 16,–

72

74

HALSKETTE, 1932
Messing vernickelt, Schraubverschluß, Galalith
Halskette: L 350
MB Bd. IX, S. 184, M-Nr. 19.034,
7.3.32, 15,–

75

CHAIN, 1932
Brass, nickel-plated; screw clasp; Galalith
Chain: L 350
PB Vol. IX, p. 184, M. no. 19.034,
7.3.32, 15,–

HALSKETTE MIT ZWEI SCHIEBERN, 1932
Gelb- und Weißmetall, Federringverschluß, Galalith
Halskette: L 400, Schieber: 35 x 20
MB Bd. IX, S. 245, M-Nr. 19.276,
2.5.32, 24,–

76

CHAIN WITH TWO SLIDES, 1932
Pinchbeck and White Metal; bolt-ring clasp; Galalith
Chain: L 400; slide: 35 x 20
PB Vol. IX, p. 245, M. no. 19.276,
2.5.32, 24,–

HALSKETTE, 1932
Messing verchromt, Federringverschluß, Galalith
Halskette: L 405
MB Bd. IX, S. 134, M-Nr. 18.840, 6.1.32, 18,–

77

CHAIN, 1932
Brass, chromium-plated; bolt-ring clasp; Galalith
Chain: L 405
PB Vol. IX, p. 134, M. no. 18.840, 6.1.32, 18,–

COLLIER, 1932
Messing verchromt, Federringverschluß »GARANTIE***«, Galalith
Halskette: L 410, Anhänger: H 48, B 42
MB Bd. IX, S.187, M-Nr. 19.044, 7.3.32

▸ 78

NECKLACE, 1932
Brass chromium-plated, bolt-ring clasp »GARANTIE***«; Galalith
Chain: L 410; pendant: H 48, W 42
PB Vol. IX, p. 187, M. no. 19.044, 7.3.32

HALSKETTE, 1932
Messing vernickelt, Federring-verschluß »GARANTIE*«, Galalith Modellanhänger 18249**
Halskette: L 400
MB Bd. IX, S. 191, M-Nr. 19.085, 18.3.32, 23,– (siehe auch S. 58, Abb. 75)

79

CHAIN, 1932
Brass, nickel-plated; bolt-ring clasp »GARANTIE***«; Galalith, model pendant 18249
Chain: L 400
PB Vol. IX, p. 191, M. no. 19.085, 18.3.32, 23,– (see also p. 58, fig. 75)

COLLIER, 1932
Messing verchromt, Schraub-verschluß, Galalith
Halsketten: L je 70, Mittelteil: H 65, B 160
MB Bd. IX, S. 233, M-Nr. 19.226, 2.5.32, 14,– (20,–)

▸ 80

NECKLACE, 1932
Brass, chromium-plated; screw clasp; Galalith
Chains: L each 70; central piece: H 65, W 160
PB Vol. IX, p. 233, M. no. 19.226, 2.5.32, 14,– (20,–)

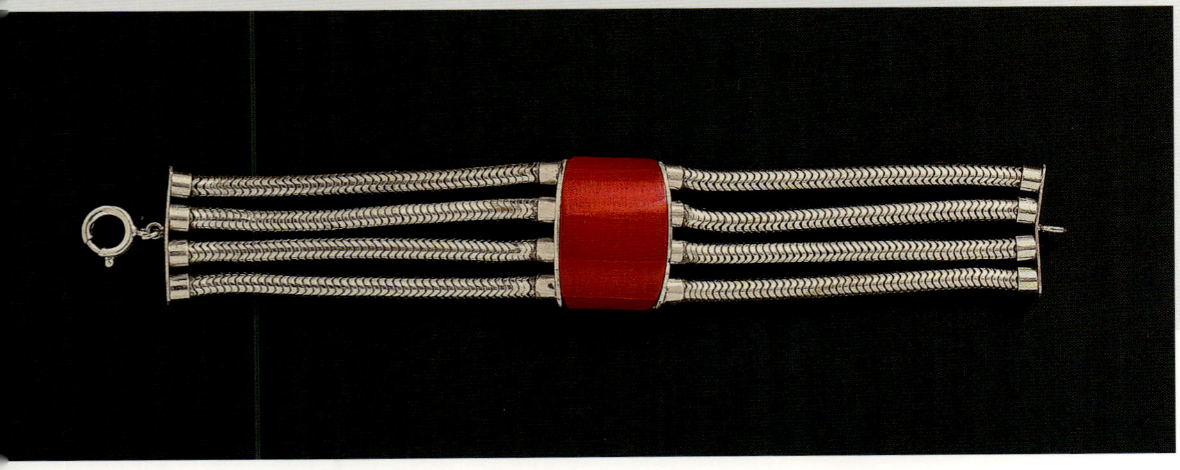

COLLIER, 1932
Metalldraht, Messing vernickelt, Schraubverschluß, Galalith (= Bernsteinimitation)
Halskette: L 420
MB Bd. IX, S. 205, M-Nr. 19.117, S. 206, M-Nr. 19.118, 18.3.32

◀ **81**

NECKLACE, 1932
Wire, nickel-plated brass; screw clasp; Galalith (= imitation amber)
Chain: L 420
PB Vol. IX, p. 205, M. no. 19.117, p. 206, M. no. 19.118, 18.3.32

COLLIER, 1932
Metalldraht, Messing vernickelt, Federringverschluß »GARANTIE*«, Galalith**
Halskette: L 410
MB Bd. IX, S. 193, M-Nr. 19.066, 18.3.32, 22,–

82

NECKLACE, 1932
Wire, nickel-plated brass; bolt-ring clasp »GARANTIE***«; Galalith
Chain: L 410
PB Vol. IX, p. 193, M. no. 19.066, 18.3.32, 22,–

ARMBAND, 1932
Messing verchromt, Federringverschluß, aufgeschraubtes Galalith
L 165, B 28
MB Bd. X, S. 9, M-Nr. 19.825, 20.8.32, 21,–

83

BRACELET, 1932
Brass, chromium-plated; bolt-ring clasp; Galalith, screwed on
L 165, W 28
PB Vol. X, p. 9, M. no. 19.825, 20.8.32, 21,–

84

COLLIER, 1932
Messing, teilweise vernickelt, Schraubverschluß, Glas
Halskette: L 390
MB Bd. IX, S. 202, M-Nr. 19.104, 18.3.32

NECKLACE, 1932
Brass, partly nickel-plated; screw clasp; glass
Chain: L 390
PB Vol. IX, p. 202, M. no. 19.104, 18.3.32

▶ 85

COLLIER, 1932
Messing vernickelt, Federringverschluß, Glas
Halskette: L 460
MB Bd. IX, S. 216, M-Nr. 19.158, 18.3.32

NECKLACE, 1932
Brass, nickel-plated; bolt-ring clasp; glass
Chain: L 460
PB Vol. IX, p. 216, M. no. 19.158, 18.3.32

86

COLLIER, 1932
Messing vernickelt, Schraubverschluß, Galalith
Halskette: L 440
MB Bd. IX, S. 194, M-Nr. 19.071, 18.3.32, 21,–

NECKLACE, 1932
Brass, nickel-plated; screw clasp; Galalith
Chain: L 440
PB Vol. IX, p. 194, M. no. 19.071, 18.3.32, 21,–

87

COLLIER, 1932
Messing vernickelt, Schraubverschluß, Glas
Halskette: L 420
MB Bd. IX, S. 312, M-Nr. 19.573, 20.6.32, 10,–

NECKLACE, 1932
Brass, nickel-plated; screw clasp; glass
Chain: L 420
PB Vol. IX, p. 312, M. no. 19.573, 20.6.32, 10,–

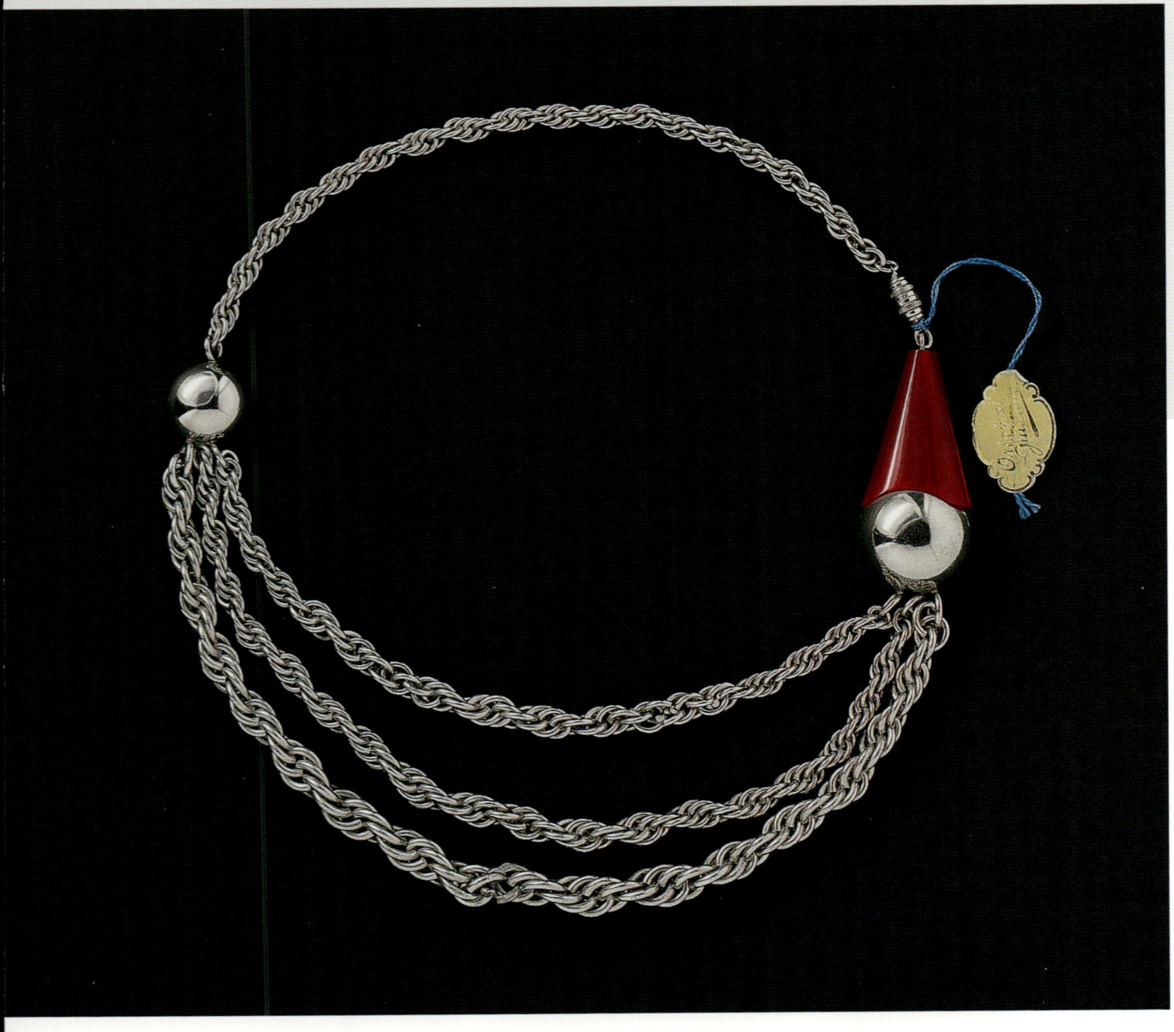

88

HALSKETTE, 1932
Messing vernickelt, Federringverschluß »GARANTIE***«, Galalith
Halskette: L 560
MB Bd. IX, S. 220, M-Nr. 19.175, 18.3.32

CHAIN, 1932
Brass, nickel-plated; bolt-ring clasp »GARANTIE***«; Galalith
Chain: L 560
PB Vol. IX, p. 220, M. no. 19.175, 18.3.32

89

HALSKETTE, 1932
Messing vernickelt, Schraubverschluß, Galalith, Etikette »Original Julienne«
Halskette: L 490
MB Bd. IX, S. 287, M-Nr. 19.451, 27.5.32

CHAIN, 1932
Brass, nickel-plated; screw clasp; Galalith; label: »Original Julienne«
Chain: L 490
PB Vol. IX, p. 287, M. no. 19.451, 27.5.32

COLLIER, 1932
Metalldraht, Messing vernickelt, Schraubverschluß, Galalith
Halskette: L 400
MB Bd. IX, S. 169, M-Nr. 18.973, 7.3.320

◄ **90**

NECKLACE, 1932
Wire, nickel-plated brass; screw clasp; Galalith
Chain: L 400
PB Vol. IX, p. 169, M. no. 18.973, 7.3.32

COLLIER, 1932
Metalldraht, Messing vernickelt, Schraubverschluß, Galalith, teilweise transparent
Halskette: L 460
MB Bd. IX, S. 359, M-Nr. 19.733, 4.8.32

91

NECKLACE, 1932
Wire, nickel-plated brass; screw clasp; Galalith, partly translucent
Chain: L 460
PB Vol. IX, p. 359, M. no. 19.733, 4.8.32

ARMBAND, 1932
Messing vernickelt, Federringverschluß, Glas
Armband: L 190
MB Bd. IX, S. 321, Nr. 19.537, 26.6.32, 10,–

92

BRACELET, 1932
Brass, nickel-plated; bolt-ring clasp; glass
Bracelet: L 190
PB Vol. IX, p. 321, M.no. 19.537, 26.6.32, 10,–

COLLIER, 1932
Messing vernickelt, Federringverschluß, Galalith
Marke: »Nickel«
Halskette: L 430
MB Bd. IX, S. 100, M-Nr. 18.694, 2.12.31, 21,–

93

NECKLACE, 1932
Brass, nickel-plated; bolt-ring clasp; Galalith
Mark: »Nickel«
Chain: L 430
PB Vol. IX, p. 100, M. no. 18.694, 2.12.31, 21,–

COLLIER MIT ANHÄNGER, 1932
Messing vernickelt, Schraubverschluß, Galalith
Halskette: L 410, Anhänger: L 90
MB Bd. IX , S. 155, M-Nr. 18.919, 6.1.32, 18,–

94

NECKLACE WITH PENDANT, 1932
Brass, nickel-plated; screw clasp; Galalith
Chain: L 410; pendant: L 90
PB Vol. IX , p. 155, M. no. 18.919, 6.1.32, 18,–

HALSKETTE MIT ANHÄNGER, 1932
Messing vernickelt, Schraubverschluß, Galalith
Halskette: L 530, Anhänger: L 65
MB Bd. IX, S. 287, M-Nr. 19.451, 27.5.32

▸ 95

CHAIN WITH PENDANT, 1932
Brass, nickel-plated; screw clasp; Galalith
Chain: L 530; pendant: L 65
PB Vol. IX, p. 287, M. no. 19.451, 27.5.32

COLLIER, 1932
Metallband, Messing vernickelt, Schraubverschluß, gesprenkeltes Galalith
Halskette: L 480
MB Bd. IX, S. 200, M-Nr. 19.095, 18.3.32, 15,–

96

NECKLACE, 1932
Metal band, nickel-plated brass; screw clasp; mottled Galalith
Chain: L 480
PB Vol. IX, p. 200, M. no. 19.095, 18.3.32, 15,–

HALSKETTE, 1932
Messing vernickelt, Wolkengalalith
Halskette: L 420
MB Bd. IX, S. 191, M-Nr. 19.058, 18.3.32, 13,–

97

CHAIN, 1932
Brass, nickel-plated; cloudy Galalith
Chain: L 420
PB Vol. IX, p. 191, M. no. 19.058, 18.3.32, 13,–

HALSKETTE, 1932
Messing verchromt, Federringverschluß, Galalith
Halskette: L 570
MB Bd. IX, S. 232, M-Nr. 19.222, 2.5.32, 12,–

▸ **98**

CHAIN, 1932
Brass chromium-plated, bolt-ring clasp; Galalith
Chain: L 570
PB Vol. IX, p. 232, M. no. 19.222, 2.5.32, 12,–

COLLIER, 1932
Messing verchromt, Schraubverschluß, Galalith, teilweise transparent
Halskette: L 410
MB Bd. IX, S. 229, M-Nr. 19.211, 2.5.32

99

NECKLACE, 1932
Brass chromium-plated; screw clasp; Galalith, partly translucent
Chain: L 410
PB Vol. IX, p. 229, M. no. 19.211, 2.5.32

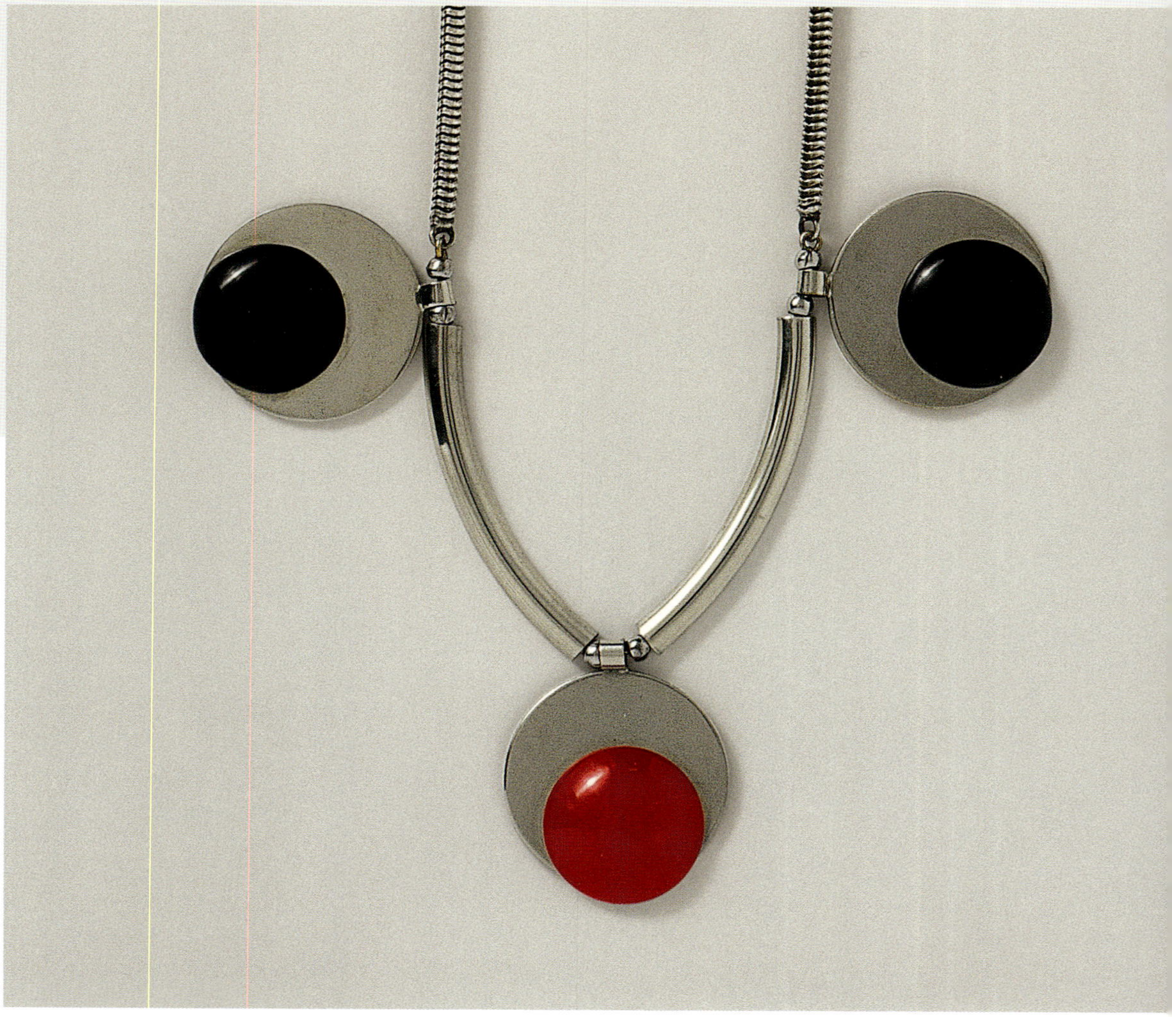

HALSKETTE, 1932
Messing verchromt bzw. vernickelt, Federringverschluß, aufgeschraubtes Galalith
Halskette: L 510, ein Glied: Ø 30
MB Bd. IX, S. 233, M-Nr. 19.226, 2.5.1932, 14,–

100

CHAIN, 1932
Brass, chrome or nickel-plated; bolt-ring clasp; Galalith, screwed on
Chain: L 510; one link: Ø 30
PB Vol. IX, p. 233, M. no. 19.226, 2.5.1932, 14,–

COLLIER, 1932
Messing verchromt, Schraubverschluß, Galalith
Halskette: L 390, Anhänger: H 59, B 49
MB Bd. IX, S. 352, M-Nr. 19.700, 30.7.32

101

NECKLACE, 1932
Brass, chromium-plated; screw clasp; Galalith
Chain: L 390; pendant: H 59, B 49
PB Vol. IX, p. 352, M. no. 19.700, 30.7.32

HALSKETTE, 1932
Messing verchromt, Federringverschluß, aufgeklebtes Galalith
Halskette: L 770, Anhänger: H 95, B 68
MB Bd. IX, S. 233, M-Nr. 19.226, 2.5.32, 14,–

102

CHAIN, 1932
Brass, chromium-plated; bolt-ring clasp; Galalith, glued on
Chain: L 770; pendant: H 95, W 68
PB Vol. IX, p. 233, M. no. 19.226, 2.5.32, 14,–

COLLIER, 1932
Messing verchromt, Schraubverschluß, aufgeklebtes zweifarbiges Galalith
Halskette: L 390
MB Bd. IX, S. 233, M-Nr. 19.226, 2.5.32, 14,–

103

NECKLET, 1932
Brass, chromium-plated; screw clasp; Galalith in two colours, glued on
Chain: L 390
PB Vol. IX, p. 233, M. no. 19.226, 2.5.32, 14,–

COLLIER, 1932
Messing verchromt/vernickelt, Federringverschluß, marmoriertes Galalith
Halskette: L 430
MB Bd. IX, S. 238, M-Nr. 19.246, 2.5.32, 9,–

▸ **104**

NECKLACE, 1932
Brass, chromium/nickel-plated; bolt-ring clasp; marbled Galalith
Chain: L 430
PB Vol. IX, p. 238, M. no. 19.246, 2.5.32, 9,–

HALSKETTE, 1932
Messing vernickelt, Schraubverschluß, Galalith
Halskette: L 430
MB Bd. IX, S. 341, M-Nr. 19.651, 15.7.32, 12,– (15,–)

105

CHAIN, 1932
Brass, nickel-plated; screw clasp; Galalith
Chain: L 430
PB Vol. IX, p. 341, M. no. 19.651, 15.7.32, 12,– (15,–)

COLLIER, 1932
Messing verchromt, Federringverschluß, Galalith
Halskette: L 420
MB Bd. IX, S. 232, M-Nr. 19.222, 2.5.32, 12,–

106

NECKLACE, 1932
Brass chromium-plated; bolt-ring clasp; Galalith
Chain: L 420
PB Vol. IX, p. 232, M. no. 19.222, 2.5.32, 12,–

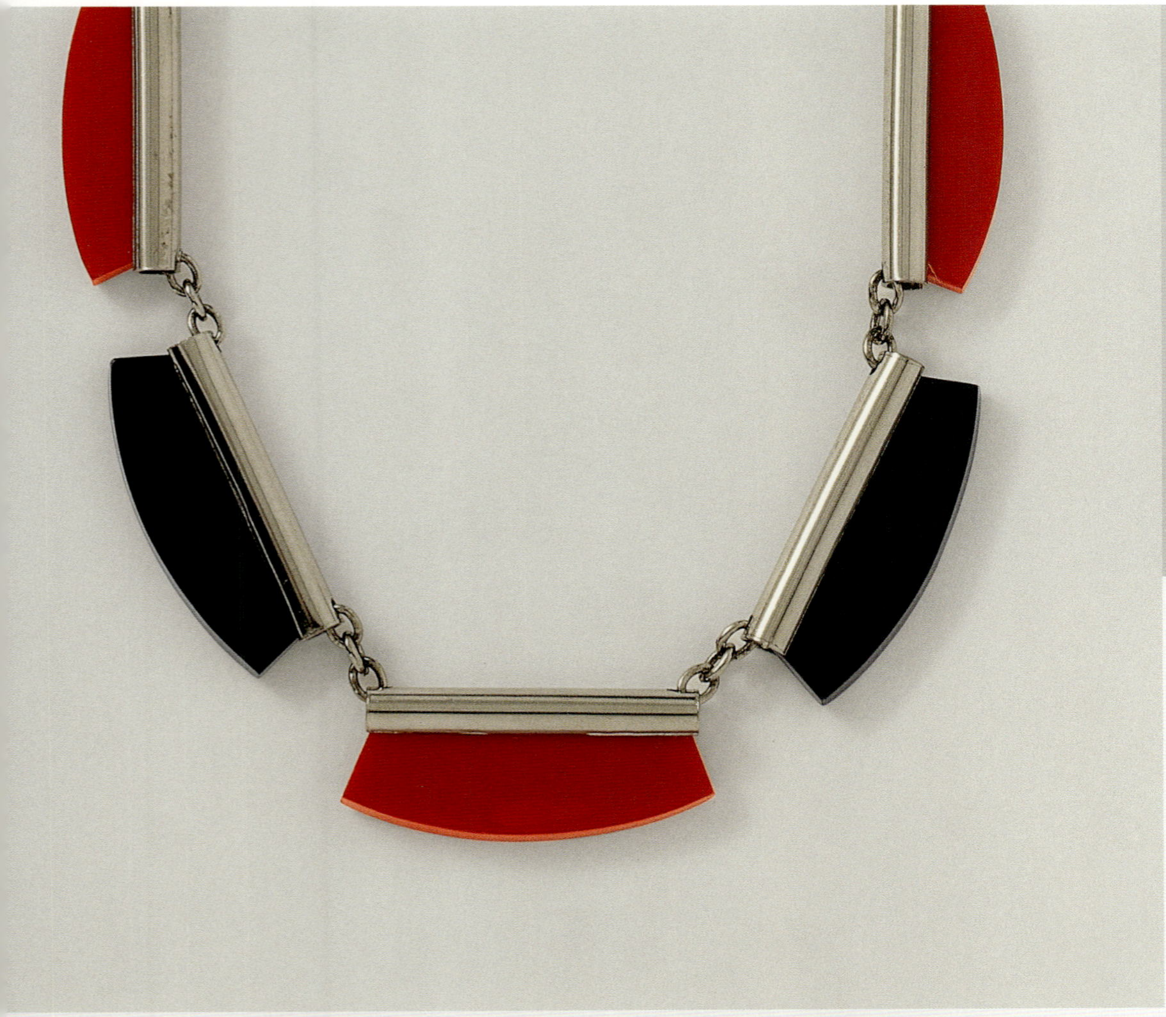

HALSKETTE, 1932
Messing verchromt, Schraubverschluß, Galalith
Halskette: L 430
MB Bd. IX, S. 238, M-Nr. 19.246, 2.5.32, 9,–

107

CHAIN, 1932
Brass, chromium-plated; screw clasp; Galalith
Chain: L 430
PB Vol. IX, p. 238, M. no. 19.246, 2.5.32, 9,–

COLLIER, 1932
Messing verchromt/vernickelt, Federringverschluß, Galalith (V, Variante in Dunkelblau vorhanden)
Halskette: L 430
MB Bd. IX, S. 238, M-Nr. 19.246, 2.5.32, 9,–

108

NECKLACE, 1932
Brass, chromium/nickel-plated; bolt-ring clasp; Galalith (V, variant available in dark blue)
Chain: L 430
PB Vol. IX, p. 238, M. no. 19.246, 2.5.32, 9,–

COLLIER, 1932
Messing verchromt, Federringverschluß, Galalith
Halskette: L 400
MB Bd. IX, S. 238, M-Nr. 19.246, 2.5.32, 9,–

109

NECKLACE, 1932
Brass, chromium-plated; bolt-ring clasp; Galalith
Chain: L 400
PB Vol. IX, p. 238, M. no. 19.246, 2.5.32, 9,–

HALSKETTE, 1932
Messing verchromt, Schraubverschluß, Galalith
Halskette: L 480
MB Bd. IX, S. 324, M-Nr. 19.589, 25.6.32

▸110

CHAIN, 1932
Brass chromium-plated; screw clasp; Galalith
Chain: L 480
PB Vol. IX, p. 324, M. no. 19.589, 25.6.32

COLLIER, 1932
Messing verchromt, Federringverschluß
»GARANTIE***«, Glas
Halskette: L 400
MB Bd. IX, S. 303, M-Nr. 19.508, 27.5.32

◂ **111**

NECKLACE, 1932
Brass, chromium-plated; bolt-ring clasp
»GARANTIE***«; glass
Chain: L 400
PB Vol. IX, p. 303, M. no. 19.508, 27.5.32

COLLIER, 1932
Messing verchromt, Kastenschloß
Halskette: L 390
MB Bd. IX, S. 303, M-Nr. 19.508, 27.5.32

112

NECKLACE, 1932
Brass, chromium-plated; box-snap clasp
Chain: L 390
PB Vol. IX, p. 303, M. no. 19.508, 27.5.32

COLLIER, 1932
Messing, Federringverschluß
Halskette: L 390
MB Bd. IX, S. 323, M-Nr. 19.221, 2.5.32, 7,–

113

NECKLACE, 1932
Brass; bolt-ring clasp
Chain: L 390
PB Vol. IX, p. 323, M. no. 19.221, 2.5.32, 7,–

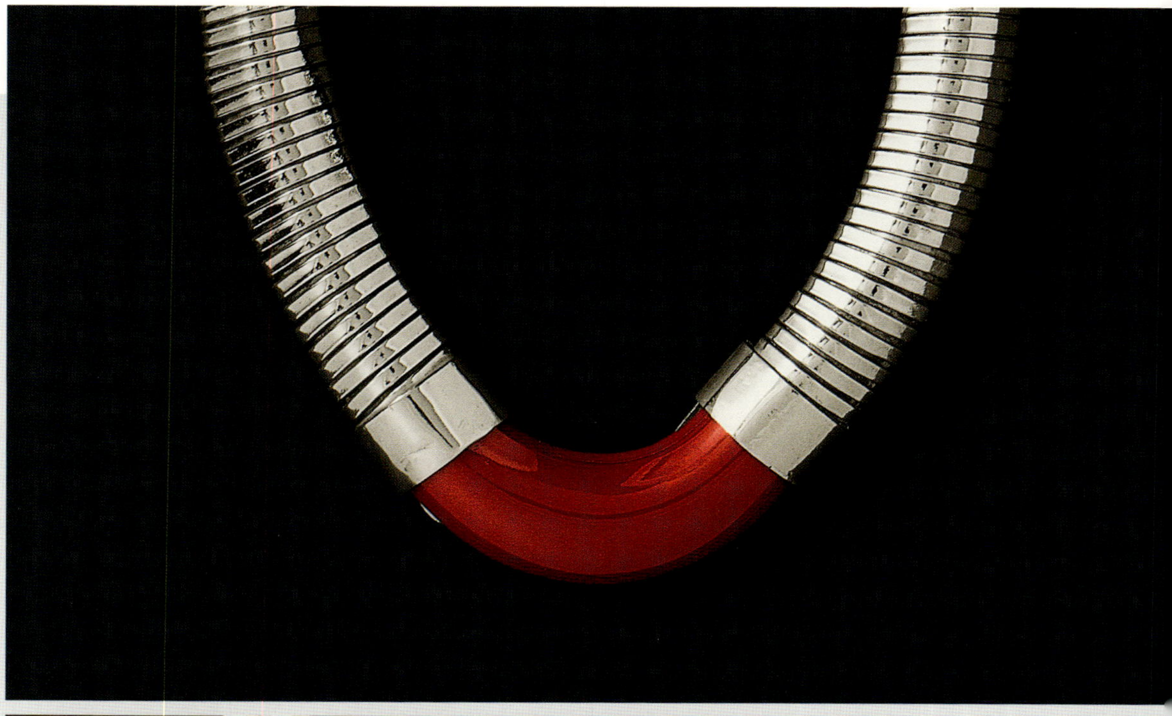

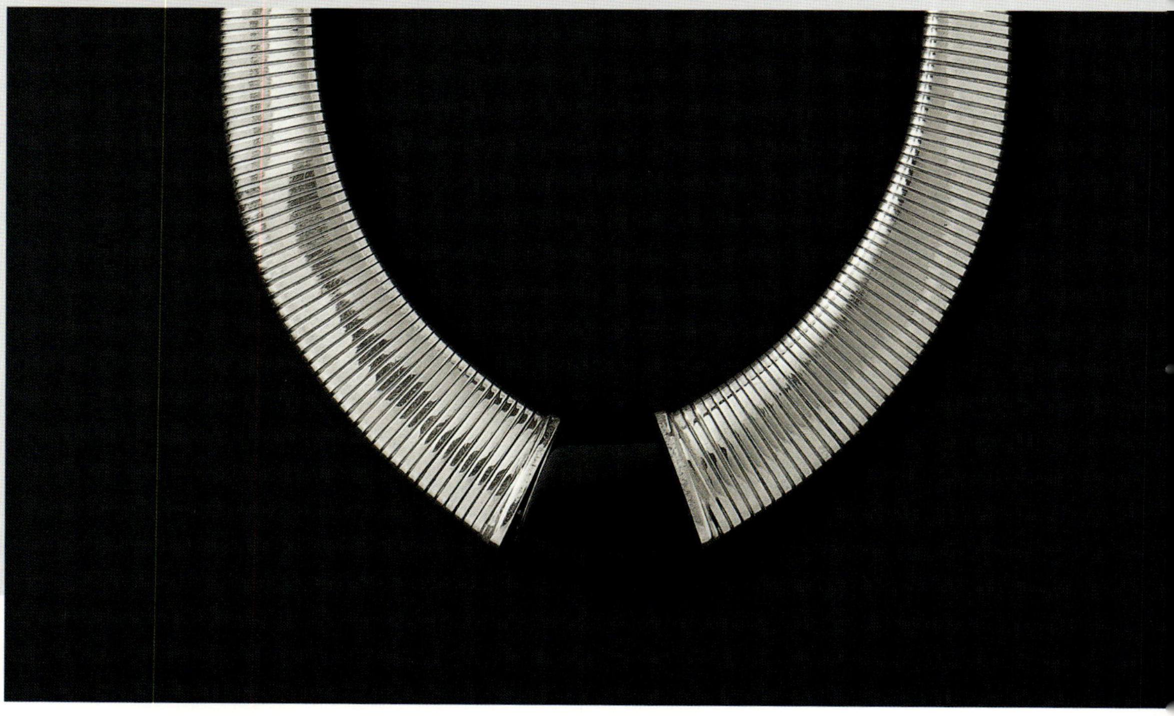

COLLIER, 1932
Messing vernickelt, Schraubverschluß, Galalith
Halskette: L 480
MB Bd. IX, S. 302, M-Nr. 19.506, 23.6.32, 30,–

114

NECKLACE, 1932
Brass, nickel-plated; screw clasp; Galalith
Chain: L 480
PB Vol. IX, p. 302, M. no. 19.506, 23.6.32, 30,–

COLLIER, 1932
Messing vernickelt, Schraubverschluß, Galalith
Halskette: L 440
MB Bd. IX, S. 363, M-Nr. 19.746, 5.8.32, 38,–

115

NECKLACE, 1932
Brass, nickel-plated; screw clasp; Galalith
Chain: L 440
PB Vol. IX, p. 363, M. no. 19.746, 5.8.32, 38,–

COLLIER, 1932
Messing verchromt, integrierter Steckverschluß, Galalith
Halskette: L 430
MB Bd. IX, S. 161, M-Nr. 18.943, 6.1.32, 15,–
MB Bd. IX, S. 248, M-Nr. 19.285, 2.5.32,
Spiraldraht gesetzlich geschützt

▸ 116

NECKLACE, 1932
Brass, chromium-plated; integrated box-snap clasp; Galalith
Chain: L 430
PB Vol. IX, p. 161, M. no. 18.943, 6.1.32, 15,–
PB Vol. IX, p. 248, M. no. 19.285, 2.5.32,
spiral wire copyright

COLLIER, 1932
Messing vernickelt, Schraubverschluß, Wolkengalalith
Halskette: L 450
MB Bd. IX, S. 329, M-Nr. 19.608, 15.7.32, 19,–

117

NECKLACE, 1932
Brass, nickel-plated; screw clasp; cloudy Galalith
Chain: L 450
PB Vol. IX, p. 329, M. no. 19.608, 15.7.32, 19,–

COLLIER »GANSGURGEL«,1932
Messing vernickelt, Schnappschloß, Galalith
Halskette: L 450
MB Bd. X, S. 71, M-Nr. 20.072, 12.11.32, 33,–

▸118

NECKLACE »GANSGURGEL«, 1932
Brass, nickel-plated; lobster clasp; Galalith
Chain: L 450
PB Vol. X, p. 71, M. no. 20.072, 12.11.32, 33,–

HALSKETTE, 1932
Messing vernickelt, Schraub-verschluß, Galalith
Halskette: L 460
MB Bd. IX, S. 370, M-Nr. 19.769, 5.8.32, 39,–
Musterschutz v. 11.VIII.32

119

CHAIN, 1932
Brass, nickel-plated; screw clasp; Galalith
Chain: L 460
PB Vol. IX, p. 370, M. no. 19.769, 5.8.32, 39,–
Pattern copyright 11.VIII.32

COLLIER, 1932
Messing vernickelt, Galalith, Schraubverschluß
Halskette: L 445
MB Bd. IX, S. 315, M-Nr. 19.550, 26.6.32, 24,–

▸120

NECKLACE, 1932
Brass, nickel-plated; Galalith; screw clasp
Chain: L 445
PB Vol. IX, p. 315, M. no. 19.550, 26.6.32, 24,–

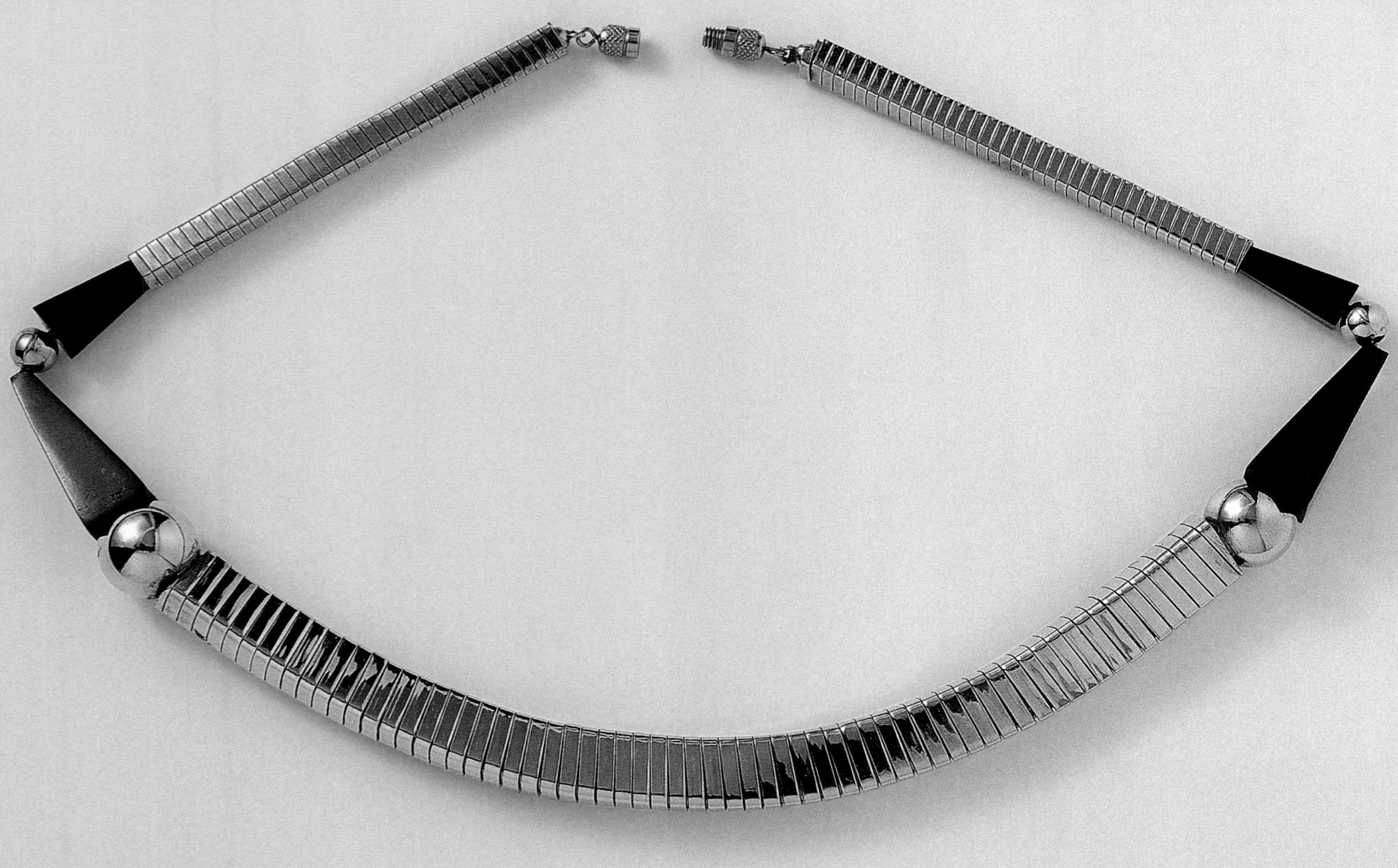

COLLIER, 1932
Messing verchromt, Schraubverschluß
Halskette: L 400
MB Bd. IX, S. 364, M-Nr. 19.752, 5.8.32

121

NECKLACE, 1932
Brass, chromium-plated; screw clasp
Chain: L 400
PB Vol. IX, p. 364, M. no. 19.752, 5.8.32

HALSKETTE MIT ANHÄNGER, 1932
Messing verchromt, Federringverschluß
Halskette: L 420, Anhänger: H 85
MB Bd. X, S. 7, M-Nr. 19.814, 18.8.32, 54,–

▶ **122**

CHAIN WITH PENDANT, 1932
Brass, chromium-plated; bolt-ring clasp
Chain: L 420; pendant: H 85
PB Vol. X, p. 7, M. no. 19.814, 18.8.32, 54,–

COLLIER, 1932
Messing verchromt, Federringverschluß
Halskette: L 420
MB Bd. IX, S. 362, M-Nr. 19.743, 5.8.32

123

NECKLACE, 1932
Brass, chromium-plated; bolt-ring clasp
Chain: L 420
PB Vol. IX, p. 362, M. no. 19.743, 5.8.32

COLLIER, 1932
Messing verchromt, Kastenschloß, Galalith
Halskette: L 430, H 40
MB Bd. X, S. 64, M-Nr. 20.046, 7.11.32, 15,–
MB Bd. IX, S. 342, M-Nr. 19.658, 15.7.32

124

NECKLACE, 1932
Brass, chromium-plated; box-snap clasp; Galalith
Chain: L 430; H 40
PB Vol. X, p. 64, M. no. 20.046, 7.11.32, 15,–
PB Vol. IX, p. 342, M. no. 19.658, 15.7.32

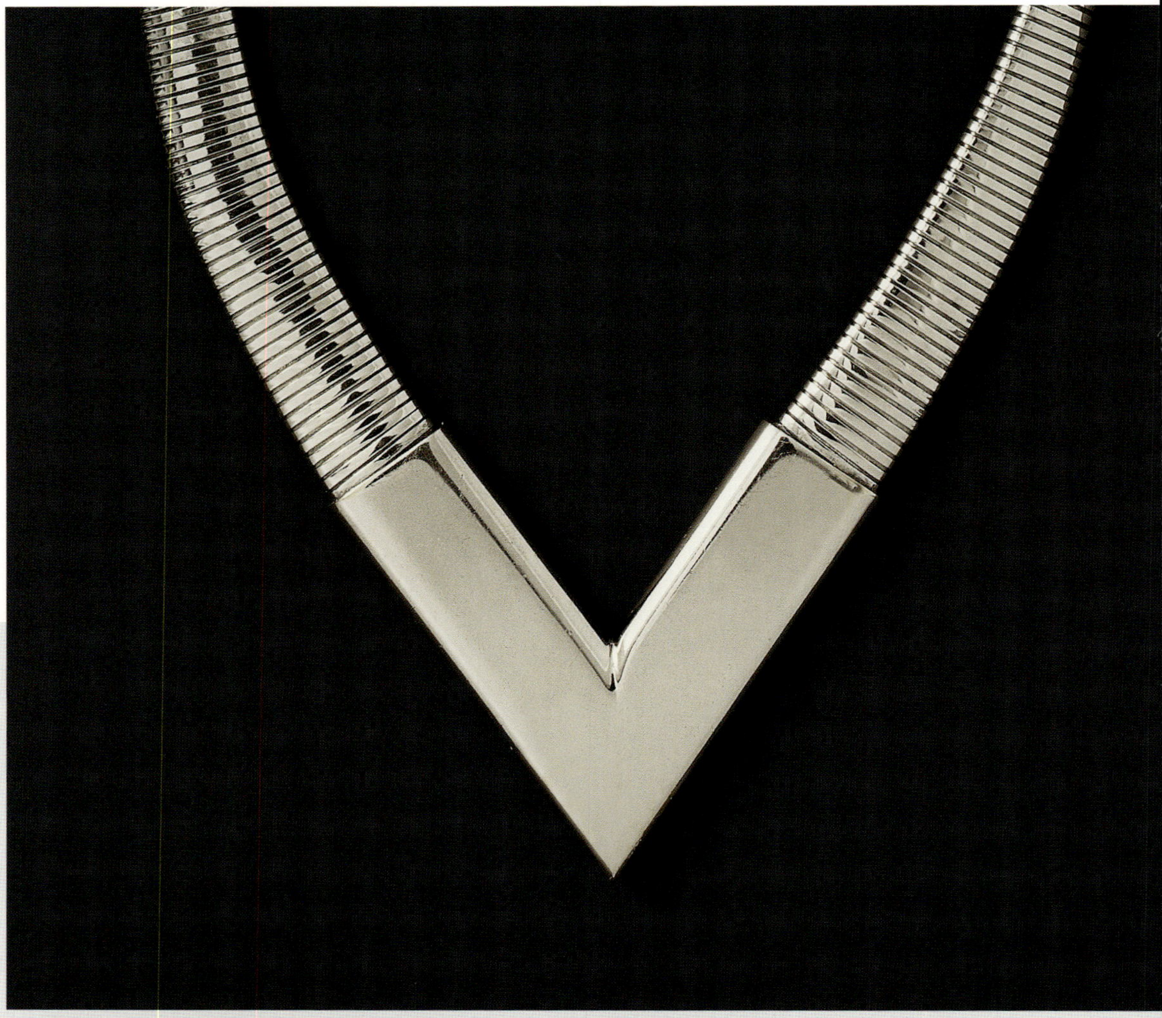

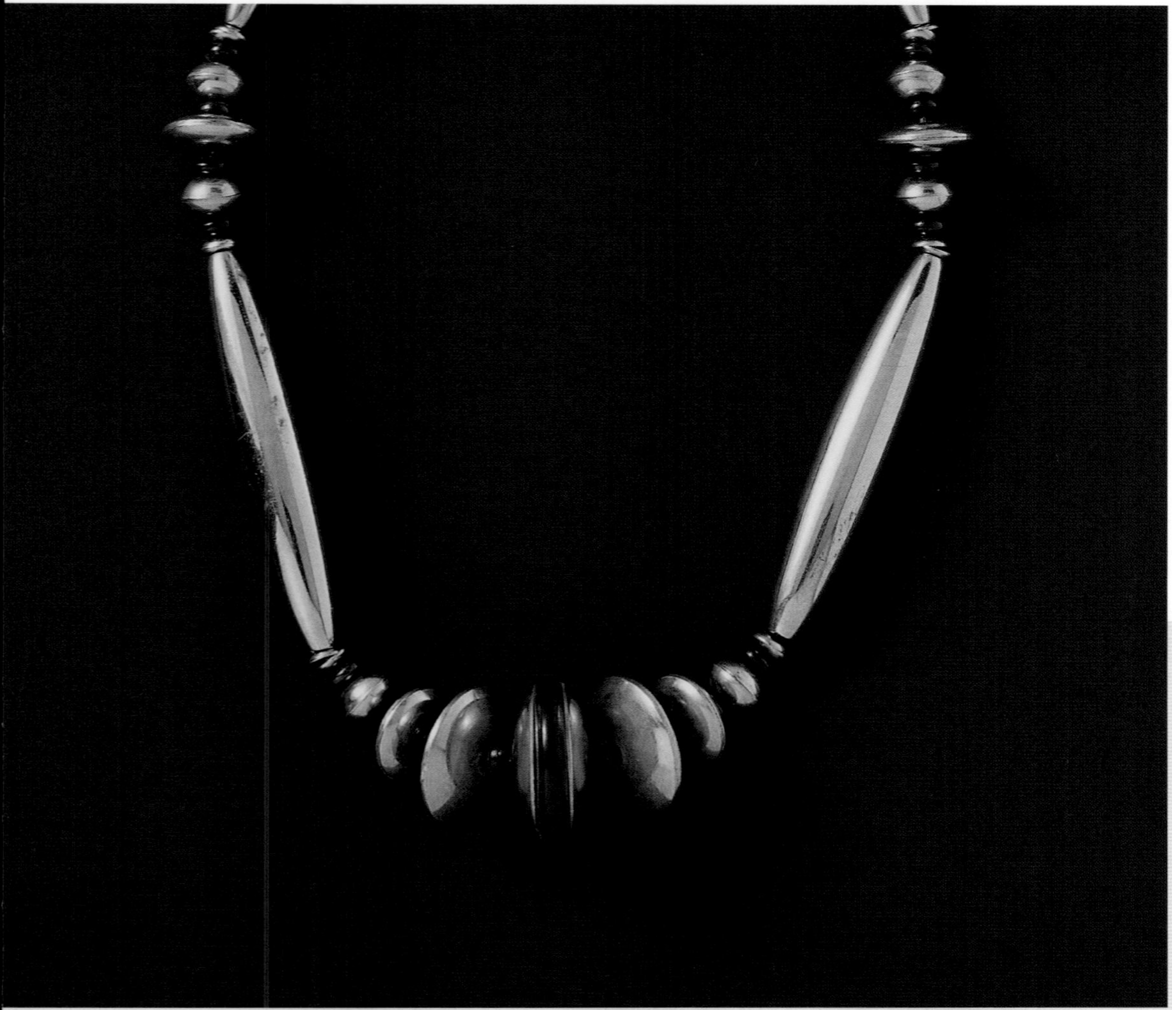

HALSKETTE, 1932
Messing vernickelt, Schraubverschluß, Galalith
Halskette: L 490
MB Bd. IX, S. 310, M-Nr. 19.537, 24.6.32, 36,–

125

CHAIN, 1932
Brass, nickel-plated; screw clasp; Galalith
Chain: L 490
PB Vol. IX, p. 310, M. no. 19.537, 24.6.32, 36,–

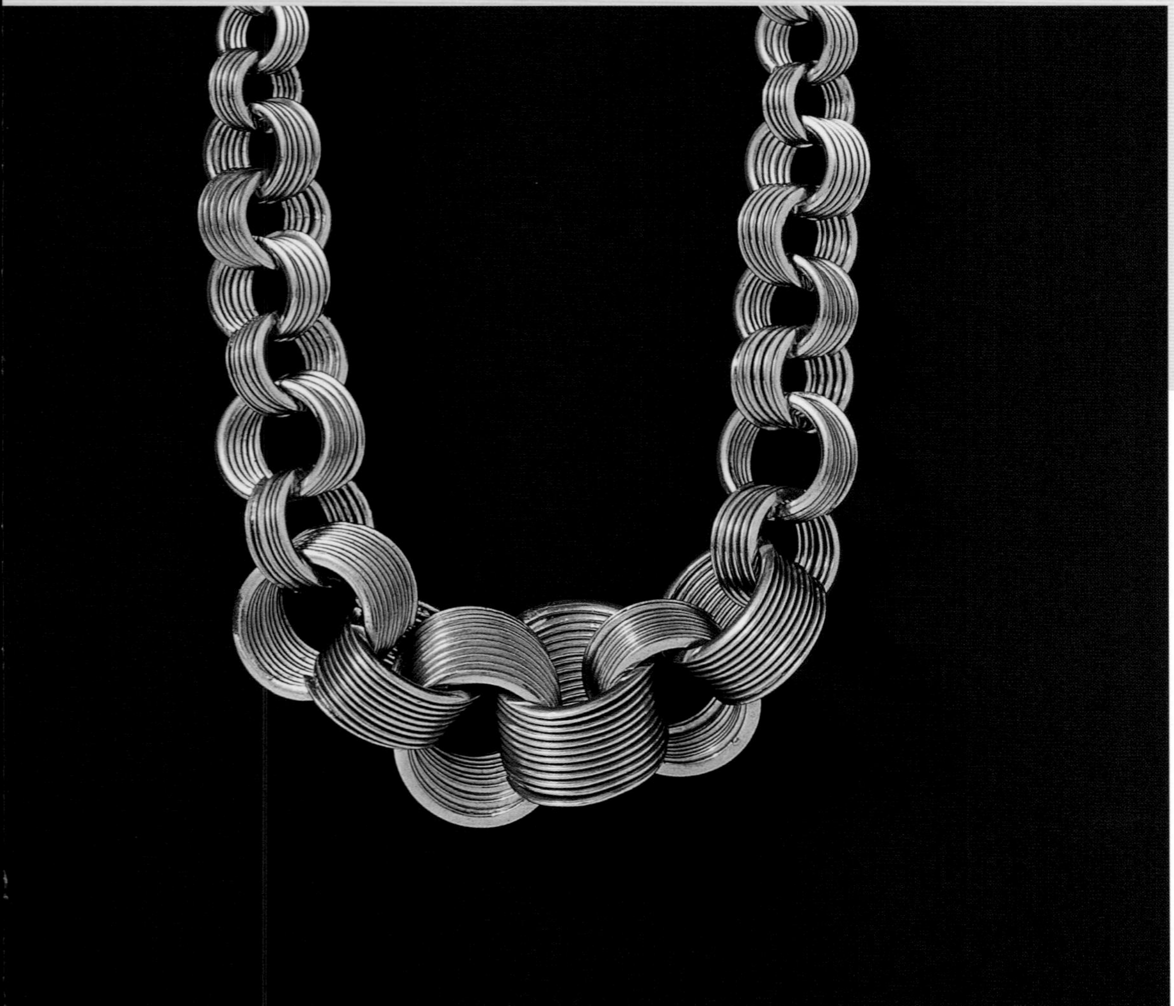

COLLIER, 1932
Messing verchromt, Federringverschluß
»GARANTIE***«
Halskette: L 420
MB Bd. IX, S. 332, M-Nr. 19.619, 15.7.32

126

NECKLACE, 1932
Brass, chromium-plated; bolt-ring clasp
»GARANTIE***«
Chain: L 420
PB Vol. IX, p. 332, M. no. 19.619, 15.7.32

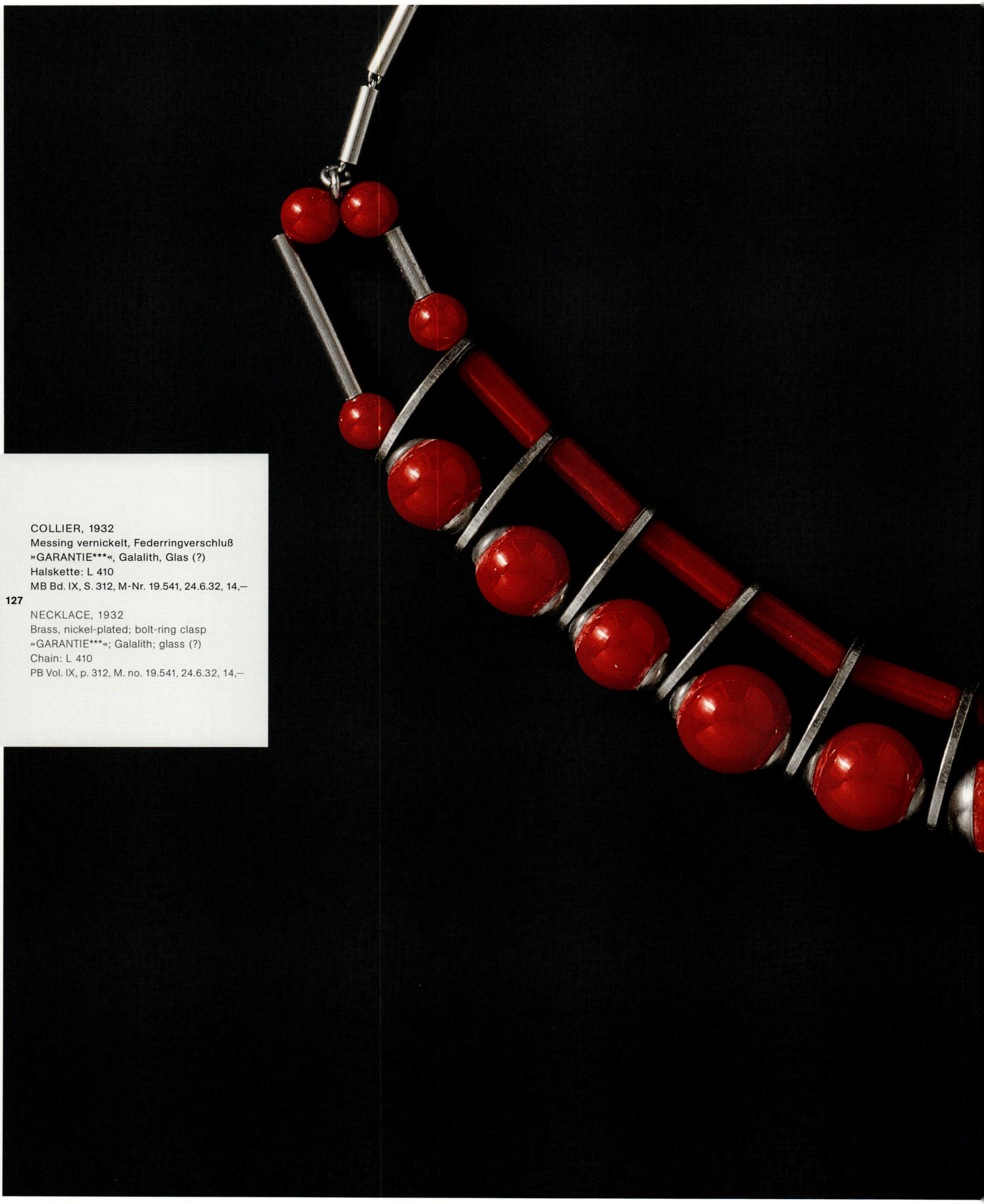

127

COLLIER, 1932
Messing vernickelt, Federringverschluß
»GARANTIE***«, Galalith, Glas (?)
Halskette: L 410
MB Bd. IX, S. 312, M-Nr. 19.541, 24.6.32, 14,–

NECKLACE, 1932
Brass, nickel-plated; bolt-ring clasp
»GARANTIE***«; Galalith; glass (?)
Chain: L 410
PB Vol. IX, p. 312, M. no. 19.541, 24.6.32, 14,–

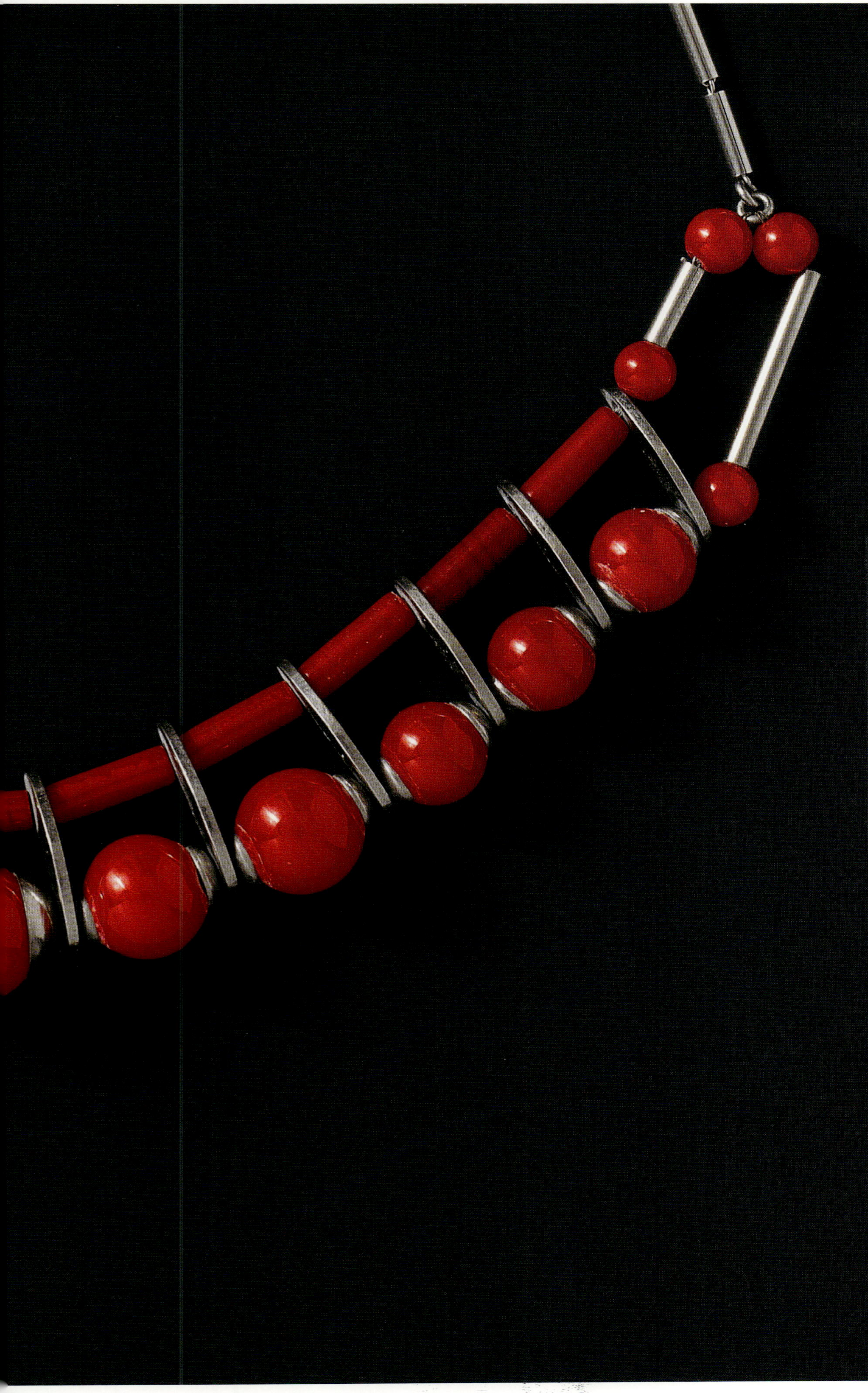

ARMREIF, 1932
Messing verchromt, Galalith
Ø 80, B 15
MB Bd. X, S. 35, M-Nr. 19.921, 23.9.32,
9,– (siehe auch S. 40, Abb. 33)

128

BANGLE, 1932
Brass, chromium-plated; Galalith
Ø 80, W 15
PB Vol. X, p. 35, M. no. 19.921, 23.9.32,
9,– (see also p. 40, fig. 33)

HALSKETTE MIT ANHÄNGER, 1932
Messing vernickelt, Glas, Galalith, Seidenkordel
Halskette: h.L 370, Anhänger: 80
MB Bd. IX, S. 314, M-Nr. 19.547, 25.6.32, 24,–

129

CHAIN WITH PENDANT, 1932
Brass, nickel-plated; glass; Galalith; silk cord
Chain: h.L 370, pendant 80
PB Vol. IX, p. 314, M. no. 19.547, 25.6.32, 24,–

HALSKETTE, 1932
Messing vernickelt, Federringverschluß, Marke »GARANTIE*«, Glas, Galalith**
Halskette: L 450, Anhänger: 70
MB Bd. IX, S. 314, M-Nr. 19.547, 25.6.32, 24,–

130

CHAIN, 1932
Brass, nickel-plated; bolt-ring clasp; marked »GARANTIE***«; glass; Galalith
Chain: L 450, pendant: 70
PB Vol. IX, p. 314, M. no. 19.547, 25.6.32, 24,–

HALSKETTE MIT ANHÄNGER, 1932
Messing vernickelt, Schraubverschluß, Galalith
Halskette: L 610, Anhänger: H 80
MB Bd. X, S.1, M-Nr. 19.789, 15.8.32, 21,–

131

CHAIN WITH PENDANT, 1932
Brass, nickel-plated; screw clasp; Galalith
Chain: L 610; pendant: H 80
PB Vol. X, p. 1, M. no. 19.789, 15.8.32, 21,–

HALSKETTE MIT ANHÄNGER, 1932
Messing verchromt, Schraubverschluß, Galalith; Anhänger beidseitig tragbar
Halskette: L 610, Anhänger: H 75
MB Bd. IX, S. 313, M-Nr. 19.544, 25.6.32, 10,–

132

CHAIN WITH PENDANT, 1932
Brass, chromium-plated; screw clasp; Galalith; pendant can be worn on both sides
Chain: L 610; pendant: H 75
PB Vol. IX, p. 313, M. no. 19.544, 25.6.32, 10,–

HALSKETTE, 1932
Messing vernickelt, Schraubverschluß, Galalith
L 430
MB Bd. IX, S. 334, M-Nr. 19.628, 15.7.32, 24,–

▶ **133**

CHAIN, 1932
Brass, nickel-plated; screw clasp; Galalith
L 430
PB Vol. IX, p. 334, M. no. 19.628, 15.7.32, 24,–

COLLIER, 1932
Gelbmetall, Federringverschluß, Galalith
Halskette: L 440
MB Bd. IX, S. 350, M-Nr. 19.693, 29.7.32

134

NECKLACE, 1932
Pinchbeck; bolt-ring clasp; Galalith
Chain: L 440
PB Vol. IX, p. 350, M. no. 19.693, 29.7.32

CLIP *KÖNIGIN LUISE-BUND*, 1932
Messing verchromt, aufgenietetes Galalith, darauf Krone und Buchstabe »L«
L 55, B 31
MB Bd. IX, S. 322, M-Nr. 19.582, 25.6.1932 (betr. Buchstaben)

▸ 135

CLIP *KÖNIGIN LUISE-BUND* [QUEEN LOUISE KNOT], 1932
Brass, chromium-plated; Galalith riveted on; on this crown and letter »L«
L 55, W 31
PB Vol. IX, p. 322, M. no. 19.582, 25.6.1932 (refers to letters)

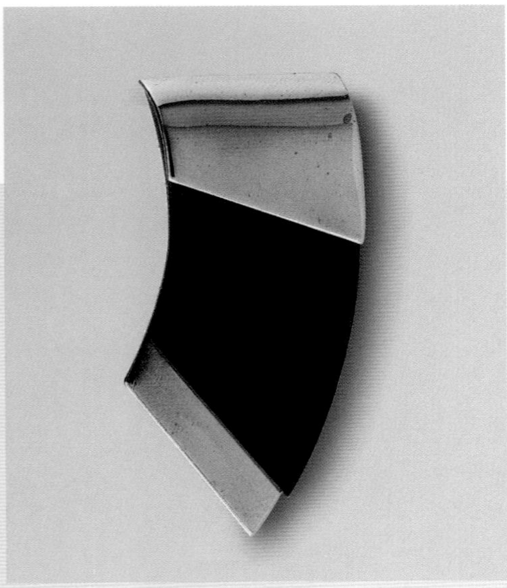

CLIP, 1932
Messing verchromt, aufgeschraubtes Galalith
Clipmechanismus: außen »187«, »Breveté« (geschützt)
L 61, B 125
MB Bd. X, S. 33, Nr. 19.916, 23.9.32, 6,–

136

CLIP, 1932
Brass, chromium-plated; Galalith, screwed on
Clip mechanism: marked externally: »187«; »Breveté« (patented)
L 61, W 125
PB Vol. X, p. 33, no. 19.916, 23.9.32, 6,–

ARMREIF, 1932
Messing verchromt, aufgeschraubtes Galalith
Ø 75, B 9, H 24
MB Bd. X, S. 34, M-Nr. 19.918, 23.9.32, 7,25

137

BANGLE, 1932
Brass, chromium-plated; Galalith, screwed-on
Ø 75, W 9, H 24
PB Vol. X, p. 34, M. no. 19.918, 23.9.32, 7,25

HALSKETTE, 1932
Messing vernickelt, Federringverschluß, Galalith
Halskette: L 410
Variante in rot (Titelabb.): Sammlung Händel
Variante in blau: Privatsammlung, München

◀ **138**

CHAIN, 1932
Brass, nickel-plated; bolt-ring clasp; Galalith
Chain: L 410
Variant in red (cover picture): Händel Collection
Variant in blue: private collection, Munich

ARMBAND, 1932
Messing vernickelt, Schnappverschluß, Galalith
L 185
Variante in rot: Sammlung Händel
Variante in blau: Privatsammlung München

◀ **139**

BRACELET, 1932
Brass, nickel-plated; lobster clasp; Galalith
L 185
Variant in red: Händel Collection
Variant in blue: private collection, Munich

HALSKETTE, 1932
Messing vernickelt, teilweise lackiert, Federringverschluß, Galalith
Halskette: L 410
MB Bd. IX, S. 136, M-Nr. 18.345, 6.10.32

140

CHAIN, 1932
Brass, nickel-plated; partly lacquered; bolt-ring clasp; Galalith
Chain: L 410
PB Vol. IX, p. 136, M. no. 18.345, 6.10.32

HALSKETTE, 1932
Messing vernickelt, Federringverschluß, Galalith
Halskette: L 400, Mittelteil: H 40

141

CHAIN, 1932
Brass, nickel-plated; bolt-ring clasp; Galalith
Chain: L 400; central piece: H 40

COLLIER, 1932
Messing vernickelt, Federringverschluß, zweifarbiges Galalith
Halskette: L 400
MB Bd. X, S. 120, M-Nr. 20.216, 16.12.32, 10,–

142

NECKLACE, 1932
Brass, nickel-plated; bolt-ring clasp; Galalith in two colours
Chain: L 400
PB Vol. X, p. 120, M. no. 20.216, 16.12.32, 10,–

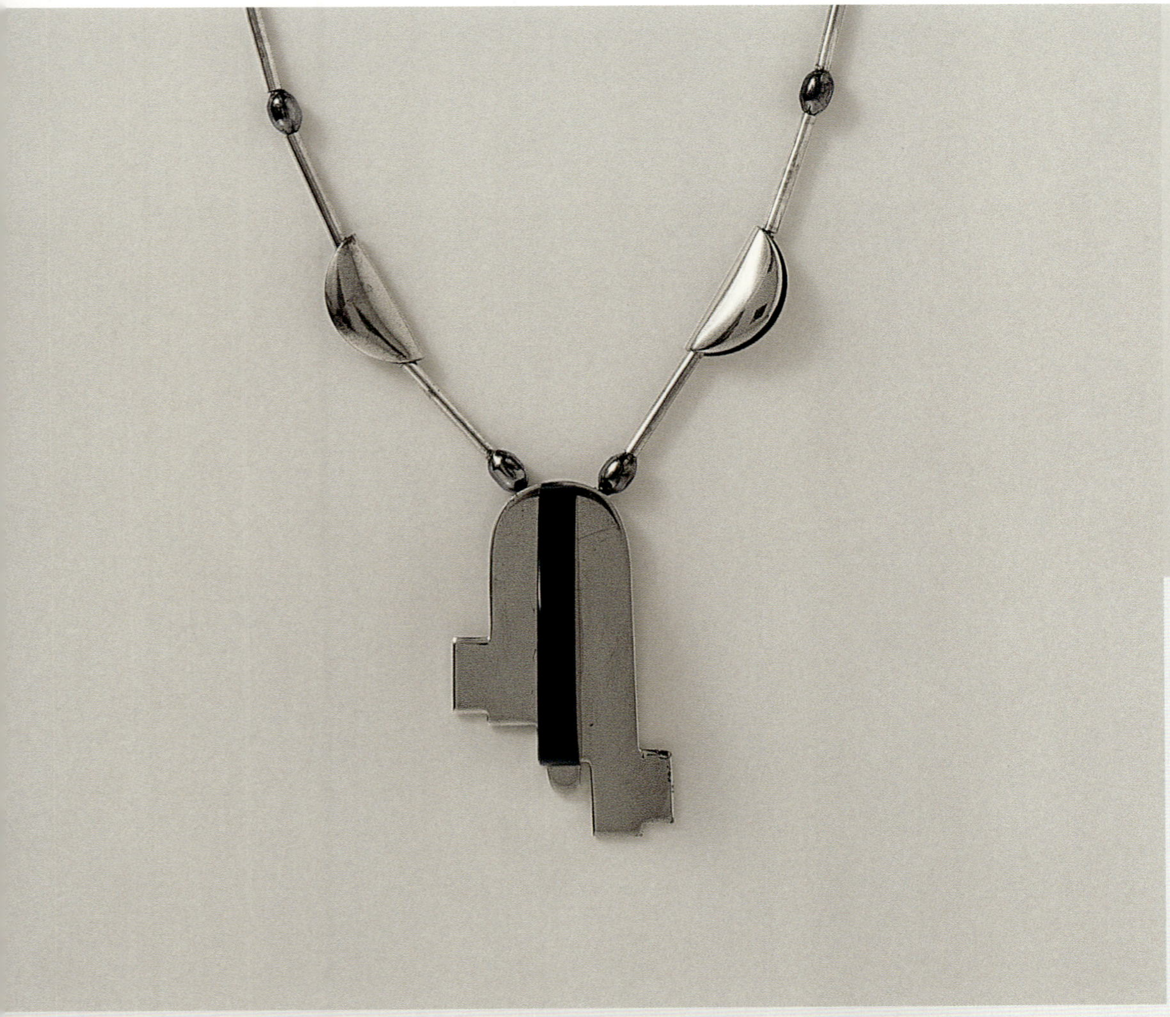

143

HALSKETTE MIT ANÄNGER, 1932
Messing verchromt, Galalith
Halskette: L 445, Anhänger: H 45
MB Bd. X, S. 98, M-Nr. 20.182, 2.12.32, 12,–

CHAIN WITH PENDANT, 1932
Brass, chromium-plated; Galalith
Chain: L 445, pendant: H 45
PB Vol. X, p. 98, M. no. 20.182, 2.12.32, 12,–

144

HALSKETTE MIT ANHÄNGER, 1932
Metallband, Messing verchromt, Federringverschluß, Glas, zweifarbiges Galalith
Halskette: L 510, Anhänger: H 58
MB Bd. X, S. 110, M-Nr. 20.218, 16.12.32, 13,–

CHAIN WITH PENDANT, 1932
Metal band, chromium-plated brass; boltring clasp; glass; Galalith in two colours
Chain: L 510; pendant: H 58
PB Vol. X, p. 110, M. no. 20.218, 16.12.32, 13,–

COLLIER, 1932
Messing vernickelt, Schraubverschluß, Galalith/Wolkengalalith
Halskette: L 430
MB Bd. X, S. 36, M-Nr. 19.926, 23.9.32, 33,–

145

NECKLACE, 1932
Brass, nickel-plated; screw clasp; Galalith/cloudy Galalith
Chain: L 430
PB Vol. X, p. 36, M. no. 19.926, 23.9.32, 33,–

COLLIER, 1932
Messing vernickelt, Federringverschluß, Galalith
Halskette: L 440
MB Bd. X, S. 36, M-Nr. 19.926 (Variante), 23.9.32, 33,–

146

NECKLACE, 1932
Brass, nickel-plated; bolt-ring clasp; Galalith
Chain: L 440
PB Vol. X, p. 36, M. no. 19.926 (variant), 23.9.32, 33,–

COLLIER, 1932
Messing vernickelt, Schraubverschluß, Galalith in untersch. Rotfärbung (V)
Halskette: L 430
MB Bd. IX, S. 371, M-Nr. 19.772/1, 5.8.32, 36,–

▸ 147

NECKLACE, 1932
Brass, nickel-plated; screw clasp; Galalith in variegated reds (V)
Chain: L 430
PB Vol. IX, p. 371, M. no. 19.772/1, 5.8.32, 36,–

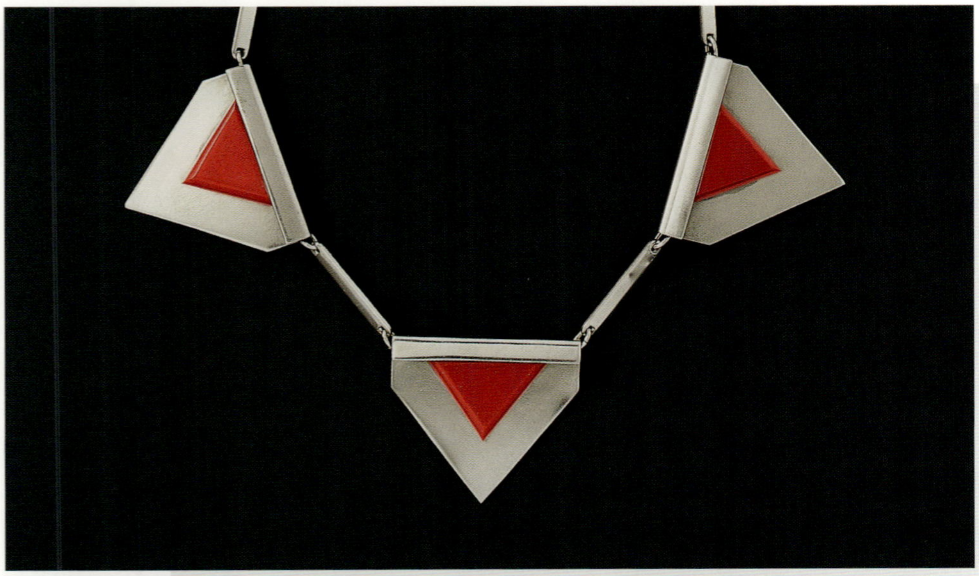

COLLIER, 1932
Messing verchromt, Federringverschluß, aufgeklebtes und aufgeschraubtes Galalith
Halskette: L 450
MB Bd. X, S. 69, M-Nr. 20.064, 8.11.32
MB Bd. IX, S. 315, M-Nr. 19.592, 1.7.32, 6,– (1 T)

◀ **148**

NECKLACE, 1932
Brass, chromium-plated; bolt-ring clasp; Galalith, glued and screwed on
Chain: L 450
PB Vol. X, p. 69, M. no. 20.064, 8.11.32
PB Vol. IX, p. 315, M. no. 19.592, 1.7.32, 6,– (1 T)

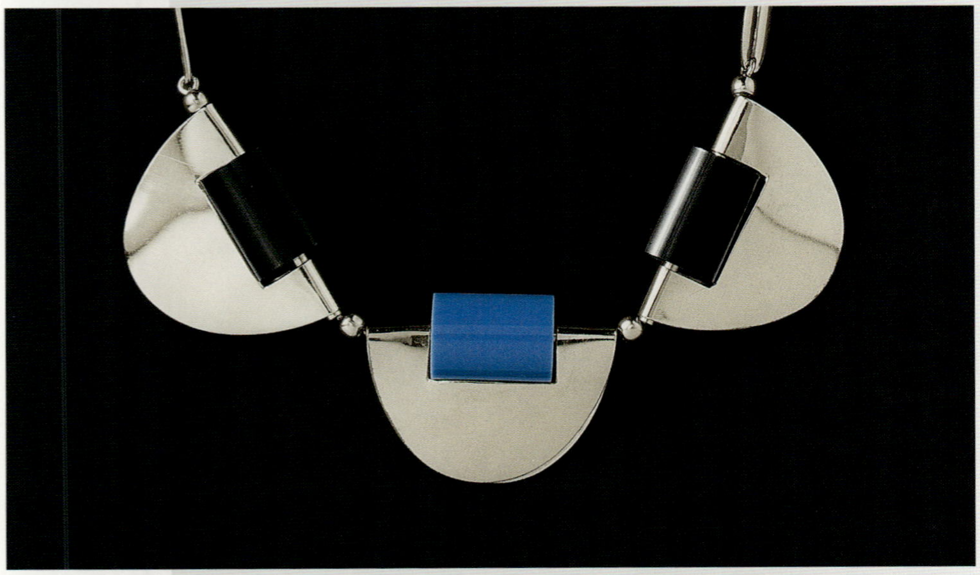

COLLIER, 1932
Messing verchromt, Federringverschluß, aufgeklebtes Galalith
Halskette: L 410, Glied: H 35
MB Bd. X, S. 69, M-Nr. 20.064, 8.11.32
MB Bd. IX, S. 325, M-Nr. 19.592, 1.7.32, 6,– (1 T.)

149

NECKLACE, 1932
Brass, chromium-plated; bolt-ring clasp; Galalith, glued on
Chain: L 410; link: H 35
PB Vol. X, p. 69, M. no. 20.064, 8.11.32
PB Vol. IX, p. 325, M. no. 19.592, 1.7.32, 6,– (1 T)

COLLIER, 1932
Messing verchromt, Federringverschluß, Galalith
Halskette: L 400
MB Bd. IX, S. 365, M-Nr. 19.755, 5.8.32

150

NECKLACE, 1932
Brass, chromium-plated; bolt-ring clasp; Galalith
Chain: L 400
PB Vol. IX, p. 365, M. no. 19.755, 5.8.32

COLLIER, 1932
Messing verchromt, Federringverschluß, marmoriertes Galalith
Halskette: L 410, Glied: H 35
MB Bd. X, S. 69, M-Nr. 20.064, 8.11.32

151

NECKLACE, 1932
Brass, chromium-plated; bolt-ring clasp; marbled Galalith
Chain: L 410; link: H 35
PB Vol. X, p. 69, M. no. 20.064, 8.11.32

COLLIER MIT ANHÄNGER, 1932
Metallband, Messing verchromt, Schraubverschluß, Galalith
Halskette: L 400, Anhänger: H 55
MB Bd. X, S. 99, M-Nr. 20.184, 2.12.32, 12,–

152

NECKLACE WITH PENDANT, 1932
Metal band, chromium-plated brass; screw clasp; Galalith
Chain: L 400; pendant: H 55
PB Vol. X, p. 99, M. no. 20.184, 2.12.32, 12,–

HALSKETTE, 1932
Messing verchromt, Galalith
Halskette: L 520
MB Bd. X, S. 122, M-Nr. 20.260, 24.12.32, 18,–

153

CHAIN, 1932
Brass, chromium-plated; Galalith
Chain: L 520
PB Vol. X, p. 122, M. no. 20.260, 2 4.12.32, 18,–

HALSKETTE MIT SCHIEBER, 1932
Messing vernickelt, Galalith,
Seidenkordel
Halskette: L 390
MB Bd. X, S. 107, M-Nr. 20.209, 2.12.32,
18,– (siehe auch S. 21, Abb. 12)

154

CHAIN WITH SLIDE, 1932
Brass, nickel-plated; Galalith, silk cord
Chain: L 390
PB Vol. X, p. 107, M. no. 20.209, 2.12.32,
18,– (see also p. 21, Abb. 12)

COLLIER, 1932
Messing verchromt, Schraubverschluß,
aufgeschraubtes Galalith
Halskette: L 490, H 68
MB Bd. X, S. 105, M-Nr. 20.205,
2.12.32, 12,–

155

NECKLACE, 1932
Brass, chromium-plated; screw clasp;
Galalith, screwed on
Chain: L 490, H 68
PB Vol. X, p. 105, M. no. 20.205,
2.12.32, 12,–

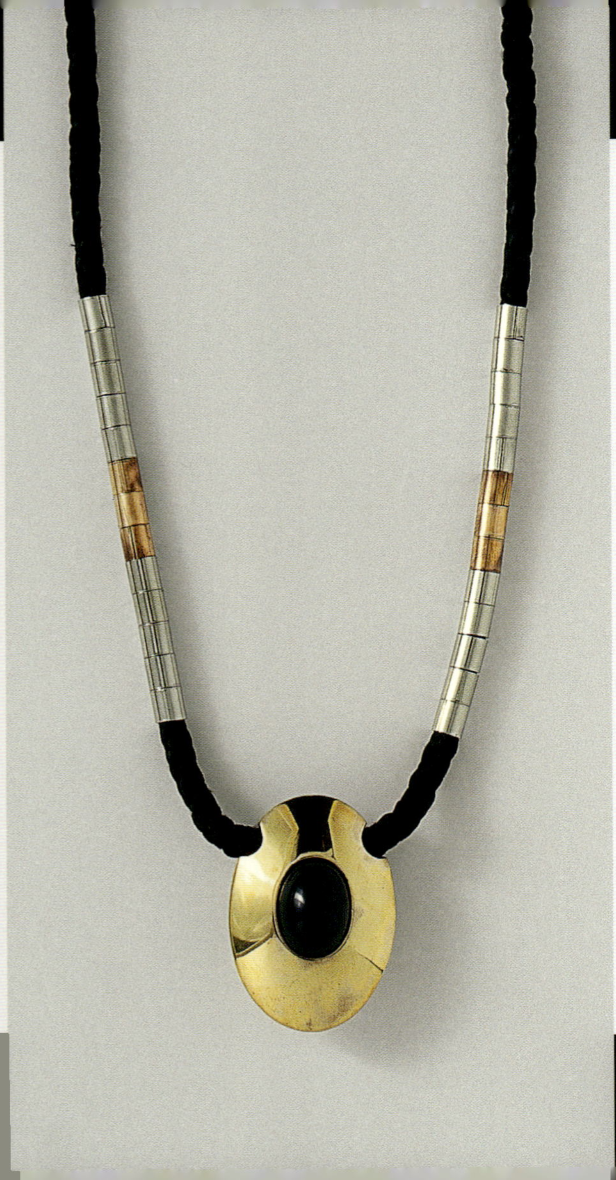

156

HALSKETTE MIT ANHÄNGER, 1932
Gelbmetall, Galalith, Seidenkordel
L 350
MB Bd. X, S. 119, M-Nr. 20.251,
17.12.32, 12,–

CHAIN WITH PENDANT, 1932
Pinchbeck; Galalith; silk cord
L 350
PB Vol. X, p. 119, M. no. 20.251,
17.12.32, 12,–

157

HALSKETTE MIT ANHÄNGER, 1932
Messing vernickelt, Rotmetall,
Gelbmetall, Seidenkordel
Halskette: L 410, Anhänger: H 50
MB Bd. X, S. 122, M-Nr. 20.261,
24.12.32, 18,–

CHAIN WITH PENDANT, 1932
Brass, nickel-plated; red brass;
pinchbeck; silk cord
Chain: L 410, pendant: H 50
PB Vol. X, p. 122, M. no. 20.261,
24.12.32, 18,–

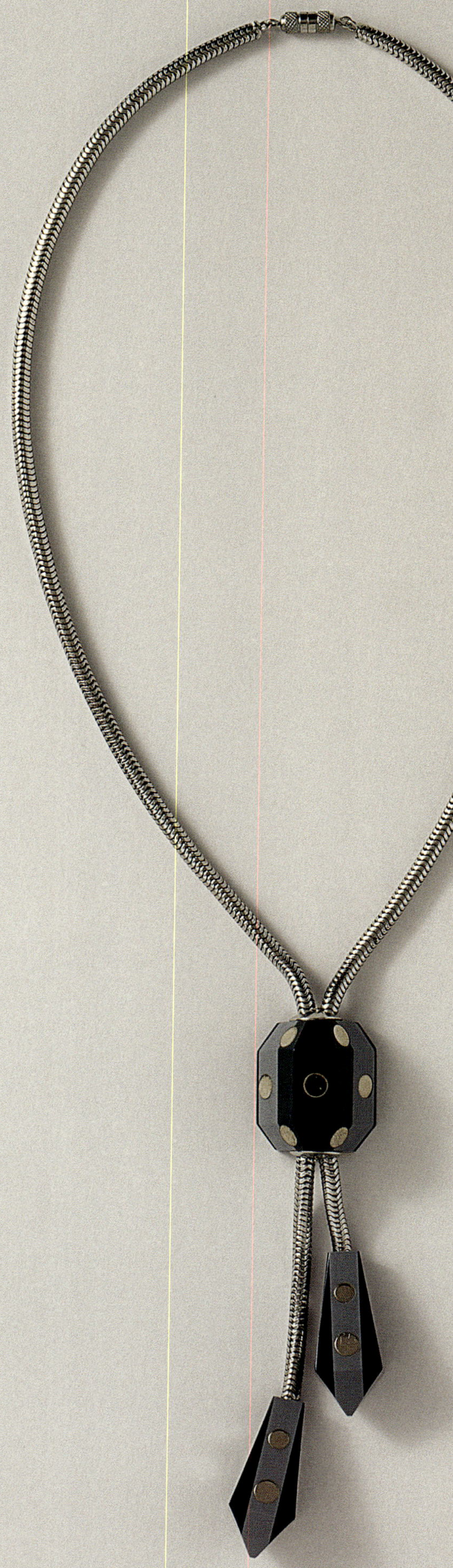

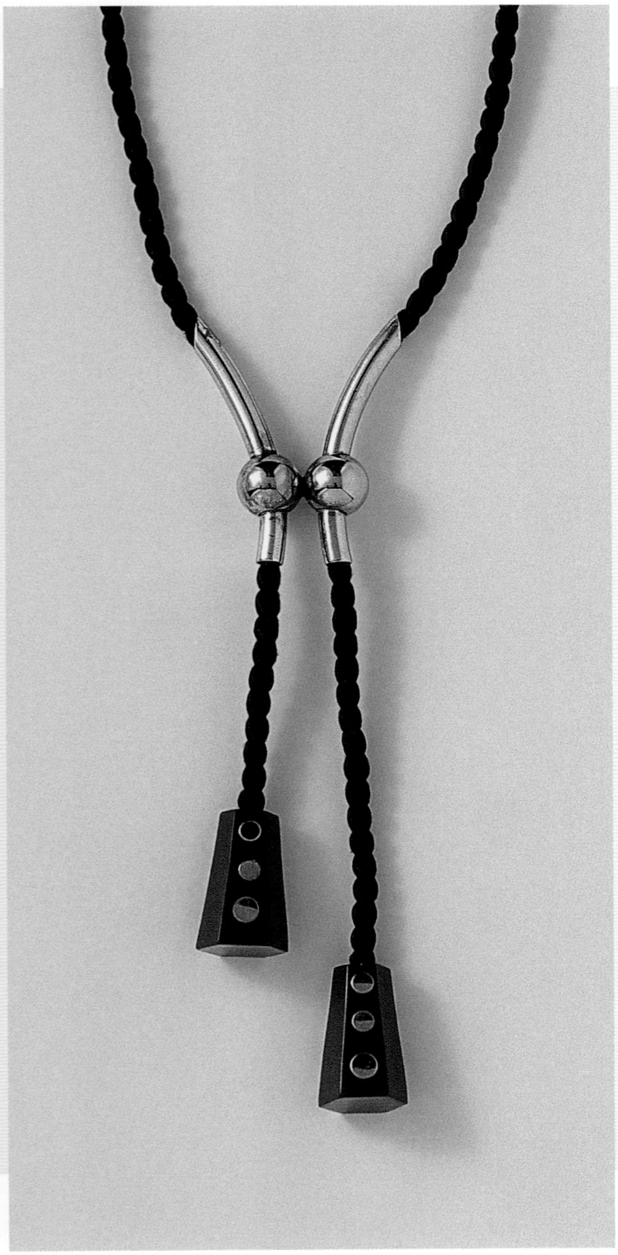

HALSKETTE MIT SCHIEBER, 1932
Messing vernickelt, Schraubverschluß, Galalith, Vermerk MB:
Schieber läuft auf Kork
Halskette: h.L 400
MB Bd. X, S. 83, Nr. 20.117, 1.12.32, 42,–

◀158

CHAIN WITH SLIDE, 1932
Brass, nickel-plated; screw clasp; Galalith; remark PB: *slide runs on cork*
Chain: h.L 400
PB Vol. X, p. 83, no. 20.117, 1.12.32, 42,–

HALSKETTE MIT SCHIEBER, 1932
Messing vernickelt, Galalith, Seidenkordel
Halskette: h.L 380
MB Bd. X, S. 122, M-Nr. 20.260, 24.12.32, 18,–

159

CHAIN WITH SLIDE, 1932
Brass, nickel-plated; Galalith; silk cord
Chain: h.L 380
PB Vol. X, p. 122, M. no. 20.260, 24.12.32, 18,–

HALSKETTE MIT SCHIEBER, 1932
Messing vernickelt, Galalith, Seidenkordel
Halskette: h.L 420
MB Bd. X, S. 127, M-Nr. 20.281, 24.12.32, 18,–

160

CHAIN WITH SLIDE, 1932
Brass, nickel-plated; Galalith; silk cord
Chain: h.L 420
PB Vol. X, p. 127, M. no. 20.281, 24.12.32, 18,–

HALSKETTE MIT ABHÄNGUNG, 1932
Messing, Federringverschluß, Galalith
Halskette: L 360, Abhängung: 110
MB Bd. IX, S. 373, M-Nr. 19.776, 5.8.32, 20,–

161

CHAIN WITH PENDANT, 1932
Brass; bolt-ring clasp; Galalith
Chain: L 360, pendant: 110
PB Vol. IX, p. 373, M. no. 19.776, 5.8.32, 20,–

A U S W A H L

COLLECTION 1933

S E L E C T I O N

HALSKETTE MIT ANHÄNGER, 1933
Messing vernickelt, Chromkugel vorne in der Mitte = Drehverschluß, Galalith, Seidenkordel
Halskette: L 290
MB Bd. X, S.183, M-Nr. 20.542, 1.2.33, 18,–

162

CHAIN WITH PENDANT, 1933
Brass, nickel-plated; central chrome sphere = slot-lock clasp; Galalith; silk cord
Chain: L 290
PB Vol. X, p. 183, M. no. 20.542, 1.2.33, 18,–

COLLIER, 1933
Messing vernickelt, Federringverschluß, Galalith, Seidenkordel
Halskette: L 410
MB Bd. X, S. 282, M-Nr. 20.956, 4.7.33, 21,– (siehe auch S. 34, Abb. 24)

▸ 163

NECKLACE, 1933
Brass, nickel-plated; bolt-ring clasp; Galalith; silk cord
Chain: L 410
PB Vol. X, p. 282, M. no. 20.956, 4.7.33, 21,– (see also p. 34, fig. 24)

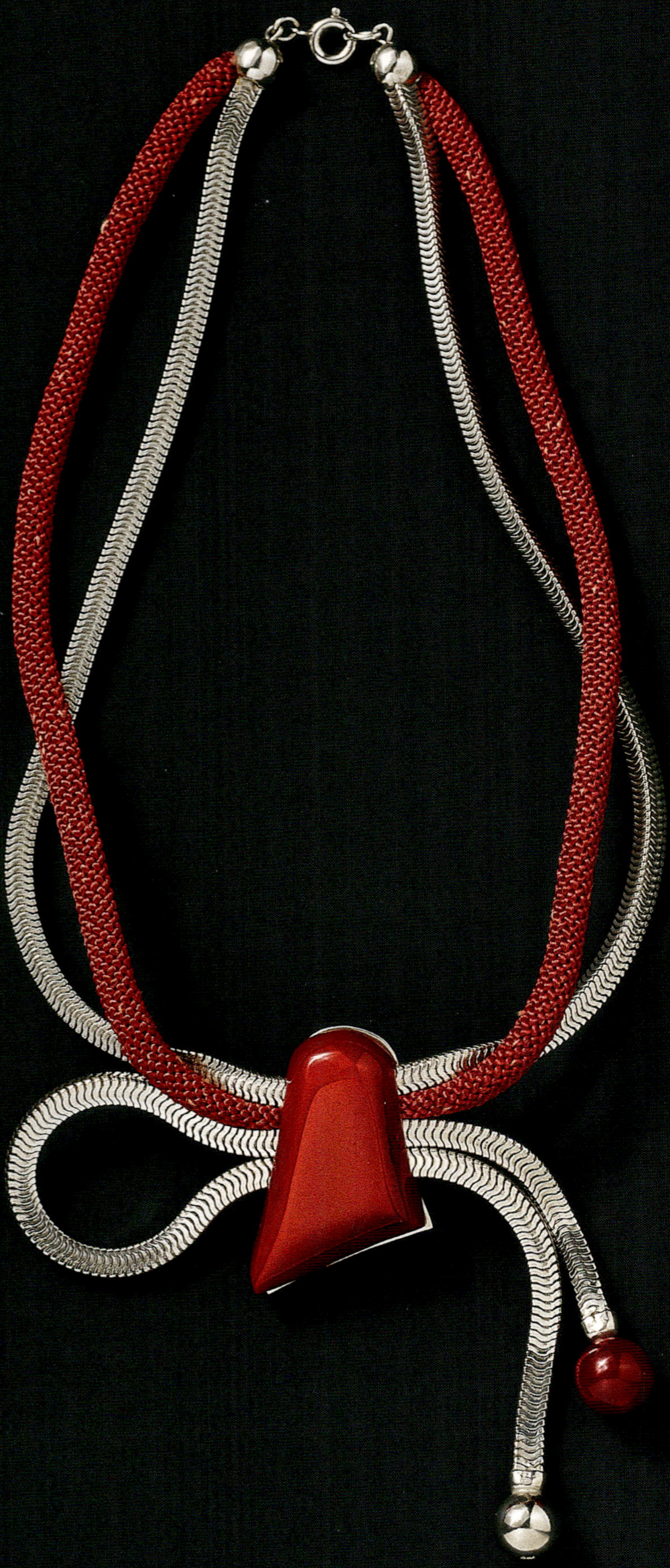

HALSKETTE MIT SCHIEBER, 1933
Messing vernickelt, Schraubverschluß, Galalith
Halskette: h.L 400
MB Bd. X, S. 323, M-Nr. 21.125/1, 29.8.33, 27,–

164 CHAIN WITH SLIDE, 1933
Brass, nickel-plated; screw clasp; Galalith
Chain: h.L 400
PB Vol. X, p. 323, M. no. 21.125/1, 29.8.33, 27,–

HALSKETTE MIT SCHIEBER, 1933
Messing vernickelt, Schraubverschluß, Galalith
Halskette: h.L 380
MB Bd. X, S. 143, M-Nr. 20.338, 13.1.33, 20,–
MB Bd. X, S. 203, M-Nr. 20.612, 22.4.33 (Schieberrückseite)

165 CHAIN WITH SLIDE, 1933
Brass, nickel-plated; screw clasp; Galalith
Chain: h.L 380
PB Vol. X, p. 143, M. no. 20.338, 13.1.33, 20,–
PB Vol. X, p. 203, M. no. 20.612, 22.4.33 (verso of slide)

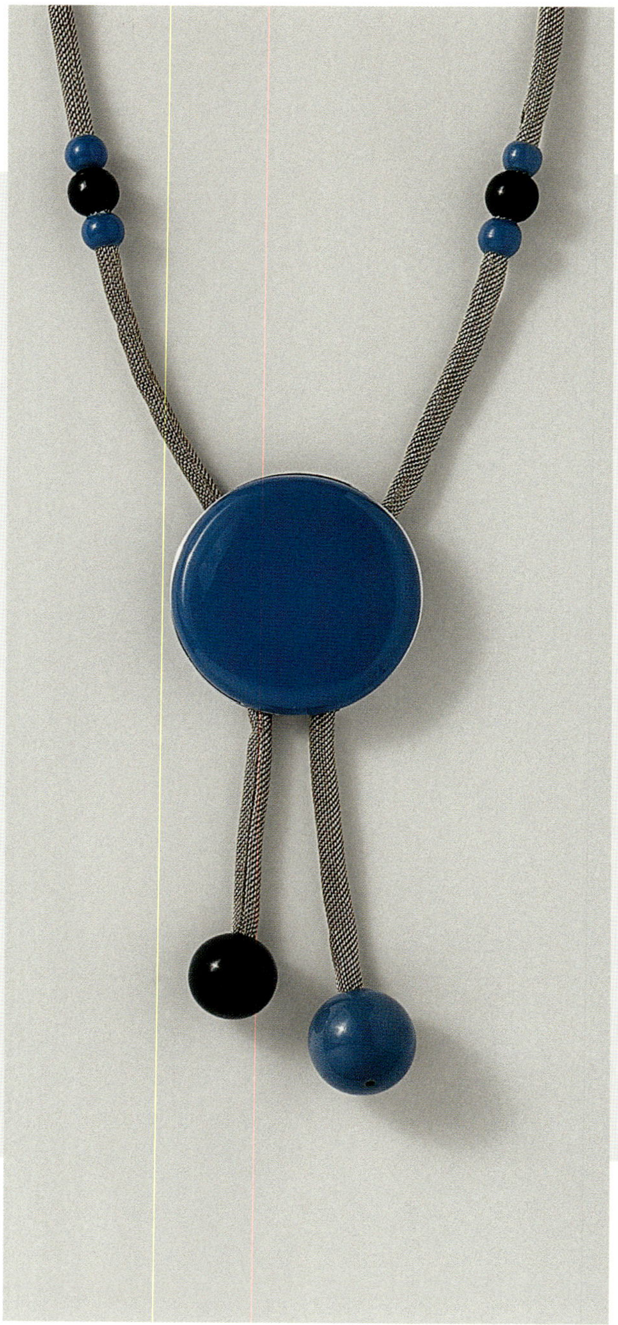

HALSKETTE MIT SCHIEBER, 1933
Kupferblech, Galalith, Seidenkordel
Halskette: h.L 430
MB Bd. X, S. 140, M-Nr. 20.331,
3.1.33, 21,–

166

CHAIN WITH SLIDE, 1933
Sheet copper; Galalith; silk cord
Chain: h.L 430
PB Vol. X, p. 140, M. no. 20.331,
3.1.33, 21,–

HALSKETTE MIT SCHIEBER, 1933
Messing vernickelt, Galalith,
Seidenkordel
Halskette: h.L 400
MB Bd. X, S. 143, M-Nr. 20.338/1,
13.1.33, 18,–
MB Bd. X, S. 203, M-Nr. 20.612,
22.4.33 (Schieberrückseite)

167

CHAIN WITH SLIDE, 1933
Brass, nickel-plated; Galalith; silk cord
Chain: h.L 400
PB Vol. X, p. 143, M. no. 20.338/1,
13.1.33, 18,–
PB Vol. X, p. 203, M. no. 20.612,
22.4.33 (verso of slide)

HALSKETTE MIT SCHIEBER, 1933
Messing vernickelt, Galalith,
Seidenkordel
Halskette: h.L 380
MB Bd. X, S. 154, M-Nr. 20.471, 19.1.33,
21,– (siehe auch S. 39, Abb. 32)

◀ 168

CHAIN WITH SLIDE, 1933
Brass, nickel-plated; Galalith;
silk cord
Chain: h.L 380
PB Vol. X, p. 154, M. no. 20.471, 19.1.33,
21,– (see also p. 39, fig. 32)

HALSKETTE, 1933
Messing vernickelt, Galalith
Halskette: h.L 340
MB Bd. X, S. 182, M-Nr. 20.539a,
1.2.33, 24,–

169

CHAIN, 1933
Brass, nickel-plated; Galalith
Chain: h.L 340
PB Vol. X, p. 182, M. no. 20.539a,
1.2.33, 24,–

HALSKETTE MIT SCHIEBER, 1933
Messing vernickelt, Galalith,
Seidenkordel
Halskette: h.L 350
MB Bd. X, S. 147, M-Nr. 20.352, 18.1.33,
21,– (siehe auch S. 39, Abb. 31)

170

CHAIN WITH SLIDE, 1933
Brass, nickel-plated; Galalith; silk cord
Chain: h.L 350
PB Vol. X, p. 147, M. no. 20.352, 18.1.33,
21,– (see also p. 39, fig. 31)

HALSKETTE MIT SCHIEBER, 1933
Messing vernickelt, Galalith,
Seidenkordel
Halskette: h.L 430
MB Bd. X, S. 167, M-Nr. 20.352/2,
18.1.33, 21,–

171

CHAIN WITH SLIDE, 1933
Brass, nickel-plated; Galalith; silk cord
Chain: h.L 430
PB Vol. X, p. 167, M. no. 20.352/2,
18.1.33, 21,–

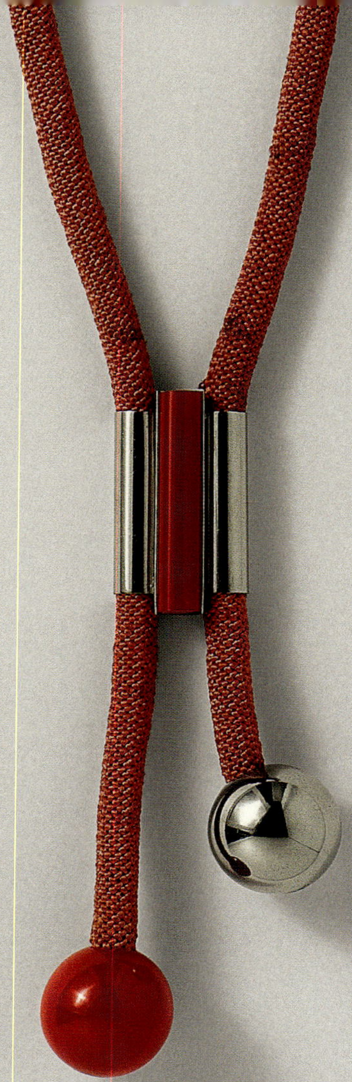

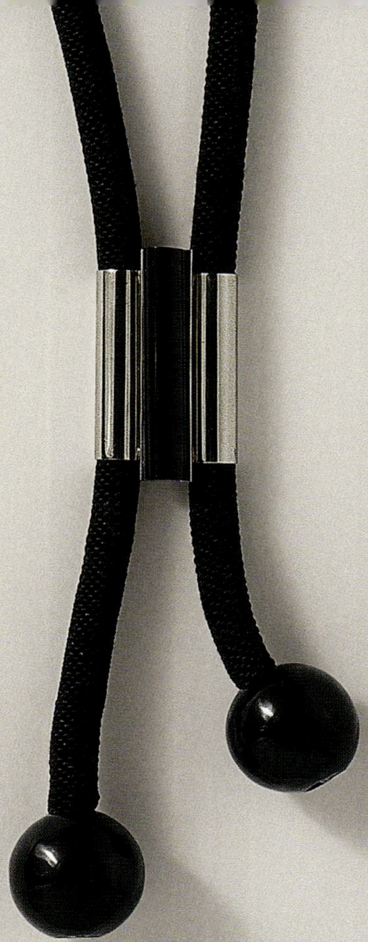

HALSKETTE MIT SCHIEBER, 1933
Messing vernickelt, Galalith,
Seidenkordel
Halskette: h.L 390
MB Bd. X, S. 142, M-Nr. 20.337, 13.1.33,
18,– (siehe auch S. 30, Abb. 22)

172

CHAIN WITH SLIDE, 1933
Brass, nickel-plated; Galalith; silk cord
Chain: h.L 390
PB Vol. X, p. 142, M. no. 20.337, 13.1.33,
18,– (see also p. 30, fig. 22)

HALSKETTE MIT ZWEI KLEINEN
SCHIEBERN, 1933
Messing vernickelt, Galalith,
Seidenkordel
Halskette: h.L 430
MB Bd. X, S. 147, M-Nr. 20.352,
18.1.33, 21,–

173

CHAIN WITH TWO SMALL SLIDES,
1933
Brass, nickel-plated; Galalith; silk cord
Chain: h.L 430
PB Vol. X, p. 147, M. no. 20.352,
18.1.33, 21,–

HALSKETTE, 1933
Messing vernickelt, Federringverschluß, Galalith, Baumwollkordel
Halskette: h.L 450
MB Bd. X, S. 154, M-Nr. 20.470, 19.1.33, 15,–

174

CHAIN, 1933
Brass, nickel-plated; bolt-ring clasp; Galalith; cotton cord
Chain: h.L 450
PB Vol. X, p. 154, M. no. 20.470, 19.1.33, 15,–

HALSKETTE MIT ANHÄNGER, 1933
Messing vernickelt, Seidenkordel
Halskette: L 470, Anhänger: H 10
MB Bd. X, S. 179, M-Nr. 20.534, 21.2.33, 12,–

175

CHAIN WITH PENDANT, 1933
Brass, nickel-plated; silk cord
Chain: L 470; pendant: H 10
PB Vol. X, p. 179, M. no. 20.534, 21.2.33, 12,–

HALSKETTE MIT SCHIEBER, 1933
Messing verchromt, Schraubverschluß, Galalith
Halskette: h.L 340

▸ **176**

CHAIN WITH SLIDE, 1933
Brass, chromium-plated; screw clasp; Galalith
Chain: h.L 340

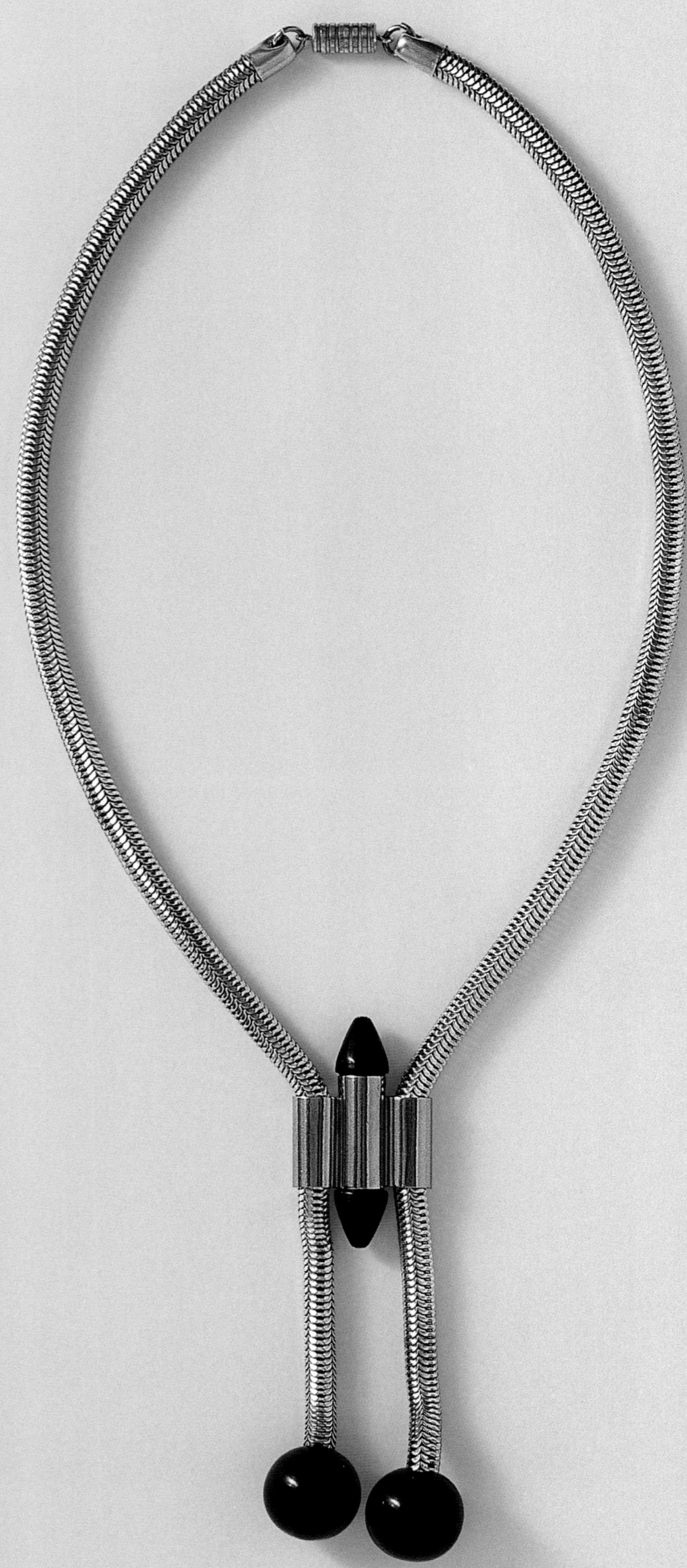

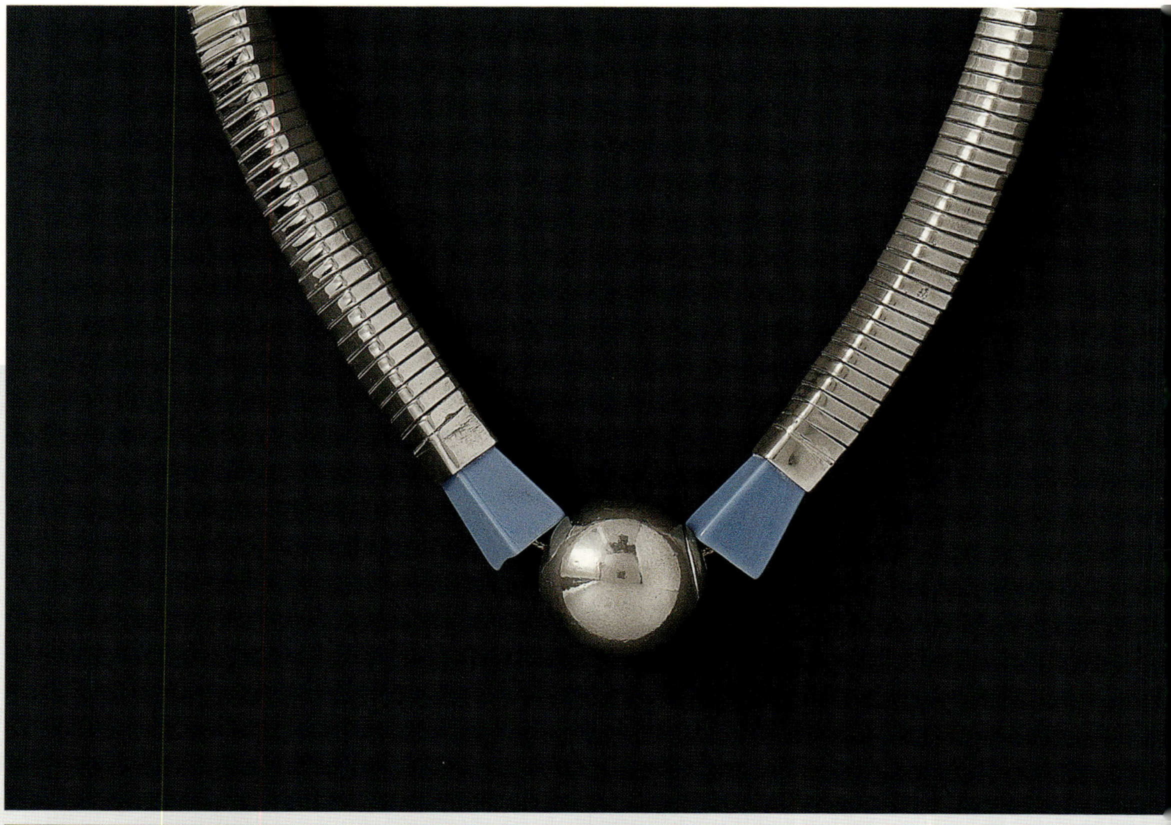

COLLIER, 1933
Messing vernickelt, Schraubverschluß, Galalith
Halskette: L 510
MB Bd. IX, S. 299, M-Nr. 19.493/1, 25.4.33, 27,–

177

NECKLACE, 1933
Brass, nickel-plated; screw clasp; Galalith
Chain: L 510
PB Vol. IX, p. 299, M. no. 19.493/1, 25.4.33, 27,–

COLLIER, 1933
Messing vernickelt, Schraubverschluß, Galalith
Halskette: L 380
MB Bd. X, S. 148, M-Nr. 20.353, 19.1.33, 18,–

178

NECKLACE, 1933
Brass, nickel-plated; screw clasp; Galalith
Chain: L 380
PB Vol. X, p. 148, M. no. 20.353, 19.1.33, 18,–

179

COLLIER, 1933
Messing vernickelt, Schraubverschluß, Galalith, Seidenkordel
Halskette: L 450
MB Bd. X, S. 294, M-Nr. 21.005, 1.7.33, 8,25

NECKLACE, 1933
Brass, nickel-plated; screw clasp; Galalith; silk cord
Chain: L 450
PB Vol. X, p. 294, M. no. 21.005, 1.7.33, 8,25

180

HALSKETTE, 1933
Messing vernickelt, Schraubverschluß, Galalith, Seidenkordel
Halskette: L 460
MB Bd. X, S. 174, M-Nr. 20.520, 14.2.33, 16,–

CHAIN, 1933
Brass, nickel-plated; screw clasp; Galalith; silk cord
Chain: L 460
PB Vol. X, p. 174, M. no. 20.520, 14.2.33, 16,–

COLLIER MIT ANHÄNGER, 1933
Messing vernickelt, Schraub-
verschluß, Galalith
Halskette: L 425, Anhänger:
H 70, B 30
MB Bd. X, S. 182, M-Nr. 20.540,
1.2.33, 21,–

181

NECKLACE WITH PENDANT, 1933
Brass, nickel-plated; screw clasp;
Galalith
Chain: L 425; pendant: H 70, B 30
PB Vol. X, p. 182, M. no. 20.540,
1.2.33, 21,–

HALSKETTE MIT SCHIEBER, 1933
Messing vernickelt, Schraubverschluß,
Seidenkordel
Halskette: h.L 280
MB Bd. X, S. 204, M-Nr. 20.614, 24.4.33, 9,–

▶ **182**

CHAIN WITH SLIDE, 1933
Brass, nickel-plated; screw clasp; silk cord
Chain: h.L 280
PB Vol. X, p. 204, M. no. 20.614, 24.4.33, 9,–

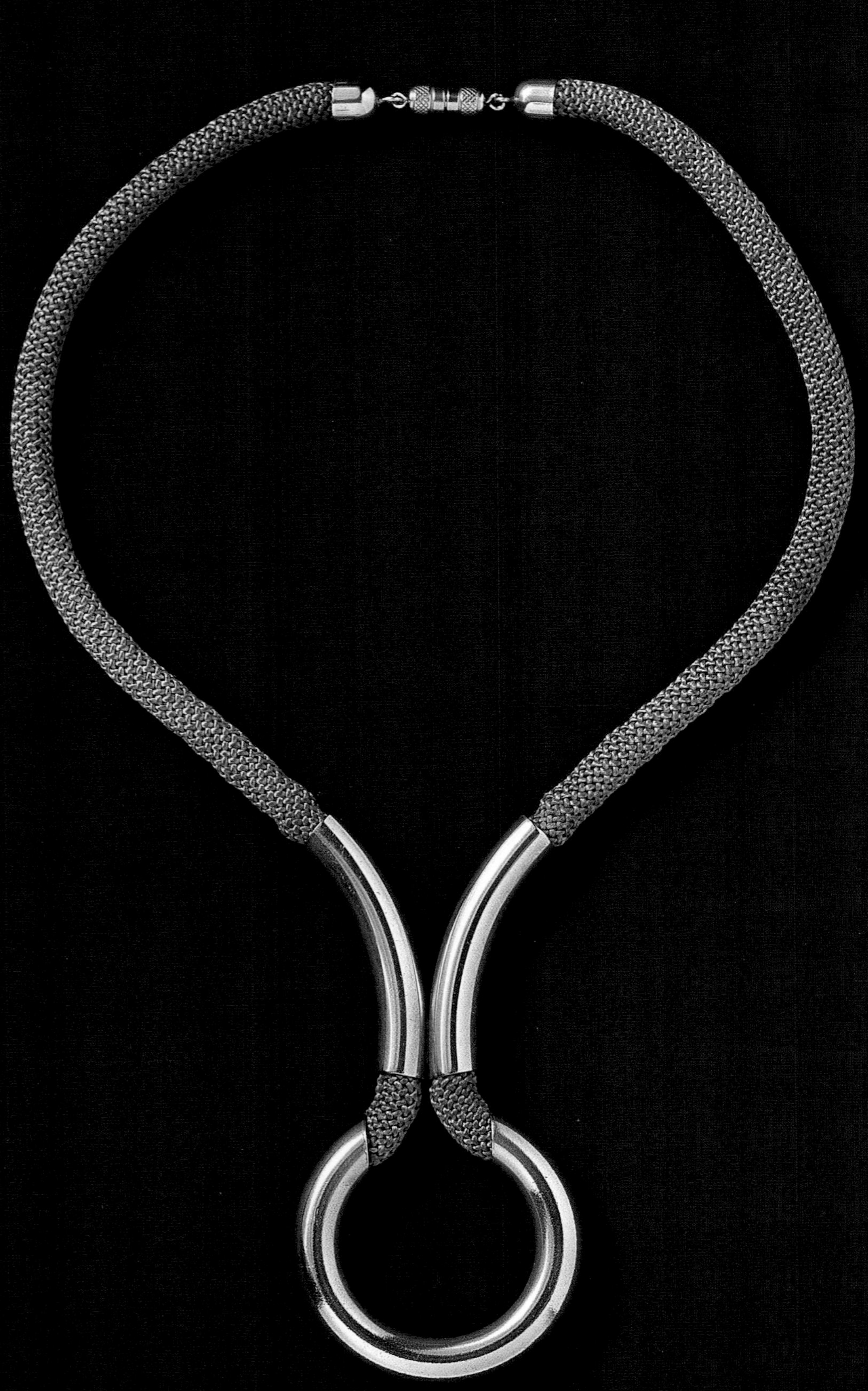

ARMREIF, 1933
Nickel, Gelbmetall
Etikett: »20.565«, Rs »GXPJ«
Ø 70, H 20
MB Bd. X, S. 189, M-Nr. 20.565,
10.3.33, 8,–

183

BANGLE, 1933
Nickel, pinchbeck
Label: »20.565«, Rs. »GXPJ«
Ø 70, H 20
PB Vol. X, p. 189, M. no. 20.565,
10.3.33, 8,–

ARMSPANGE, 1933
Messing verchromt, genutetes Band, eingeklebtes Galalith
Ø 70, B 17
MB Bd. X, S.188, M-Nr. 20.560, 10.3.33, 12,–
Vermerk MB: *Zeichnung nicht mehr bemustern, ist geschützt von H+Gr*
(= Henkel & Grosse, Pforzheim)

184

BANGLE, 1933
Brass, chromium-plated, chased band; Galalith, glued in
Ø 70, W 17
PB Vol. X, p. 188, M. no. 20.560, 10.3.33, 12,–
Remark PB: *Drawing no longer to be patterned, copyright by H+Gr*
(= Henkel & Grosse, Pforzheim/Germany)

185
COLLIER »GANSGURGEL«, 1933
Messing vernickelt, Federring-verschluß, Galalith
Halskette: L 450
MB Bd. X, S. 147, M-Nr. 21.351, 18.1.33, 18,–

NECKLACE »GANSGURGEL« (CHOKER), 1933
Brass, nickel-plated; bolt-ring clasp; Galalith
Chain: L 450
PB Vol. X, p. 147, M. no. 21.351, 18.1.33, 18,–

186
COLLIER MIT ANHÄNGER, 1933
Messing vernickelt, Kastenschloß, aufgeschraubtes Galalith
Halskette: L 440, Anhänger: H 55, B 24
MB Bd. X, S. 351, M-Nr. 21.231, 3.10.33

NECKLACE WITH PENDANT, 1933
Brass, nickel-plated; box-snap clasp; Galalith, screwed on
Chain: L 440, pendant: H 55, B 24
PB Vol. X, p. 351, M. no. 21.231, 3.10.33

▸ 187
COLLIER, 1933
Messing verchromt, Kastenschloß
Halskette: L 410
MB Bd. X, S. 351, M-Nr. 21.231, 3.10.33

NECKLACE, 1933
Brass, chromium-plated, box-snap clasp
Chain: L 410
PB Vol. X, p. 351, M. no. 21.231, 3.10.33

COLLIER, 1933
Silber/Bronze, Nickel, Federring-verschluß
Halskette: L 450
MB Bd. X, S. 151, M-Nr. 20.362, 19.1.33

188

NECKLACE, 1933
Silver/bronze; nickel; bolt-ring clasp
Chain: L 450
PB Vol. X, p. 151, M. no. 20.362, 19.1.33

COLLIER, 1933
Gelbmetall
Halskette: L 400
MB Bd. X, S. 300, M-Nr. 21.033, 3.8.33, 9,–

▶ **189**

NECKLACE, 1933
Pinchbeck
Chain: L 400
PB Vol. X, p. 300, M. no. 21.033, 3.8.33, 9,–

COLLIER MIT ANHÄNGER, 1933
Messing vernickelt, Schraubverschluß,
Galalith, Seidenkordel
Halskette: L 420, Anhänger: H 80
MB Bd. X, S. 190, M-Nr. 20.569,
15.3.33, 16,– (siehe auch S. 22, Abb. 15)

190

NECKLACE WITH PENDANT, 1933
Brass, nickel-plated; screw clasp;
Galalith; silk cord
Chain: L 420; pendant: H 80
PB Vol. X, p. 190, M. no. 20.569, 15.3.33,
16,– (see also p. 22, fig. 15)

COLLIER MIT ANHÄNGER, 1933
Messing vernickelt, Chrom, Schraub-
verschluß, Galalith, Seidenkordel
Halskette: L 430, Anhänger: H 60
MB Bd. X, S. 190, M-Nr. 20.568/2,
15.3.33, 16,– (siehe auch S. 22, Abb. 15)

191

NECKLACE WITH PENDANT, 1933
Brass, nickel-plated; chromium; screw
clasp; Galalith; silk cord
Chain: L 430; pendant: H 60
PB Vol. X, p. 190, M. no. 20.568/2,
15.3.33, 16,– (see also p. 22, fig. 15)

192

HALSKETTE MIT ANHÄNGER, 1933
Messing vernickelt, Chromband, Schraubverschluß, Galalith, Seidenkordel
Halskette: L 460, Anhänger: B 75
MB Bd. X, S. 201, M-Nr. 21.605, 21.4.33, 15,– Variante

CHAIN WITH PENDANT, 1933
Brass, nickel-plated; chromium band; screw clasp; Galalith; silk cord
Chain: L 460; pendant: B 75
PB Vol. X, p. 201, M. no. 21.605, 21.4.33, 15,– Variant

193

COLLIER MIT ANHÄNGER, 1933
Messing vernickelt/Nickel, Chromnickelband, Galalith, Seidenkordel
Halkette: L 420, Anhänger: H 65
MB Bd. X, S. 201, M-Nr. 20.606, 21.4.33, 18,–

NECKLACE WITH PENDANT, 1933
Brass, nickel-plated/nickel; chromium nickel band; Galalith; silk cord
Chain: L 420; pendant: H 65
PB Vol. X, p. 201, M. no. 20.606, 21.4.33, 18,–

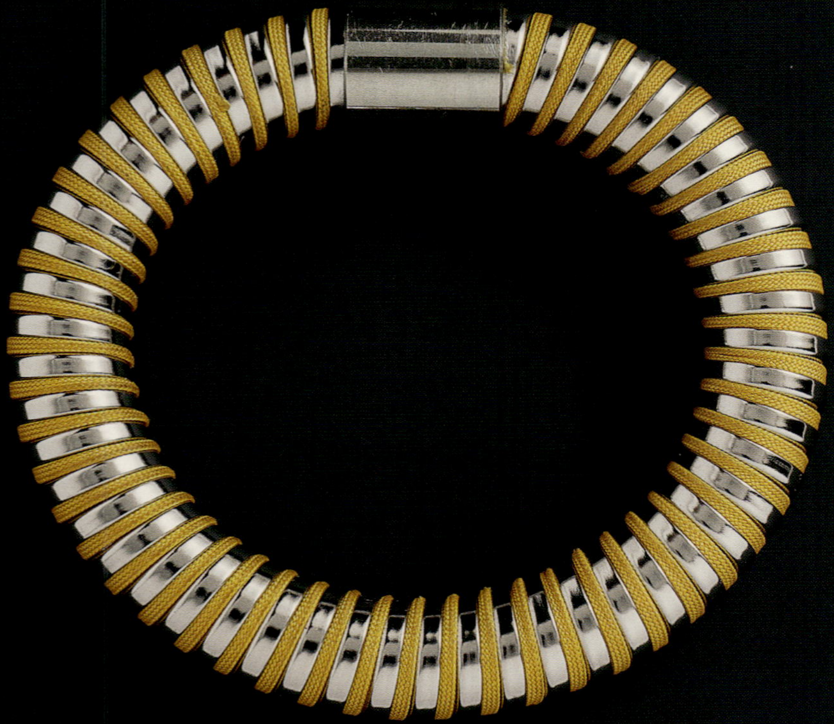

HALSREIF, 1933
Messing verchromt, Hakenverschluß,
Seidenband (V)
Reif: L 380
MB Bd. X, S. 178, M-Nr. 20.529/2, 21.2.33

◀ 194

TORQUE, 1933
Brass, chromium-plated; strung-bead
hook clasp; silk ribbon (V)
Torque: L 380
PB Vol. X, p. 178, M. no. 20.529/2, 21.2.33

ARMREIF, 1933
Messing verchromt, ohne Verschluß,
Seidenband (V)
Ø 90
MB Bd. X, S. 178, M-Nr. 20.529/1, 21.2.33

195

BANGLE, 1933
Brass, chromium-plated; no clasp;
silk ribbon (V)
Ø 90
PB Vol. X, p. 178, M. no. 20.529/1, 21.2.33

HALSKETTE MIT MITTELTEIL, 1933
Messing vernickelt, Galalith, Seidenkordel
Halskette: L 390
MB Bd. X, S. 200, M-Nr. 20.601, 21.4.33, 9,–

196

CHAIN WITH CENTRAL PIECE, 1933
Brass, nickel-plated; Galalith; silk cord
Chain: L 390
PB Vol. X, p. 200, M. no. 20.601, 21.4.33, 9,–

COLLIER MIT MITTELTEIL, 1933
Messing verchromt, Federringverschluß, Galalith
Halskette: L 410, Mittelteil: H 70, B 75
MB Bd. X, S. 313, M-Nr. 21.089, 23.8.33, 20,–

197

NECKLACE WITH CENTRAL PIECE, 1933
Brass, chromium-plated; bolt-ring clasp; Galalith
Chain: L 410; central piece: H 70, W 75
PB Vol. X, p. 313, M. no. 21.089, 23.8.33, 20,–

198

COLLIER MIT MITTELTEIL, 1933
Messing verchromt, Schraubverschluß, zweifarbiges Galalith
Halskette: L 430, Mittelteil: H 45
MB Bd. X, S. 194, M-Nr. 20.583, 17.3.33, 6,– (1Pl.)

NECKLACE WITH CENTRAL PIECE, 1933
Brass, chromium-plated; screw clasp; Galalith two coloured
Chain: L 430; central piece: H 45
PB Vol. X, p. 194, M. no. 20.583, 17.3.33, 6,– (1Pl.)

199

COLLIER MIT MITTELTEIL, 1933
Messing verchromt, Federringverschluß, Galalith
Halskette: L 400, Mittelteil: H 55
MB Bd. X, S. 224, M-Nr. 20.698, 5.5.33

NECKLACE WITH CENTRAL PIECE, 1933
Brass, chromium-plated; bolt-ring clasp; Galalith
Chain: L 400, central piece: H 55
PB Vol. X, p. 224, M. no. 20.698, 5.5.33

HALSKETTE MIT ANHÄNGER, 1933
Messing verchromt, Federringverschluß, Galalith
Halskette: L 610, Anhänger: H 65
MB Bd. X, S.171, M-Nr. 20.513/3, 14.2.33, 13,– (siehe auch S. 40, Abb. 34)

200

CHAIN WITH PENDANT, 1933
Brass, chromium-plated; bolt-ring clasp; Galalith
Chain: L 610; pendant: H 65
PB Vol. X, p. 171, M. no. 20.513/3, 14.2.33, 13,– (see also p. 40, fig. 34)

HALSKETTE MIT MITTELTEIL, 1933
Messing verchromt, Federringverschluß, aufgeschraubtes Galalith
Halskette: L 500, Mittelteil: H 45
MB Bd. X, S. 357, M-Nr. 21.258, 4.10.33, 15,–

201

CHAIN WITH CENTRAL PIECE, 1933
Brass, chromium-plated; bolt-ring clasp; Galalith, screwed on
Chain: L 500; central piece: H 45
PB Vol. X, p. 357, M. no. 21.258, 4.10.33, 15,–

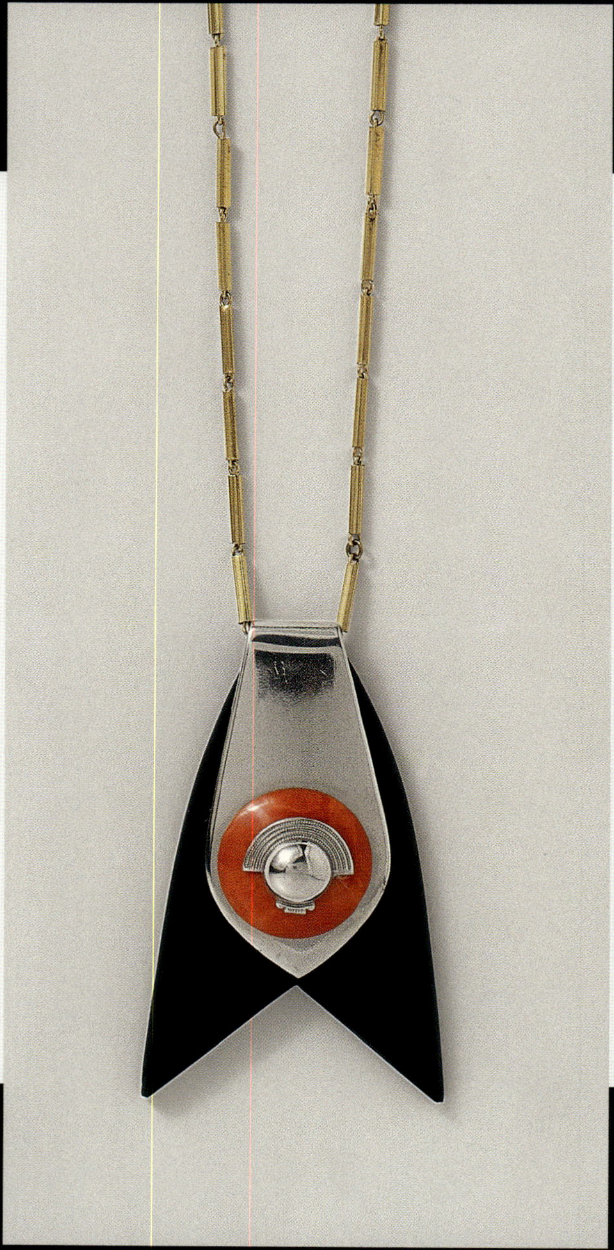

202

HALSKETTE MIT MITTELTEIL, 1933
Messing verchromt, Federringverschluß, Oberfläche teilweise geriffelt, aufgeschraubtes Galalith
Halskette: L 510, Mittelteil: H 60
MB Bd. X, S. 257, M-Nr. 20.855, 8.6.33

CHAIN WITH CENTRAL PIECE, 1933
Brass, chromium-plated; bolt-ring clasp, surface partly grooved; Galalith, screwed on
Chain: L 510; central piece: H 60
PB Vol. X, p. 257, M. no. 20.855, 8.6.33

ARMSPANGE, 1933
Messing verchromt, aufgeschraubtes Galalith
außen Signatur: »R. DOLMAN 210 ABBEY LANE LEICESTER R.E. B.C. 23/1«
Ø 70, B 11, H 55
MB Bd. X, S. 229, M-Nr. 20.715, 12.5.33, 7,25

203

BANGLE, 1933
Brass, chromium-plated; Galalith, screwed on
Exterior signature: »R. DOLMAN 210 ABBEY LANE LEICESTER R.E. B.C. 23/1«
Ø 70, B 11, H 55
PB Vol. X, p. 229, M. no. 20.715, 12.5.33, 7,25

HALSKETTE MIT ANHÄNGER, 1933
Messing verchromt, Federringverschluß, Galalith, teilweise marmoriert
Halskette: L 490, Quadrat: 43 x 43
MB Bd. X, S. 135, M-Nr. 20.548, 1.12.33

▶ **204**

CHAIN WITH PENDANT, 1933
Brass, chromium-plated; bolt-ring clasp; Galalith, partly marbled
Chain: L 490; square piece: 43 x 43
PB Vol. X, p. 135, M. no. 20.548, 1.12.33

205

HALSKETTE MIT MITTELTEIL, 1933
Messing vernickelt, Federringverschluß, Galalith
Halskette: L 500, Mitte: H 47

CHAIN WITH CENTRAL PIECE, 1933
Brass, nickel-plated; bolt-ring clasp; Galalith
Chain: L 500; central piece: H 47

206

COLLIER MIT ANHÄNGER, 1933
Messing verchromt, teilweise ziseliert, Federringverschluß, Galalith
Halskette: L 430, Anhänger: H 44
MB Bd. X, S. 139, M-Nr. 20.329, 3.1.33, 12,–

NECKLACE WITH PENDANT, 1933
Brass, chromium-plated; partly chiselled; bolt-ring clasp; Galalith
Chain: L 430; pendant: H 44
PB Vol. X, p. 139, M. no. 20.329, 3.1.33, 12,–

COLLIER MIT ANHÄNGER, 1933
Metallband, Messing vernickelt, Federringverschluß, Galalith, in Metall gefaßte Straßsteine
Halskette: L 420, Anhänger: H 45

207

NECKLACE WITH PENDANT, 1933
Metal band, nickel-plated brass; bolt-ring clasp; Galalith; strass stones set in metal
Chain: L 420; pendant: H 45

HALSKETTE MIT ANHÄNGER (fest montiert), 1933
Messing vernickelt, Schraubverschluß, Galalith
Halskette: L 390, Anhänger: H 50, B 38
MB Bd. X, S. 168, M-Nr. 20.509, 13.2.33, 21,–

208

CHAIN WITH PENDANT (mounted), 1933
Brass, nickel-plated; screw clasp; Galalith
Chain: L 390; pendant: H 50, W 38
PB Vol. X, p. 168, M. no. 20.509, 13.2.33, 21,–

BROSCHEN »SEGELBOOT«, 1933
Messing vernickelt, Drahtkordel, Galalith
ca. H 54, B 57
MB Bd. X, S. 267, M-Nr. 20.899/1, 5.4.33, 6,–; MB Bd. X, S. 305, M-Nr. 21.053, 5.8.33, 6,–; MB Bd. X, S. 248, M-Nr. 20.816/1, 22.5.33, 8,–

209

SAILING-BOAT BROOCHES, 1933
Brass, nickel-plated; wire cord, Galalith
ca. H 54, W 57
PB Vol. X, p. 267, M. no. 20.899/1, 5.4.33, 6,–; PB Vol. X, p. 305, M. no. 21.053, 5.8.33, 6,–; PB Vol. X, p. 248, M. no. 20.816/1, 22.5.33, 8,–

HALSKETTE MIT ANHÄNGER »ANKER«, 1933
Messing vernickelt, Goldringe (?), Schraubverschluß, Seidenband
Halskette: L 310, Anhänger: H 60
MB Bd. X, S. 245, M-Nr. 20.806, 22.5.33, 16,–

▸ **210**

CHAIN WITH ANCHOR PENDANT, 1933
Brass, nickel-plated; gold rings (?); screw clasp; silk ribbon
Chain: L 310; pendant: H 60
PB Vol. X, p. 245, M. no. 20.806, 22.5.33, 16,–

COLLIER, 1933
Messing verchromt, teilweise gehämmert, Federringverschluß, Galalith
Halskette: L 420, Glied: H 40
MB Bd. X, S. 330, M-Nr. 21.152,
8.9.33, 20,–

211

NECKLACE, 1933
Brass, chromium-plated, partly beaten; bolt-ring clasp; Galalith
Chain: L 420, link: H 40
PB Vol. X, p. 330, M. no. 21.152,
8.9.33, 20,–

COLLIER, 1933
Messing verchromt, Federringverschluß, aufgeklebtes Galalith, teilweise gewolkt
Halskette: L 410, Glied: H 35
MB Bd. 10, S. 256, M-Nr. 20.853,
8.6.33, 6,–

▸ 212

NECKLACE, 1933
Brass, chromium-plated; bolt-ring clasp; Galalith, glued on, partly cloudy
Chain: L 410, link: H 35
PB Vol. 10, p. 256, M. no. 20.853,
8.6.33, 6,–

HALSKETTE MIT ANHÄNGER, 1933
Messing verchromt, Federringverschluß, aufgeschraubtes Galalith, Perle
Halskette: L 650, Anhänger: H 70
MB Bd. X, S. 296, M-Nr. 21.014, 30.8.33, 9,–

213

CHAIN WITH PENDANT, 1933
Brass, chromium-plated; bolt-ring clasp; Galalith, screwed on; bead
Chain: L 650; pendant: H 70
PB Vol. X, p. 296, M. no. 21.014, 30.8.33, 9,–

HALSKETTE, 1933
Messing verchromt, Federringverschluß, aufgeschraubtes Galalith
Halskette: L 545, H 70
MB Bd. X, S.285, M-Nr. 20.973, 4.7.33

214

CHAIN, 1933
Brass, chromium-plated; bolt-ring clasp; Galalith, screwed on
Chain: L 545, H 70
PB Vol. X, p. 285, M. no. 20.973, 4.7.33

215
HALSKETTE MIT ANHÄNGER, 1933
Messing vernickelt, Federringverschluß, Galalith
Halskette: L 425, Anhänger: H 50, B 28
MB Bd. X, S. 313, M-Nr. 21.089, 23.8.33, 6,–

CHAIN WITH PENDANT, 1933
Brass, nickel-plated; bolt-ring clasp; Galalith
Chain: L 425; pendant: H 50, B 28
PB Vol. X, p. 313, M. no. 21.089, 23.8.33, 6,–

216
HALSKETTE MIT ANHÄNGER, 1933
Messing vernickelt, Schraubverschluß, Galalith
Halskette: L 500, Anhänger: H 80, B 35
MB Bd. X, S. 285, M-Nr. 20.973, 4.7.33

CHAIN WITH PENDANT, 1933
Brass, nickel-plated; screw clasp; Galalith
Chain: L 500; pendant: H 80, B 35
PB Vol. X, p. 285, M. no. 20.973, 4.7.33

COLLIER MIT ANHÄNGER, 1933
Messing verchromt, Federringverschluß »GARANTIE***«, aufgeschraubtes Galalith
Halskette: L 430, Anhänger: H 55
MB Bd. X, S. 266, M-Nr. 20.895, 5.7.33, 15,–

◀ 217

NECKLACE WITH PENDANT, 1933
Brass, chromium-plated; bolt-ring clasp »GARANTIE***«; Galalith, screwed on
Chain: L 430; pendant: H 55
PB Vol. X, p. 266, M. no. 20.895, 5.7.33, 15,–

COLLIER, 1933
Messing vernickelt, Schraubverschluß, Galalith (V)
Anhänger »Original Julienne«, Rs: 20.975
Halskette: L 510
MB Bd. X, S. 286, M-Nr. 20.975, 4.7.33, 22,–

218

NECKLACE, 1933
Brass, nickel-plated; screw clasp; Galalith (V)
Pendant »Original Julienne«, B. 20.975
Chain: L 510
PB Vol. X, p. 286, M. no. 20.975, 4.7.33, 22,–

CLIP, 1933
Gelbmetall, Galalith, teilweise
gewolkt, Rs: Clipmechanismus
L 52, B 42

219

CLIP, 1933
Pinchbeck; Galalith, partly cloudy;
B: clip mechanism
L 52, W 42

ARMBAND, 1933
Messing verchromt, Kastenverschluß,
aufgeschraubtes Galalith
L 170, B 26
MB Bd. X, S. 326, M-Nr. 21.135, 29.8.33

220

BRACELET, 1933
Brass, chromium-plated; box-snap
clasp; Galalith, screwed on
L 170, W 26
PB Vol. X, p. 326, M. no. 21.135, 29.8.33

221

COLLIER MIT ANHÄNGER, 1933
Messing verchromt, z.T. gehämmert, Schraubverschluß, Galalith, Etikett mit Nr. 21127
Halskette: L 420, Anhänger: H 85
MB Bd. X, S. 324, M-Nr. 21.127, 29.8.33, 18,–

NECKLACE WITH PENDANT, 1933
Brass, chromium-plated, partly beaten; screw clasp; Galalith; Label with no. 21127
Chain: L 420; pendant: H 85
PB Vol. X, p. 324, M. no. 21.127, 29.8.33, 18,–

HALSKETTE MIT ANHÄNGER, 1933
Messing verchromt, Schraubverschluß, aufgeschraubtes Galalith
Halskette: L 410, Anhänger: H 55
MB Bd. X, S. 324, M-Nr. 21.126, 29.8.33, 15,–

◀ 222

CHAIN WITH PENDANT, 1933
Brass, chromium-plated; screw clasp; Galalith, screwed on
Chain: L 410; pendant: H 55
PB Vol. X, p. 324, M. no. 21.126, 29.8.33, 15,–

HALSKETTE, 1933
Messing verchromt, Federringverschluß, aufgeklebtes Galalith
Halskette: L 530
MB Bd. X, S. 324, M-Nr. 21.126, 29.8.33, 15,–

223

CHAIN, 1933
Brass, chromium-plated; bolt-ring clasp; Galalith, glued on
Chain: L 530
PB Vol. X, p. 324, M. no. 21.126, 29.8.33, 15,–

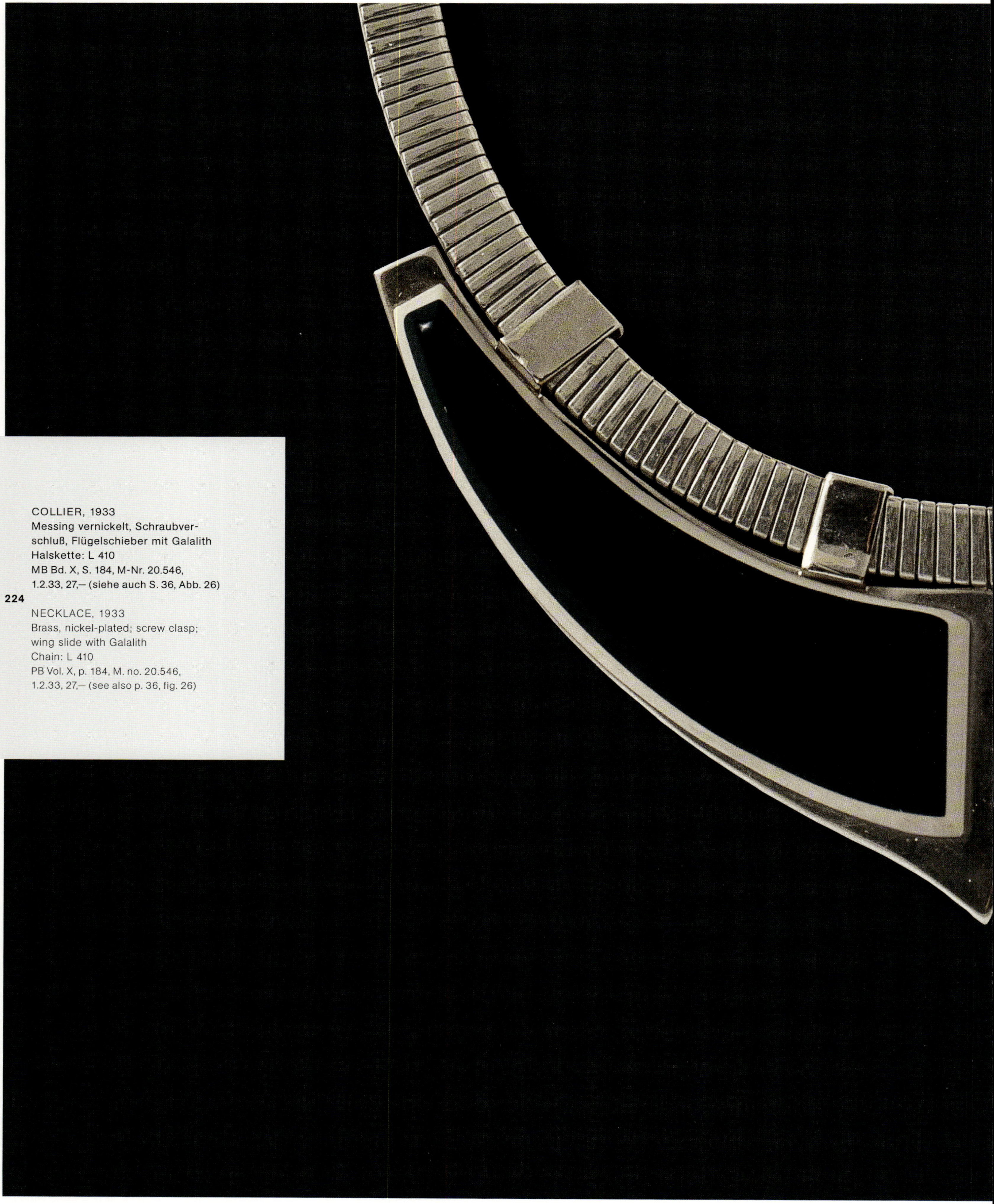

224

COLLIER, 1933
Messing vernickelt, Schraubverschluß, Flügelschieber mit Galalith
Halskette: L 410
MB Bd. X, S. 184, M-Nr. 20.546, 1.2.33, 27,– (siehe auch S. 36, Abb. 26)

NECKLACE, 1933
Brass, nickel-plated; screw clasp; wing slide with Galalith
Chain: L 410
PB Vol. X, p. 184, M. no. 20.546, 1.2.33, 27,– (see also p. 36, fig. 26)

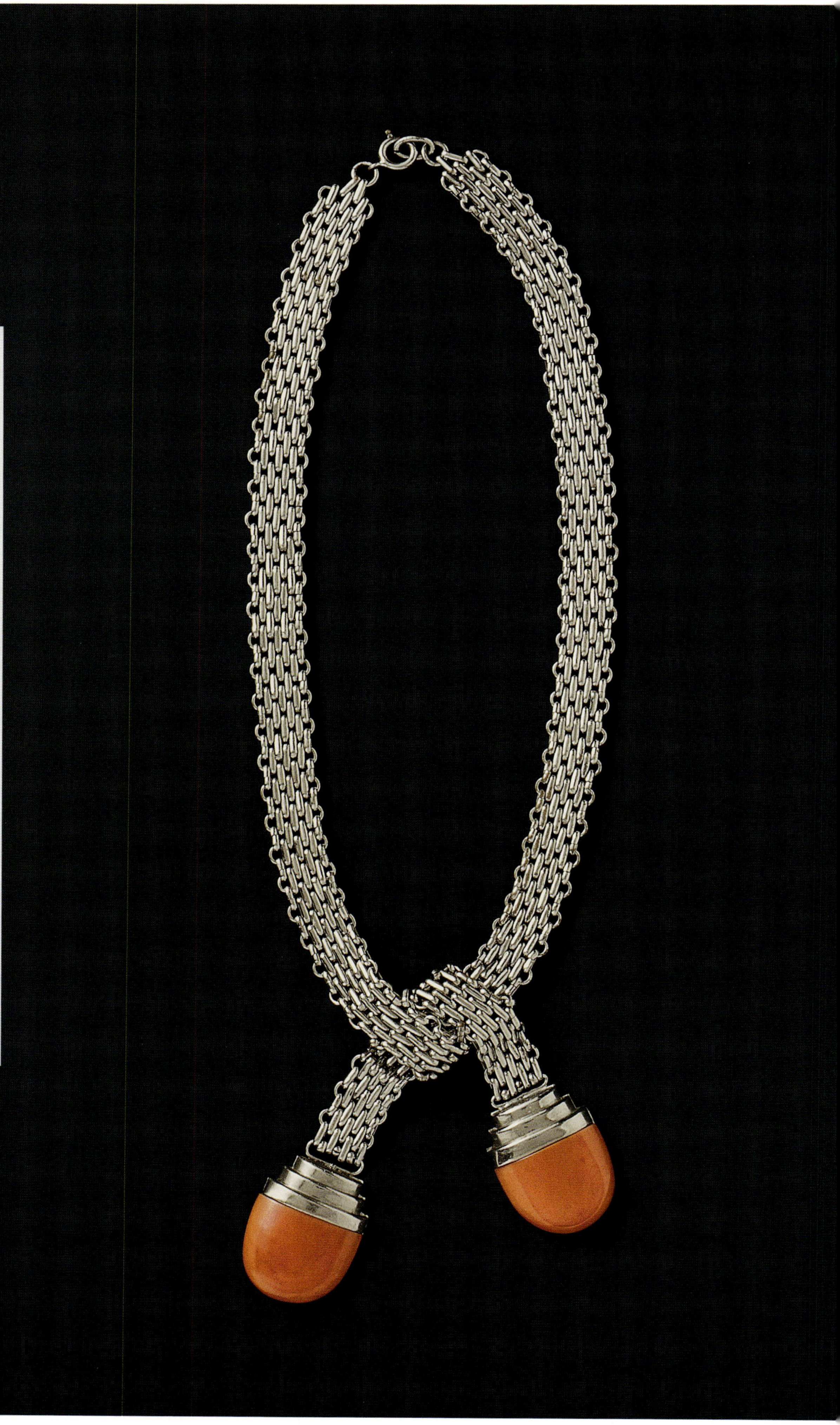

COLLIER, 1933
Messing verchromt, Federringverschluß, aufgeschraubtes Galalith
Halskette: L 430, H 70
MB Bd. X, S. 335, M-Nr. 21.169, 15.9.33, 14,–
MB Bd. X, S. 351, M-Nr. 21.231, 3.10.33, 6,–

225

NECKLACE, 1933
Brass, chromium-plated; bolt-ring clasp; Galalith, screwed on
Chain: L 430, H 70
PB Vol. X, p. 335, M. no. 21.169, 15.9.33, 14,–
PB Vol. X, p. 351, M. no. 21.231, 3.10.33, 6,–

COLLIER, 1933
Messing verchromt, (Fehler im Mauerwerk), gesamte Oberfläche lackiert, Federringverschluß
Halskette: L 390
MB Bd. X, S. 335, M-Nr. 21.169, 15.9.33, 14,–

▸ **226**

NECKLACE, 1933
Brass, chromium-plated (defect in flexible mesh), entire surface lacquered; bolt-ring clasp
Chain: L 390
PB Vol. X, p. 335, M. no. 21.169, 15.9.33, 14,–

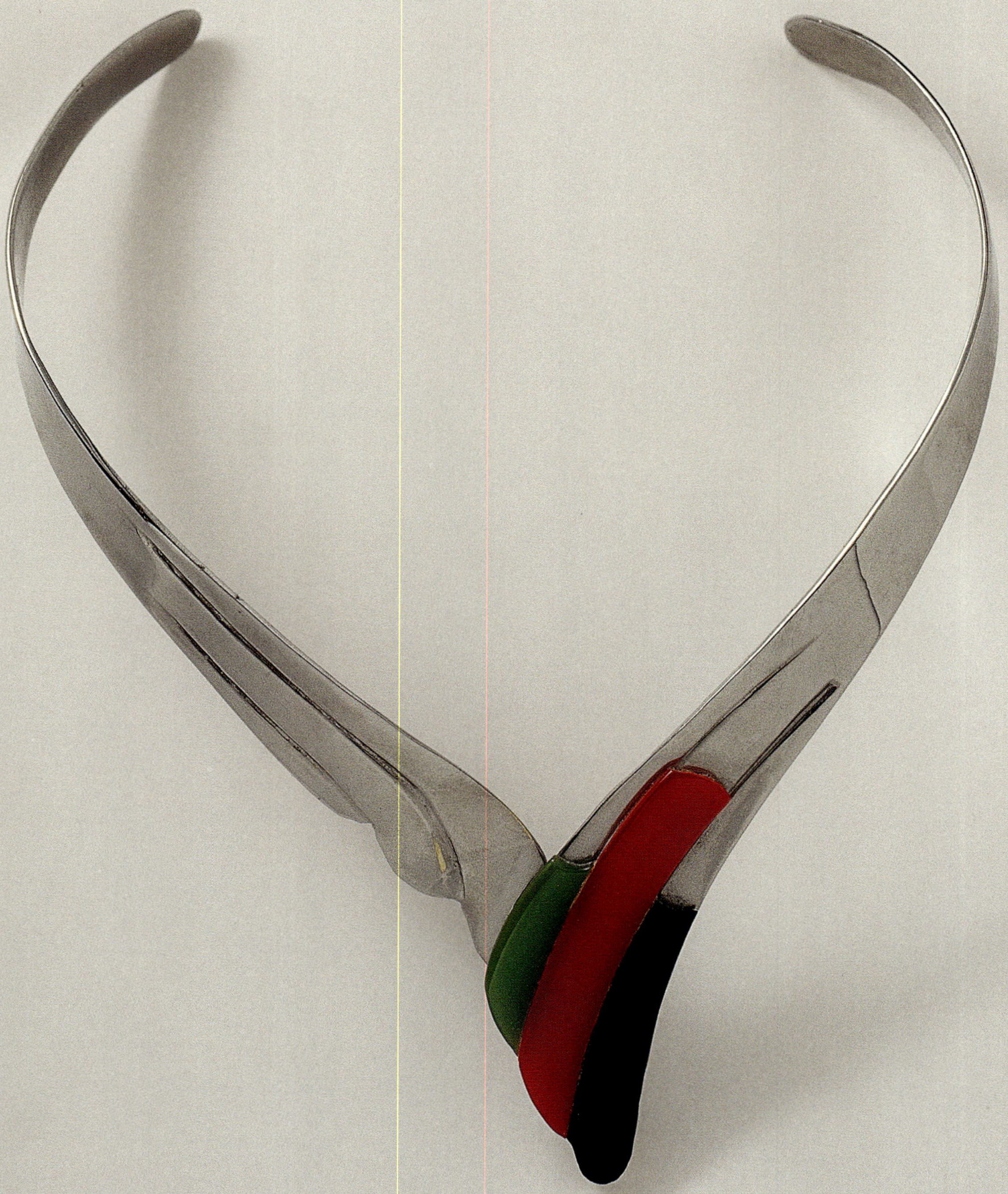

OFFENER HALSREIF, 1933
Messing verchromt, Galalith
Reif: H 145, B 110
MB Bd. X, S. 372, M-Nr. 21.334, 20.10.33

◂ **227**

OPEN TORQUE, 1933
Brass, chromium-plated; Galalith
Torque: H 145, B 110
PB Vol. X, p. 372, M. no. 21.334, 20.10.33

ARMBAND, 1933
Metall, Metallfeder, Galalith
ø 70, H 35

228

BRACELET, 1933
Metal; metal spring; Galalith
ø 70, H 35

HALSKETTE, 1933
Messing vernickelt, Federringverschluß, Galalith
L 500
MB Bd. X, S. 355, M-Nr. 21.250, 4.10.33, 15,– (siehe auch S. 40, Abb. 35)

229

CHAIN, 1933
Brass, nickel-plated; bolt-ring clasp; Galalith
L 500
PB Vol. X, p. 355, M. no. 21.250, 4.10.33, 15,– (see also p. 40, fig. 35)

COLLIER, 1933
Messing verchromt, teilweise gehämmert, Fedrringverschluß, aufgeschraubtes Galalith
Halskette: L 420
MB Bd. X, S. 355, M-Nr. 21.248, 4.10.33, 10,– (siehe auch S. 40, Abb. 35)

230

NECKLACE, 1933
Brass chromium-plated, partly beaten; bolt-ring clasp; Galalith, screwed on
Chain: L 420
PB Vol. X, p. 355, M. no. 21.248, 4.10.33, 10,– (see also p. 40, fig. 35)

HALSKETTE, 1933
Messing verchromt, Federringverschluß, zweifarbiges Galalith
Halskette: L 600

▸ **231**

CHAIN, 1933
Brass, chromium-plated; bolt-ring clasp; Galalith two-colored
Chain: L 600

ARMREIF, 1933
Messing verchromt, Metallspirale, Galalith
Signatur: »TCHECHOSLOVAQUIE« (Innenrand)
Ø 70, B 15

232

BANGLE, 1933
Brass, chromium-plated; metal spiral; Galalith
Signature: »TCHECHOSLOVAQUIE« (inner edge)
Ø 70, W 15

BROSCHE, 1933
Messing verchromt, Galalith,
Rs: Broschierung
L 80

▶ **233**

BROOCH, 1933
Brass, chromium-plated; Galalith;
B: pin
L 80

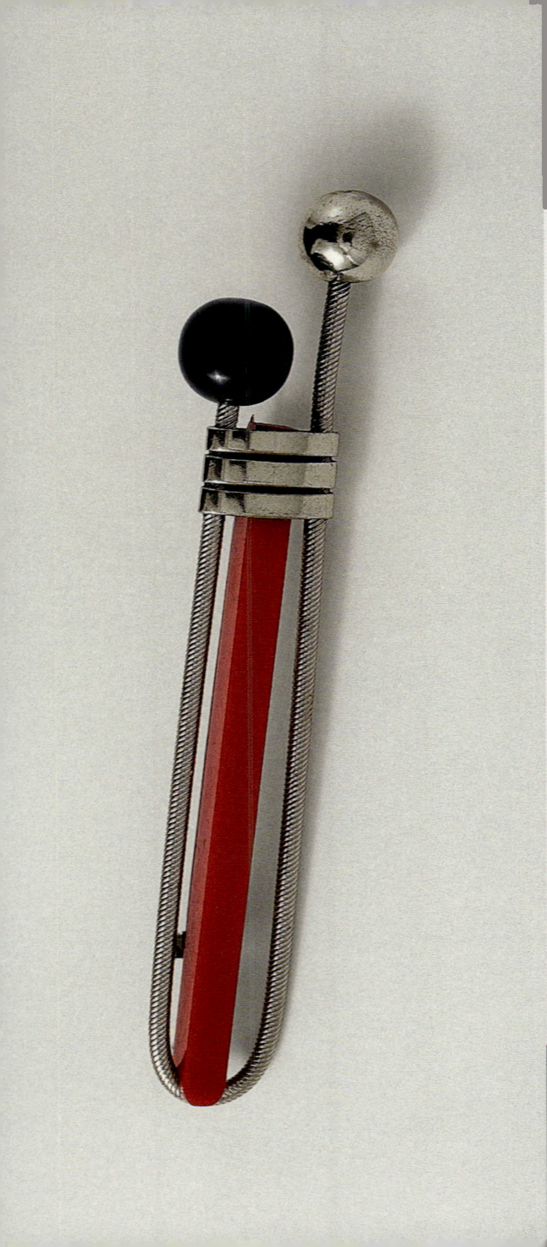

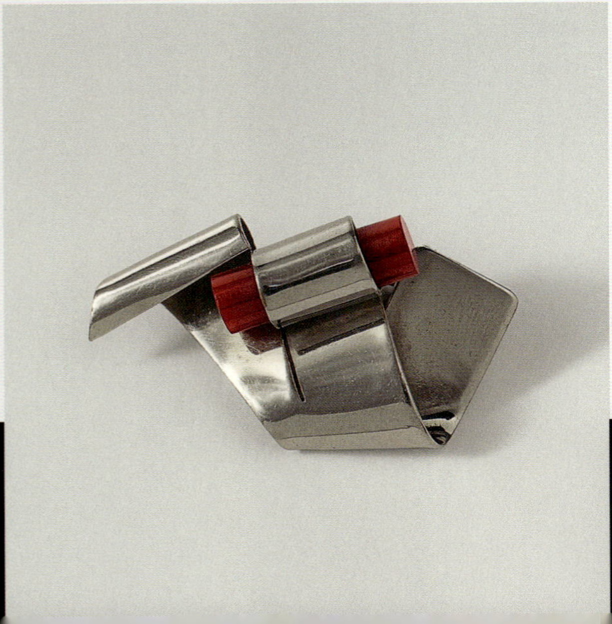

BROSCHE »ANKER«, 1933
Messing vernickelt, Galalith
H 75, B 60
Marke »Tcheco Slovaquie«
MB Bd. X, S. 237, M-Nr. 20.746/2 und 4a, 22.5.33, 3,50

234

ANCHOR BROOCH, 1933
Brass, nickel-plated; Galalith
H 75, W 60
Mark »Tcheco Slovaquie«
PB Vol. X, p. 237, M. no. 20.746/2 and 4a, 22.5.33, 3,50

BROSCHE, 1933
Messing verchromt, aufgeschnittene und gebogene Metallplatte, aufgeschraubtes Galalith
L 54, B 30

235

BROOCH, 1933
Brass, chromium-plated; cut and bent metal plate; Galalith, screwed on
L 54, W 30

HALSKETTE MIT QUASTEN-ANHÄNGER, 1930er JAHRE
Gelbmetall, teilweise geschwärzt, Federringverschluß, Galalith
Halskette: L 650, Quaste: H 60

236

CHAIN WITH PENDENT TASSELS, 1930S
Pinchbeck, partly blackened; bolt-ring clasp; Galalith
Chain: L 650; tassels: H 60

HALSKETTE MIT ANHÄNGER UND QUASTE, 1930er JAHRE
Messing verchromt, Schraubverschluß, Galalith (eine Perle fehlt)
Halskette: L 500, Anhänger: H 135

237

CHAIN WITH PENDANT AND TAS-SELS, 1930S
Brass, chromium-plated; screw clasp; Galalith (a bead is missing)
Chain: L 500; pendant: H 135

HALSKETTE MIT ANHÄNGER, 1933
Messing verchromt, Federringverschluß »GARANTIE***«, Galalithröhrchen (1 Röhrchen fehlt)
Halskette: L 580, H 80

▸ **238**

CHAIN WITH PENDANT, 1933
Brass, chromium-plated; bolt-ring clasp »GARANTIE***«, Galalith tubes (1 tube missing)
Chain: L 580, H 80

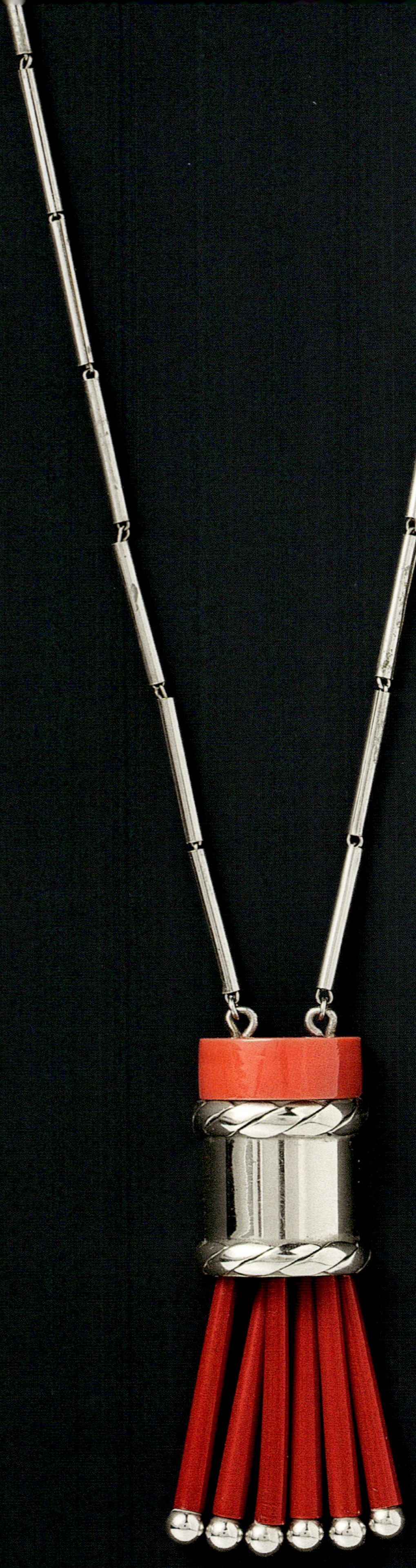

COLLIER, 1933
Messing verchromt, Federringverschluß, gemasertes Galalith, aufgeschraubt
Halskette: L 420
MB Bd. X, S. 347, M-Nr. 21.218, 19.9.33, 21,–

239

NECKLACE, 1933
Brass, chromium-plated, bolt-ring clasp; streaky Galalith, screwed on
Chain: L 420
PB Vol. X, p. 347, M. no. 21.218, 19.9.33, 21,–

CLIP, 1933
Messing, aufgeschraubtes Galalith, verchromt, Clipbroschur
L 50, B 45

240

CLIP, 1933
Brass, chromium-plated; Galalith, screwed on; clip fastening
L 50, W 45

CLIP, 1933
Messing verchromt, genietetes und geklebtes Galalith
Clipbroschur: »Tcheco-Slovaquie«
L 75, B 18

241

CLIP, 1933
Brass, chromium-plated; Galalith, riveted and glued on
Clip fastening: »Tcheco-Slovaquie«
L 75, W 18

COLLIER, 1933
Messing verchromt, Schraubverschluß, Galalith
Halskette: L 430

242

NECKLACE, 1933
Brass, chromium-plated; screw clasp; Galalith
Chain: L 430

A U S W A H L

COLLECTION

S E L E C T I O N

1935
1936
1938

ARMSPANGE, 1935/36
Messing gehämmert, aufgeschnitten
und gebogen
Ø 70, H 52

243

BANGLE, 1935/36
Brass, beaten, cut and bent
Ø 70, H 52

BROSCHE, 1935
Messing versilbert, gehämmert,
aufgelötete Spirale, Rs: Broschierung
Ø 61
MB Bd. XII, S. 25, M-Nr. 23.354,
9.4.35, 5,50

244

BROOCH, 1935
Brass, silvered, beaten; soldered
spiral; B: fastening
Ø 61
PB Vol. XII, p. 25, M. no. 23.354,
9.4.35, 5,50

HALSKETTE MIT ANHÄNGER, 1935
Gelbmetall, Schraubverschluß,
Wolkengalalith, facettierter Glasstein
Halskette: L 225, Anhänger: H 70, B 53
MB Bd. XII, S. 155, M-Nr. 24.015,
17.12.35, 18,–

▸ 245

CHAIN WITH PENDANT, 1935
Pinchbeck; screw clasp; cloudy Galalith;
faceted glass stone
Chain: L 225; pendant: H 70, W 53
PB Vol. XII, p. 155, M. no. 24.015,
17.12.35, 18,–

HALSKETTE MIT ANHÄNGER, 1935
Gelbmettall gehämmert, Wabenstruktur, Federringverschluß, facettierter Glasstein
Halskette: L 260, Anhänger: H 55, B 38
MB Bd. XII, M-Nr. 23.864/1, 26.9.35, 14,–

246

CHAIN WITH PENDANT, 1935
Pinchbeck, beaten, cloison cells; bolt-ring clasp; faceted glass stone
Chain: L 260, pendant: H 55, W 38
PB Vol. XII, M. no. 23.864/1, 26.9.35, 14,–

HALSKETTE MIT ANHÄNGER, 1935
Gelbmetall, Federringverschluß
Halskette: L 250, Anhänger: H 52, B 55
MB Bd. XII, S. 119, M-Nr. 23.863, 26.9.35, 21,–

247

CHAIN WITH PENDANT, 1935
Pinchbeck, bolt-ring clasp
Chain: L 250; pendant: H 52, W 55
PB Vol. XII, p. 119, M. no. 23.863, 26.9.35, 21 ,–

248

HALSKETTE MIT ANHÄNGER, 1935
Gelbmetall, Federringverschluß, transparentes Galalith, facettierter Glasstein
Halskette: L 270, Anhänger: H 65, B 45
MB Bd. XII, S. 118, M-Nr. 23.859, 26.9.35, 15,–

CHAIN WITH PENDANT, 1935
Pinchbeck; bolt-ring clasp; translucent Galalith; faceted glass stone
Chain: L 270; pendant: H 65, W 45
PB Vol. XII, p. 118, M. no. 23.859, 26.9.35, 15,–

HALSKETTE MIT ANHÄNGER, 1936
Gelbmetall, Federringverschluß,
Wolkengalalith, facettierter Glasstein
Halskette: L 300, Anhänger: H 75, B 55
MB Bd. XII, S. 191, M-Nr. 24.177,
23.1.36, 22,–

249

CHAIN WITH PENDANT, 1936
Pinchbeck; bolt-ring clasp; cloudy
Galalith; facetted glass stone
Chain: L 300; pendant: H 75, W 55
PB Vol. XII, p. 191, M. no. 24.177,
23.1.36, 22,–

ANHÄNGER MIT SEIDENKORDEL, 1936
Gelbmetall z.T. gehämmert, Wolkengalalith, facettierter Glasstein, Seidenkordel
H 70, B 58 (Anhänger), L 320 (Kordel)
MB Bd. XII, S. 190, M-Nr. 26.172, 23.1.36, 21,–

250

PENDANT WITH SILK CORD, 1936
Pinchbeck, partly beaten;
cloudy Galalith; faceted glass stone, silk cord
H 70, W 58 (pendant); L 320 (cord)
PB Vol. XII, p. 190, M. no. 26.172, 23.1.36, 21,–

COLLIER »OLYMPIA-RINGE«, 1936
Nickel, Federringverschluß,
Trophäenmotiv mit Olympia-Ringen
Halskette: L 410
MB Bd. XII, S. 235, M-Nr. 24.400,
9.5.36, 9,–

251

NECKLACE OLYMPIC RINGS, 1936
Nickel; bolt-ring clasp; trophy motif
with Olympic Rings
Chain: L 410
PB Vol. XII, p. 235, M. no. 24.400,
9.5.36, 9,–

COLLIER »OLYMPIA-RINGE«, 1936
Gelbmetall, Federringverschluß
Halskette: L 480
MB Bd. XII, S. 235, M-Nr. 24.399,
9.5.36, 9,–

252

NECKLACE OLYMPIC RINGS, 1936
Pinchbeck; bolt-ring clasp
Chain: L 480
PB Vol. XII, p. 235, M. no. 24.399,
9.5.36, 9,–

ARMBAND, 1938
Messing, Kastenverschluß, aufge-
schraubtes Galalith
Kastenschloß Rs: »BTE (breveté,
geschützt) S.G.D.G.«, Vs: »X«
L 180, B 21

253

BRACELET, 1938
Brass; box-snap clasp; screwed-on
Galalith
Collet clasp B: »BTE (breveté, ge-
schützt [patented]) S.G.D.G.«; F: »X«
L 180, W 21

ANHANG I

(siehe hierzu Seite 93):

Auftragsbuch Jakob Bengel, Bd. I, Frankreich 1928–35

Die Firmen sind in alphabetischer Reihenfolge aufgeführt, an erster Stelle werden die großen Pariser Kaufhäuser genannt. In der Regel sind nur der Name des Kunden, die Adresse und das Jahr der Geschäftsbeziehung aufgeführt. Gelegentliche Anmerkungen weisen auf einen Firmen- oder Ortswechsel der Firma hin.

Pariser Kaufhäuser

GRANDS MAGASINS DU »LOUVRE«, Paris 11, Rue Croix de petits Champs

GRANDS MAGASINS DE LA »SAMARITAINE«, Paris, Boul.d Capucines 27

GRANDS MAGASINS DU »PRINTEMPS«, 64 Caumartin, Paris IX *1930*

SOCIÉTÉ ANONYME PARISIENNE D'ACHATS EN COMMUN S.A.P.A.C, Paris 41, Rue Faubert

SOCIÉTÉ PARISIENNE D'ACHATS ET DE MANUTENTION AUX GALERIS »LAFAYETTE«, Paris 9, 36 Rue Blanche

Firmen

ADRY, 75 Rue Turbigo, Paris *1931*

DANDOR, 94 Boulevard Haussmann, Paris 9e, Inh. J. Pepo Dänon (früher Adry) *1935*

LEON BLOCH, 6 Quai, Bouget de l'Isle, Straßburg (Herbert Lautenbach) *1931*

J. BLUM – SCHWOB FILS, 60 Boulevard de Straßbourg, Paris *1932*

H. BONNOUVRIER, 2 Rue Carnot, Montceau-les-Mines (Saone et Loire) *1930*

FR. BRABLIK, 28 Rue des Petites Ecuries, Paris *1931*

(TSCHECHE) seit Mitte 1933: TTURCIANSKY-SVATY-MARTIN (Tschechoslowakei)

ETABLISSEMENTS CHAB, 11–12 Rue Pierre Picard, Paris (18) *1932* Inhaber: Bloch & Bodenheimer

JOSEPH E. COHEN, 80 Faubourg St. Denis, Paris X *1930*

VIDAL COHEN, 34 Rue Bergère, Paris *1935*

COMPTOIRE DES FARBRICANTS, 85 Rue des Archives und 2, Rue Portefoin, Paris *1933*

F. EDBERG, Comptoir General Parisien, 62 Rue du Temple *1929*

CURT S. DAVID, Parkstraße 9, Frankfurt a. Main *1933* (David & Co. Paris)

DESENNE & FILS, 113, 116, 118 Rue du Temple, Paris 3e *1931*

ESSÈS, 70 Rue Amelot, Paris XI *1930*

FABRIQUE DE BIJOUTERIE »IMITATION PARFAITE«, 18 Boulevard St. Denis, Passage du Prado, Paris *1931*

JEAN FAYERSTERN, 42 Rue de Marsi, Paris *1933*

M. FEFERMAN, 36 Rue de la Paix, Lens, Pas-de-Calais *1929*

L. FIEDLER, 37 Rue de Paradis, Paris *1931*

VICTOR FINZI, 46 Rue de la Victoire, Paris *1932*

EMILE FOUQUET, 30 Rue de Picardi, Paris 3e *1930*

N. FUILLA SUCC., 27 Av. Thiers, Le Mans *1931*

E. GISSINGER SUCC., 27 Rue Pastourelle, Paris 3 *1928*

LUCIEN GOUBET, 33 Rue Charlot, Paris 3e *1933*

GRANDS MAGASINS DU LOUVRE, 11 Rue Croix des Petits Champs *1931*

GEORGES GRUMBACH, 60 Faubourg de France, Belfort *1931*

J. HAIM & CIE, 23 Rue du Remard, Paris *1930*

SAMUEL HONIGBAUM, Nachf. v. M. Feferman, 14 Rue des Jardins, Metz *1928*

J. JOANNON, 8 Rue Pasteur, Rue Séb. Lechre 1, Metz *1928*

APPENDIX I

(see on this p. 91):

Order Book Jakob Bengel, Vol. I, France 1928–35

The firms are listed in alphabetical order. The great Paris department stores come first. As a rule, only the client's name, address and the year in which the business contact took place are listed. Occasional notes refer to a change of firm name or location of headquarters.

Paris department stores

GRANDS MAGASINS DU »LOUVRE«, Paris 11, rue Croix de petits Champs

GRANDS MAGASINS DE LA »SAMARITAINE«, Paris, Boul. d. Capucines 27

GRANDS MAGASINS DU »PRINTEMPS«, 64 Caumartin, Paris IX *1930*

SOCIÉTÉ ANONYME PARISIENNE D'ACHATS EN COMMUN S.A.P.A.C, Paris 41, rue Faubert

SOCIÉTÉ PARISIENNE D'ACHATS ET DE MANUTENTION AUX GALERIES »LAFAYETTE«, Paris 9, 36 rue Blanche

Firms

ADRY, 75 rue Turbigo, Paris *1931*

DANDOR, 94 Boulevard Haussmann, Paris 9e, proprietor. J. Pepo Dänon (formerly Adry) *1935*

LEON BLOCH, 6 Quai, Bouget de l'Isle, Strasbourg (Herbert Lautenbach) *1931*

J. BLUM – Schwob Fils, 60 Boulevard de Strasbourg, Paris *1932*

H. BONNOUVRIER, 2 rue Carnot, Montceau-les-Mines (Saône-et-Loire) *1930*

FR. B RABLIK, 28 rue des Petites Écuries, Paris *1931*

(TSCHECHE = Czech) since mid-1933: TTURCIANSKY-SVATY-MARTIN (Czechoslovakia)

ÉTABLISSEMENTS CHAB, 11–12 rue Pierre Picard, Paris (18) *1932* Proprietor: Bloch & Bodenheimer

JOSEPH E. COHEN, 80 Faubourg St. Denis, Paris Xe *1930*

VIDAL COHEN, 34 rue Bergère, Paris 1935

COMPTOIRE DES FARBRICANTS, 85 rue des Archives and 2 rue Portefoin, Paris *1933*

F. EDBERG, Comptoir General Parisien, 62 rue du Temple *1929*

CURT S. DAVID, Parkstrasse 9, Frankfurt a. Main *1933* (David & Co. Paris)

DESENNE & FILS, 113, 116, 118 rue du Temple, Paris 3e *1931*

ESSÈS, 70 rue Amelot, Paris XIe *1930*

FABRIQUE DE BIJOUTERIE »IMITATION PARFAITE«, 18 Boulevard St. Denis, Passage du Prado, Paris *1931*

JEAN FAYERSTERN, 42 rue de Marsi, Paris *1933*

M. FEFERMAN, 36 rue de la Paix, Lens, Pas-de-Calais *1929*

L. FIEDLER, 37 rue de Paradis, Paris *1931*

VICTOR FINZI, 46 rue de la Victoire, Paris *1932*

EMILE FOUQUET, 30 rue de Picardi, Paris 3e *1930*

N. FUILLA SUCC., 27 Av. Thiers, Le Mans *1931*

E. Gissinger Succ., 27 rue Pastourelle, Paris 3e 1928

LUCIEN GOUBET, 33 rue Charlot, Paris 3e *1933*

GRANDS MAGASINS DU LOUVRE, 11 rue Croix des Petits Champs *1931*

GEORGES GRUMBACH, 60 Faubourg de France, Belfort *1931*

J. HAIM & CIE, 23 rue du Remard, Paris *1930*

N.S. KAPLAN, 25 Rue Louis le Grand, Paris *1931*

LES FRERES H. & W. KAHN, 61 Rue de Chabrol, Paris 10e *1933*

MAISON HECTOR LACHELIN, 249 Rue St. Martin, Paris 3e *1930*

SOCIÉTÉ PARISIENNE D'ACHATS ET DE MANUTENTION, 36 Rue Blanche, Paris 9e *1930*

ETABLISSEMENTS LANCEL, 3 Impasse de la Planchette, Paris IIIe Goethestraße 35, Pforzheim *1931*

LÈAUTAND STE. AME, 8 Cité d'Hauteville, Paris *1929*

LEDER FRÈRES, 175 Rue du Temple, Paris 3e *1931*

ARMAND LEWIN, 1 Passage de Prado, 20 Boulevard St. Denis, Paris *1931*

LIASER, 136 Rue du Temple, Paris *1932*

E. LOURIÉ, 142 Faubourg St. Denis, Paris X *1934*

J. LUKES, 95 Rue de Turenne, Paris 3e *1931*

ARMAND MEYER, 8 Rue Sleidan Straßburg *1930*

MARCEL MEYER, 11 Rue Oberlin, Straßburg *1930*

MICO, 19 Rue Bleue, Paris IXe *1935*

C. MONCHAUSSÉ, 44 Rue d'enghien, Paris X *1932*

VICTOR MOSCHENROSS FILS SUCCESSEUR, 75 Rue des Archives, Paris *1929*

D. NETTER & FRÈRES, 44 Vieux Marche aux Poissons, Straßburg *1929*

J. NETTER & FRÈRES, 14 Rue Mesley, Paris 3e *1930*

GUSTAV NISSE, Straßburg *1929*

LA PERLE-SEIVEL, 5 Rue St. Georges, Paris *1931*

PICARD FRERES & OZANNE, 187 Rue du temple, Paris 3e *1931*

MAISON PLANARD GIRARDIN, 61 Grandes Arcades, Straßburg *1929*

D. POLITI, 11 Rue Condorcet, Paris 9e *1931*

JEAN RAAB, 12 Rue Bouchardon, Paris X *1935*

C. RAABE, Rue de Salis 1, Metz *1928*

M. RAND, 45 Boulevard St. Martin, Paris 3e *1931*

H. RAYERS, 10 Rue jean-Jaurès, Toulon-sur-Mer *1932*

RECHT & CO., 19 Rue des Orfèvres, Straßburg *1928*

D. SAPRITCH, 17 Rue Cadet, Paris IX *1931*

JULES SAPY, 91 Rue de Turenne, Paris 3 *1931*

SONIA, 10 Cité Condorcet, Paris *1932*

CHARLES SOUKUP, 11 Rue Mesley, Paris *1934*

E. SPIERE, 57 Boulevard Montparnasse, Paris VI *1930*

A. SOURY & CO., 56 Faubourg Poissonniere, Paris *1929*

HERMANN SCHIFF, Passage Prado, Bouleverd St. Denis 18–20, Paris *1932*

JÉROME SCHOENER, Kronenburgerstr. 24, Straßburg Inh. Ab 1.1.32 Roméo Bertani *1929*

AD. SCHWENK FILS, 57/59 Rue Reaumur, Paris 2e *1930*

STYL, Art, 43 Rue du Caire, Paris *1932*

VEITH, Lecordier & Co. S.A. Rue du Jeu-des-Enfants, Straßburg *1929*

ANDRÉ WOLF, 17 Faubourg Montmarte, Paris IX *1929*

WORMS, Frères, 24 Rue Richer, Paris *1931*

GUSTAVE WUNSCH, Rue du Temple, Paris *1930*

ZIMBACCA, 70 Rue du Temple, Paris *1929*

SAMUEL HONIGBAUM, M. Feferman, successor, 14 rue des Jardins, Metz *1928*

J. JOANNON, 8 rue Pasteur, rue Séb. Lechre 1, Metz *1928*

N.S. KAPLAN, 25 rue Louis le Grand, Paris *1931*

LES FRERES H. & W. KAHN, 61 rue de Chabrol, Paris 10e *1933*

MAISON HECTOR LACHELIN, 249 rue St. Martin, Paris 3e *1930*

SOCIÉTÉ PARISIENNE D'ACHATS ET DE MANUTENTION, 36 rue Blanche, Paris 9e *1930*

ÉTABLISSEMENTS LANCEL, 3 Impasse de la Planchette, Paris IIIe Goethestrasse 35, Pforzheim *1931*

LÉAUTAND STE. AME, 8 Cité d'Hauteville, Paris *1929*

LEDER FRÈRES, 175 rue du Temple, Paris 3e *1931*

ARMAND LEWIN, 1 Passage de Prado, 20 Boulevard St. Denis, Paris *1931*

LIASER, 136 rue du Temple, Paris *1932*

E. LOURIÉ, 142 Faubourg St. Denis, Paris X *1934*

J. LUKES, 95 rue de Turenne, Paris 3e *1931*

ARMAND MEYER, 8 rue Sleidan Strasbourg *1930*

MARCEL MEYER, 11 rue Oberlin, Strasbourg *1930*

MICO, 19 rue Bleue, Paris IXe *1935*

C. MONCHAUSSÉ, 44 rue d'Enghien, Paris X *1932*

VICTOR MOSCHENROSS FILS SUCCESSEUR, 75 rue des Archives, Paris *1929*

D. NETTER & FRÈRES, 44 Vieux Marche aux Poissons, Strasbourg *1929*

J. NETTER & FRÈRES, 14 rue Mesley, Paris 3e *1930*

GUSTAV NISSE, Strasbourg *1929*

LA PERLE-SEIVEL, 5 rue St. Georges, Paris *1931*

PICARD FRERES & OZANNE, 187 rue du temple, Paris 3e *1931*

MAISON PLANARD GIRARDIN, 61 Grandes Arcades, Strasbourg *1929*

D. POLITI, 11 rue Condorcet, Paris 9e *1931*

JEAN RAAB, 12 rue Bouchardon, Paris Xe *1935*

C. RAABE, rue de Salis 1, Metz *1928*

M. RAND, 45 Boulevard St. Martin, Paris 3e *1931*

H. RAYERS, 10 rue Jean-Jaurès, Toulon-sur-Mer *1932*

RECHT & CO., 19 rue des Orfèvres, Strasbourg *1928*

D. SAPRITCH, 17 rue Cadet, Paris IXe *1931*

JULES SAPY, 91 rue de Turenne, Paris 3e *1931*

SONIA, 10 Cité Condorcet, Paris *1932*

CHARLES SOUKUP, 11 rue Mesley, Paris *1934*

E. SPIERE, 57 Boulevard Montparnasse, Paris VIe *1930*

A. SOURY & CO., 56 Faubourg Poissonnière, Paris *1929*

HERMANN SCHIFF, Passage Prado, Boulevard St. Denis 18–20, Paris *1932*

JÉROME SCHOENER, Kronenburgerstr. 24 Strasbourg Proprietor from 1 Jan. 1932 Roméo Bertani *1929*

AD. SCHWENK FILS, 57/59 rue Réaumur, Paris 2e *1930*

STYL, ART, 43 rue du Caire, Paris *1932*

VEITH, LECORDIER & CO. S.A. rue du Jeu-des-Enfants, Strasbourg *1929*

ANDRÉ WOLF, 17 Faubourg Montmarte, Paris IXe *1929*

WORMS, FRÈRES, 24 rue Richer, Paris *1931*

GUSTAVE WUNSCH, rue du Temple, Paris *1930*

ZIMBACCA, 70 rue du Temple, Paris *1929*

Auftragsbuch Jakob Bengel, Bd. II, Nichtfranzösische Länder, 1928–1935 (Auszug)

Die Länder mit denen die Firma Bengel Geschäftsbeziehungen pflegte, sind weitgehend in alphabetischer Reihenfolge genannt. Gelegentlich ist auch der Kunde, d.h., das Geschäft genannt, bzw. der Vertreter, über den das Geschäft abgewickelt wurde. Die Jahreszahlen verweisen auf den Zeitraum, in dem Geschäftskontakte bestanden.
Es ist unklar, warum Stockholm, Malmö und Göteborg unter Rußland aufgeführt sind.
In der Regel sind unter den einzelnen Ländern nur einige Auftragsabwicklungen genannt, bei den mit * gekennzeichneten Ländern sind sehr viele Eintragungen zu finden.

AUSTRALIEN: Melbourne

MAROKKO: Meknes, Rabat, Casablanca (1928/31/33/34/35), Casablanca, Pierre Salesne (1929/30/31) Casablanca: Magasins Modernes, Succursale des Galeries Lafayette de Paris (1934/35) (Einkäufer: Ernst Winkler, Durlacherstr. 29, Pforzheim) Casablanca, Abdel Vahab (1934) (Vertreter: Heinz Marx), Gibraltar (1933) Centa (1933)

MEXIKO: Tampa, Casa de Curiosidades e Importadora (Curt Baronsky)

NORDAMERIKA: Arnold, Constable & Cie., New York (Einkäufer: Loewenstein & Hecht, A.G. Berlin) (1933)

CANADA: Montreal, Henry Birks & Sons Ltd. (1931/32) The European Novelty Cie. Ltd. (Einkäufer: Friedrich Engert, Annaberg & Herbert Lautenbach) (1930/31/32)

NEUSEELAND: Auchland

NORDAMERIKA: New York: The Royal Jewelry M.f.G. Cie. Inc. (Einkäufer: A. Rosenfeld, Pforzheim) (1929/30/31) Chicago, Illinois: Marshall Field & Company (Einkaufshaus in Deutschland: Chemnitz, Lohstr. 17) (1928/29/30)

NORWEGEN: Oslo (1929), Drämmen (1929/31), Aalesund (1935), Trondhjiem (1935)

ÖSTERREICH: Wien, VI. Bezirk: Leo Baum 1932/33, Wien, XVI. Bezirk: Franz Goldstein, Gold- & Metallwarenfabrik, Engros Export, Bijouterie & Knopffabrik Großmann & Cie., Nachfolger Schüller + C.

PALÄSTINA, Jerusalem (1929) Tel Aviv (1932/33), Jaffa (1935)

POLEN: Warschau, A. Katz (1920), Krakau (1928/30)

PORTUGAL: Lissabon (1934)

RUMÄNIEN: Bucarest, Arad, Cernanti, Beclean, Chisjnan (1934)

RUSSLAND: Stockholm (1932) Malmö (1932/33) Göteborg (1933)

SCHWEIZ: Biel (1927/29), Bern, Zürich, Luzern, Genf, Basel

SPANIEN*: Barcelona, Madrid, Sevilla, Malaga

SÜDAMERIKA*: Brasilien: Rio de Janeiro, Sao Paulo Santo; Santiago de Chile (1928), Buenos Aires, Uruguay, Montevideo, Kolumbien: Bogota (1933/35)

SÜDAFRIKA: Johannesburg (1929)

SMYRNA*: Rodolfo, Penzo & Cie. (1928–1935), mehrere Lieferungen pro Jahr, manchmal sogar mehrere Lieferungen pro Monat

SYRIEN: Beirut (1935), Aleppo (1931)

TSCHECHOSLOWAKEI*: Gablonz (1931), Prag

TÜRKEI: Konstantinopel (1929/30)

UNGARN*: Budapest, Rakospalota

PERSIEN: Tabris (1928), Teheran (1934)

»REST AFRIKA«*: Dakar: Mohamed ben Ahmed Cheraiby (1930), Senegal: SAHBIB BEN AMOUR; Rufisque

MESOPOTAMIEN*: Bagdad (1930–35)

Order Book Jakob Bengel, Vol. II, Non-French countries, 1928–1935 (excerpt)

The countries with which the firm of Bengel maintained business contacts are listed in alphabetical order. Occasionally the client, i.e., the client's firm or its representative, with whom business was conducted, is mentioned. The dates refer to the period of time during which business contacts were maintained.
It is not clear why Stockholm, Malmö and Göteborg are listed under Russia instead of Sweden.
As a rule only a few business dealings are listed under the individual countries; there are a great many entries under the countries marked with an asterisk*.

AUSTRALIA: Melbourne

MOROCCO: Meknes, Rabat, Casablanca (1928/31/33/34/35), Casablanca, Pierre Salesne (1929/30/31) Casablanca: Magasins Modernes, Succursale des Galeries Lafayette de Paris (1934/35) (Buyer: Ernst Winkler, Durlacherstr. 29, Pforzheim) Casablanca, Abdel Vahab (1934) (Representative: Heinz Marx), Gibraltar (1933) Ceuta (1933)

MEXICO: Tampa, Casa de Curiosidades e Importadora, (Curt Baronsky)

NORTH AMERICA: Arnold, Constable & Cie., New York (Buyer: Loewenstein & Hecht, A.G. Berlin) (1933)

CANADA: Montreal, Henry Birks & Sons Ltd. (1931/32) The European Novelty Cie. Ltd. (Buyers: Friedrich Engert, Annaberg & Herbert Lautenbach) (1930/31/32)

NEW ZEALAND: Auckland

NORTH AMERICA: New York: The Royal Jewelry M.f.G. Cie. Inc. (Buyer: A. Rosenfeld, Pforzheim) (1929/30/31); Chicago, Illinois: Marshall Field & Company (Buyers in Germany: Chemnitz, Lohstr. 17) (1928/29/30)

NORWAY: Oslo (1929), Drämmen (1929/31), Aalesund (1935), Trondheim (1935)

AUSTRIA: Vienna, VIth District: Leo Baum 1932/33; Vienna, XVIth District: Franz Goldstein, Gold- & Metallwarenfabrik, Engros Export, Bijouterie & Knopffabrik Großmann & Cie., Successors Schüller + C.

PALESTINE, Jerusalem (1929) Tel Aviv (1932/33), Jaffa (1935)

POLAND: Warsaw, A. Katz (1920), Kraková (1928/30)

PORTUGAL: Lisbon (1934)

ROMANIA: Bucharest, Arad, Cernanti, Beclean, Chisjnan (1934)

RUSSIA: Stockholm (1932) Malmö (1932/33) Göteborg (1933)

SWITZERLAND: Biel (1927/29), Bern, Zurich, Luzern, Geneva, Basle

SPAIN*: Barcelona, Madrid, Seville, Malaga

SOUTH AMERICA*: Brazil: Rio de Janeiro, Sao Paulo Santo; Santiago de Chile (1928), Buenos Aires; Uruguay: Montevideo; Colombia: Bogota (1933/35)

SOUTH AFRICA: Johannesburg (1929)

SMYRNA*: Rodolfo, Penzo & Cie. (1928–1935): several deliveries annually, sometimes even several deliveries monthly

SYRIA: Beirut (1935), Aleppo (1931)

CZECHOSLOVAKIA*: Gablonz (1931), Prague

TURKEY: Constantinople (1929/30)

HUNGARY*: Budapest, Rakospalota

PERSIA: Tabriz (1928), Teheran (1934)

»REST OF AFRICA«*: Dakar: Mohamed ben Ahmed Cheraiby (1930), Senegal: SAHBIB BEN AMOUR; Rufisque

MESOPOTAMIA*: Baghdad (1930–35)

ANHANG II

(siehe hierzu Seite 93)

Bei der Manufaktur Rudolf Löwy in Gablonz wurden 1932 Lampendurchlochperlen und Druckperlen aus Glas bestellt.
Zur Erleichterung der technischen Produktion wurden gerade in den 1930er Jahren unzählige Hilfsmittel angeboten: Bei der Firma Wilhelm Paff in Wuppertal-Barmen bestellte man Hilfsmittel zum Weichlöten, bei Reinhold Schüler in Leipzig »Brünofix«.
Die Lack- und Farbenfabrik Hallack in Halle-Nietlebenbot bietet 1937 den Metallveredler »Halliol« und seine Imitationslacke an. In der Broschüre heißt es: »Messing-Kupfer, Nickel- und Chromlackierungen werden täuschend ähnlich erzielt.«
Der Katalog der Fabrik Dr. Leopold Rostosky, Ausgabe 17 (1.11.1937), weist auf die Vorteile von FIRNIT hin, ein Autogenschweißstoff und Lötstoff für Aluminium, Kupfer, Nickel, u.a. Der einst nur aus Kettenmaschinen, Pressen und Stanzen bestehende »Maschinenpark« konnte im Laufe der Zeit durch immer mehr technische Hilfsmittel erweitert werden. Bei den Unterlagen haben sich Prospekte der Firma »Igetro«, Maschinenfabrik und Trockenapparaturen, Stuttgart, Zuffenhausen aus dem Jahre 1938 erhalten sowie der Firma Helmbrecht & Co. »Helma Farbspritz-Apparate«.

ANHANG III

(siehe hierzu Seite 94)

»Bei meinem Eintritt (in die Firma), am ersten Tag der Lehre, kam die Frage auf: Wo setzen wir den Bub denn überhaupt hin? ›Natürlich gleich an meine Seite‹, sagte der Chef. ›Stellt einen Tisch seitlich von mir auf, damit ich ihn immer im Blickfeld habe.‹ Oft hörte ich ihn dann immer leise vor sich hinsprechen: ›Jetzt hast du ihn, lasse ihn nicht mehr los, auf ihn, auf ihn.‹ Meinen fragenden Blick beantwortete er nur: ›Ja, ja, Dich meine ich, arbeite, arbeite.‹«
Auch mit seinem eigenen Sohn war Ernst Hartenberger sen. sehr streng, Emil Schmidt schätzte aber sein faires Verhalten ihm gegenüber: »War dem Chef sein Sohn gleich morgens noch nicht an seinem Arbeitsplatz, erklang der Ruf ›Feikert (= Otto Feikert) gehe mal sofort den Ernst wecken.‹ Nach kurzer Zeit kam der dann, um unter den Mißblicken seines Vaters, wie ein geprügelter Hund, an seinen Schreibtisch zu schleichen. Aber nie bekam er einen Rüffel vor versammelter Belegschaft, was ich dem ›Alten‹ damals hoch anrechnete.«
Eine andere Begebenheit zeigte deutlich das Verhältnis zwischen Dienstherr und Arbeiter, und das durchaus nicht zu gering schätzende Selbstbewußtsein des Firmeninhabers: »Otto Feikert, der niemals mit Herr angeredet wurde, kommt vom Empfangsbüro: ›Herr Hartenberger, gerade ist Herr sowieso gekommen, er möchte Sie sprechen‹, ›Wer ist gekommen?‹ Feikert sagte erneut: ›Herr sowieso.‹ Der Chef dann in seinen Bart murmelnd: ›Es kann doch nicht schon jeder ein Herr sein.‹«
Das strenge Regiment Ernst Hartenberger sen. fürchteten alle, so war man hoch erfreut, wenn dieser verkündete er fahre mit seiner Frau in Urlaub. »Dabei gab es zu dieser Zeit überhaupt noch keinen offiziellen Urlaub für die Belegschaft, weshalb auch ein gewisser Zweifel aufkam, zumal der Chef sein Büro nur in den aller seltensten Fällen verließ. Kurzum, an diesem Samstag wurde mindestens bis 17.00 Uhr, anstatt wie sonst, bis 13.00 oder 14.00 gearbeitet – es durfte ja nichts liegenblei-

APPENDIX II

(see on this p. 91)

In 1932 lamp-hole beads and pressed glass beads were ordered from the Rudolf Löwy factory in Gablonz.
To facilitate production, in the 1930s especially, a great many technical aids were available from other firms: equipment and materials for soft soldering were ordered from the firm of Wilhelm Paff in Wuppertal-Barmen and »Brünofix« from Reinhold Schüler in Leipzig.
Hallack, Manufacturers of Lacquers and Paints in Halle-Nietlebenbot advertised a metal finisher, »Halliol« and imitation lacquers in 1937.
In their brochure it says: »Brass, copper, nickel and chrome lacquer finishes look so genuine they cannot be distinguished from the real thing.«
The catalogue issued by the Dr. Leopold Rostosky Factory, 17th edition (1 Nov. 1937) points out the advantages of FIRNIT, an autogenic material used for welding and soldering aluminium, copper, nickel and other metals. The »plant«, which had once consisted of only chain-making machines, presses and punches, was enlarged with time to include an ever broader range of technical aids. The Bengel records include brochures from the firm of Igetro, Maschinenfabrik und Trockenapparaturen [dryers], Stuttgart, Zuffenhausen dated 1938 as well as Helmbrecht & Co. Helma Farbspritz-Apparate [sprayers].

APPENDIX III

(see on this p. 93)

»When I entered (the firm), on the first day of my apprenticeship, the question arose of where could we let the boy sit? ›Right at my side, of course,‹ said the boss. ›Set up a table next to me so I can always keep an eye on him.‹ I often heard him muttering softly to himself: ›Now you've got him, don't let him go, at him, at him.‹ All he would say in answer to my questioning glance at him was: ›Yes, yes. I mean you, work, work.‹«
Ernst Hartenberger, sen., was very strict with his own son as well. Emil Schmidt, however, appreciated the fair treatment he gave to his son: »If the Boss's son wasn't at work on time in the morning, he'd yell ›Feikert (= Otto Feikert), go wake up Ernst.‹ A bit later he would arrive and, under his dad's frowns, would sneak to his desk like a dog that's had a hiding. But he was never reprimanded in front of the personnel, which I thought was greatly to the ›old man's‹ credit.«
Another incident illustrates the relationship between boss and worker and the self-confidence of the proprietor of the firm, which certainly should not be underrated: »Otto Feikert, who was never addressed as ›Herr‹, comes from the reception: ›Herr Hartenberger, Herr Thingummy has just arrived, he'd like to talk to you.‹ ›Who has arrived?‹ Feikert said again: ›Herr Thingummy.‹ The boss, muttering in his beard: ›Surely not everyone is a gentleman by now.‹«
Everyone was afraid of Ernst Hartenberger, sen., because he was so strict. Consquently, people were delighted when he announced he was going on holiday with his wife. »At that time there wasn't any official holiday for the personnel so doubts arose about this since the Boss only left the office very seldom. In short, on that Saturday, work went on until 5pm at least instead of 1pm or 2pm – nothing could be left undone. Monday morning I went to work in a good mood and was horrified to see the Boss sitting at his desk as usual. He realized straight

ben. Montags in der Früh ging ich wohlgelaunt zur Arbeit und sah zu meinem Entsetzen den Chef an seinem Arbeitsplatz sitzen. Er erkannte sofort mein versteinertes Gesicht und bemerkte ganz genüßlich: ›Komm, komm nur, ich habe es im Urlaub nicht ausgehalten.‹«
Oberstes Gebot in der Firma Jakob Bengel war die Sparsamkeit. Sicher wurde diese bei Bengels gelegentlich etwas übertrieben, allgemein hatte sie aber in den 1930er Jahren einen anderen Stellenwert – die Sorglosigkeit unserer heutigen Wegwerfgesellschaft war damals unmöglich. Emil Schmidt weiß zu berichten: »Eingehende Päckchen oder Pakete wurden, sofern sie mit Kordel verschnürt waren, sorgsam aufgeknotet, die Schnur über den Fingern aufgewickelt und in einem Karton auf dem Packtisch aufbewahrt, um dann bei der ersten Gelegenheit wieder verwendet zu werden. Die Kordel mit dem Messer oder der Schere aufzuschneiden und dadurch unbrauchbar zu machen, war eine Todsünde. Schon schrie der Chef: ›Der Kerl bringt mich um mein Vermögen.‹ Das gleiche galt für das Packpapier. Die aufgeklebte Adresse des Lieferanten wurde mit dem Messer ausradiert, das Papier glatt gestrichen und natürlich für unsere ausgehenden Pakete wieder verwandt; eine Selbstverständlichkeit. Neue Kartons zum Verpacken der Ware, gab es nur in den allerseltensten Fällen. Üblich war: Herr Feikert ging mit seinem Handkarren zur Drogerie Kröninger auf dem Marktplatz, die ihre leeren Kartons für uns aufbewahrte. Herr Feikert nahm die Kartons mit und brachte sie in einem extra dafür vorgesehenen Raum in der Firma Bengel unter. Je nach Bedarf wurden diese Kartons dann zugeschnitten um dann, so die Ware umhüllend, die Reise in die weite Welt anzutreten. Das gleiche galt für Holzkisten, die wir von der Firma Fritz Hartenberger, einem jüngeren Bruder unseres Chefs, erhielten.«
Die sprichwörtliche Sparsamkeit des Ernst Hartenberger sen. schlug nicht selten in puren Geiz um: Der Mustermacher Albert Roos wußte davon noch in den 50er Jahren zu berichten: »Hartenberger forderte ihn einst auf: ›Morgen in aller Früh, nimmst Du dir zwei Mann und fährst mit dem Postkarren an die Mosel, die Pakete aufgeben.‹ Zu welchem Ort dies genau geschah, hat er (= Albert Roos) nie erwähnt, er wurde aber auch nicht danach gefragt. Bis Bernkastel sind es immerhin runde 50 km, so daß mit Hin- und Rückfahrt mindestens eine Übernachtung anstand. Nach seiner Rückkehr präsentierte er dem Chef seine Spesenabrechnung. Der war entsetzt und schrie: ›Statt in einer schönen, ruhigen Scheune auf frischem Stroh zu schlafen, übernachten die Kerle im besten Hochwaldhotel und dinieren dazu noch wie die Fürsten, aber der Hartenberger, der hat's ja, der kann's ja bezahlen!‹«
Die Firma Bengel hatte einen umfangreichen Paketversand, einige Geschichten von Emil Schmidt geben auch hierüber Aufschluß: »Fast jeden Abend fuhren wir mit Paketen zur Post. Wir waren Selbstkleber. Die Packkammer schloß um 18.00 Uhr. Leider konnten wir nicht immer pünktlich sein, aber auf ein bestimmtes Klopfzeichen wurde uns die Tür wieder geöffnet. Nun bekam die Packkammer einen neuen Mitarbeiter, der um 18.00 Uhr froh verkündete: ›Endlich Schluß für heute‹, worauf ihn sein älterer Kollege belehrte: ›Noch nicht ganz, Bengels waren noch nicht da.‹«
Als Lehrling mußte man 3 Jahre einmal wöchentlich die kaufmännische Berufsschule besuchen. Der Unterricht begann um 7.30 Uhr in der Flurschule. Während für alle Schulkameraden der Arbeitstag auch (erst) um diese Zeit begann, waren Bengels Lehrbuben von 7.00 bis 7.25 Uhr noch in der Firma beschäftigt. Dann aber hieß es: vite, vite, macht schnell, damit ihr nicht zu spät zur Schule kommt. Die Flurschule lag etwa 5 Minuten von unserem Büro entfernt. Die damals einem Lehrling zukommenden Aufgaben mögen heute auf völliges Unverständnis stoßen: »Als besondere Anerkennung durfte ich den ›Alten‹ noch in den Hunde-Zwinger, zu seinen Tauben und in den Hühnerstall begleiten, wobei es eine große Ehre war, denselben auch ausmisten zu dürfen. Auch sah er es als eine Auszeichnung an, die Schlachtabfälle für seine Hunde in einem Eimer bei der Metzgerei Worst in der Wilhelmstraße abzuholen. Die einzelnen Rationen für die Hunde teilte er selbst ein.«
Mit Emil Schmidt war auch Anton Bückler aus Bärenbach, ein Nachkomme des Schinderhannes, Lehrling

off why I looked so stony-faced and said with relish: ›Come, come, I just couldn't stand being on holiday.‹«
Thrift was writ large at Jakob Bengel. Perhaps the Bengels occasionally took this approach too far but in the 1930s the virtue of economy enjoyed an entirely different status – the carelessness with which we throw everything away nowadays would have been unthinkable then. As Emil Schmidt tells: »Incoming packages or parchels were, if they were tied up with twine, carefully untied, the twine was wrapped round a finger and then put into a box on the packing table, ready for reuse whenever it might be needed. Making twine useless by cutting it with a knife or scissors was a mortal sin. If he saw anyone doing this, the Boss would shout: ›The chap's robbing me of everything I have!‹ The same held for wrapping paper. The address on the label glued on by the sender would be erased with a knife, the paper smoothed out and naturally reused for the parcels we sent out, as a matter of course. Only very rarely were there new boxes for packing wares in. The usual procedure was: Herr Feikert would go with his wheelbarrow to Drogerie Kröninger in Marktplatz, who used to keep their empty boxes for us. Herr Feikert would take the boxes and store them in a special box room provided for that purpose at Bengel. They were cut down as needed to send the wares out, wrapped in them, across the world. Wooden crates were treated the same way; they were given to us by Fritz Hartenberger, a younger brother of the Boss.«
The legendary thrift practized by Ernst Hartenberger, sen., often turned into pure stinginess. Albert Roos the pattern maker described it back in the 1950s: »Hartenberger once demanded of him: ›Tomorrow morning as early as possible you take two men and goes with the post cart to the Mosel to send off the parcels.‹ He (= Albert Roos) never divulged the name of the town where this took place but, after all, he was never asked. At any rate, it's at least 50 km to Bernkastel so, to go there and come back, you had to count on staying overnight. After his return he presented the boss with his bill for expenses. The Boss was horrified and bellowed: ›Instead of bedding down on fresh straw in a nice, quiet barn, the chaps spend the night in the best upland hotel and even enjoy a princely dinner but old Hartenberger, he's rolling in money so he can foot the bill!‹«
The firm sent out a great many orders and Emil Schmidt has some enlightening stories to tell about this: »Almost every evening we drove with the parcels to the post office. We stuck on our labels ourselves. The packing-room closed at about 6pm. Unfortunately, we couldn't always make it on time but the door would be opened for us if we gave a certain knock as a signal. Now one day the packing-room got a new worker, who announced cheerfully at 6pm: ›That's it for today then‹ and a senior colleague told him off: ›Not quite, Bengels haven't been here yet.‹
As an apprentice you had to attend commercial school for three years. Classes began at 7.30 am at the Flurschule. Although the work day (only) began then for all our schoolmates, Bengels' apprentices were kept busy working in the firm from 7.00 to 7.25. But then the word was: ›vite, vite, quick, see you don't get to school late.‹ The Flurschule was about 5 minutes from our office. The tasks piled on an apprentice in those days would probably meet with complete incomprehension nowadays: As a special acknowledgement I was allowed to accompany the ›Old Man‹ to his dovecote and chickens, where it was a great honor to be allowed to muck them out, too. He also saw it as a distinction [for apprentices] to be allowed to pick up scraps and offal for his dogs in a bucket from Worst the Butcher's in Wilhelmstrasse. He fed the dogs their rations himself.«
Anton Bückler from Bärenbach, a descendant of the famous Schinderhannes, served his apprenticeship at Bengel with Emil Schmidt. »Young Bückler had to walk to Fischbach-Weierbach train station every morning and arrived at Oberstein at about 6.30 am. The work day was from 7.00 am – 6 pm. The train left at 6.30. By the time he reached home it was always later than 8 pm. He was often so exhausted that he fell asleep at work, only to be rudely awakened by the Boss.«
Emil Schmidt also remembers Herr Späth, the foreman: »I see him in front of me, always struggling to carry a huge sieve, which brought electroplated ware from being electro-

bei der Firma Bengel. Der junge Bückler mußte jeden Morgen zu Fuß zur Bahnstation Fischbach-Weierbach laufen und kam um 6.30 Uhr in Oberstein an. Die Arbeitszeit war von 7.00–18.00 Uhr. Sein Zug ging dann um 18.30 Uhr. Bis er wieder zu Hause ankam, war es immer nach 20.00 Uhr. Dementsprechend müde, schlief er des öfteren während der Arbeitszeit ein, um dann immer unsanft durch den Chef geweckt zu werden.
Emil Schmidt erinnert sich auch an den Vorarbeiter, Herrn Späth:
»Ich sehe ihn vor mir, wie er immer in einem großen Sieb, schwer tragend, die galvanisierte Ware aus der Galvanisation ins Büro brachte.
In den geheizten Sägemehlkästen wurde die Ware, wenn sie aus dem Bad kam, getrocknet. Aber auch die Essens-Kesselchen wurden hier erwärmt, um die Mahlzeit dann im Speiseraum einzunehmen.
Das betraf vor allem die auswärtigen Mitarbeiter.«

ANHANG IV

(siehe hierzu Seite 95)

Zur Führung eines Arbeitsbuches war man laut Gesetz vom 26. Februar 1935, RGBl. I S. 311 verpflichtet. Diesen Arbeitsbüchern sind Geburtsdatum, weitere persönliche Daten und alle Arbeitgeber sowie die Funktion des Beschäftigten genannt. In einzelnen Fällen ist auch ein Hinweis zur Ausbildung zu finden.

ERNST BENDER, *geb. 1895*
Ausbildung zum Metallschmuckwarenarbeiter, 1909 bis 1912 bei der Firma Bengel
Tätigkeit bei der Firma Bengel: 11. 4.1909–17. 3.1945 als Metallschmuckwarenarbeiter

OTTO HUGO BENDER, *geb. 2.10.1903*
Ausbildung zum Metallschmuckwarenarbeiter, 1918 bis 1921
Tätigkeit bei der Firma Bengel: 27. 9.1939–2. 3.1940 als Goldschmied, ab 9.4.1947 als Goldschmied; um 1930 als Lagerverwalter tätig

GÜNTER REINHOLD BENDER, *geb. 15.1.1923*
Ausbildung zum Werkzeugschlosser, 1937 bis 1940
Tätigkeit bei der Firma Bengel: 24. 3.1937–23. 9.1938 als Schlosserlehrling

OTTO CAESAR, *geb. 22.6.1884*
Lehre als Büroangestellter, 1898 bis 1901
Tätigkeit bei der Firma Bengel: ab 27. 6.1900 als Buchhalter; erledigte die Korrespondenz

LIESELOTTE DISTLER, *geb. 2.9.1928*
Keine abgeschlossene Berufsausbildung
Tätigkeit bei der Firma Bengel: 25. 3.1946–30. 6.1946 als Hilfsarbeiterin

LUDWIG GROSSARDT, *geb. 21. 7. 1885*
Ausbildung zum Goldschmied, 1900 bis 1903
Tätigkeit bei der Firma Bengel: 27. 9.1939–27. 9.1940 als Goldschmied

HERBERT HANNSCHER (?), *geb. 16. 11. 1914*
Ausbildung zum Diamantschleifer, 1929 bis 1932
Tätigkeit bei der Firma Bengel: 27. 12. 1943–17. 3.1945, 13.1.1947–8. 4.1947 und ab 13. 7.1948 als Hilfsarbeiter

LUDWIG HAMSCHER (?), *geb. 3.11.1894*
Ausbildung zum Metallschmuckwarenarbeiter, 1909 bis 1912
Tätigkeit bei der Firma Bengel: 6. 6.1933–6. 1.1939 als Metallschmuckwarenarbeiter

ANNI JÄGER, *geb. 17. 7. 1913*
Tätigkeit bei der Firma Bengel 23. 9.1935–25. 1. 1941 als Metallschmuckwarenarbeiterin

WILHELM RUDOLF JUNG, *geb. 31. 1. 1883*
Tätigkeit bei der Firma Bengel: 18. 11.1943–17. 3.1945 als Rüstungsarbeiter

RUDOLF KNAU, *geb. 1920*
Ausbildung zum Metallschmuckwarenarbeiter, 1935–1938
Tätigkeit bei der Firma Bengel: 6. 5.1946–24. 5.1946 als Goldschmied

HUGO KNEBES, *geb. 29.1.1903*
Ausbildung zum Metallschmuckwarenarbeiter, 1918 bis 1920
Tätigkeit bei der Firma Bengel: 15. 7. 1929–29. 10. 1937 als Metall-

galvanized to the office. The wares were dried in crates of heated sawdust after they came out of the bath. But the little pot with our food was warmed up here, too, so that it could be eaten in the dining-room. That mainly affected workers from outside.«

APPENDIX IV

(see on this p. 91)

The law that came into force on 26 February 1935, RGBl. I S.311, required employees to keep a works log. Such logs give birth dates, other personal data and all employers as well as job descriptions. In some cases reference is also made to training.

ERNST BENDER, *b. 1895*
Trained as a metalworker in jewelry; at Bengel from 1909 to 1912
Job description at Bengel: 11 April 1909 – 17 March 1945 metalworker in jewelry

OTTO HUGO BENDER, *b. 2 Oct. 1903*
Trained as a metalworker in jewelry, 1918 to 1921
Job description at Bengel: 27 Sept. 1939 – 2 March 1940 goldsmith; from 9 April 1947 goldsmith; ca. 1930 stores supervisor

GÜNTER REINHOLD BENDER, *b. 15 Jan. 1923*
Trained as a tool-maker and machinist, 1937 to 1940
Job description at Bengel: 24 March 1937 – 23 Sept. 1938 as a machinist's apprentice

OTTO CAESAR, *b. 22 June 1884*
Trained as an office worker, 1898 to 1901
Job description at Bengel: from 27 June 1900 accountant; handled the correspondence

LIESELOTTE DISTLER, *b. 2 Sept. 1928*
No training
Job description at Bengel: 25 March 1946 – 30 June 1946 unskilled worker

LUDWIG GROßARDT, *b. 21 July 1885*
Trained as a goldsmith, 1900 to 1903
Job description at Bengel: 27 Sept. 1939 – 27 Sept. 1940 goldsmith

HERBERT HANNSCHER(?), *b. 16 Nov. 1914*
Trained as a diamond grinder and polisher, 1929 to 1932
Job description at Bengel: 27 Dec. 1943 – 17 March 1945, 13 Jan. 1947 – 8 April 1947 and from 13 July 1948 unskilled worker

LUDWIG HAMSCHER(?), *b. 3 Nov. 1894*
Trained as a metalworker in jewelry, 1909 to 1912; Job description at Bengel: 6 June 1933 – 6 Jan. 1939 metalworker in jewelry

ANNI JÄGER, *b. 17 July. 1913*
Job description at Bengel 23 Sept. 1935 – 25 Jan. 1941 metalworker in jewelry

WILHELM RUDOLF JUNG, *b. 31 Jan. 1883*
Job description at Bengel: 18 Nov. 1943 – 17 March 1945 armaments worker

RUDOLF KNAU, *b. 1920*
Trained as a metalworker in jewelry, 1935–1938
Job description at Bengel: 6 May 1946 – 24 May 1946 goldsmith

HUGO KNEBES, *b. 29 Jan. 1903*
Trained as a metal worker in jewelry, 1918 to 1920
Job description at Bengel: 15 July 1929 – 29 Oct. 1937 metalworker in jewelry, 3 March 1938 – 17 March 1945 metalworker in jewelry, turner and milling cutter; goldsmith from 23 Aug. 1948

schmuckwarenarbeiter, 3.3.1938–17.3.1945 als Metallschmuckwarenarbeiter, Dreher und Fräser, Aufnahme der Tätigkeit am 23.8.1948 als Goldschmied

ANNA LAUER, verh. Popp, *geb. 1.6.1917*
Tätigkeit bei der Firma Bengel: 19.9.–16.12.1944 als Rüstungshilfsarbeiterin

ALBERT LOCH, *geb. 1893*
Ausbildung zum Metallschmuckwarenarbeiter, 1908 bis 1911
Tätigkeit bei der Firma Bengel: 4.6.1942–22.2.1943 und 22.3.1943–17.3.1945 als Goldschmied

EMIL FRIEDRICH LOCH, *geb. 1905*
Ausbildung als Werkzeugmacher, 1920 bis 1924
Tätigkeit bei der Firma Bengel: 27.1.1941–10.4.1942 und 5.5.1942–30.8.1944 als Schlosser

OSKAR HEINRICH LOCH, *geb. 1900*
Ausbildung als Werkzeug-Maschinenschlosser, 1915 bis 1919
Tätigkeit bei der Firma Bengel: 5.12.1934–30.12.1938 als Lagerhalter

LONI MAYER, verh. Leidecker, *geb. 12.5.1924*
Tätigkeit bei der Firma Bengel: 12.4.1938–5.9.1940 als Metallschmuckwaren-Anlernmädchen

EMIL MOSER, *geb. 22.7.1884*
Ausbildung zum Goldschmied von 1899 bis 1902
Tätigkeit bei der Firma Bengel: 30.7.1934–17.3.1945 als Metallschmuckwarenarbeiter

WALTER MOSER, *geb. 19.8.1920*
Ausbildung zum Werkzeugschlosser, 1935 bis 1939
Tätigkeit bei der Firma Bengel: 1.4.1946–29.7.1946 als Werkzeugmacher

RUDOLF ORTH, *geb. 8.12.1895*
Ausbildung zum Goldschmied und Fasser, 1910 bis 1914
Tätigkeit bei der Firma Bengel: 26.8.1935–22.11.1935 als Metallschmuckwarenarbeiter

RUDOLF REIDENBACH, *geb. 28.7.1921*
Ausbildung zum Werkzeugschlosser bei der Firma Bengel, 30.3.1936 bis 31.10.1939, Facharbeiterprüfung 1939
Tätigkeit bei der Fa. Bengel: 1.11.1939–29.3.1940 als Schlosser

HUGO RISCH, *geb. 13.8.1928*
Ausbildung zum Goldschmied bei der Firma Bengel, 12.4.1943–17.3.1945

HULDA SCHNEIDER, verh. Petry, *geb. 1.6.1900*
Ausbildung zur Metallschmuckarbeiterin, 1914 bis 1916
Tätigkeit bei der Firma Bengel: 28.4.1919–11.8.1937 als Metallschmuckwarenarbeiterin, ab 14.7.1947 als Goldschmiedsgehilfin

HARRY SCHNEPF, *geb. 20.6.1927*
Tätigkeit bei der Firma Bengel: 22.6.1942–4.2.1944 als Hilfsarbeiter

WALTER SCHRAMM, *geb. 18.4.1922*
Tätigkeit bei der Firma Bengel: 1.3.–22.9.1939 als Hilfsarbeiter

RICHARD SCHUCHARDT, *geb. 20.9.1896*
Ausbildung zum Metallschmuckarbeiter, 1911 bis 1914
Tätigkeit bei der Firma Bengel: 23.8.1939–7.9.1940 und 9.9.1940–19.3.1945 als Goldschmied

ERNST SOHNI, *geb. 6.11.1906*
Ausbildung zum Edelsteinschleifer, 1921 bis 1924
Tätigkeit bei der Firma Bengel: 29.1.–17.4.1940 als Hilfsarbeiter

HELMUT SPÄTH, *geb. 25.11.1923*
Lehre bei der Firma Bengel als Metallschmuckarbeiter bzw. Goldschmied, 19.4.1938–11.7.1939 und 15.8.1939–31.10.1939, Facharbeiterprüfung 1941

WILLI STUMM, *geb. 5.12.1908*
Ausbildung zum Werkzeugschlosser, 1923 bis 1926
Tätigkeit bei der Firma Bengel: 4.4.1926–6.4.1934 als Werkzeugschlosser

WALTER WITTMANN, *geb. 11.2.1903*
Ausgelernter Metallschleifer
Tätigkeit bei der Firma Bengel: 12.3.1928–5.1.1944 als Metallschleifer, 19.1.1944–17.3.1945 als Rüstungsarbeiter, ab 8.6.1946 als Presser

HANS ZIMMERMANN, *geb. 26.3.1925*
Ausbildung zum Goldschmied bei der Firma Bengel: 3.4.1939 bis 1942

LONI LEIDECKER, née Mayer, *b. 12 May 1924*
Job description at Bengel: 12 April 1938 – 5 Sept. 1940 trainee metalworker in jewelry

ALBERT LOCH, *b. 1893*
Trained as a metalworker in jewelry, 1908 to 1911
Job description at Bengel: 4 June 1942 – 22 Feb. 1943 and 22 March 1943 – 17 March 1945 goldsmith

EMIL FRIEDRICH LOCH, *b. 1905*
Trained as a tool-maker and machinist, 1920 to 1924
Job description at Bengel: 27 Jan. 1941 – 10 April1942 and 5 May 1942 – 30 Aug. 1944 mechanic

OSKAR HEINRICH LOCH, *b. 1900*
Trained as a tool-maker and machinist, 1915 to 1919
Job description at Bengel: 5 Dec. 1934 – 30 Dec. 1938 keeper of stores

EMIL MOSER, *b. 22 July 1884*
Trained as a goldsmith from 1899 to 1902 Job description at Bengel: 30 July 1934 – 17 March 1945 metalworker in jewelry

WALTER MOSER, *b. 19 Aug. 1920*
Trained as a tool-maker and machinist, 1935 to 1939
Job description at Bengel: 1 April 1946 – 29 July 1946 tool-maker

RUDOLF ORTH, *b. 8 Dec. 1895*
Trained as a goldsmith and setter, 1910 to 1914
Job description at Bengel: 26 Aug. 1935 – 22 Nov. 1935 metalworker in jewelry

HULDA PETRY, née Schneider, *b. 1 June 1900*
Trained as a metalworker in jewelry, 1914 to 1916
Job description at Bengel: 28 April 1919 – 11 Aug. 1937 metalworker in jewelry, from 14 July 1947 journeyman goldsmith

ANNA POPP, née Lauer, *b. 1 June 1917*
Job description at Bengel: 19 Sept. – 16 Dec. 1944 unskilled armaments worker

RUDOLF REIDENBACH, *b. 28 July 1921*
Trained at Bengel as a tool-maker and machinist, 30 March 1936 to 31 Oct. 1939, skilled worker's certificate 1939
Job description at Bengel: 1 Nov. 1939 – 29 March 1940 machinist

HUGO RISCH, *b. 13 Aug. 1928*
Trained as a goldsmith at Bengel, 12 April 1943 – 17 March 1945

HARRY SCHNEPF, *b. 20 June 1927*
Job description at Bengel: 22 June 1942 – 4 Feb. 1944 unskilled worker

WALTER SCHRAMM, *b. 18 April 1922*
Job description at Bengel: 1 March – 22 Sept. 1939 unskilled worker

RICHARD SCHUCHARDT, *b. 20 Sept. 1896*
Trained as a metalworker in jewelry, 1911 to 1914
Job description at Bengel: 23 Aug. 1939 – 7 Sept. 1940 and 9 Sept. 1940 – 19 March 1945 goldsmith

ERNST SOHNI, *b. 6 Nov. 1906*
Trained as a gem-grinder and polisher, 1921 to 1924
Job description at Bengel: 29 Jan. – 17 April 1940 unskilled worker

HELMUT SPÄTH, *b. 25 Nov. 1923*
Apprenticeship at Bengel as a metalworker in jewelry and goldsmith, 19 April 1938 – 11 July 1939 and 15 Aug. 1939 – 31 Oct. 1939, skilled worker's certificate 1941

WILLI STUMM, *b. 5 Dec. 1908*
Trained as a tool-maker and machinist, 1923 to 1926
Job description at Bengel: 4 April 1926 – 6 April 1934 tool-maker and machinist

WALTER WITTMANN, *b. 11 Feb. 1903*
Skilled metal-burnisher and polisher
Job description at Bengel: 12 March 1928 – 5 Jan. 1944 metal-burnisher and polisher, 19 Jan. 1944 – 17 March 1945 armaments worker, from 8 June 1946 presser

HANS ZIMMERMANN, *b. 26 March 1925*
Trained as a goldsmith at Bengel: 3 April 1939 to 1942

STAMMBAUM BENGEL + HARTENBERGER

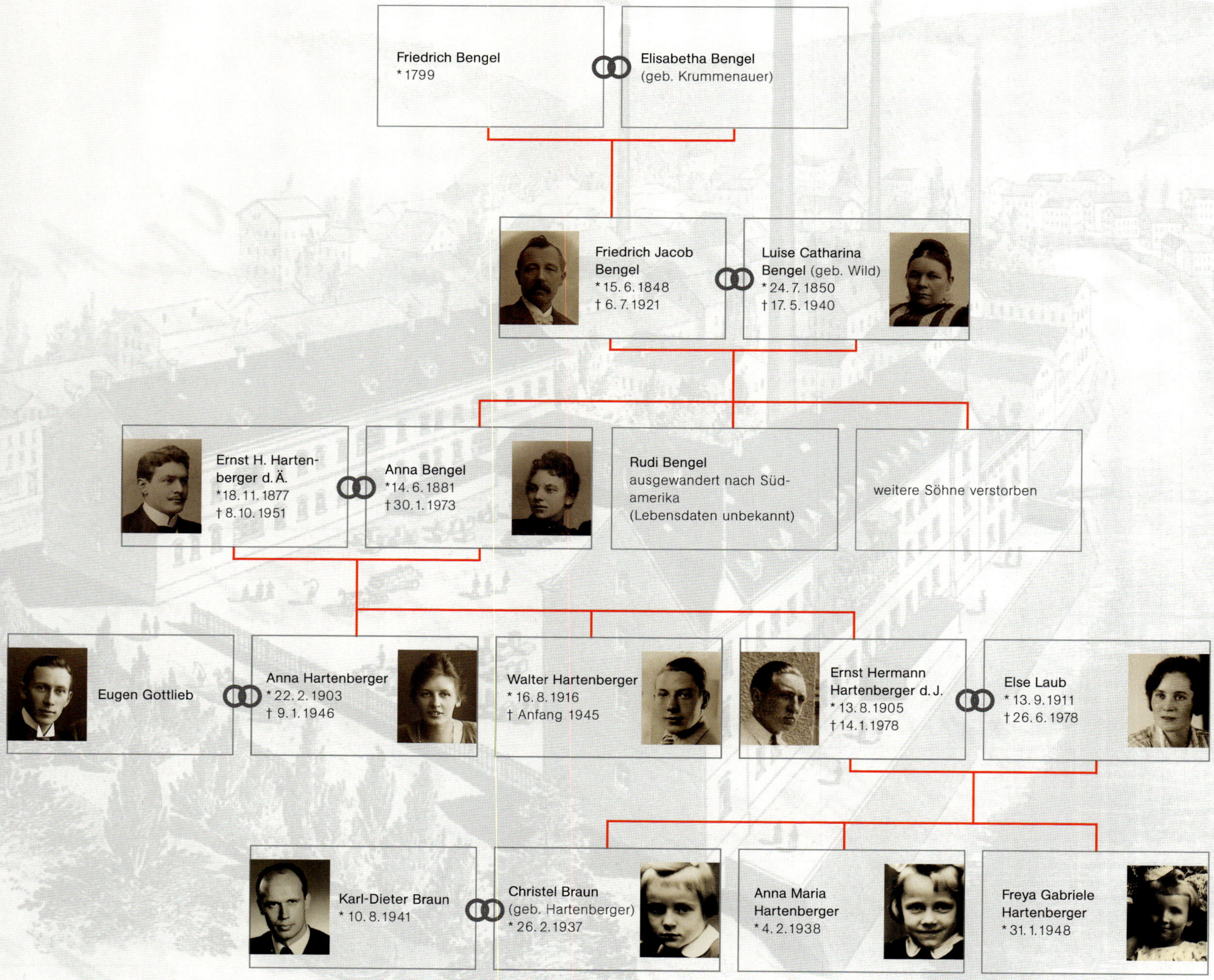

BIBLIOGRAPHIE
BIBLIOGRAPHY

BAUM 1988
Baum, Vicki: Menschen im Hotel. Köln 1988

BECKER 1961
Becker, Kurt: Idar-Oberstein im Landkreis Birkenfeld. Köln 1961 (S. 195–222)

BECKER 1991
Becker, Vivienne: Modeschmuck im Wandel der Zeit. Strass, Phantasie-Schmuck und Imitation. München 1991

BRUNIALTI/BRUNIALTI 1997
Ginelli Brunialti, Carla/Brunialti, Roberto: American Costume Jewelry 1935–1950. Mailand 1997

CASPER o.J. (1975)
Casper, Rudolf: Anekdoten und Schnurren aus dem Landkreis des Schinderhannes. Bad Kreuznach o. J. (1975)

DAVIDOV/REDINGTON 1988
Davidov, Corinne/Redington Dawes, Ginny: The Bakelite Jewelry Book. New York 1988

DE BEAUVOIR 1969
de Beauvoir, Simone: In den besten Jahren. Reinbek 1969

FARNETI 1991
Farneti Cera, Deanna (Hrsg.): Glanzstücke. Modeschmuck vom Jugendstil bis zur Gegenwart. München 1991

FARNETI 1995
Farneti Cera, Deanna (Hrsg.): Bijoux. Mailand 1995

GABARDI 1999
Gabardi, Melissa: Jean Després maestro orafo tra art déco e avangardie. Mailand 1999

GORDON 1990
Gordon, Angie: Twentieth Century Costume Jewellery. London 1990

HUFNAGL 1997
Hufnagl, Florian (Hrsg.): Plastics + Design. Stuttgart 1997

KELLEY/SCHIFFER 1987
Kelley, Lyngerda/Schiffer, Nancy: Plastic Jewelry. West Chester/PA 1987

KEUN 1992
Keun, Irmgard: Das kunstseidene Mädchen. München 1992

LEHNERT 2000
Lehnert, Gertrud: Geschichte der Mode im 20. Jahrhundert. Köln 2000

LEXIKOTHEK 1993
Lexikothek: Die 30er Jahre. Gütersloh 1993

LOSCHEK 1994
Loschek, Ingrid: Reclams Mode- & Kostümlexikon. Stuttgart 1994

MÖLLER 1996
Möller, Renate: Modeschmuck aus drei Jahrhunderten. München/Berlin 1996

RAULET 1985
Raulet, Sylvie: Schmuck. Art Déco. München 1985

ROTH 1986
Roth, Ulrike: Die Entwicklung des Achat- und Edelsteinschleiferei-gewerbes und der Schmuck- und Metallwarenindustrie Idar-Obersteins vom ausgehenden Mittelalter bis zum 2. Weltkrieg. Idar-Oberstein 1986

RUDOLPH 1990
Rudolph, Monika: Naum Slutzky, Meister am Bauhaus, Goldschmied und Designer. Stuttgart 1990

TRIOLET 1999
Triolet, Elsa: Colliers de Paris. Dortmund 1999

TSCHIMMEL 1989
Tschimmel, Udo: Die Zehntausend-Dollar-Idee. Kunststoff-Geschichte vom Zelluloid zum Superchip. Düsseldorf/Wien/New York 1989

VON REZZORI 1999
von Rezzori, Gregor: Mir auf der Spur. München 1999

SCHNURNBERGER 1991
Schnurnberger, Lynn: Let There Be Clothes. New York 1991

SIGMUND 2002
Sigmund, Anna Maria: Die Frauen der Nazis II. München 2002

TUCHOLSKY 1980
Tucholsky, Kurt: Gesammelte Werke, Band 8, 1930. Reinbek 1980

WEBER 1990
Weber, Christianne: Schmuck der 20er und 30er Jahre in Deutschland. Stuttgart 1990

WEBER 2000
Weber, Christianne: Art Déco Schmuck. Die internationale Schmuckszene der 20er und 30er Jahre. München 2000

WEBER/MÖLLER 1999
Weber, Christianne/Möller, Renate: Mode und Modeschmuck. Fashion and Jewelry 1920–1970. Stuttgart 1999

WINSLOW 1999
Winslow, Christa: Mädchen in Uniform. Göttingen 1999

WORRESCHKE, 1925
Worreschke, Hans: Die Metall verarbeitende Industrie in Oberstein (Diss.). Frankfurt a. M. 1925

Kataloge
Catalogues

BERLIN 1972
20er Jahre Neuerwerbungen. Ausstellungskatalog, Staatliche Museen Preußischer Kulturbesitz. Berlin 1972

BERLIN 1977
Metropolen machen Mode. Haute Couture der Zwanziger Jahre. Ausstellungskatalog, Staatliche Museen Preußischer Kulturbesitz. Berlin 1977

BERLIN 1992
Die Metallwerkstatt am Bauhaus. Ausstellungskatalog, Bauhaus-Archiv Museum für Gestaltung. Berlin 1992

DÜSSELDORF 1986
Dekorative Polymere: Schmuck aus Kunststoff 1860–1960. Sammlung Kölsch. Ausstellungskatalog, Stadtmuseum Düsseldorf 1986

ERFURT 1987
Modeschmuck vom Biedermeier bis zur Bauhauszeit. Sammlung Dr. Wartmann. Ausstellungskatalog, Galerie am Fischmarkt. Erfurt 1987

GALALITH 1954
Galalith. Die Geschichte eines Kunststoffes 1904–1954. Gedenkschrift, herausgegeben unter Mitwirkung des Verbandes kunststofferzeugende Industrie und verwandte Gebiete e.V., o.O., o. J. (1954)

JUNKER 1999
Junker, Almut (Hrsg.): Frankfurt Macht Mode 1933–45. Ausstellungskatalog, Historisches Museum. Marburg 1999

LEIPZIG 1913
Deutsches Goldschmiedejahrbuch 1913 ff.

LEIPZIG 1940
Deutscher Goldschmiedekalender. Geschäftshandbuch für das Juwelier- und Goldschmiedegewerbe. Leipzig 1940

PFORZHEIM 1982
75 Jahre Henkel & Grosse. Max Geisenheyner: Werden und Wirken einer Pforzheimer Schmuckmanufaktur. Festschrift. Pforzheim 1982

WORMS 1993
Denkmaltopograhie Bundesrepublik Deutschland, Kulturdenkmäler in Rheinland-Pfalz, Band 11, Kreis Birkenfeld. Bearb. von Ulrike Weber-Karge und Maria Wenzel. Worms 1993

Artikel
Articles

FISCHER, WALTER:
»Vom ›Schorschtegold‹ zum Eloxal«. Aus der Geschichte der Obersteiner Schmuck- und Metallwarenindustrie, in: Heimatkalender des Landkreises Birkenfeld, Birkenfeld 1956, S. 46–56

GERBER, OTTO: »Die Idar-Obersteiner metallverarbeitende Hilfsindustrien«, in: Die Aufgabe, Zeitschrift für Wirtschaft und Forschung, 2. Jg. 1949, S. 35

HARTLEB, RENATE: »Schmuck der zwanziger und dreißiger Jahre. Teil 2, Schmuck aus Kunststoffen und Industriemetallen«, in: Uhren und Schmuck, Heft 22, Berlin 1985, S. 6–8

HISSERICH, L.TH.: »Entstehung der Fabrikindustrie«, in: Hausindustrie im Gebiete der Schmuck- und Ziersteinverarbeitung, die Idar-Obersteiner Industrie. Im Anschluß an die Veröffentlichungen des Vereins für Sozialpolitik, Oberstein 1890, S. 147–150

Jahresberichte der Handelskammer zu Trier, 1893, S. 34

Jahresberichte der Handelskammer zu Trier, 1905, S.34

KLINGENSTEIN, EVA: »Buntes Symbol der Moderne«. Bakelitschmuck der zwanziger und dreißiger Jahre, in: Weltkunst 20/1995, S. 2762–2764

KREUTER, P.: »Die Entwicklungsgeschichte der Obersteiner Industrie«, in: Festschrift anläßlich der 27. Tagung des Reichsverbandes deutscher Juweliere, Gold-, und Silberschmiede in Idar-Oberstein, 17.–20.9.1928 (Hrsg. v. Oldenburgischen Industrie- und Handelskammer für den Landesteil Birkenfeld), Idar 1928, S. 39–45

KURZ, SABINE: »Modeschmuck aus Kunststoff«, in: Trödler, Nr. 246, Mai 2000, S. 32–40

KURZ, SABINE: »Modeschmuck im Bauhaus-Stil«, in: Schmuck-Magazin, Heft 6, 1997/98, S. 92f.

DR. M.: »Die volkswirtschaftliche Bedeutung Idar-Oberstein«, in: Deutsche Goldschmiedezeitung (DGZ), Nr. 5, 1950, S. 116

NATIONALE ZEITUNG, 11.12.1934, Stadtarchiv Idar-Oberstein

N.N.: »Die Obersteiner Uhrketten- und Metallwarenindustrie unter den Einwirkungen des Krieges«, in: Deutsche Goldschmiedezeitung (DGZ), Nr. 35–36, 24. 8. 1918, S. 178 f.

N.N.: »Die deutsche Schmuckkettenindustrie«, in: Deutsche Goldschmiedezeitung (DGZ), Nr. 24, 1920, S. 406 f.

O.F.: »Die wirtschaftliche Entwicklung der Oberstein-Idarer Industrie«, in: Deutsche Goldschmiedezeitung (DGZ), Nr. 37, 8. 9. 1928, S. 387 f.

R.R. (= Rudolf Rücklin?): »Modeschmuck«, in: Deutsche Goldschmiedezeitung (DGZ), Nr. 27, 1938

RÜCKLIN, RUDOLF: »Nationaler Schmuck«, in: Deutsche Goldschmiedezeitung (DGZ), Nr. 49, 1933, S. 528

SABEL, EUGEN: »Oberstein und seine Bijouterie-Industrie«, in: Die Schaulade vereinigt mit Kunst und Kunstgewerbe, 10. Jg. 1934, Heft 3, S. 141 f.

STANCLIFFE, JANE: »Costume and Fashion Jewellery of the Twentieth Century«, in: Victoria and Albert Album, London 1985, S. 112–124

REGISTER
INDEX

Alle Seitenzahlen beziehen sich auf den deutschen Text.
All page numbers refer to the German text.

ADRIAN 15
Althoff, Theodor 92
Altmann 52
Altmann, B. 59

BAAROVA, Lida 18
Bailly, Marguerite Marie 57
Baltin, Karl 39
Bauer, Alfred 54
Baum, Vicki 8, 10, 12
Beauvoir, Simone de 18
Bender, Ernst 284
Bender, Günter Reinhold 284
Bender, Otto Hugo 284
Bengel, Anna 78
Bengel, Elisabetha 74
Bengel, Friedrich 74
Bengel, Luise 74, 75
Bengel, Rudi 75
Bergdorf Goodman 59
Bogner, Willy 18
Bonaz, Auguste 57, 59
Bonaz, César 57
Braun, Christel 95
Braun, Eva 15
Breuer, Marcel 56
Bückler, Anton 283, 284

CAESAR, Otto 93, 284
Calder, Alexander 56
Chanel 18
Chanel, Coco 16, 20, 59
Cocteau, Jean 16
Cohn & Rosenberger 59, 60
Colbert, Claudette 16
Collomb, Louis 59
Collomb, Paul 59
Contreau, Pierre 20
Crawford, Joan 11

DALÍ, Salvador 16, 18
Després, Jean 44, 46
Deutsch, Ernst (Dryden) 15
Dietrich, Marlene 15
Distler, Lieselotte 284
Dryden 15

ELISABETH (Queen Mom), Königin 18

FEIKERT, Otto 83, 93, 94, 282, 283
Ferragamo, Salvatore 15
Fessler 39
Fischer, Walther 68
Fouquet, Jean 45

GALA 18
Garbo, Greta 11
Gerson, Berlin 8
Goebbels, Joseph 18
Goebbels, Magda 12
Gottlieb, Eugen 78
Gottlieb & Söhne 21, 78
Gottlieb & Söhne, Louis 61
Gottlieb & Wagner 61, 62
Grant, Cary 16
Gropius, Walter 44
Grossardt, Ludwig 284
Grosse, Adalbert 56
Grosse, Artur 55, 56
Grosse, Florentin 55
Grosse, Heinrich 55, 56
Grusinskaja 11

HAMSCHER, Ludwig 284
Hannscher, Herbert 284
Harlow, Jean 15
Hartenberger, Anna Maria 78, 83
Hartenberger, Christel 83, 95
Hartenberger, Ernst jun. 78, 80, 81, 83
Hartenberger, Ernst sen. 57, 78, 80, 81, 83, 89, 91, 94, 282, 283
Hartenberger, Freya Gabriele 83
Hartenberger, Fritz 283
Hartenberger, Hugo 78
Hartenberger, Walter 80
Harvey, Lillian 16
Hauschild 69
Heinz 94
Henkel, Heinrich 55
Henkel & Grosse, Pforzheim 21, 54, 55, 56,
Hepburn, Katherine 16
Hermann, Gottlieb 62
Hirsch 39
Hirsch & Sohn 52
Hitler, Adolf 12, 15
Hoppe, Marianne 16
Hügel, Albert 93, 94

JÄGER, Anni 284
Jager, Max 83
Jung, Wilhelm Rudolf 284

KARSTADT, Rudolph 92
Keller Christian Sohn, Carl 21, 54, 55
Keller Sohn, Leopold 62
Keun, Irmgard 8, 11, 12
Klein, Robert 54
Klein & Quenzer, Oberstein 21, 54, 55
Kleine, Herta 93
Knapp, Hilde 94
Knau, Rudolf 284
Knebes, Hugo 284
Kreuter & Co., Hans, Hanau 41, 44
Krische, Wilhelm 24

LAUB, Else 80, 83
Lauer, Anna 285
Leigh, Vivian 18
Leoni, Ercole 92
Leven, Hugo 41
Levy, Gebrüder 80
Loch, Albert 285
Loch, Emil Friedrich 285
Loch, Oskar Heinrich 285
Loch & Cie 39
Lord & Taylor 59

MARCH, Werner 18
Martin, Willy 41
Mayer, Loni 285
Meyer, Leon 57
Minn, R. 83
Mitford, Unity 15
Moser, Emil 285
Moser, Walter 285
Muth, Lotte 93

ORTH, Rudolf 285

PUIFORCAT, Jean 44, 45

QUENZER, Alfred 54

REIDENBACH, Rudolf 285
Rezzori, Gregor von 15
Rink 94
Risch, Hugo 285
Roos, Albert 41, 94, 283

SANDOZ, Gérard 44, 45, 46
Sartre, Jean-Paul 18
Schiaparelli, Elsa 16
Schmidt, Emil 78, 91, 93, 94, 282, 283
Schmidt, Gebrüder 63
Schneider, Hulda 285
Schnepf, Harry 285
Schramm, Walter 285
Schuchardt, Richard 285
Simpson, Wallis 18
Slutzky, Naum 44, 45, 47, 53
Sohni, Ernst 285
Späth, Helmut 284, 285
Spitteler, Adolf 24
Stumm, Willi 93, 285
Summer, Charles 92
Swanson, Gloria 15

TAYLOR, Elizabeth 18
Templier, Raymond 44, 45, 46
Thiele, Hertha 12
Tracy, Spencer 16
Triolet, Elsa 59
Tucholsky, Kurt 12

VIONNET, Madeleine 15

WAGENFELD, Wilhelm 41
Wales, Prince of 18
Weimarer Republik 10
Weinrodt 39
Westwood, Vivienne 8
Wieck, Dorothea 12
Wigman, Mary 18
Wild, Luise Catharina 74
Wilhelm, Klara 93
Winslow, Christa 8, 11, 12
Wittmann, Walter 285
Wittmer, W. 41
Woolworth Co. GmbH, F.W. 55, 59, 92

ZIEHER, Ottmar 41, 44
Zimmermann, Hans 285